GRAND DECEPTION

Anthologies by Alexander Klein:

GRAND DECEPTION

THE EMPIRE CITY

COURAGE IS THE KEY

GRAND DECEPTION

The World's Most Spectacular and Successful
HOAXES, IMPOSTURES, RUSES and FRAUDS

Collected and Edited by

ALEXANDER KLEIN

J. B. LIPPINCOTT COMPANY

Philadelphia   *New York*

Printed in the United States of America

Library of Congress Catalog Card Number 55-6302

Second Impression

ACKNOWLEDGMENTS

Grateful appreciation is expressed herewith to all authors, publishers, magazines and agents who courteously granted permission to include copyrighted material: OREGON'S SECRET LOVE CULT by Stewart H. Holbrook. Copyright, 1937, by The American Mercury, Inc. Reprinted by permission of the author. THE VERMONT RAFFLES WHO TRANSCENDED THE TOMB, from *You Can Escape* by Edward H. Smith. Copyright, 1929, by Edward H. Smith. Reprinted by permission of The Macmillan Company. MEXICO'S DECEPTIVE MILLIONAIRE by Bernard Hilton. Copyright, 1950, by Fawcett Publications, Inc. Reprinted from *True, The Man's Magazine*. THE MEN FROM MARS by John Houseman. Copyright, 1948, by Harper & Brothers. Reprinted by permission of the author. THE INSPECTOR GENERAL WAS A LADY: THE FACTS IN THE CASE by David Porter. Copyright, 1955, by Alexander Klein. THE FABULOUS FRAUD FROM BROOKLYN by Alan Hynd. Copyright, 1952, by Fawcett Publications, Inc. Reprinted from *True, The Man's Magazine*. THE MANY LIVES OF SALLY BEAUCHAMP reprinted from *The Dissociation of a Personality* by Morton Prince. Copyright, 1905, by Longmans, Green & Co., Inc. Permission of publisher. THE CASE OF ROMAN MALINOVSKY, from *Three Who Made a Revolution* by Bertram D. Wolfe. Copyright, 1948, by Bertram D. Wolfe. Reprinted by permission of The Dial Press and the author. THE DOUBLE LIFE OF HANS VAN MEEGEREN by Klaus Mann. Copyright, 1948, by J. B. Lippincott Co. Reprinted from *Town and Country* by permission of Erika Mann and The Hearst Corporation. LIFE AMONG THE AUSTRALIAN CANNIBALS, from *The English Eccentrics* by Edith Sitwell. Published in England by Dennis Dobson, Ltd. Originally published by Faber and Faber, Ltd. Reprinted by permission of Pearn, Pollinger & Higham, Ltd. THE WONDROUS BOX OF DR. ABRAMS by Robert Yoder. Copyright, 1940, by The Curtis Publishing Company. Reprinted from *The Saturday Evening Post*. THE REAL STORY OF THE CARDIFF GIANT by Alan Hynd. Copyright, 1951, by Fawcett Publications, Inc. Reprinted from *True, The Man's Magazine*. THE GREAT FRITZ KREISLER HOAX by Louis Biancolli. Copyright, 1951, by Theodore Presser Co. Reprinted by permission of the author and *Etude, The Music Magazine*. ATOMIC ENERGY, 1872-1899: R.I.P. by Alexander Klein. Copyright, 1955, by Alexander Klein. PSALMANAZAR: THE MAN WHO INVENTED FORMOSA, from *Literary Forgeries* by J. A. Farrar. Copyright, 1907, by Longmans, Green & Co., Inc. Reprinted by permission of the publisher. THE ROYAL CANADIAN NAVY'S MYSTERY SURGEON (The Master Impostor: An Incredible Tale) by Joseph McCarthy. Copyright, 1952, by Time, Inc. Reprinted from *Life* by permission of William Morris Agency. THE ABYSSINIAN PRINCES WHO OUTWITTED THE BRITISH NAVY by Joseph

4

M. Hone. Copyright, 1940, by The Living Age, Inc. Reprinted by permission of the author. THE SAWING-OFF OF MANHATTAN ISLAND, from *All Around the Town*, by Herbert Asbury. Copyright, 1934, by Alfred A. Knopf, Inc. Reprinted by permission of the publisher. THE MASKED MEDIUM SPOOF, from *Crimes That Made News* by Bernard O'Donnell. Reprinted by permission of Burke Publishing Company, Ltd., London. OUTER BALDONIA *vs.* SOVIET RUSSIA (He Invented a New Country) by William Bancroft Mellor. Copyright, 1954, by The American Mercury Magazine, Inc. UNDEFEATED AND UNDETECTED by Lloyd Mann. Copyright, 1949, by Esquire, Inc. Reprinted by permission of the author and *Esquire*. THE LEGENDARY MIZNERS, from *The Legendary Mizners* by Alva Johnston. Copyright, 1942, 1950, 1952, The New Yorker, Inc. Copyright, 1953, by Evelyn Johnston. Reprinted by permission of Farrar, Straus & Young, Inc. THE NEXT NOEL COWARD, from "Fabulous Phonies" by Joseph McCarthy. Copyright, 1951, by Hearst Magazines, Inc. Reprinted by permission of William Morris Agency and *Cosmopolitan Magazine*. JOHN BARRYMORE HYDE, from *Good Night, Sweet Prince* by Gene Fowler. Copyright, 1943, 1944, by Gene Fowler. Reprinted by permission of The Viking Press, Inc., New York. PHANTOM FAME by Harry Reichenbach, with David Freedman. Published by Simon & Schuster, Inc. Copyright, 1931, by Lucinda Reichenbach and David Freedman. Reprinted by permission of Lucinda Reichenbach. THE MERRY PRANKS OF KANONIER SCHMIDT (The Man Who Fooled Hitler) by Joseph Wechsberg. Copyright, 1951, by The Atlantic Monthly Company, Boston 16, Massachusetts. Reprinted by permission of Paul R. Reynolds & Son. THE INVISIBLE ACCOMPLICE by E. H. Jones, reprinted from *Escapers All* (1932) by permission of the publisher, John Lane, The Bodley Head. THE BIG DEAL by David Copeland. Copyright, 1955, by Alexander Klein. MASTER OF THE DOUBLE CROSS by William C. White. Copyright, 1934, by North American Review Corporation. WONG DUCK IS WRONG DUCK, from *The Case of Erle Stanley Gardner* by Alva Johnston. Copyright, 1947, by William Morrow & Co. Reprinted by permission of Evelyn Johnston. BILL FALLON, from "The Redheaded Mouthpiece of Broadway" by Avery Hale. Copyright, 1953, by Fawcett Publications, Inc. Reprinted from *True, The Man's Magazine*. THE AMERICAN GOLCONDA by A. J. Liebling. Copyright, 1940, The New Yorker Magazine, Inc. ABANDON ALL BEASTS!, from *The Tax Dodgers* by Elmer L. Irey, with William J. Slocum. Copyright, 1948, by Greenberg Publisher. BONBONNE D'URANIUM! by Toni Howard. Copyright, 1953, The Curtis Publishing Co. and 1954, by Toni Howard under the title, "The Great Uranium Hoax." Reprinted by permission of Ann Watkins, Inc. THE 70,000 HEIRS OF SIR FRANCIS DRAKE by Bill Slocum. Copyright, 1950, by The Crowell-Collier Publishing Company. Reprinted from *Collier's* by permission of the author. THE MAN WHO TOOK JAY GOULD TO THE CLEANERS by Alexander Klein. Copyright, 1955, by Alexander Klein. THE RED BARON OF ARIZONA by Clarence Buddington Kelland. Copyright, 1947, by The Curtis Publishing Company. UP AND DOWN WITH SAM INSULL by John T. Flynn. Copyright, 1932, by The Crowell-Collier Publishing Company. Reprinted from *Collier's* by permission of the author. THE LAST OF THE FREEBOOTERS by Alexander Klein. Copyright, 1955, by Alexander Klein. THE GREAT CORPORATION SWINDLE by Craig Thompson. Copyright, 1953, by The Curtis Publishing Company. Reprinted by permission of Brandt & Brandt. HOW MADAME HUMBERT TOOK FRANCE by Alexander Klein. Copyright, 1955, by Alexander Klein.

CONTENTS

III FOR THE DEVIL OF IT

IV IN THE LINE OF DUTY

V THE PROFIT MOTIVE

INTRODUCTION

Everything that deceives may be said to enchant.——Plato

Things are seldom what they seem
Skim milk masquerades as cream.——W. S. Gilbert

A Hair perhaps divides the False and True.——Omar Khayyám

If this were played upon a stage now,
I could condemn it as an improbable fiction.——William Shakespeare

There is a short period of infancy when, psychologists tell us, every human being feels himself omnipotent and unlimited. During this halcyon time the infant does not distinguish between himself and other objects: they are all himself, he is the whole universe. But, in due time, each infant makes the painful discovery that he is a limited being, dependent on others whose wishes do not always coincide with his own, imprisoned within his own skin, fated to live within the circumscribed orbit of his own experience. This loss of omnipotence is balanced, however, by the rise of the faculty of imagination, of dreaming and by the consequent creation of illusion and myth. A man is only as limited as his imagination.

Thurber's Walter Mitty lives in each one of us. We all wish to play many more parts than we actually achieve—and in our imaginations we do play many roles, we do improve on reality. And to some extent we all deceive ourselves as well as others. Who can say that he knows the whole truth about himself, much less that he lives the whole truth, that he conveys to others the literal truth and nothing but that truth at all times? Indeed, would not the reduction of life to such rigid, literal limitations—excluding all fantasy—constitute a falsehood by omission?

Thus, deception is universal. So is credulity, the necessary ground for the success of deception. For successful deception is dependent on human optimism, on belief in the goodness of our fellow-man, on the wish that the fairy tale be more than an expression of human aspiration, that reality match the visions of the mind and heart. "I'm not lying, I'm dreaming," is the gist of the little child's protest when

11

he is caught in what appears a fib to the literal-minded. And all humanity echoes him.

Man's ingenuity at deception is linked with his imaginativeness, with the talents that make possible his achievements in art, science, religion and love. Indeed, a man who could never be fooled and who would never fool anyone else, even in jest, would in all probability be a man bereft of fancy, lacking the salt which is of the essence of humanity.

Inevitably, deception is an important thread in all human history, and in the mythology and literature of every culture. I do not hold with those misogynists who consider the creation of Eve out of Adam's rib—while Adam was unsuspectingly slumbering—the quintessential ruse from which stems all our troubles. But certainly the snake's tempting of Eve to try the little apple is a hoax with far-reaching, ambiguous consequences. (On the one hand, essential phases of our humanity— self-consciousness, the search for truth, the yearning for perfection —stem from the snake's ironic apple-hoax. On the other hand, one must concede more than a grain of truth in the pessimistic view that, after the fall of man, human life itself became a hoax, in the sense that it forever promises more than it delivers, grants us all a reach that far exceeds our grasp.)

The Old Testament, thereafter, is replete with stories of deception. Jacob, at his mother's bidding, dons kid skins to aid him in impersonating his hirsute brother, Esau, and steals blind Isaac's paternal blessing. However, Jacob himself appears more than once in the role of the deceived victim. After he has labored for seven years to earn the hand of his beloved Rachel, her father, Laban, substitutes her older sister, Leah, to consummate the marriage in the darkness of the bridal chamber. Years later, Joseph's brethren cruelly hoax their father, Jacob, when they sell Joseph into bondage and bring home his rent and bloody garments as proof that he has been slaughtered by some wild beast—proxy for their own aggression and jealousy. In turn, when Joseph's brothers eventually come to Egypt, the Provider—whom they fail to recognize—counters with a hoax which, though it ends happily, for a while sets their lives in jeopardy.

One could go on citing instances indefinitely. From the earliest recorded folk-tales on through Homer, the Greek plays, the medieval romances, Tyll Eulenspiegel, Robin Hood, Shakespeare, down to the latest novel or play—in all appear the deceiver and the deceived, in all the perennial riddle of appearance and reality is the universal underlying theme.

Deeply rooted in human impulses as they are, it is little wonder that true stories of deception—of hoaxes, impostures, ruses and frauds, and the fabulous people who perpetuate them—have had a perennial fascination for mankind. For in such accounts—in such true, amazing stories—are revealed the fantastic possibilities of the human personality. The impulses involved are related to those which are the essence of every practical joke, every piece of wit, every flight of imagination, every act of aggression. Above all, every deception, every imposture is an assumption of power; the person deceived is reduced in stature, symbolically nullified, while the impostor is temporarily powerful, even greater than if he were the real thing.

The deceptions in this volume are all taken from the realm of fact; these are all lies that lived, improvements on reality that were not only imagined but acted out with remarkable success. Where Walter Mitty left off, the masters of illusion in this book really swung into action.

Naturally, in view of the omnipresence of deception in human affairs, no volume in this field could claim to be extensively complete either in specific accounts or even in categories. My basic criterion of selection was, frankly, entertainment, the excitement of the action, the ingenuity of the role-playing involved, the fabulousness of the characters in the drama. Secondarily came the matter of representativeness.

The immediate motivations for these deceptions vary widely: patriotism, monetary gain, fame, power, revenge, love, fun, the puncturing of a stuffed shirt, achieving one's goal in the line of duty or the practice of one's profession, or maintaining one's personality in perilous balance from chaos. In addition to adventure, wonder and suspense, these accounts strike a gamut of varied notes, ranging from pathos to rollicking humor. Many spheres of action and diverse locales are represented. Although there is diversity in time, too—from the Renaissance to the 1950's—modern accounts dealing with occurrences in the nineteenth and twentieth centuries predominate. The accounts are arranged in sections broadly based on motivation, the immediate goal of the deception, as well as the field in which it operated. There are heroes of deception who aided their country or a cause, or escaped from the enemy in wartime. There are hoaxes where sheer deviltry is the most prominent element, even though other motivations may also be intermingled (such as when Virginia Woolf helped hoax the British Navy to show up the pompousness of its ceremonials). One section is devoted to swindles, but only frauds involving unusually ingenious deception or executed on a grand scale were included. Another section comprises hoaxes in the arts and sciences, in literature and journalism. And one section, "The Fabulous People," is, admittedly, a catch-all for accounts of deceptions in which the motivation is clouded or the area indefinite; but the stories in that section are of the sort that make one particularly pause to wonder.

Some notable hoaxes and frauds, such as the recently confirmed Piltdown Man fake, and various celebrated masters of deception, such as Cagliostro, Titus Oates, Chatterton and Arthur Ornton, have been excluded either because their stories have been told too often or because the facts involved or the accounts available were not deemed of sufficient narrative interest. Wherever possible I have selected accounts that carry the reader through the deception with the chief actor in sufficient detail to make for full participation. In some instances, though, the marvelousness or uniqueness of a feat of deception qualified it for inclusion despite paucity of detail. In a number of cases, when no appropriate account of a remarkable deception was available, I have undertaken to remedy the omission.

I owe thanks for helpful suggestions to Lenwood Bowman, Jay Dreyer, Imie Lane, Charles Neider and Dr. Herman Tannenbaum. Particularly do I wish to thank Alan Williams for his comments during numerous editorial consultations. Greatest of all is my debt to my wife, Virginia Copeland, for her invaluable patience and counsel, and her generous aid.

ALEXANDER KLEIN

New York
February 1, 1955

1

THE FABULOUS PEOPLE

OREGON'S SECRET LOVE CULT

by Stewart H. Holbrook

When Joshua Elijah Creffield got the call, one day in 1903, the Pacific Northwest discovered once for all the true potentials of the female libido—and the male. Stewart Holbrook recounts the fascinating details. As to who fooled whom and why, each reader will have to judge for himself.

When Joshua Elijah Creffield of Oregon raised his voice in holy anger, the vast city of San Francisco shook horribly in the grip of an Act of God and then went down, writhing and smoking, in one of the greatest disasters within the memory of living man. Impious folk may not believe this, but there were many in Oregon who did, and before this amazing backwoods prophet and prodigious fornicator was done, he had filled the State insane asylum nigh to bursting and had added measurably to the work of undertakers of the time.

Oregon, of course, has like other West Coast States been exposed to the workings of Christian medicine men since the earliest times. By the very power of his eye, back in the 'Forties, the Rev. Jason Lee could make a sinner twitch and groan mightily, and the later and also Rev. Billy Sunday caused multitudes of the ungodly to grovel in repentant sawdust. But these worthies were engaged in the simple saving of souls, whereas Joshua Elijah Creffield was engrossed in search for a second, and not necessarily a virgin, Mother of Christ. His destruction of San Francisco was a mere incident.

Edmund Franz Creffield made his first appearance in the role of

16

Joshua sometime in 1903 and in the then country village of Corvallis in Western Oregon. Born in Germany thirty-five years before, he had come to the United States as a youth and had joined the Salvation Army. As a commander in that group he came to Corvallis in 1902. A year later a sudden revelation broke over him like a great light and he was Edmund Creffield no longer but Joshua Elijah, sole prophet and for a short time sole communicant of the Church of the Bride of Christ. He had no learning beyond that he absorbed from a weekly reading of the Salvation Army's *War Cry*. He was not of imposing physical stature, nor was he, strangely enough, what connoisseurs in demonology would term a bull-roarer. He confined his bellowing to direct commands and to the bringing down of curses from on high. But he could and did grow a beard that was a lulu and he allowed his hair to tumble down over his shoulders.

It must have been, despite its several churches, that the town of Corvallis was lacking something in spiritual life, at least so far as the women were concerned, for presently the new Joshua had a notable flock of females at his heels. Yet he went about the business so quietly that I have always thought he had subscribed to one of those correspondence courses in hypnotism which were so popular with lonely hired men, rutty village youths, and others of the time. If you're old enough you will readily recall the appeal of the advertisements: "Make Women Bend to Your Will."

In any case, Joshua Creffield was soon holding secret meetings in the homes of members, with the blinds pulled down. Afternoon, when grubby menfolk were away at work, was the time. Girls in their 'teens skipped school. Housewives left their bread in dough, while unseen yet positive horns sprouted from the unsuspecting heads of solid male citizens.

Joshua became bolder, or at least careless, and the surprised parents of a fifteen-year-old girl learned how she got that way. Pulling down all the blinds at the meeting place, this girl said, Joshua began to chant, swaying his arms and body in unison, and calling upon the Full Spirit to descend and to designate her who was to be the mother of a second Christ.

The girls and women swayed, twelve of them on this occasion. They chanted as they swayed, they spoke in tongues, and they cried aloud, while Joshua seemed to gain in stature and his normally pale eyes sank deep into his head where they glowed like two pits of fire. Then, like a thunderbolt, Joshua roared: "Vile clothes, begone!" The whiskered fellow disrobed, and, without urging on his part, all the women present did likewise. There was no coyness about it, no sense of shame. They threw off their peekaboo waists and their skirts, and they tore wildly at whalebone corsets, meanwhile moaning like all get-out. "Roll, ye sinners, roll!" thundered Joshua, and roll they did, some in chemises, some without, all over the bare floor, with Joshua rolling happily among them.

The subsequent orgies of this particular meeting could not here be reported and go through the mails. Never had there been such manifest workings of the Spirit, and it was clear that Joshua was going about his quest for a mother of Christ in a thorough and a searching manner.

News of the Joshuan search got around in small Corvallis in a hurry, and more than one wife and daughter was put on the domestic grill. Four girls, ranging in age from fourteen to sixteen years, were sent away to the Oregon Boys and Girls Aid Society. One married woman was committed to the State asylum at Salem. A committee of two men called on the Prophet and requested him to leave town. He simply sneered a Joshuan sneer and laughed quietly in his beard.

For by now the Prophet felt himself strong enough to defy all the male scoffers in town. The meetings grew wilder and much larger, until it was common for a score of girls and women to attend. Joshua invented some rites new even to Corvallis matrons, and on at least two occasions he led a whole harem of them, like a Pied Piper suffering from acute satyriasis, to a spot in some river-bottom land south of town. Here the lot of them stripped and rolled their sins away in the lush grass. Some unbeliever whose name is lost to history but whose Brownie had a good lens, took a candid camera shot of one of these gatherings in the wildwood. The film was small but clear as crystal, and it was all but worn out in the making of prints which circulated by the hundreds in Corvallis and nearby towns.

No movie ever made created such a furor as this two inches of Brownie film. There was an immediate uproar, as enraged fathers and injured husbands had their kids and wives packed off to the State asylum and the home for wayward girls. Fifteen of Joshua's tribe were at once taken out of circulation, while others got warnings to which they paid little if any heed. Joshua remained. He not only remained but he took to wife, in an orthodox manner, one Maude Hurt, the twenty-year-old daughter of an old and respected family; and the meetings continued, albeit with greater secrecy.

Then, on the coolish evening of January 4, 1904, a band of men made a call on the Prophet. They escorted him to the edge of town, gave him a coat of tar and feathers, and told him to begone. For a while he dropped out of sight, though not out of mind of those of his followers who had not yet been locked up. These took to pining openly for Joshua, nor did they pine in vain. The Prophet secretly returned and was soon taken in *flagrante delicto* with the wife of a prominent citizen, but got away with no buckshot in his pants. The husband swore out a warrant charging adultery.

The police had been waiting for something tangible like this to work on. But they couldn't find the Prophet. To stimulate the hunt, Victor Hurt, father-in-law of Joshua, offered a reward of $150 for his arrest. Maude Hurt Creffield secured a divorce. Things looked dark for the Prophet.

Nearly three months passed with Creffield at large. Then, on a day in June, young Roy Hurt, adopted son of Victor, made a startling discovery. Crawling under the Hurt home in search of a tin can in which to carry worms on a fishing trip, the youngster was frightened near out of his wits when he suddenly found himself looking into the great blazing eyes of a bearded man. Backing out of the hole as fast as he could, the boy called his foster-father. Victor Hurt came and peered into the dark hole and then called the police.

The cops came and hauled the Prophet from his den. He was, as one of the officers recalls thirty years after, a sight to behold. Naked as to clothes, and dirty as a Berkshire hog, the Prophet was as hairy all over as a black water spaniel—and most gloriously endowed by Mother Nature withal. His beard grew down to his stomach and was bushy as a clump of alder. But he was as thin as a fence rail. He was weak, too, and could scarcely stand.

"You're Creffield, ain't you?" asked a doubtful cop, recalling the old stories of surviving cave men.

"I am Joshua." The voice that came from the beard was weak, yet obviously the voice of a prophet.

They pieced together a weird story. For nearly three months Creffield had lived, naked, in the hole under the house of the very man who had offered a reward for his arrest, emerging only when the menfolk were away, and being fed scraps of food that the women could smuggle from the cupboard.

Put on trial on the adultery charge previously mentioned, a jury of men found Joshua guilty and old Judge Sears threw the book at him.

"Two years in State's prison," said the judge.

"God bless you and forgive you, for ye know not what ye do," responded the Prophet.

With Creffield behind bars, menfolk slept more soundly than for a year past. Gradually there was a trickle back from the asylum and detention homes of the girls and women who had wanted to become the Second Mother, and the town regained something of its former quiet. So forgotten was the whole affair that the press failed to mark the release of Creffield from the pen in December, 1905.

Shaved clean now, and his hair cut, Creffield at once dug out for Los Angeles—then as now a lodestone for prophets of all kinds—and immediately began a correspondence with some of his former devotees in Corvallis. He also sent a note of warning to Victor Hurt, his ex-father-in-law:

> God has resurrected me. I have now got my feet on your neck. God has restored me to my own. I will return to Oregon and gather together all my followers. Place no obstruction in my way, or God will smite you.—Joshua Creffield.

To Esther Mitchell, fair and seventeen-year-old girl who had been one of the youngest of his flock before his incarceration, Creffield wrote at length. The Lord, he confided, had now definitely chosen her to become the Second Mother, and had commanded Creffield to bring it about. What young Esther replied is not known, but later events indicated that her answer had been favorable.

Creffield now went north, stopping neither in Corvallis nor in Oregon, but going direct to Seattle where, by pre-arrangement, his former wife awaited him. They were remarried by an orthodox preacher and went to live with Mrs. Creffield's brother and his wife, Mr. and Mrs. Frank Hurt of Seattle.

Joshua presently let them into a secret. He had, he said, made up his mind to call down the wrath of God upon Seattle, Portland, Corvallis, and San Francisco. He had also sent this warning to his faithful followers in Corvallis. He would loose the Lord's anger just as soon as he could establish a colony for those who cared to be saved from the coming devastation. He told Frank Hurt that he, Joshua, knew of a wonderful spot for a true Garden of Eden; all he needed was a little financial help.

Creffield painted a gaudy picture. He, with Frank Hurt as his Gabriel, would buy a piece of land known to Creffield at a remote spot on the Oregon coast. Here, amidst the green and lush vegetation, the Prophet would lead all his followers (female), and the whole outfit of them, with Frank Hurt as lieutenant, would live free from the profane gaze of scoffers—while the great cities on the coast, and Corvallis, too, groveled in penitent ashes.

It was a pretty swell picture. Frank Hurt sold his Seattle property and went, as directed, to Waldport, ninety miles west of Corvallis on the wild Pacific shore. Mrs. Creffield went ahead with the Hurts. Joshua was to follow alone.

On the afternoon of April 18, 1906, the Prophet again laid foot on Oregon soil. He skirted Corvallis in a buggy, and then took the train for Newport, end of the line and nearest railroad station to Waldport and Eden. When passengers got off at Newport, they found the town in great excitement. Telegraphic dispatches told that the city of San Francisco lay in smoking ruins.

"I knew it," the bearded man said quietly to the little group who now fairly trembled at sight of the Man of Wrath. "Didn't I tell you I would call down God's curse? This is only the beginning. I have warned the faithful at Corvallis. They are coming."

And come they did. Within twenty-four hours, trainmen on the C. & E. were struck by the beauty of a fair-haired girl who said she was going to join the Prophet at Waldport. It was Esther Mitchell, soon to be in headlines throughout the West. There were two trains daily out of Corvallis, and for the next week every train carried at least two pilgrims on their way to Eden, and sometimes as many as six.

Back in troubled Corvallis, females were in ferment, while fathers and husbands were desperate. Girls started for school and never got there. Housewives disappeared, two of them carrying babies. When the man who had once had Creffield arrested for adultery awoke one morning, he found a note in his wife's handwriting pinned to the pillow beside his own. It read:

I don't want to leave in the daytime because the children will cry and want to go with me. I must leave while they are asleep. I have taken $3.50 of your money. This will not pay all my fare and I will have to walk ninety miles to where I want to go.

That's how they came when Joshua called. That woman walked much of the way to Waldport—ninety miles up through a mountain pass where cougars stalked the very roadside, and then down to the beach and the Prophet. Praise Joshua and great day in the morning!

Exodus was on. Fathers of two runaway girls took guns and got aboard a train for the beach. But Joshua, undoubtedly warned by the Lord, had flown. Young George Mitchell, brother to Esther, heard that the Prophet had fled to Seattle. Mitchell went at once to Seattle, and there on the morning of May 7, 1906, he sighted Joshua and Mrs. Creffield at the corner of Second and Columbia streets. Stepping up behind him, Mitchell pressed the muzzle of a .38 revolver to the Prophet's neck and pulled the trigger. Creffield fell in a welter of blood.

Despite the protests of the widow and the Hurts, all of whom said he was as ageless as Time and immune to the ills and accidents of mortal man, a cynical undertaker stuffed cotton into the hole in Creffield's neck and they laid him away tenderly in Lake View Cemetery in Seattle.

George Mitchell's trial for murder would have got front-page space all over the country had it not been that the Thaw case was concurrently on view in New York. The revelations concerning the lusty doings of the Prophet, as brought out by defense counsel, were juicier than anything offered at the Thaw trial, in comparison a Dorcus Society meeting; and Mitchell was found not guilty.

Free again, with the man who had seduced his sister in the grave, Mitchell went to Seattle's Union Station to get a train back to Oregon. There, while hundreds of tourists watched, Esther Mitchell walked up behind her brother, pulled a gleaming nickel-plated gun from her cloak, and shot him through the head.

"My brother killed an innocent man," Esther told a court, "and that is why I shot him." She wouldn't plead insanity, so a jury had her committed to the State hospital. The Prophet's widow took poison while awaiting trial; she had bought the gun Esther used.

A month after the Prophet's death, old George Hodges, Oregon timber cruiser, emerged from the woods after running a "Forty" south of Waldport. Hodges couldn't know that he was in Garden of Eden country, so it is not strange that he swallowed the chew of *Climax* he was working on; he had run fair into a camp of what looked to him to be wild women. Ragged, almost naked, and little better than half-starved, he found five females and a baby grouped about a tattered old tent on the beach. They told him they were waiting for Joshua, the man who had just destroyed San Francisco and was now on his way to do likewise for Corvallis, Portland, and Seattle. Hodges told them that their Prophet was dead. They merely laughed wildly and those who could still stumble around went off in search of more mussels, their only food in weeks.

The startled timber cruiser notified authorities who came and removed the crazed women back to Corvallis which, as they were surprised to find, was still standing. For a time there was talk that Joshua had been resurrected, but, if so, he never showed up in his old haunts. And to this day the city of Corvallis . . . remains on guard. In October of 1936, even so seemly and mild-mannered a prophet as Dr. Norman Thomas was refused permission to address the burghers there.

THE VERMONT RAFFLES WHO TRANSCENDED THE TOMB

by Edward H. Smith

For some seventeen years, from 1885 to 1902, Clarence Adams lived a double life, a sort of odd, continual practical joke on his neighbors. But his greatest feat of deception came after his first hoax was exposed.

Clarence A. Adams, born to a name as illustrious as any in the annals of New England, was a farmer and the son of a farmer, having a moderate landed property on the outskirts of the little town of Chester, not far from the Connecticut River in Windsor County. He had been appraiser, selectman, and member of the legislature, and he was for more than fifteen years the chief trustee of the public library and the person who selected the books for its shelves.

Chester, and all the surrounding territory of his narrow little State, knew him for a solid, careful, and studious man, who had inherited enough property and money to be fixed for life. He lived on his suburban farm, which was about a mile from the heart of the town. Here he superintended the work and submitted to the tender and somewhat intrusive ministrations of an elderly woman housekeeper. He was in town almost every day, sometimes attending meetings and sessions of political bodies, sometimes working at the library, and occasionally running up to Montpelier when the legislature was in session.

Not only had he collected in the public library an array of books uncommon to such repositories, but he had in his home shelf after shelf of volumes, some of them devoted to strange and mystifying subjects. For he had got together the stories of Poe, Stevenson, Hugo, Sue, Dumas, Balzac, Gaboriau, Hoffmann, Conan Doyle and many other writers of criminal, detective, and mystery stories. Beside these ranged a patiently acquired list of books on hypnotism, occultism, magic, and necromancy. He was held to be merely a devotee, an innocent fanatic. No one regarded his absorption in the grotesque and arabesque, as Poe would have said, as anything but a hobby on which a man of substance was surely entitled to ride.

Sometimes, it was true, Clarence Adams could be a little annoying. When a store was burglarized or the night prowlers invaded a home and made off with the family plate and jewelry, Adams would be on hand within a day or two, weaving strange theories and applying to these ordinary yet mysterious village thefts all the curious and devious hypotheses he had learned from his reading. But this, too, was passed off as a mere vagary of the student-farmer's.

But the burglaries became more and more numerous and annoying as time went on. Beginning about 1885, Chester and several of the close-clustered surrounding towns and villages had been visited at irregular and shortening intervals by night raiders who broke into houses, shops, and factories, held up pedestrians on the darkened streets, and generally kept the entire neighborhood apprehensive and in tumult. The local police, after their usual formula, had picked up tramps and laggards here and there, and some of these undermen had been packed off to the prison at Windsor, but the burglaries had not ceased. Year after year they seemed to grow in number and mystery till, in the spring of 1902, the whole community was in a ferment and special precautions were being taken on all sides.

One of the chief sufferers by the petty depredations of the undiscoverable marauders was C. H. Waterman, who owned the grist mill and principal feed-store. Every little while someone broke into the plant at night and stole a few bags of grain or feed. On one occasion some clothing had been taken, and again some office equipment, mere trifling stuff that should have suggested the presence of someone other than a professional burglar. The mill owner endured these annoyances for years without much grumbling. He was more mystified than anything else, for the method by which the intruder had got into the place was often not to be discovered. Only after careful watching and minute search was it possible to clear up this point. The robber was in the habit of taking the screws out of locks, removing the whole contrivance, getting what he wanted from the mill, and then putting the locks back into place, so carefully, in most instances, that the police looked everywhere but at the fastenings.

Other merchants and householders were nearly as badly treated, and sorely troubled. J. E. Pollard's clothing store had been entered from time to time, and a suit or two of ready-made garments had gone away to a mysterious ownership on each occasion. Finally, there was a real burglary, in which half the stock of the store was carted off. As a result, a reward was offered and Adams, as a friend of the merchant, helped to post the signs all about the countryside. A few nights afterward, however, masked men entered the clothing man's residence, held up the family at the points of revolvers, and took all the cash, jewelry, silver, and ornaments in the place. And the offers of added rewards did no good.

Finally, to add a touch of pain, the burglar went back, entered the Waterman mill again, and opened the safe, taking fifteen hundred dollars in cash. Now the mill owner employed a secret watchman, but so long as the man was on duty nothing happened. The miller got tired of paying this man for nothing and dismissed him. The very next night the burglar came again and helped himself to some sacks of feed.

Apparently this criminal or band of criminals was local and in the confidence of the townsmen and their police, for too much intimate knowledge of local affairs had been displayed, and too certain information of the movements of officers and watchmen. The officials arrested and examined every one in or near the town who might possibly have seemed a worthy object of suspicion, but no good came of it. The Waterman mill was robbed once more. The whole matter had become too bad a joke.

Old man Waterman set to work on his own plans, and on the night of July 29, 1902, they bore strange fruit. When the mill owner opened his place of business in the morning he discovered that a spring-gun, which he had set to cover the entrance usually used by the intruder, had been discharged and traces of blood near by showed that its charge had found a mark. In so small a community it was not hard to discover the culprit-victim. Imagine the astonishment of the whole population when Clarence Adams, model citizen, public official and custodian of juvenile morals through his superintendency of the library, was found in bed with the charge of Waterman's woodcock shot in his left leg. He was too sorely wounded to be taken to jail at the time, and guards were appointed to watch him day and night.

Adams confessed that he had committed all the burglaries which had annoyed the town for more than fifteen years, and a search of his place disclosed the hiding places of many curious objects whose loss their original owners had forgotten. Adams said that he had taken many of these worthless trinkets because there was nothing else that he could carry away conveniently in his pockets.

"I never robbed because I needed money," he went on, "but simply because robbery, and afterwards listening to the comments and theories of the people and the police, amused me. It was great sport. I was never amused by the recreations that please most men. I always sought pleasure in some unusual way, and robbing for the fun of it was unusual, wasn't it?"

Adams also admitted that many of the methods he had used had been learned from his reading of criminal tales, and that his constant offering of involved hypotheses to explain his simple burglaries had been part of his curious sport—to exaggerate the stupidity of the police and victims. Asked which of his books had influenced him most, he replied by saying that he had been fascinated by *Dr. Jekyll and Mr. Hyde.*

The town gave short shrift to this contradictory man. He was tried less than three weeks after the spring-gun had done its work and sentenced to serve ten years in the State prison at Windsor.

Clarence Adams took his place in the prison in the dress of a celebrity, a rare bird, an extravagance. No one took him seriously in the prison. He was set down as peculiar, a crank, and a trifler, but this judgment was no more correct than the average estimate of the learned man at the hands of his practical brothers.

Adams was put to work in the prison library and in the school. He became at once what is termed a model prisoner, and not the least fear of him was entertained by the officials. But Clarence Adams began to plan his escape the day he set foot inside the walls, and he worked on his plans with unremitting energy, although his labor and his scheme were of so subtle a sort that no one saw or guessed.

No mere jail break could have availed him anything, even if he had been able to accomplish it, which is doubtful. The prison is a strong one, and Adams was not a member of the professional criminal world. He would have had no aid from sources that prove invaluable to the usual escaper. However, his problem lay even deeper. He was so well known personally all through his State and the surrounding New England territory that he would almost certainly be picked up before he could get far from his prison. His wide acquaintance and the notoriety of his case would handicap him the rest of his life, even if he did manage to get away and stay away. Accordingly, Adams set his mind, saturated as it was with strange lores and love of the bizarre and mysterious, to work on a scheme that would divorce him completely from the past, and at the same time carry him out of prison to freedom. It was probably Stevenson who suggested to this necromantic reader and strange criminal the course he took, and it was not the account of *Dr. Jekyll and Mr. Hyde,* but *The Master of Ballantrae,* ›from which the inspiration was drawn.

For the plan he eventually adopted, he needed aid both within and without the prison. Outside aid was at hand. The people of Chester knew, though he himself could nowise be made to confess it, that Adams had not been without accomplices in some of his burglaries. On one occasion, four men participated in a holdup, the sole responsibility for which was admitted by Adams after his capture. It was undoubtedly to one or more of these old aides that the convict resorted for outside co-operation.

› More important still was the co-operation of one man in the prison, locked away like the escaper himself to expiate some crime against the people. This man was the convict physician, and Adams came to know him because he also was studious, a lover of books and a constant reader in the prison library where Adams presided.

The only obstacle in the way was the visiting doctor—for the Vermont prison was not wholly dependent on the services of the immured medicus. Dr. John D. Brewster, a local practitioner, called at the institution at regular intervals, or was summoned whenever there was special need of his services. Thus, whatever plot the librarian and the imprisoned doctor might form must be subtle enough to circumvent the vigilance of the outside man of medicine. Dr. Brewster was, for instance, required to sign the death certificates of all men who perished inside the walls, and they could not be legally buried without his certification. This was important, for Adams planned to die and be born again.

On the afternoon of Washington's birth anniversary, 1904—about eighteen months after his imprisonment—Adams reported to Dr. Brewster, who called at the prison that day, that he was suffering from inflammatory rheumatism. The physician ordered him into the hospital and placed him in care of the convict doctor, with instruction as to his treatment. Though he complained of rheumatism and was sent to the infirmary on that plea, he told the physician that he thought the grippe was coming on, and that he was not long for this world.

On the following day, the 23rd, Adams repeated this dismal prophecy to the deputy warden and still later to the warden himself, but these officials laughed at him and assured him he would be "up and about" in a few days, a prophecy that must have made the plotter smile. Despite Adams' complaining, no grave symptoms set in either on the 24th or on the 25th, and the deputy warden, who was watching the case closely and was repeatedly asking the convict doctor for reports, did not think it necessary to send for Dr. Brewster. But at three o'clock on the afternoon of February 26th, the prison doctor announced that Adams had died of œdema of the lungs, otherwise pneumonia. He made out a death certificate and sent it to Dr. Brewster, together with his report of treatment and examination, and the visiting surgeon promptly signed the document. It might have struck him that pneumonia rarely kills in three and a half days, especially when there have been no violent symptoms even twelve hours before the end, but he probably was busy with his own affairs and did not think it worth while to inquire.

The prison doctor laid out the body himself, washed the corpse, removed it to a slab in a side room, and covered it with sheets and a blanket. No one else had any dealings with the dead Adams, save that the deputy warden came and viewed the body in a perfunctory way. Ordinarily, one of the convict nurses would have been ordered to perform the last unpleasant offices on the body, but the prison doctor explained that Adams had been his friend and had requested him to treat his corpse in a certain way.

The peculiar incidents began now to multiply. Though Adams was related to scores of persons in Chester and in the prison town of Windsor itself, and though he had named as executor his uncle, Samuel Adams, of Chester, he left a hastily drawn testament in which he willed his body to a certain William Dunn, and gave special instructions that it was to be entrusted to no one else. And Dunn appeared at the prison to take charge of it before it was cold. Word of Adams' death had been sent out, it was true, but Dunn appeared so promptly that he felt compelled to explain that Adams had sent him word of his illness and approaching death.

Warden Oakes had previously telephoned to relatives of the dead burglar in Chester, asking whether they would come for the body. Having been given a negative answer, he felt no hesitation in complying with Dunn's demand, backed as he was by the convict's own will. A local undertaker was called, the body was dressed in what is termed a death robe, and laid in a casket. After a brief funeral ceremony it was carried out of the prison, loaded into the undertaker's wagon, and driven twenty-five miles over the hill roads to Cavendish, a small town adjoining Chester, where there was a cemetery and a receiving vault. Into the latter the casket was put, the plan being to bury it in the spring after the frost was out of the earth. The sexton locked the vault carefully and went his way. The casket supposed to contain the body of Adams had not been in its vault more than two months when a well-known traveling man, returning from a trip to Canada, went to the sexton of the cemetery and reported in awed whispers that he had seen and talked to Adams, in Nova Scotia.

As a result of this report, and of other rumors that reached Chester, Samuel Adams, the executor of the dead man's will and trustee of his estate, commanded the sexton to open the casket before burial and make sure that the body was inside. There was a body in the casket, beyond question, and it was that of a man who bore some outward resemblance to Adams, but the death-growth of beard had partly obscured the face and slow decomposition had done the rest, so that no man could have been certain without a more detailed examination. This the sexton did not make. He seems merely to have peeped hastily under the lid, seen the ruined face of what had once been a man, and dropped the coffin quickly into the prepared grave in the Adams cemetery plot.

The statement of the sexton stilled the rumors for a time, but a few months later the mysterious Adams was again seen in Canada, and the renewed report of his presence in the flesh started a fresh tremor in the veins of the people of Chester. The result was a demand for a State investigation, including an inquiry into the conduct of the prison, and the happenings just before Adams' reputed death. At the same time the newspapers set up a hue-and-cry for the exhumation of the body. Then, through the activity of mysterious powers, the Adams story dropped suddenly out of the newspapers, the talk of a State commission ceased, and the relatives of Adams refused permission to have the body taken from the earth. Writers for metropolitan newspapers who went to Vermont to clear up the mystery found themselves balked at every turn. Vermont had decided that it wanted no investigation, and none was made.

Some time ago an associate of the writer who has a large acquaintance in the criminal world and the confidence of many ex-convicts, was summering in Vermont and amused himself by making numerous inquiries among the local people. Eventually he found an old prisoner who had been confined at Windsor at the time of Adams' supposed death, and got from him the prison version of the affair. According to this man, Adams used a sum of money, said to have been three thousand dollars, to aid him in his plot. This sum is said to have been brought to the prison in cash by one of the burglar's intimates and turned over to the convict doctor.

Adams, according to the prison story, was actually able to induce hypnotic suspension of animation in himself, and talked at great length on the subject with the convict doctor and with another intimate of his inside the walls. He made experiments on these friends and on himself, and the three were constantly reading books on the subject which Adams had brought from his library in Chester. He worked on himself for more than a year, previous to the escape, and repeatedly threw himself into states of suspension, from which the convict doctor roused him after short intervals. Finally, after he had made the experiment many times and gradually got himself into a physical and mental condition to risk a longer sleep, he simulated illness, was admitted to the hospital and, after allowing a few days to elapse, put himself to sleep by hypnosis and was pronounced dead by his confederate.

The convict doctor now barred everyone else from touching or approaching the body and personally prepared it for the ordeal of deathlike sleep. He stopped the ears in the manner usual with undertakers, and he apparently filled the nasal passages with cotton, but this was done in such a way that the passage of air was not greatly hindered and the slumbering Adams was thus able to do the almost imperceptible breathing necessary under a hypnotic trance. In this condition he was placed in the coffin and driven to Cavendish, where he was locked into the receiving vault.

To cover this point, the plotters had calculated carefully. Adams knew, warned by his reading of Stevenson, that great cold is likely to prove fatal to experimenters with this death-sleep. Accordingly, it would have been better to make the escape in the summer, but they were faced with the necessity of permitting the body to be buried, if death came in the warm season. On the other hand, if Adams were to die in the middle of the bitter New England winter, his body would undoubtedly be placed in the vault, whence it might be rescued at the proper time without the risk of temporary burial. So the month of February was chosen for the escape.

The body was taken to Cavendish cemetery, locked into the vault and subjected to no watching. The next night the aides of the sleeper appeared and took off the vault locks with a screw driver, exactly as Adams had done in burglarizing the Waterman mill. They entered the place, opened the coffin, and revived their daring brother, who was supplied with clothing and food, and carried overland to a remote railway station, where he was aided to get to Canada in disguise. In Canada the man lived quietly until he was discovered, when he moved his residence, only to encounter again those who knew him. Eventually, he went West and settled down on a ranch. Later still, he is said to have drifted down into Mexico, and there all trace of him was lost.

The matter of the body found in the casket when the sexton opened it before interment was explained readily enough. The town of Hanover, New Hampshire, the seat of Dartmouth College, is only sixteen miles distant from Windsor. Cadavers for use in the medical school are necessarily procured and taken to Dartmouth from time to time, for the use of the medical students and instructors. It was, the old convict said, no difficult matter to procure a body from those who supplied them to the college, and to transport it to the lonely cemetery at Cavendish, where it was placed in the coffin which Adams had quitted a few minutes before. Adams' confederates had balked at this part of the scheme, the old convict said, but the hero of the adventure insisted that an examination might be made and that a body would have to be in the casket to convince the neighbors that the strange burglar of Chester was indeed dead and in his grave.

Apparently, then, Clarence Adams put his reading of Stevenson's strange story into the dress of reality and, unlike James Durrisdeer, the hero of the romance, he survived the experiment and escaped from his enemies.

MEXICO'S DECEPTIVE MILLIONAIRE

by Bernard Hilton

In the Panteón de Dolores, on the outskirts of Mexico City, is a tomb built of colorful Talavera tiles. Here, inseparable as they were in life, lie Don Carlos Balmori and Señorita Concepción Jurado. They died together November 27, 1931.

Thousands of strangers visit the grave every year. On each anniversary of their death a memorial service is broadcast over the leading networks. The participants include not only outstanding Mexican actors but also government officials, generals, scientists, businessmen, noted artists and writers.

For in Mexico, Don Carlos Balmori is as immortal as his Spanish predecessor, Don Quixote de la Mancha. But while Don Quixote took himself and his world seriously, Don Carlos took nothing seriously, least of all himself.

"Nothing is as it appears to be," was his refrain. "Nothing is real. Not even I."

And he proved it.

A portrait on the tomb, done in colored tiles, shows Don Carlos Balmori as a little man with enormous glasses and a fierce mustache. His gloved hands are folded over a walking stick. In his white scarf is a pin with a huge diamond.

Don Carlos was reported to have been one of the world's richest men, holding the Cuban sugar concession, the Bolivian tin concession and the Chinese opium concession. He owned a fabulous castle outside of Mexico City, vast estates elsewhere in the republic and luxurious villas in European resorts.

Contradicting his appearance, Don Carlos was one of the great lovers of all times. In less than ten years this astounding philanderer was engaged to marry or actually married no fewer than fifty women. But the woman who shares his tomb was neither his wife nor his mistress.

Concepción Jurado was sixty-seven when she died. The full-length

tile portrait shows she was rather thin, with intelligent eyes behind
steel-rimmed glasses. Her tightly drawn black hair was streaked
with gray.

She never married, but shared her brother's home in one of the older
sections of the city. Modest and soft-spoken, she had little social life.
Until the day of her death her name had never appeared in any newspaper. No more incongruous mate for Don Carlos in his tomb could
be imagined.

How, then, did it happen that these utterly different human beings
were joined in death?

One evening in 1927 some thirty people were crowded into the two
small rooms of the house of Ignacio Jurado, gardener to Don Carlos
Balmori. Most of the ladies wore evening gowns, the men well-
tailored dark suits. Expensive cars were parked outside.

Two men were making their first visit to the home of Jurado. One
was Señor Martínez, a prominent manufacturer, who hoped to interest
Don Carlos in financing a new plant. The other was Carlos González,
a tall young man with a luxuriant black beard. A real-estate developer,
his aim was to get the backing of Don Carlos for a large project. Both
men had been assured by friends of Don Carlos that he was most
receptive during his weekly visit to the gardener's house.

Conversation stopped abruptly when there was a brusque knock on
the door. The guest of honor paused briefly in the doorway, behind
him a troop of secretaries, lawyers and other attendants.

Deferentially taking the great man's arm, his host led him from
guest to guest. Don Carlos was overly gallant with the younger and
prettier ladies, chucking them under the chin and rolling his eyes in
admiration.

A secretary touched Don Carlos' elbow. "Here is the well-known
industrialist, Señor Martínez, who wishes to speak to you about a confidential matter."

The guests directed curious glances to the millionaire's corner as
Don Carlos listened to the description of a new factory the petitioner
wanted to build in Monterey.

"Very interesting, very interesting," the Spaniard declared. "Allow
me to congratulate you on your astuteness, Señor Martínez. And how
much capital do you require?"

"I think," Martínez hesitated, "we might begin construction with
two hundred and fifty thousand pesos."

"You can't build a decent chicken coop for two hundred and fifty thousand pesos! I'll tell you what. I'll buy a half interest in your business for a half million pesos. You can arrange the details with my attorney tomorrow. Meanwhile, to seal the bargain—"

The secretary extended checkbook and pen. Don Carlos started to write, then paused and gave his new partner a long look. "Señor," he asked accusingly, "do you belong to the Masons?"

"No, sir. The only fraternal order I profess is the Lions Club."

"Oh-ho, so you are a Lion! Well, then, tonight you can roar with satisfaction over the deal we have just made. Come now, let's hear you roar!"

Martínez smiled uncertainly. "Don Carlos, we call ourselves Lions. But we do not roar."

The Spaniard showed contempt. "You are all liars, every one of you. First you tell me you are a lion, then you say you cannot roar. Perhaps you are not a manufacturer, either."

The embarrassed manufacturer saw no escape. He roared, feebly. Don Carlos shook his head in disgust. "My house cat can do better. Come on, get down on your hands and knees and let's hear a real roar."

The reluctant Lion dropped to the floor and roared as if a pitchfork had prodded him. Amid the laughter of the startled company he then received his check and retired.

González, the real-estate developer, had watched these proceedings with divided emotions. His musings were interrupted by the approach of the secretary to Don Carlos. It was his turn to meet the financial genius.

Don Carlos was attentive as he acknowledged the introduction.

"Carlos González," he repeated in his Spanish accent. "I have heard the name before—in connection with real estate, if I am not mistaken."

"The Lomas de Chapultepec developments," said González, with pride. "The fastest-growing section of the city. In ten years' time—"

Don Carlos laughed harshly. "Like all salesmen, Señor González, you make extravagant claims. I myself live in the Colonia del Valle and I maintain that is the most desirable section of the city."

The young man tugged at his rich beard for an inspired reply. None came to him. Don Carlos laughed again.

"So, my friend, for the moment you are that rarity—a salesman without an argument! But I think I could use a young and ambitious man with experience in real estate."

González was in the clouds again as Don Carlos continued. "Sever your ties with the Lomas de Chapultepec people. I want to corner all the available property in Colonia del Valle. It must be done smoothly and secretly, by a man of your caliber. I'll give you a check for sixty thousand pesos now to start picking up options. If you are half the man you seem to be, you'll make more in commissions in the next month than you would in ten years out in Chapultepec."

Percentages and profits danced happily in his mind as González weighed the proposal.

"Come, come!" Don Carlos snapped. "I thought you were a man of decision." Once again the secretary was handing over the checkbook and pen.

"I was only trying to find the proper words of appreciation," the young man said.

Don Carlos smiled. "Your full name?"

"Carlos González."

The millionaire put down his pen. "I am very sorry, but I will not employ anyone whose given name is the same as mine. You must change your name."

González swallowed. "Very well, sir. My middle name is Manuel. I shall use the name Manuel González."

"Good! I like a man who will compromise when he must." Don Carlos wrote the new name on the draft, then fixed his eyes distastefully on the young man's full beard.

"Why do you insist on wearing that beard? Even I, Carlos Balmori, do not permit myself the luxury of more than a mustache. Every time I see a man with a beard I am reminded of a goat!"

The one-time Carlos González clutched involuntarily at his beautiful beard. "It is a personal matter, Don Carlos," he explained weakly. "I—it is a matter of dignity. All during my manhood I have worn a beard. Even for my wife, who objects to it, I would not. . . ."

"Nonsense! When you are as wealthy as I am you can afford to grow yourself another one, down to your knees if you wish, and change your name back to Carlos again. For the present, Manuel, you must be satisfied with a clean-shaven face."

González was in agony. But those commissions! Sixty thousand pesos! After all, it wouldn't be the same as losing an arm or leg.

The young man surrendered. "All right, sir. I shall shave my beard in the morning."

"Splendid!" cried the aging tyrant. "But *mánana* never comes. It shall be done now. Don Ignacio! Bring me shears."

"But Don Carlos!" González protested. "Surely tomorrow—with the proper barber . . ."

"Any fool with a peso can go to a barber," Balmori retorted. "But what man can say that Don Carlos himself has cut his whiskers?"

Don Carlos took the scissors as the young man knelt before him. In a few minutes only an untidy stubble was left.

Carlos Manuel González was a changed man. Gone was the pompous dignity and solemnity. Here was a man who looked like other men—a little nervous and uncertain, it was true, but the check that the secretary handed him would make quite a difference.

"Look at him!" the old man roared. "Once again my money has accomplished a miracle! For a handful of pesos they abandon their names, give up their jobs and change their faces!"

González tried to take the insult with a smile. The smile vanished as Don Carlos, in the act of straightening his tie, began to fumble frantically.

"My pin!" he cried. "My diamond pin! It's gone! I have been robbed! Luis—call the police!"

The secretary hurried outside.

It was the shorn González who spoke next. "I think we should all agree to be searched," he declared. "I will be the first to offer myself!"

The lawyer who had been close by Don Carlos all evening stepped up to González and calmly began the search. It was over in a few seconds. From the breast pocket of the young man's jacket he pulled the glittering pin and held it up. The company gasped.

At the same instant Luis the secretary appeared with two policemen.

"Arrest that man!" screamed Don Carlos. "Arrest that ungrateful thief!"

Not until he felt the pressure of the policemen's hands was González able to speak.

"No!" he shouted. "No! I swear I didn't take it! Somebody must have planted it on me."

The lawyer who had searched González, the impeccably correct Eduardo Delhumeau, former member of the Chamber of Deputies, spoke freezingly. "Are you suggesting, señor, that I would be a party to such a thing?"

The policemen started hustling González to the door. He struggled, like a drowning man. A few minutes ago he had been on the threshold of wealth. Now everything was gone the way of his beard.

"Don Carlos!" he cried in his despair. "Don Carlos, I beg you—"

As if it were a miracle, the ruthless financier seemed to heed the cry. He raised a hand. The policemen stopped, still gripping González.

Don Carlos smiled with strange benevolence as he climbed on a chair so everyone could see and hear him.

"Ladies and gentlemen," he began. "Just as my precious stone reappeared, so must the truth eventually come out. The truth is always hidden. The lesson we must take from the events tonight is that nothing is real, nothing is what it appears to be," Don Carlos continued. Then, after a long pause, he pointed at González. "This man is not a thief! Just as this diamond is not a diamond. Just as Don Carlos Balmori, the famous Spanish multimillionaire, is neither Spanish nor a millionaire. Nor, for that matter, even a man!"

He raised his hat with a flourish. Down cascaded the flowing hair of a woman. Another swift movement and the bristling mustache was off; then the distinctive eyeglasses. In place of the arrogant Spaniard was a modestly smiling, elderly woman.

"I am Conchita Jurado, the humble sister of your host," she said softly. "Here to help you pass a pleasant evening."

Applauding, the guests moved forward and surrounded her.

But how could it have happened that only González and Martínez were fooled by the impostor? And what of the *real* Don Carlos Balmori—the fabulous person whose exploits provided columns of newspaper copy, whose escapades and financial coups supplied gossip for the entire city? Where was he?

Cayetano Guerrero, the newspaperman, walked over to the two men and gave the answer.

"Balmori is imaginary," he said. "He is an illusion created by men's greed and ambition. He is kept alive because no man wishes to believe he is alone in the depths to which avarice will send him."

Every person in the room, Guerrero continued, had been through a similar ordeal. All were sworn to secrecy. González and Martínez now belonged to the most exclusive club in Mexico. In the weeks to come they would enjoy rare diversion. Moreover, each had the right to pick a victim for the next *balmoreada*.

This is but a single episode in the drama in which Don Carlos Balmori played the leading role. During half a century close to three thousand individuals, some famous and others little known, were victimized by the masterly performance of Conchita Jurado.

There was the proud, much-decorated general who was induced by Don Carlos (and a check for 20,000 pesos) to part with his medals.

A prominent jeweler had been told by friends that Don Carlos was seeking seven matched pearls for a Spanish duchess and that the eccentric Spaniard could not recognize imitations. Before the evening was over the jeweler confessed publicly that his pearls were paste.

Even Mexico's famous detective, Valente Quintana, was fooled. Introduced to Don Carlos, Quintana readily accepted a retainer of 5,000 pesos a month to protect the millionaire from a man who threatened him. Don Carlos warned that this fellow would be hard to deal with even for Quintana, because he was such a clever impersonator. Quintana said not to worry; disguises were schoolboy stuff that couldn't fool him.

"So, for example, a man dressed as a woman could never fool you?" asked Don Carlos.

"Of course not," replied Quintana.

"Well," said Don Carlos, "take a good look." And Don Carlos swept off his hat, revealing Conchita Jurado's graying locks.

Who was this remarkable woman?

Concepción Jurado was born in Mexico City in 1874. Her family was poor. By the time she was eighteen Conchita had a reputation for her skill in mimicry. Her favorite subject was an elderly Spaniard, actually named Carlos Balmori, who lived nearby. Her imitations of Balmori's mincing gait, lordly bearing and truculent voice were the delight of the neighborhood.

One day Conchita and her sister, Angela, plotted a practical joke on their father. Conchita borrowed a black suit from her brother and a hat that came down over her ears. She made up her face in the Spaniard's image, including a huge black mustache.

That evening there was a knock on the door. Angela came to her father and announced that Don Carlos Balmori desired the pleasure of an interview. Admitted to the parlor and invited to sit down, the fierce Spaniard refused.

"You will excuse me," he growled in a deep baritone, "but I can make my desires better known on my feet. I shall ask your forbearance if I keep my hat on. I caught a slight cold last evening at the Casino and it is infernally draughty here."

Don Carlos paced the room in silence for several moments. Then, fixing his eyes on his host, he declared with the utmost solemnity:

"Señor, for some time now I have had the pleasure of knowing your young daughter, the beautiful, spiritual but flighty Conchita. We have passed many delightful hours together in the park and in—ahem!—the privacy of her room."

At these words the outraged father leaped to his feet. "I do not believe you!" he shouted. "Furthermore, I demand that you show more respect in my house for my daughter and for me!"

A malicious glint showed in the Spaniard's eyes. "Well," he drawled, "let's make a wager. This night, with your permission or without it, I shall pass the night in Conchita's bed—in this house!"

This was too much for Jurado. With a smothered cry he ran at the visitor, who nimbly ducked behind a sofa. Angela burst into the room, laughing. Don Carlos yanked off the false mustache and the hat, then asked sweetly:

"Well, Papa, where shall I sleep, if not in my own bed?"

It was some moments before the stupefied father could join in the laughter.

That was the first appearance of Don Carlos Balmori on his private stage in Mexico—a stage he was to occupy for fifty years.

Conchita thought up new roles for Don Carlos and tried the act on other relatives. People who had known the girl from infancy were completely fooled. The audience was gradually enlarged to include friends. One by one they met Don Carlos, were insulted and drawn into quarrels. In the end the hoax was revealed.

It was not until 1925 that the great names of Mexico were brought into the game, one after another. Cayetano Alfonso Guerrero, the newspaperman who was also Conchita's nephew, had invited his good friend Eduardo Delhumeau to dinner at the home of a relative. Delhumeau, then a member of the Chamber of Deputies, had listened closely as Guerrero described the mimicry of Don Carlos.

Delhumeau thought it was a pity that such an exceptional farce should play before so small an audience. Why not expand the game?

Conchita was willing. The first step was to equip Don Carlos with an extravagant wardrobe from one of the most expensive shops. A fine malacca stick was bought. The fake diamond stickpin was a happy afterthought.

Semiweekly performances at the Jurado home or at the elaborate Army Club were decided upon. The victims, known as *puerquitos* (little pigs), were to be picked with care. Conchita would be thoroughly briefed on the background and weaknesses of each *puerquito*. Since secrecy was vital, each victim would be sworn to silence in exchange for a pledge that his downfall would never be publicized. Up until Conchita's death not a single word of the farce ever leaked out —and this despite the fact that among the victims were the leading newspapermen, publishers, writers and political figures of Mexico.

In fact, these distinguished personages lent their talents and connections to the task of convincing the public that the eccentric multimillionaire actually existed. News of Balmori's financial coups and private activities was seriously printed in the newspapers. Photographs frequently appeared—and certainly the camera cannot lie. By skillfully superimposing the head of Don Carlos on news pictures from all over the world, the papers showed Don Carlos with his foot on an elephant he had killed in Africa, Don Carlos with the tiger he had shot in India, Don Carlos leaning over a fallen antagonist on the field of honor, Don Carlos conversing intimately with the Shah of Persia, and so on for year after year. Nobody could doubt his existence.

Conchita herself was modest, gentle and unpretentious. But as Don Carlos she was haughty, boastful and cruel. And although Conchita was always a virtuous spinster, Don Carlos was a lecherous old goat who never missed a chance to fondle and proposition a pretty girl.

One memorable evening Major Salvador Martínez Cairo, who had been an early victim, introduced the famous millionaire to a beautiful sixteen-year-old girl named María Antonieta. Fashionably gowned, with a pert red hat on a luxuriant hair-do, the girl was a born coquette.

Don Carlos fell on his knees before this promising dish. He seized the girl's hands and kissed them ardently. Finally, like dozens before her, the girl succumbed.

Came the end of the evening and the showdown. Don Carlos removed his hat and mustache, and Conchita Jurado smiled at the horrified girl.

But María Antonieta had her own contribution to make. The girl pulled off her red hat. Then she tore off her wig, revealing a young boy who got busy at once wiping lipstick off his mouth and powder from his face. Don Carlos was not a man and María Antonieta was no lady.

Most of Conchita Jurado's hoaxes were intended to illustrate her cynical belief that people will do anything for money, that they will give up honor, self-respect, love, for gold. In a sense, however, Conchita, herself, disproved her own theory. For she refused to utilize her talents for gain, turned down numerous legitimate and shady schemes, and lived her materially humble, strangely dedicated existence to the end. Once when Conchita Jurado was really hard up, Don Carlos called up the Minister of Education and influenced him to have the poor, deserving old woman hired as janitress in a school near her home. Throughout her life, Conchita Jurado refused to be dependent on the charity of her friends.

In 1931, at the age of sixty-seven, Conchita Jurado began to complain of severe pain, dizziness and general weakness. Physicians found she had cancer. In spite of their objections she continued to appear regularly at the *balmoreadas*. Only two weeks before her death she gave her last performance. Those who saw it say she was as brilliant as ever.

On November 27, 1931, surrounded by relatives and many friends, Conchita Jurado died. The ban on revealing secrets of the *balmoreadas* was ended. Every newspaper in Mexico devoted entire pages to feature articles on the amazing exploits of Don Carlos Balmori.

Conchita Jurado was buried in the Panteón de Dolores the day after her death. The services were broadcast. Among the mourners were scores of important persons, all of whom had been *puerquitos*. No less than twenty beautiful, young women who had in the course of an evening either married or promised to marry the elderly unattractive Don Carlos Balmori—thus proving themselves gold-diggers —assisted at the burial.

A year after Conchita's death her friends and admirers collected money to build the monument that now stands above her grave, a tomb of tiles bearing portraits of both Concepción Jurado and Don Carlos Balmori in addition to scenes from many of the famous *balmoreadas*.

And each year since, on the anniversary of her death, survivors of the fantastic hoax have gathered at the tomb to honor the memory of Mexico's greatest actress.

PANIC: THE MEN FROM MARS

by John Houseman

Most of our accounts deal with consciously created deceptions. The famous Mercury Theater radio broadcast that panicked America differs somewhat, for its creators sought to create the illusion of reality only within the legitimate framework of a dramatic performance. But, through a combination of historical timing, brilliant craftsmanship and certain human failings shared by millions of listeners, this particular radio drama was accepted by a huge audience as stark reality. In this fascinating account, theatrical and film producer John Houseman, founding partner of the Mercury Theater with Orson Welles, and editor of the theater's radio series enables us to watch the show's development from the inside, as well as portraying its impact on the audience and analyzing why such startling reactions occurred.

RADIO WAR TERRORIZES U. S.—N. Y. *Daily News*, October 31, 1938.

Everybody was excited I felt as if I was going crazy and kept on saying what can we do what difference does it make whether we die sooner or later? We were holding each other. Everything seemed unimportant in the face of death. I was afraid to die, just kept on listening.—*A listener*

Nothing about the broadcast was in the least credible.
                                              —*Dorothy Thompson*

The show came off. There is no doubt about that. It set out to dramatize, in terms of popular apprehension, an attempted invasion of our world by hostile forces from the planet Mars. It succeeded. Of the several million American citizens who, on the evening of October 30, 1938, milled about the streets, clung sobbing to one another or drove wildly in all directions to avoid asphyxiation and flaming death, approximately one-half were in terror of Martians—not of Germans, Japanese, or unknown enemies—but, specifically, of Martians. Later, when the excitement was over and the shadow of the gallows had lifted, some of us were inclined to take credit for more deliberate and premeditated villainy than we deserved. The truth is that at the time, nobody was more surprised than we were. . . .

In later years, when the Men from Mars had passed into history, there was some bickering among members of the Mercury as to who, exactly, had contributed precisely what, to that particular evening's entertainment. The truth is that a number of us made a number of essential and incalculable contributions to the broadcast. (Who can accurately assess, for instance, the part played by Johnny Dietz's perfect engineering, in keeping unbroken the shifting illusion of imperfect reality? How much did the original old H. G. Wells, who noisily repudiated us, have to do with it? Or the second assistant sound man? Or individual actors? Or Dr. Goebbels? Or Charlie McCarthy?) Orson Welles had virtually nothing to do with the writing of the script and less than usual to do with its preliminary rehearsals. Yet first and last it was his creation. If there had been a lynching that night, it is Welles the outraged populace would have strung up—and rightly so. Orson was the Mercury. "The War of the Worlds," like everything we did, was his show.

Actually, it was a narrow squeak. Those Men from Mars barely escaped being stillborn. Tuesday afternoon—five days before the show—Howard Koch telephoned. He was in deep distress. After three days of slaving on H. G. Wells' scientific fantasy he was ready to give up. Under no circumstances, he declared, could it be made interesting or in any way credible to modern American ears. Koch was not given to habitual alarmism. To confirm his fears, Annie, our secretary, came to the phone. She was an acid and emphatic girl from Smith College with fine blond hair, who smelled of fading spring flowers. "You can't do it!" she whined. "Those old Martians are just a lot of nonsense. It's all too silly! We're going to make fools of ourselves! Absolute fools!"

For some reason which I do not clearly remember our only possible alternative for that week was a dreary one—"Lorna Doone." I tried to reach Welles. He was at the theater and wouldn't come to the phone. . . . I called Koch back. I was severe. I taxed him with defeatism. I gave him false comfort. I promised to come up and help.

When I finally got there—around two the next morning—things were better. He was beginning to have fun laying waste the State of New Jersey. Annie had stopped grinding her teeth. We worked all night and through the next day. Wednesday at sunset the script was finished.

Thursday, as usual, Paul Stewart rehearsed the show, then made a record. We listened to it rather gloomily, long after midnight in Orson's room at the St. Regis, sitting on the floor because all the chairs were covered with coils of unrolled and unedited film. We agreed it was a dull show. We all felt its only chance of coming off lay in emphasizing its newscast style—its simultaneous, eyewitness quality.

All night we sat up, spicing the script with circumstantial allusions and authentic detail. Friday afternoon it went over to CBS to be passed by the network censor. Certain name alterations were requested. Under protest and with a deep sense of grievance we changed the Hotel Biltmore to a non-existent Park Plaza, Trans-America to Intercontinent, the Columbia Broadcasting Building to Broadcasting Building. . . .

Saturday afternoon Paul Stewart rehearsed with sound effects but without Welles. He worked for a long time on the crowd scenes, the roar of cannon echoing in the Watchung Hills and the sound of New York Harbor as the ships with the last remaining survivors put out to sea.

Around six we left the studio. Orson, phoning from the theater a few minutes later to find out how things were going, was told by one of the CBS sound men, who had stayed behind to pack up his equipment, that it was not one of our better shows. Confidentially, the man opined, it just didn't come off. . . .

On Sunday, October 30, 1938, at 8:00 P.M., E.S.T., in a studio littered with coffee cartons and sandwich paper, Orson swallowed a second container of pineapple juice, put on his earphones, raised his long white fingers and threw the cue for the Mercury theme—the Tchaikovsky Piano Concerto in B Flat Minor #1. After the music dipped, there were routine introductions—then the announcement that a dramatization of H. G. Wells' famous novel, *The War of the Worlds*, was about to be performed. Around 8:01 Orson began to speak, as follows:

WELLES

We know now that in the early years of the twentieth century this world was being watched closely by intelligences greater than man's and yet as mortal as his own. We know now that as human beings busied themselves about their various concerns they were scrutinized and studied, perhaps almost as narrowly as a man with a microscope might scrutinize the transient creatures that swarm and multiply in a drop of water. With infinite complacence people went to and fro over the earth about their little affairs, serene in the assurance of their dominion over this small spinning fragment of solar driftwood which by chance or design man has inherited out of the dark mystery of Time and Space. Yet across an immense ethereal gulf minds that are to our minds as ours are to the beasts in the jungle, intellects vast, cool, and unsympathetic regarded this earth with envious eyes and slowly and surely drew their plans against us. In the thirty-ninth year of the twentieth century came the great disillusionment.

It was near the end of October. Business was better. The war scare was over. More men were back at work. Sales were picking up. On this particular evening, October 30, the Crossley service estimated that thirty-two million people were listening in on their radios. . . .

Neatly, without perceptible transition, he was followed on the air by an anonymous announcer caught in a routine bulletin:

ANNOUNCER

. . . for the next twenty-four hours not much change in temperature. A slight atmospheric disturbance of undetermined origin is reported over Nova Scotia, causing a low pressure area to move down rather rapidly over the northeastern states, bringing a forecast of rain, accompanied by winds of light gale force. Maximum temperature 66; minimum 48. This weather report comes to you from the Government Weather Bureau. . . . We now take you to the Meridian Room in the Hotel Park Plaza in downtown New York, where you will be entertained by the music of Ramon Raquello and his orchestra.

At which cue, Bernard Herrmann led the massed men of the CBS house orchestra in a thunderous rendition of "La Cumparsita." The entire hoax might well have exploded there and then—but for the fact that hardly anyone was listening. They were being entertained by Charlie McCarthy—then at the height of his success.

The Crossley census, taken about a week before the broadcast, had given us 3.6 per cent of the listening audience to Edgar Bergen's 34.7

per cent. What the Crossley Institute (that hireling of the advertising agencies) deliberately ignored, was the healthy American habit of dial-twisting. On that particular evening, Edgar Bergen in the person of Charlie McCarthy temporarily left the air about 8:12 P.M., E.S.T., yielding place to a new and not very popular singer. At that point, and during the following minutes, a large number of listeners started twisting their dials in search of other entertainment. Many of them turned to us—and when they did, they stayed put! For by this time the mysterious meteorite had fallen at Grovers Mill in New Jersey, the Martians had begun to show their foul leathery heads above the ground, and the New Jersey State Police were racing to the spot. Within a few minutes people all over the United States were praying, crying, fleeing frantically to escape death from the Martians. Some remembered to rescue loved ones, others telephoned farewells or warnings, hurried to inform neighbors, sought information from newspapers or radio stations, summoned ambulances and police cars.

The reaction was strongest at points nearest the tragedy—in Newark, New Jersey, in a single block, more than twenty families rushed out of their houses with wet handkerchiefs and towels over their faces. Some began moving household furniture. Police switchboards were flooded with calls inquiring, "Shall I close my windows?" "Have the police any extra gas masks?" Police found one family waiting in the yard with wet cloths on faces contorted with hysteria. As one woman reported later:

> I was terribly frightened. I wanted to pack and take my child in my arms, gather up my friends and get in the car and just go north as far as we could. But what I did was just sit by one window, praying, listening, and scared stiff, and my husband by the other sniffling and looking out to see if people were running. . . .

In New York hundreds of people on Riverside Drive left their homes ready for flight. Bus terminals were crowded. A woman calling up the Dixie Bus Terminal for information said impatiently, "Hurry please, the world is coming to an end and I have a lot to do."

In the parlor churches of Harlem evening service became "end of the world" prayer meetings. Many turned to God in that moment:

> I held a crucifix in my hand and prayed while looking out of my open window for falling meteors. . . . When the monsters were wading across the Hudson River and coming into New York, I wanted to

run up on my roof to see what they looked like, but I couldn't leave my radio while it was telling me of their whereabouts. . . .

The panic moved upstate. One man called up the Mt. Vernon Police Headquarters to find out "where the forty policemen were killed." Another took time out to philosophize:

> I thought the whole human race was going to be wiped out—that seemed more important than the fact that we were going to die. It seemed awful that everything that had been worked on for years was going to be lost forever.

In Rhode Island weeping and hysterical women swamped the switchboard of the Providence *Journal* for details of the massacre, and officials of the electric light company received a score of calls urging them to turn off all lights so that the city would be safe from the enemy. The Boston *Globe* received a call from one woman "who could see the fire." A man in Pittsburgh hurried home in the midst of the broadcast and found his wife in the bathroom, a bottle of poison in her hand, screaming, "I'd rather die this way than that." In Minneapolis a woman ran into church screaming, "New York destroyed this is the end of the world. You might as well go home to die I just heard it on the radio." . . .

In San Francisco the general impression of listeners seemed to be that an overwhelming force had invaded the United States from the air—was in process of destroying New York and threatening to move westward. "My God," roared an inquirer into a telephone, "where can I volunteer my services, we've got to stop this awful thing!"

As far south as Birmingham, Alabama, people gathered in churches and prayed. On the campus of a Southeastern college——

> The girls in the sorority houses and dormitories huddled around their radios trembling and weeping in each other's arms. They separated themselves from their friends only to take their turn at the telephones to make long distance calls to their parents, saying goodbye for what they thought might be the last time. . . .

There are hundreds of such bits of testimony, gathered from coast to coast.

At least one book* and quite a pile of sociological literature has

---

* *The Invasion from Mars* by Hadley Cantril, Princeton University Press, from which many of the above quotations were taken.

appeared on the subject of "The Invasion from Mars." Many theories
have been put forward to explain the "tidal wave" of panic that swept
the nation. I know of two factors that largely contributed to the
broadcast's extraordinarily violent effect. First, its historical timing.
It came within thirty-five days of the Munich crisis. For weeks, the
American people had been hanging on their radios, getting most of
their news no longer from the press, but over the air. A new technique
of "on-the-spot" reporting had been developed and eagerly accepted
by an anxious and news-hungry world. The Mercury Theater on the
Air by faithfully copying every detail of the new technique—including its imperfections—found an already enervated audience ready to
accept its wildest fantasies. The second factor was the show's sheer
technical brilliance. To this day it is impossible to sit in a room and
hear the scratched, worn, off-the-air recording of the broadcast, without feeling in the back of your neck some slight draft left over from
that great wind of terror that swept the nation. . . .

Radio drama was taken seriously in the thirties—before the Quiz
and the Giveaway became the lords of the air. In the work of such
directors as Reis, Corwin, Fickett, Welles, Robson, Spier, and Oboler
there was an eager, excited drive to get the most out of this new, all
too rapidly freezing medium. But what happened that Sunday, up on
the twentieth floor of the CBS building was something quite special.
Beginning around two, when the show started to take shape under
Orson's hands, a strange fever seemed to invade the studio—part
childish mischief, part professional zeal.

First to feel it were the actors. I remember Frank Readick (who
played the part of Carl Phillips, the network's special reporter) going
down to the record library and digging up the Morrison recording of
the explosion of the Hindenburg at Lakehurst. This is a classic re-
portage—one of those wonderful, unpredictable accidents of eyewitness description. The broadcaster is casually describing a routine
landing of the giant gasbag. Suddenly he sees something. A flash of
flame! An instant later the whole thing explodes. It takes him time—
a full second—to react at all. Then seconds more of sputtering ejacu-
lations before he can make the adjustment between brain and tongue.
He starts to describe the terrible things he sees—the writhing human
figures twisting and squirming as they fall from the white burning
wreckage. He stops, fumbles, vomits, then quickly continues. Readick
played the record to himself, over and over. Then, recreating the emotion in his own terms, he described the Martian meteorite as he saw it

lying inert and harmless in a field at Grovers Mill, lit up by the head-lights of a hundred cars—the coppery cylinder suddenly opening, revealing the leathery tentacles and the terrible pale-eyed faces of the Martians within. As they begin to emerge he freezes, unable to trans-late his vision into words; he fumbles, retches—and then after a second continues.

A few moments later Carl Phillips lay dead, tumbling over the microphone in his fall—one of the first victims of the Martian Ray. There followed a moment of absolute silence—an eternity of waiting. Then, without warning, the network's emergency fill-in was heard—somewhere in a quiet studio, a piano, close on mike, playing "Clair de Lune," soft and sweet as honey, for many seconds, while the fate of the universe hung in the balance. Finally it was interrupted by the manly reassuring voice of Brigadier General Montgomery Smith, Commander of the New Jersey State Militia, speaking from Trenton, and placing "the counties of Mercer and Middlesex as far west as Princeton and east to Jamesburg" under Martial Law! Tension—re-lease—then renewed tension. For soon after that came an eyewitness account of the fatal battle of the Watchung Hills; and then, once again, that lone piano was heard—now a symbol of terror, shattering the dead air with its ominous tinkle. As it played, on and on, its effect became increasingly sinister—a thin band of suspense stretched almost beyond endurance.

That piano was the neatest trick of the show—a fine specimen of the theatrical "retard," boldly conceived and exploited to the full. It was one of the many devices with which Welles succeeded in com-pelling, not merely the attention, but also the belief of his invisible audience. "The War of the Worlds" was a magic act, one of the world's greatest, and Orson was just the man to bring it off.

For Welles is at heart a magician whose particular talent lies not so much in his creative imagination (which is considerable) as in his proven ability to stretch the familiar elements of theatrical effect far beyond their normal point of tension. . . .

Among the columnists and public figures who discussed the affair during the next few days (some praising us for the public service we had rendered, some condemning us as sinister scoundrels) the most general reaction was one of amazement at the "incredible stupidity" and "gullibility" of the American public, who had accepted as real, in this single broadcast, incidents which in actual fact would have taken days or even weeks to occur. "Nothing about the broadcast," wrote

Dorothy Thompson with her usual aplomb, "was in the least credible." She was wrong. The first few minutes of our broadcast were, in point of fact, strictly realistic in time and perfectly credible, though somewhat boring, in content. Herein lay the great tensile strength of the show; it was the structural device that made the whole illusion possible. And it could have been carried off in no other medium than radio.

Our actual broadcasting time, from the first mention of the meteorites to the fall of New York City, was less than forty minutes. During that time men traveled long distances, large bodies of troops were mobilized, cabinet meetings were held, savage battles fought on land and in the air. And millions of people accepted it—emotionally if not logically.

There is nothing so very strange about that. Most of us do the same thing, to some degree, most days of our lives—every time we look at a movie or listen to a broadcast. Not even the realistic theater observes the literal unities; motion pictures and, particularly, radio (where neither place nor time exists save in the imagination of the listener) have no difficulty in getting their audiences to accept the telescoped reality of dramatic time. Our special hazard lay in the fact that we purported to be, not a play, but reality. In order to take advantage of the accepted convention, we had to slide swiftly and imperceptibly out of the "real" time of a news report into the "dramatic" time of a fictional broadcast. Once that was achieved—without losing the audience's attention or arousing their skepticism, if they could be sufficiently absorbed and bewitched not to notice the transition—then, we felt, there was no extreme of fantasy through which they would not follow us. We were keenly aware of our problem; we found what we believed was the key to its solution. And if, that night, the American public proved "gullible," it was because enormous pains and a great deal of thought had been spent to make it so.

In the script, "The War of the Worlds" started extremely slowly —dull meteorological and astronomical bulletins alternating with musical interludes. These were followed by a colorless scientific interview and still another stretch of dance music. These first few minutes of routine broadcasting "within the existing standards of judgment of the listener" were intended to lull (or maybe bore) the audience into a false security and to furnish a solid base of realistic time from which to accelerate later. Orson, in making over the show, extended this slow movement far beyond our original conception. "La Cumparsita,"

rendered by "Ramon Raquello, from the Meridian Room of the Hotel
Park Plaza in downtown New York," had been thought of as running only a few seconds; "Bobby Millette playing 'Stardust' from the
Hotel Martinet in Brooklyn," even less. At rehearsal Orson stretched
both these numbers to what seemed to us, in the control room, an
almost unbearable length. We objected. The interview in the Princeton Observatory—the clockwork ticking monotonously overhead, the
woolly-minded professor mumbling vague replies to the reporters'
uninformed questions—this, too, he dragged out to a point of tedium.
Over our protests, lines were restored that had been cut at earlier
rehearsals. We cried there would not be a listener left. Welles
stretched them out even longer.

He was right. His sense of tempo, that night, was infallible. When
the flashed news of the cylinder's landing finally came—almost fifteen
minutes after the beginning of a fairly dull show—he was able suddenly to spiral his action to a speed as wild and reckless as its base
was solid. The appearance of the Martians; their first treacherous act;
the death of Carl Phillips; the arrival of the militia; the battle of the
Watchung Hills; the destruction of New Jersey—all these were telescoped into a space of twelve minutes without overstretching the listeners' emotional credulity. The broadcast, by then, had its own reality, the reality of emotionally felt time and space.

At the height of the crisis, around 8:31, the Secretary of the
Interior came on the air with an exhortation to the American people.
His words, as you read them now, have a Voltairean ring. . . .

THE SECRETARY

Citizens of the nation: I shall not try to conceal the gravity of the
situation that confronts the country, nor the concern of your Government in protecting the lives and property of its people. However, I
wish to impress upon you—private citizens and public officials, all of
you—the urgent need of calm and resourceful action. Fortunately, this
formidable enemy is still confined to a comparatively small area, and
we may place our faith in the military forces to keep them there. In
the meantime placing our trust in God, we must continue the performance of our duties, each and every one of us, so that we may
confront this destructive adversary with a nation united, courageous,
and consecrated to the preservation of human supremacy on this earth.
I thank you.

Toward the end of this speech (*circa* 8:32 E.S.T.), Davidson Taylor, supervisor of the broadcast for the Columbia Broadcasting System, received a phone call in the control room, creased his lips, and hurriedly left the studio. By the time he returned, a few moments later —pale as death—clouds of heavy smoke were rising from Newark, New Jersey, and the Martians, tall as skyscrapers, were astride the Pulaski Highway preparatory to wading the Hudson River. To us in the studio the show seemed to be progressing splendidly—how splendidly Davidson Taylor had just learned outside. For several minutes now, a kind of madness had seemed to be sweeping the continent— somehow connected with our show. The CBS switchboards had been swamped into uselessness but from outside sources vague rumors were coming in of deaths and suicides and panic injuries.

Taylor had requests to interrupt the show immediately with an explanatory station-announcement. By now the Martians were across the Hudson and gas was blanketing the city. The end was near. We were less than a minute from the Station Break. The organ was allowed to swirl out under the slackening fingers of its failing organist and Ray Collins, superb as the "last announcer," choked heroically to death on the roof of Broadcasting Building. The boats were all whistling for a while as the last of the refugees perished in New York Harbor. Finally, as they died away, an amateur shortwave operator was heard, from heaven knows where, weakly reaching out for human companionship across the empty world:

> 2X2L Calling CQ
> 2X2L Calling CQ
> 2X2L Calling CQ
> Isn't there anyone on the air?
> Isn't there anyone?

Five seconds of absolute silence. Then, shattering the reality of World's End—the Announcer's voice was heard, suave and bright:

ANNOUNCER

You are listening to the CBS presentation of Orson Welles and the Mercury Theater on the Air in an original dramatization of *The War of the Worlds,* by H. G. Wells. The performance will continue after a brief intermission.

The second part of the show was extremely well written and most sensitively played—but nobody heard it. It recounted the adventures of a lone survivor, with interesting observations on the nature of human society; it described the eventual death of the Martian Invaders, slain—"after all man's defenses had failed by the humblest thing that God in his wisdom had put upon this earth"—by bacteriological action; it told of the rebuilding of a brave new world. After a stirring musical finale, Welles, in his own person, delivered a charming informal little speech about Halloween, which it happened to be.

I remember, during the playing of the final theme, the phone starting to ring in the control room and a shrill voice through the receiver announcing itself as belonging to the mayor of some Midwestern city, one of the big ones. He is screaming for Welles. Choking with fury, he reports mobs in the streets of his city, women and children huddled in the churches, violence and looting. If, as he now learns, the whole thing is nothing but a crummy joke—then he, personally, is coming up to New York to punch the author of it on the nose! Orson hangs up quickly. For we are off the air now and the studio door bursts open. The following hours are a nightmare. The building is suddenly full of people and dark blue uniforms. We are hurried out of the studio, downstairs, into a back office. Here we sit incommunicado while network employees are busily collecting, destroying, or locking up all scripts and records of the broadcast. Then the press is let loose upon us, ravening for horror. How many deaths have *we* heard of? (Implying they know of thousands.) What do *we* know of the fatal stampede in a Jersey hall? (Implying it is one of many.) What traffic deaths? (The ditches must be choked with corpses.) The suicides? (Haven't you heard about the one on Riverside Drive?) It is all quite vague in my memory and quite terrible.

Hours later, instead of arresting us, they let us out a back way. We scurry down to the theater like hunted animals to their hole. It is surprising to see life going on as usual in the midnight streets, cars stopping for traffic, people walking. At the Mercury the company is still stoically rehearsing—falling downstairs and singing the "Carmagnole." Welles goes up on stage, where photographers, lying in wait, catch him with his eyes raised up to heaven, his arms outstretched in an attitude of crucifixion. Thus he appeared in a tabloid that morning over the caption, "I Didn't Know What I Was Doing!" The New York *Times* quoted him as saying, "I don't think we will choose anything like this again."

We were on the front page for two days. Having had to bow to radio as a news source during the Munich crisis, the press was now only too eager to expose the perilous irresponsibilities of the new medium. Orson was their whipping boy. They quizzed and badgered him. Condemnatory editorials were delivered by our press-clipping bureau in bushel baskets. There was talk, for a while, of criminal action.

Then gradually, after about two weeks, the excitement subsided. By then it had been discovered that the casualties were not as numerous or as serious as had at first been supposed. One young woman had fallen and broken her arm running downstairs. Later the Federal Communications Commission held some hearings and passed some regulations. The Columbia Broadcasting System made a public apology. . . .

As to the Mercury—our new play, *Danton's Death,* finally opened after five postponements. Not even our fantastic publicity was able to offset its generally unfavorable notices. On the other hand, that same week the Mercury Theater on the Air was signed up by Campbell Soups at a most lavish figure.

Of the suits that were brought against us—amounting to over three quarters of a million dollars for damages, injuries, miscarriages, and distresses of various kinds—none was substantiated, or legally proved. We did settle one claim, however, against the advice of our lawyers. It was the particularly affecting case of a man in Massachusetts, who wrote:

"I thought the best thing to do was to go away. So I took three dollars twenty-five cents out of my savings and bought a ticket. After I had gone sixty miles I knew it was a play. Now I don't have money left for the shoes I was saving up for. Will you please have someone send me a pair of black shoes size 9B!"

We did.

By way of footnote: *In 1939 an adaptation of* The Men from Mars, *broadcast in Ecuador, caused similar panic. Afterwards, an angry mob burned down the radio station, killing six of the show's participants.*

THE WOMAN WHO MARRIED FOURTEEN WIVES

from The Newgate Calendar

MARY HAMILTON, ALIAS CHARLES HAMILTON, ALIAS GEORGE HAMILTON, ALIAS WILLIAM HAMILTON

Polygamy, or a man marrying two or more wives, and, *vice versa,* a woman marrying two or more husbands, is a crime frequently committed; but a woman, according to the rites of the established Church, marrying a woman, is something strange and unnatural. Yet did this woman, under the outward garb of a man, marry fourteen of her own sex!

At the quarter-sessions held at Taunton, in Somersetshire, this woman was brought before the Court; but under what specific charge, or upon what penal statute she was indicted, we can neither trace by the mention of the circumstance, nor could we frame an indictment to meet the gross offense, because the law never contemplated a marriage among women. She was, however, tried, whether or not her case might have been cognizable, and Mary Price, the fourteenth wife, appeared in evidence (in such a case as this we must be pardoned for ambiguity) against her female husband. She swore that she was lawfully married to the prisoner, and that they bedded, and lived together as man and wife, for more than a quarter of a year; during all which time, so well did the impostor assume the character of man, that she still actually believed she had married a fellow-creature of the right and proper sex. At length, the prosecutrix added, she became mistrustful, and, comparing certain circumstances with the married Goodies, her neighbours, she was convinced that Mary had acted the part of Charles towards her by the vilest and most deceitful practices.

The learned quorum of justices,

> In full-blown dignity of wigs,
> Mounted on blocks, thus cogitated—

"That the he, she, prisoner at the bar, is an uncommon notorious cheat; and we, the Court, do sentence her or him, whichever he or she may be, to be imprisoned six months, and, during that time, to be whipped in the towns of Taunton, Glastonbury, Wells, and Shipton-Mallet, and to find security for good behaviour as long as they, the learned justices aforesaid, shall or may, in their wisdom and judgment, require"; and Mary, the monopolizer of her own sex, was imprisoned and whipped accordingly, in the severity of the winter of the year 1746.

THE INSPECTOR GENERAL WAS A LADY

In his More Tramps Abroad, *Mark Twain wrote a brief account
of an amazing imposture which he heard about in South Africa.*

A CURIOUS ROMANCE

by Mark Twain

I saw some of the fine old Dutch mansions, pleasant homes of the
early times, pleasant homes to-day, and enjoyed the privilege of their
hospitalities. And just before I sailed I saw in one of them a quaint
old picture which was a link in a curious romance—a picture of a pale,
intellectual young man in a pink coat with a high black collar. It was
a portrait of Dr. James Barry, a military surgeon who came out to the
Cape fifty years ago with his regiment. He was a wild young fellow,
and was guilty of various kinds of misbehavior. He was several times
reported to headquarters in England, and it was in each case expected
that orders would come out to deal with him promptly and severely,
but for some mysterious reason no orders of any kind ever came back
—nothing but just an impressive silence. . . .

Next, he was promoted—away up. He was made Medical Super-
intendent-General, and transferred to India. Presently he was back
at the Cape again and at his escapades once more. There were plenty
of pretty girls, but none of them caught him, none of them could get
hold of his heart; evidently he was not a marrying man. And that was
another marvel, another puzzle, and made no end of perplexing talk.
Once he was called in the night, on obstetric service, to do what he
could for a woman, who was believed to be dying. He was prompt
and scientific, and saved both mother and child. There are other instances of record which testify to his mastership of his profession;
and many which testify to his love of it and his devotion to it. Among
other adventures of his was a duel of a desperate sort, fought with
swords, at the Castle. He killed his man.

The child heretofore mentioned as having been saved by Dr. Barry so long ago, was named for him, and still lives in Cape Town. He had Dr. Barry's portrait painted, and gave it to the gentleman in whose old Dutch house I saw it—the quaint figure in the pink coat and high black collar.

The story seems to be arriving nowhere. But that is because I have not finished. Dr. Barry died in Cape Town thirty years ago. It was then discovered that he was a *woman.*

THE FACTS IN THE CASE

by David Porter

Dr. James Barry died in an apartment at 14 Margaret Street, London (not in Cape Town as Twain reports), on July 25, 1865, and Hart's Army List, as well as the newspaper announcements of that month, give the Inspector General's age as seventy-one. The first person known to have discovered Dr. Barry's true sex was the physician who examined the body and signed the death certificate. It must have been a startling discovery, indeed, for the young Army doctor, as he, himself, had served several years under the Inspector General.

The astonishing news was officially reported to the Horse Guards. An autopsy yielded the further startling news that Dr. James Barry had been a mother, probably early in life. Since Dr. Barry's real name and origin remain a mystery, we do not know whether she was married nor what happened to the child. Dr. Barry's motherhood is, however, the only clue we have as to the chain of events that might have been instrumental in leading her to discard women's clothes for those of a man. Possibly she was loved and left, with or without her acquiescence, and gave birth to an illegitimate child, which, either conveniently died or was disposed of in some fashion. Then, having found, through unhappy experience, that it was a man's world, she may have decided to *be* a man for the rest of her life. Or else she was married at a very tender age and found it a disillusioning experience.

At any rate, she either contrived to get hold of some money or she was supported in her masquerade by her family or some benefactor. For in 1808, when she was sixteen, she was accepted as a student in Edinburgh University, under the name of James Barry. According to the testimony of fellow-students, who were contacted after her death, no one had apparently suspected James Barry to be other than she appeared. James was somewhat nervous at going through certain

rough neighborhoods in Edinburgh at night, and often asked a fellow-
student to accompany her. Also she absolutely refused to box. And
she had an odd manner of keeping her arms folded over her chest that
the other students found quite amusing.

After obtaining her medical degree at Edinburgh, Dr. Barry disappears from the records for several years. Then in 1816 she reappears
as an Army surgeon. For a time Dr. Barry was stationed at Quebec.
There she became notorious for her sharp temper. Once when a man
taunted her by calling her voice squeaky and effeminate, Dr. Barry—
despite her lack of practice in boxing and the dangers of exposure
involved—took the man on with bare fists and gave a good account
of herself.

She later served in the Mediterranean, the West Indies and South
Africa. She was promoted regularly and once was particularly commended "for assiduity and skill during a small-pox epidemic."

At the Cape of Good Hope, Dr. James Barry seems to have been
something of a medical pioneer, a battler against ignorance and care-
lessness. In her civil post as Inspector of the Colonial Medical Board,
she strongly opposed the prevailing practice of allowing anyone who
wished to set up as a chemist and dispense medicines and drugs. She
insisted that every chemist pass an examination. The chemists fought
this idea and a long-drawn out, inconclusive conflict ensued. The records also show that Dr. Barry devoted a lot of attention to the lepers.
Afterwards, when the facts about her true sex reached South Africa,
people recalled her special interest in one child suffering from leprosy
and conjectured that this might have been her own.

In his memoirs, the Earl of Albemarle describes Dr. Barry:

> In this learned pundit I beheld a beardless lad, apparently of my
> own age, with an unmistakable Scotch type of countenance, reddish
> hair, and high cheek-bones. There was a certain effeminacy in his
> manner which he seemed to be always striving to overcome. His style
> of conversation was greatly superior to that one usually heard at a
> mess-table in those days of non-competitive examinations.

We get an idea of the constant care Dr. Barry had to exercise to
avoid disclosing her imposture, from the report of a young man who
once shared a cabin with the doctor on an intercolonial steamer ply-
ing between St. Thomas and the Barbados. The young man occupied
the top bunk; Dr. Barry, then Deputy-Inspector of Hospitals, had the
lower. Dr. Barry solved the delicate problem by peremptorily order-

ing the young man out of her cabin every morning: "Now youngster, you clear out while I dress."

This same young man's report informs us that a goat was kept on board to provide Dr. Barry with milk. The doctor's diet apparently was strictly vegetarian, and she never touched intoxicating drinks. But, at the General's table, where she and the young man both sat, Dr. Barry had everyone in stitches with her amusing tales about her powers as a lady-killer.

One of the last reports about Dr. Barry comes from two ladies who met her at an inn. Given a room adjoining the Doctor's, the ladies were warned to be very quiet as the gentleman next door was crotchety. They found Dr. Barry, on the contrary, an agreeable, witty companion, though somewhat querulous-voiced. Pale and wizened, Dr. Barry wore a flaxen wig and was invariably accompanied by a small white dog.

Investigation after Dr. Barry's death, indicated that neither her servants nor her comrades-at-arms, despite close daily fellowship, had had an inkling of the truth. The facts about Dr. Barry's real origin were either never uncovered by the British Army or were hushed up through high-level intervention. In later years, British feminists adopted Dr. Barry as one of their heroes. As one of them put it: "In her numerous reports she proved herself a skilled doctor, and an enthusiast at her work. She wrote fearlessly and frankly, always ready to expose incompetence and charlatanism, even though it involved her in controversy and opposition. For high courage nothing could exceed the spirit of this woman who was so far ahead of her time that, to achieve her purpose, she renounced her sex."

The fragments available to us of this amazing woman's life open up innumerable, fascinating lines of conjecture. What an incredible inner life she must have led. What secret fears, triumphs, conflicts must have been her lot. What innumerable stratagems she must have practiced. One wonders, too, what sexual outlets she resorted to, or did her whole life serve as a single, sustained sublimation? At any rate, this unique woman, whose tombstone inscription still bills her as "Dr. James Barry," successfully competed with men in a profession denied to her fellow-women for more than half a century after she took the Hippocratic Oath.

THE FABULOUS FRAUD FROM BROOKLYN

by Alan Hynd

Some years ago when I was laid low in a Connecticut hospital, I was pulling every trick out of the bag in an effort to find out just what was wrong with me—with notable lack of success.

Then one day when things were getting more mysterious than ever, the door of my room opened and in walked a dark, neatly turned-out little man chasing sixty but not looking it. The day nurse looked at him as a guard would look at a spy in a top-secret missile factory, but the visitor quickly put her at her ease. "I'm Dr. Weyman from New York," he said to the nurse.

There stood Stanley Clifford Weyman, the man who had been for a hilarious third of a century the country's number-one impostor.

I just lay there, entranced by the spectacle of the little man about whom I had heard so much but had never seen, except in newspaper photos. With considerable aplomb he dismissed the nurse, laid his hat and stick on the bureau and drew a chair up to my bed. "I saw in the New York papers you were here," he told me, "and so I thought I'd come up and pay my respects." It seemed that Weyman had long been a reader of my stories and, since I had long followed his career, we had formed a sort of mutual admiration society.

I didn't know what Weyman really had come for and didn't bother to ask him right then. I had something more urgent in mind. I wanted to find out just what was wrong with me, and what, to be more specific, my chances of survival were, and I knew that Stanley Clifford Weyman was just the boy to clear things up.

"Just leave it to me," he said. He went down the hall and returned with the charts on my case. "I'll just take these out to lunch with me," he said, "and study them while I eat. Where's the physicians' dining room?"

After Weyman left, one of the real doctors came in, inquiring about the charts. "Oh," I explained, "a specialist friend of mine from New York stopped by and took them out to lunch with him."

"Who's the specialist?" asked the doctor.

"His name is Weyman—Dr. Stanley Clifford Weyman."

Now the day nurse fell to thinking. "It seems to me," she said, "that I read something in the papers about Dr. Weyman. And not long ago, either."

And of course the nurse was right. Only two years previously, Weyman had turned up at Lake Success, New York, then the assembly hall of the United Nations. Loaded down with fake credentials, he had sold himself to Robert Erwin, head of the Erwin News Service, an agency servicing small-time papers, as an experienced correspondent. He was promptly accredited as a working journalist at the United Nations.

A man of Olympian impartiality, Weyman was soon on cordial footing with such political opposites as Warren Austin, the chief American delegate to Lake Success and with Andrei Gromyko, the Russian representative. A linguist of notable ability, Weyman conversed with several of the foreign diplomats in their native tongues.

One of Weyman's greatest admirers at Lake Success was Ambassador Wan Waithayakon of Thailand. Early in 1950, after Weyman had interviewed His Excellency on the radio several times, he suggested to the Ambassador that he could help Thailand's cause, if the Ambassador could wangle him an appointment as a special public-relations counselor with diplomatic status. The Ambassador considered the suggestion a sound one.

Weyman got off a long night letter to the State Department in Washington. He wanted to know if his American citizenship would be placed in jeopardy if he became an accredited diplomat from Thailand. Presently the striped-pants boys were hustling through the hushed precincts of the Department carrying memorandums of dreadful import. The memorandums were about Stanley Clifford Weyman. The FBI had a plump dossier on the little man.

So Weyman not only missed out on becoming a genuine diplomat but he also lost his job with the Erwin News Service.

The whole hilarious business of the little impostor's almost becoming an accredited diplomat hit the papers not long before Weyman showed up in my hospital room, and that was what the nurse vaguely remembered. But as I lay there waiting to find out what Dr. Weyman would glean from the charts, my mind went back to the many phases of the little man's career even before he pulled the wool over the official eyes at Lake Success.

Born in Brooklyn under the name of Stephen Weinberg, he was an under-sized precocious kid who wanted to be a doctor. Since his parents were too poor to send him through college and to medical school, he was obliged to earn a livelihood at such mundane tasks as clerking in stores and working as a drudge in counting houses.

He never cleared more than operating expenses out of his impersonations, playing his roles merely for the joy of basking, however temporarily, in the ego-nourishing rays of the limelight.

Weyman got off to a dreary start in his career as an impostor. At the age of twenty-one he quit his job in a Brooklyn counting house and crossed into Manhattan decked out in a purple uniform and proclaiming himself the United States Consul Delegate to Morocco. He ran up a few tabs in the swank restaurants and, by way of getting some cash for incidental expenses, stole a camera and hocked it. That indiscretion got him a term in the Elmira Reformatory.

Out on parole the following year, Weyman walked the streets of Brooklyn and Manhattan in a double role—that of a military attaché from Serbia and a lieutenant in the United States Navy. Caught, he went back to prison for a couple of years.

Out on parole a second time, Weyman gave himself a double promotion. He became a lieutenant commander in the Rumanian Army and Rumanian Consul General in New York. Aware of his new responsibilities, he decided to inspect a battleship.

Pulling the various wires that eventually set off his escapades was never a problem to Stanley Clifford Weyman. He usually operated on such a high level that the victims of his impostures took it for granted that he had hurdled the lower-level barriers. When he decided to inspect a battleship he simply telephoned to the United States Navy Department in Washington, introduced himself in his double Rumanian role, and announced that the Queen of Rumania had instructed him to pay his informal respects to the United States Navy.

Thus one day in 1915, decked out in a stunning light-blue uniform, dripping with gold braid and wearing an admiral's hat, he boarded a launch that took him out to the U.S.S. *Wyoming*, lying at anchor in the Hudson River. Although the distinguished little visitor was at the time only twenty-four years old, his severe mien and dignity made him appear much older.

As the *Wyoming's* captain hustled him past the rows of sailors standing at attention, Weyman would stop occasionally to request that a sailor raise his chin a trifle, stand more erectly or shift his hat to a more becoming angle. He found a big smudge on the toe of one gob's shoe and just stood there, looking first at the shoe, then at the gob's face, then at the shoe, then at the face again.

Although Weyman was severe with the enlisted men, he was most cordial to the brass. The tour over, he announced that he wished to throw a dinner for the officers. He went to the Astor Hotel in Times Square, still all decked out in the sky-blue uniform, the gold braid and the admiral's hat, and hired a private dining room. The bill? "Just send it to me at the Rumanian Consulate in Washington."

The day the banquet was to be held, a detective down at Police Headquarters was reading the New York *Times* when he came to an item which had been sent to the paper by the Astor's publicity department, announcing that Consul General Stanley Clifford Weyman of Rumania was going to be host at a banquet for the officers of the U.S.S. *Wyoming*.

So two dicks crashed the party. The consul general, gold braid and all, was plucked from the center of festivities, and sent back to prison for violating his parole. "All I can say," the captain of the *Wyoming* later told a reporter, "is the little guy put on one hell of a tour."

When the United States entered the first World War, Weyman, adorned with the name of Royal St. Cyr, commissioned himself a lieutenant in the Army Air Corps. He pranced around Brooklyn and Manhattan in a spanking, custom-tailored uniform. Then one day, apparently feeling that he was not getting enough attention, he turned up at the Forty-seventh Regiment Armory in Brooklyn. "You may announce in the papers," he instructed the commanding officer in the armory, "that I am about to make a formal inspection of the Forty-seventh Regiment."

Weyman was conducting the inspection with his usual thoroughness when a couple of dicks turned up. "That's him, all right."

In 1920, Weyman, out of jail and sunk in a job in a Brooklyn counting house, read an advertisement in the New York *Times* for a physician to go to Lima, Peru, to supervise sanitation conditions for a New York development company. He stuffed a brief case with spurious credentials and applied for the job. A genuine doctor interviewed the applicants and, after looking at Dr. Weyman's credentials, became so captivated by the little fellow's personality that he recommended him for the post.

So, as he approached his thirtieth birthday, Brooklyn's Walter Mitty left the New York cops behind him and sailed away. Once in Lima, he rented a palace, hired a large staff of servants, imported two American cars, threw lavish parties—and put everything on an expense account forwarded to the New York development company. In the performance of his duties as a sanitation expert, he played it safe; he just nodded wisely when a local official made what appeared to be a constructive suggestion.

It was the expense accounts that did him in. There was, somehow, an unprofessional tinge about them. So Dr. Weyman's employers decided to hold the man's credentials up to the light. When the awful truth came out, little Dr. Weyman was quietly recalled.

In the summer of 1921, Weyman read an item in the public prints to the effect that Princess Fatima of Afghanistan was getting an official brush off during a visit to the United States.

Under the circumstances, Walter Mitty would have simply dreamed of helping a princess in distress. Weyman, on the other hand, decked himself out in striped pants, cutaway, top hat and cane and presented himself at the suite of Her Royal Highness as Under Secretary Stanley Clifford Weyman of the State Department.

The Princess, dark, squat, was swathed in billowing satin of many hues, and she wore a large diamond in, of all places, the fleshy part of her nose. He informed her, through one of her sons who spoke English that he had come to apologize on behalf of Secretary of State Charles Evans Hughes for having been remiss in according her a proper reception.

"Tell Her Highness," Weyman said to the son, "that I am going to take her to Washington to meet the Secretary of State and the President." That, answered Her Highness through the interpreter, was more like it. Under Secretary Weyman coughed. There would be, he said, a little matter of money—$10,000, say. What for? Why, to observe an old American custom: to purchase gifts for attachés of the State Department and the personnel at the White House.

Weyman took the ten grand and hired a private railroad car to run him and Her Royal Highness down to Washington. He ensconced Fatima in a suite in the Willard Hotel then hustled over to the State Department. By now he was decked out in the summer whites of a lieutenant commander in the United States Navy. He informed a State Department under secretary that a group of influential U.S. Senators, whose names he reeled off, had sent him over to arrange that Her Highness be received by Secretary Hughes.

The reception of the Princess by the Secretary of State was quickly arranged. During the course of Fatima's reception by Hughes, Brooklyn's Mitty chatted pleasantly with the Secretary of State.

When the little visit was coming to an end, Weyman whispered to a State Department attaché that Her Highness wished to pay her respects to President Warren G. Harding.

So Fatima and the Brooklyn boy crossed the street from the State Department to the White House and were ushered in to see the President.

The President was flanked by half a dozen naval lieutenants who snapped to attention when the lieutenant commander entered. "At ease," said Lieutenant Commander Weyman. Then, when he had introduced Fatima to the President, Weyman began to pass little pleasantries with Harding. That caused the naval attachés to get suspicious.

That night, while Weyman and Fatima were on the way back to New York, a high-level inquiry got under way. Next day the awful truth came out. But by the time Naval Intelligence hit the Waldorf-Astoria to lay hands on the little man, Weyman had gone back to his prosaic labors in Brooklyn.

In 1922, Weyman read in the papers about the impending visit to this country of Dr. Adolf Lorenz, the world-renowned bloodless surgeon of Vienna. On the day that Dr. Lorenz's boat came in, Dr. Clifford Weyman, special representative of the Health Commissioner of New York, went down the bay on the revenue cutter that carried reporters and photographers who met distinguished arrivals.

The impostor, who spoke German, greeted the doctor—a kindly big bear of a man—on behalf of New York City. When the reporters arrived and started interviewing Lorenz, Dr. Weyman acted as interpreter. Once in awhile, when a reporter popped a question that Dr. Weyman deemed inappropriate, he frowned and put the fellow in his place.

By the time the liner had reached its berth in the North River, Dr. Lorenz had come to regard little Dr. Weyman as indispensable. Weyman told Lorenz that he would be glad to disentangle himself from his official city duties and help Lorenz any way he could during the noted visitor's stay. Lorenz, baffled by American ways, was delighted. So when Lorenz set up a clinic at the New York Hospital for Joint Diseases, Weyman was right there with him, decked out in operating-room garb, in charge of everything.

After extensively observing the Lorenz method, Weyman decided to personally minister to the afflicted one day when Lorenz was out for a bite to eat. He put a little boy up on the table and began to manipulate the child's deformed foot. The child yelled bloody murder and Weyman got rid of him, looked up at a nurse and said, "Next patient."

By the time Weyman had treated four patients, it was obvious to the doctor witnesses that the man was an authentic fraud. One of the medicos began a quiet investigation and quickly turned up the fact that Weyman wasn't a doctor at all. The cops heard about that and connected him with the fellow who had impersonated a naval officer in Washington. So one afternoon, a couple of men from Naval Intelligence dropped into the Lorenz clinic and started Weyman on a two-year term for impersonating a federal officer.

After his release, he turned up outside the gates of Sing Sing in the role of prison-reform expert. An execution was about to be held and there were quite a few reporters hanging around. Weyman was giving out an interview, protesting not only the execution that was about to take place, but *all* executions.

Warden Lewis E. Lawes became curious about what was going on outside the gates. Investigating, Lawes recognized Weyman and, as the cliché experts would say, the jig was up.

Not long afterward a group of prominent physicians was included among those in attendance at the dedicatory exercises of Middlesex University, a former Massachusetts medical school. The program listed Dr. Stanley Clifford Weyman, "Penal Authority," as scheduled to read a paper on "Insanity: Its Defense in Crime."

The Weyman paper went fine for awhile . . . but as the impostor got further into his paper, he began to find fault with alienists. "Some alienists," he read, "are far from perfect. I know some, in fact, who, when they go into a certain prison to probe the minds of the prisoners, are by all odds on the wrong side of the bars." Now Dr. Weyman digressed from his prepared text. He glanced up and smiled coldly. "To be specific, gentlemen," he said, "I think that the average alienist should himself be subjected to a searching mental examination."

Weyman was dwelling in comparative obscurity in 1926 when Rudolph Valentino, the Great Lover of the silent-movie era, died in a New York Hospital. Pola Negri, the Polish tragedienne of the flickers, appeared in New York, ensconced herself in a suite in the Ambassador Hotel and announced that she was practically out of her mind with grief over Valentino's death. She and the Great Lover had, she announced, been informally engaged.

Weyman, out in the wilderness of Brooklyn, decided to do something about La Negri's plight. He asked for a few days' vacation from the counting house and, carrying a medical kit, crossed the river to Manhattan and hustled up to the Ambassador. There, announcing himself to a maid as Dr. Weyman, a personal friend of the late Valentino, he was quickly shown into Negri's boudoir. "Rudy," said Dr. Weyman to the actress, who was propped up in a luxurious bed, the symbol of tragic beauty, "would have wanted me to take care of you."

Negri sighed, obviously touched. But Weyman, professionally brisk, had little time for emotion. "Put out your tongue," he said. "Ah, a little coated." He popped a thermometer into Negri's mouth, took out a watch and counted her pulse. "You're running quite a temperature."

The doctor sat down, wrote out a prescription and summoned a maid. "Have this filled immediately," he said. "A teaspoonful every three hours in a little water."

Weyman asked the actress if she had an extra bedroom in the suite. It so happened she had. "Fine," he said. "I'll just remain with you until you're through this terrible ordeal." Negri gasped her heartfelt appreciation.

Now Weyman began issuing bulletins to the reporters on Negri's condition. The New York *Times,* which even then had a fat dossier on the fellow in its clipping library, didn't get around to making any connection between Negri's physician and the little impostor. It printed sober accounts of Negri's condition, as given out by Dr. Weyman. It even went so far as to describe the good doctor as the author of a non-existent volume called *Weyman on Medico-Jurisprudence.*

It wasn't until the day of Valentino's funeral that Dr. Weyman really got going. The actor's body lay in state in Campbell's Funeral Home on upper Broadway and the tens of thousands of the morbid and sentimental lined up to get a last look at the corpse. And there was Brooklyn's Mitty, right in the middle of the whole thing. He escorted Miss Negri when she went to have a last look at the remains and, after taking her back to the Ambassador, returned to the funeral home.

Weyman set up a little first-aid booth outside of Campbell's. He bustled around, looking at the tongues and feeling the pulses of the curious. When somebody swooned, he was right there with the smelling salts. Brooklyn's Mitty was living one of his shining hours.

There is only one instance on record wherein Stanley Clifford Weyman made a legitimate dollar in his career as an impostor. Back in the Twenties there was a tabloid newspaper in New York, published by Bernarr Macfadden, called the *Evening Graphic*. It was edited by Emile Gauvreau.

Queen Marie of Rumania—an autocratic woman and something of an old fake herself—hit New York and ensconced herself on an entire floor of the Ambassador Hotel and barricaded herself against the press. Gauvreau determined that the *Evening Graphic* should scoop the town in getting an interview with Her Majesty even though he had to fake one. He was visited by a bright thought: it would take a fraud to snare a fraud. So Gauvreau got in touch with Weyman. "I want you to get in to see the Queen," he told Weyman.

Weyman, wearing striped pants, cutaway and top hat, breezed into the Ambassador lobby. The entrance to one elevator, reserved for the Queen's exclusive use, was blocked by several Secret Service men.

Weyman appeared to be surprised. He smiled briskly and reached into his wallet for a name card. "Which one of you is in charge here?" he asked pleasantly. A Secret Service man said *he* was. Weyman handed the man the card.

"Oh," said the Secret Service man, "I beg your pardon."

"Quite all right, my good fellow," said Weyman.

"I knew he was somebody," the Secret Service man said to another operative. "He's an under secretary of State. Name's Weyman."

The Queen was in the parlor, sitting in the center of a group of top-level society figures. Weyman edged his way to the royal presence. He clicked his heels, bowed, kissed Her Majesty's hand then inquired, "Does Your Highness find everything completely to your royal satisfaction?" The Queen, taking the little man to be the hotel's director of protocol, replied in perfect English that her quarters were just fine. Now Weyman, pouring on the oil, remarked that the hotel staff had requested him to convey to her a somewhat personal observation. And what, the Queen inquired, was that? "Simply, Your Majesty," said Weyman, "that you look so remarkably young and beautiful." The Queen was simply enchanted.

Now Weyman took over the whole show. He asked Her Highness the standard questions—what she thought of American men. American girls, bobbed hair and sex. That evening, the subway set was reading the *Evening Graphic's* great scoop.

Late in the Twenties, Weyman opened an office on Broadway. He was now posing as an attorney at law. There is not much of a record as to how long Weyman had his shingle hung up, or just who his clients were, or precisely what he said he could do for them. But one day an investigator for the Bar Association stopped in to see Weyman the barrister. "And how may I be of service?" asked Weyman. "Just show me your license to practice," said the man.

After coming out of jail, Weyman was quiescent for a few years. Then, when World War II broke out, he established himself in a midtown New York Hotel as Dr. Stanley Clifford Weyman and opened up consulting rooms for draft dodgers. He instructed them in how to simulate deafness and he schooled the more stupid-looking candidates in how to look even more stupid and fake feeble-mindedness.

What Weyman needed, in company with his co-conspirators, the FBI decreed, was about seven years in jail.

Released in 1948, Brooklyn's Mitty, now fifty-seven, began casting about for a new role. That was when he appeared at the United Nations, there to function for two years before being exposed.

When Stanley Clifford Weyman returned from lunch to my room in the hospital that day he was all smiles. "You haven't a thing to worry about," he assured me.

"But what's wrong with me?"

"Well, the doctors don't exactly know. It seems to be a virus of some kind. But it doesn't amount to anything. They'll knock it out with one of those drugs they're injecting in you."

They finally did knock it out—a couple of months later—but strangely enough, the fraudulent Mr. Weyman's reassuring words did ease me over the hump.

What had he originally come to see me about? It seems that he wanted me to collaborate with him on a book about his life as an impostor. I refused, for the time being anyway. Something tells me the little man with the brass-band front hasn't expunged all the devious exploits from his doughty system. And it just could be that the next one might make the biggest chapter of them all.

THE MANY LIVES OF SALLY BEAUCHAMP

by Morton Prince

*This piece stands somewhat apart from the others in this volume
in several respects. The deceptions of Miss Beauchamp's several
personalities were practiced chiefly on one another—that is, on
herself. And these excerpts from Dr. Morton Prince's remarkable
study,* The Dissociation of a Personality (1905), *do not relate one
or two striking instances of dissimulation, but rather present the
fascinating pattern of a case of multiple personality in action. In a
sense, of course, we are all many people; certainly each of us has
many moods and is aware that nuances of his personality differ in
different situations. Thus, the persistent, intricate and thorough
self-deception carried on by Miss Beauchamp reflects the incredible but universal role-playing potentials of the human psyche.*

*Miss Christine Beauchamp—which, of course, is not her real
name—was an intelligent, neurasthenic New England college girl,
shortly before the turn of the century. Soon after she came for
treatment to Dr. Prince, he became aware that she possessed
several distinct personalities, whose actions and thoughts were in
some cases partially, in others wholly, concealed from one another. The reader should keep in mind that every one of the
personalities—B I, Sally, B IV, etc.—belongs to the same person
and that, except for her immediate family, nobody—fellow-
students, friends, teachers—suspected the true state of affairs.
After several years of treatment, Dr. Prince succeeded in largely
unifying and harmonizing the various personalities and recon-
stituting the true Miss Beauchamp. Thus, eventually the many
became one. But at the start of these excerpts Sally and Miss
Beauchamp are in conflict.*

Miss Beauchamp . . . was punished by being put upon an allowance which was doled out to her in amounts of from five to ten cents
a day. It was about twenty-four hours after returning home that she
received a note from Sally with the first instalment. The note said, in
substance, that she could have ten cents to amuse herself with, but no

more, and that henceforth the writer was going to take charge of her finances. The rest of her money was thereupon confiscated. . . . No amount of pleading would induce Sally to allow Miss Beauchamp to have more money than her allowance. . . .

But this was only a small part of the torment to which she was subjected. . . . Her postage stamps were taken, and with her small allowance she did not have money enough to buy them or to pay street-car fares. So, in the want of the latter, she walked; and as for letters, when she wrote one, she was compelled by her tyrant to place it on the table for approval. If it was approved, she found it stamped and was allowed to post it; if not approved, it did not go, and that was the end of it. "She writes too many letters," said Sally. "She sha'n't write, excepting to people whom I choose, and she sha'n't have any money excepting what I give her."

Miss Beauchamp has a nervous antipathy to spiders, snakes, and toads; she abhors them to a degree that contact with them throws her into a condition of terror. One day she found in her room a small box neatly tied up, as if it were a present for herself. On opening it six spiders ran out. "She screamed," said Sally, "when she opened the box, and they ran out all over the room." It turned out that Sally had gone into the country and gathered these spiders as a treat for Miss Beauchamp. . . .

One of Miss Beauchamp's constant trials was to find a piece of worsted work she was making unravelled as fast as she made it. She had been asked by a very dear friend to make a baby's blanket. Her heart was in the work and she was anxious to finish it. She had worked at it for months, but often complained to me that whenever it neared completion she would find it almost wholly unravelled. Then, like Sisyphus, she would have to begin her task all over again. Finally, when at last the blanket was finished and ready to send, the climax came. Sally pulled the whole of it to pieces, and drawing out the yarn wound it round about the furniture, carrying it from picture to picture, back to the different articles of furniture, then round herself many times, then back to the furniture, finally hiding the ends somewhere in the bed. Then Sally, standing in the midst of this perfect tangle of yarn, wakened Miss Beauchamp, who came to herself in the maze. So great was the tangle that she had to cut the yarn to get out.

Another of Sally's pranks which had serious consequences to Miss Beauchamp's health was to take her on walks too long for her strength. On one occasion she went out into a suburban town (Watertown) and there took a long walk, so far beyond Miss Beauchamp's strength that it left the latter exhausted. Miss Beauchamp came to herself in this suburb, weary and helpless, unable to recognize the place, and ignorant of the way home.

One very curious phenomenon was the difference between the physical condition of Sally and that of Miss Beauchamp after a fatiguing walk of this kind. On this occasion two days later Miss Beauchamp was still extremely fatigued and worn out. Then suddenly changing in my presence to Sally, this personage appeared perfectly fresh and unaffected by the walk. Then changing back to Miss Beauchamp, the fatigue returned with the change of personality.

Sally enjoyed making Miss Beauchamp tell nonsensical lies. . . . Sally also took advantage of Miss Beauchamp's sense of dignity. Knowing this feeling was acute, Sally, to punish her, would make her sit with her feet on another chair, or even on the mantelpiece. Miss Beauchamp could not take her feet down, but would have to sit there undergoing the torture of mortification. On numerous occasions Sally tore up many manuscript pages of her school work, the product of much labor. . . .

Although it amused her to make Miss Beauchamp miserable, nevertheless at times, when she went too far and Miss Beauchamp became ill from anxiety, Sally would be alarmed and would write me a letter asking for help, saying she could "not do anything with Miss Beauchamp"; and that I "really must help" her. . . .

Of all the trials which Miss Beauchamp had to undergo, I think what she minded most were the letters she received from her other self. She was deluged with letters; and if she refused to read them Sally would pin upon the wall sheets of paper with messages written thereon, and so placed that she could not help seeing them. Sally knew her sensitiveness, her keen sense of honor, as well as all her little weaknesses, and these she played upon in a highly artistic manner. Then again Sally would write letters to different people, telling all sorts of things about Miss Beauchamp's private affairs, exaggerating and distorting them beyond recognition, and even telling things not true. She would describe extraordinary and impossible things she proposed to do, pretended engagements objectionable to Miss Beauchamp—all of which was sufficient to frighten the latter out of her senses. These letters Sally had no intention of sending, but she would leave them open where they could be read by Miss Beauchamp, who, taking them seriously, would be made to feel she lived over a dynamite magazine. Sometimes, however, Sally would actually send letters which expressed her own peculiar ideas. These naturally would be extremely disagreeable to Miss Beauchamp, who would learn of them from her friends or from the letters received in reply.

Of all these letters, the most troublesome for me were those in which Sally misrepresented my attitude towards Miss Beauchamp. For instance, she wrote B I that I accused her of not keeping her word and of telling untruths, and that I was so annoyed with her that I wished her never to come again for treatment. Sally's game was to prevent Miss Beauchamp's being the object of care. In spite of constant warnings not to believe Sally's statements, B I* always accepted them as true. A despairing letter from her would follow, declaring her ignorance of everything she had ever done in her "lapses," and asking forgiveness for anything that was displeasing. . . .

Sally hated Miss Beauchamp, and the secret of her hatred was unquestionably jealousy, as Miss Beauchamp suspected. Sally frequently complained that everybody seemed to care about what was going to become of Miss Beauchamp, but nothing about her own fate. She felt hurt too that she was told she was childish and irresponsible and broke her promises, while Miss Beauchamp was treated with great respect. "Nobody cares what becomes of me," she would repeat. . . .

[Notebook] *April 28, 1899.* "As Sally had been tormenting Miss Beauchamp, I took occasion to upbraid her. . . .

"'But why do you hate her? You are only hating yourself, for she is yourself.'

"'No, she isn't.' [With resentment.] 'I won't have it so! We are not the same person. We don't think alike, and we don't have the same thoughts,' etc., etc. Her indignation increased, and she ended again with, 'I certainly hate her. She thinks she won't let me come [that is, into active existence as Sally]. . . . I am going to do everything I can think of . . . I tried to cut off her hair the other day, but she woke up before I could do it. I think the scissors waked her up.'

"'You will cut off your own hair; it is your hair.'

[Laughing.] "'I don't care. She will look a guy—just like one of those monkeys. I don't care how I look.'

"At such times Sally has no consciousness of Miss Beauchamp's existence. 'Where is she now?' Sally often asks."

[Later another self appeared to complicate matters.—A. K.]

* Miss Beauchamp.

During the following summer B IV came and went, changing places with Sally and Miss Beauchamp as in a stage comedy. The complications had been bad enough when there were only two persons, but now that there were three, the situations became wofully tangled. I saw nothing of any of them during July and August, though in frequent correspondence with Miss Beauchamp and Sally, but I learned afterwards of their doings. A pretty mess they made of it, each playing her own game regardless of the others. Poor Miss Beauchamp was in despair, and got into a hopeless state of mind not to be wondered at.

She had not only "lost much time"—the greater part of the summer, in fact—but had also lost a number of valuables, including some rings, a necklace, a watch, and several borrowed books. . . . To cap the climax, she learned from one of Sally's letters that she had borrowed quite a sum of money and had promptly lost it. Miss Beauchamp, of course, was in the dark about the way all this had happened, and ignorant of the fate of her valuables. Whatever meagre information she had came from Sally's letters. For she did not realize that there were now in the family besides herself two others, instead of one. . . .

It was B IV who had borrowed the money, and it was also B IV who had lost a ring which Miss Beauchamp treasured, wearing it on a chain around her neck. . . . The other rings were not lost, as Miss Beauchamp supposed, although she (B I) could not find them; this was owing to negative hallucinations. They were literally directly under her nose—yet, owing to this psychical phenomenon, she could not see or feel them. Sally had strung them for safety on a ribbon about her neck, where they were later found. . . .

Miss Beauchamp had disappeared for weeks during the summer, leaving Sally and B IV to alternate with each other and to run the campaign. B IV managed the family affairs according to her own ideas, which agreed with those of Miss Beauchamp about as well as Katharine agreed with Petruchio. Then Sally would just drop a line to B I that she might know what IV had done, if it happened to be particularly galling to I's feelings. . . .

[*Dr. Prince quotes here directly from his notes.—A. K.*]

"Miss Beauchamp, being unable to discover the whereabouts of her missing property, decided that she would go to New York to earn some money for the purpose of paying back that which had been borrowed. . . . For some reason she took tickets to New Haven, instead of to New York. On arrival in New Haven, she went to the Young Women's Christian Association, and applied to the matron for work. . . . The matron asked if she could wait on table. Miss Beauchamp thought she could, so a place was obtained for her at a hotel . . . Her stay here lasted about two days . . . All went well until the 'Idiot' * suddenly appeared and found herself waiting upon table, a position which she looked upon with the utmost disgust. Nevertheless, angry and disgusted as she was, she went on doing the work for a time.

"Finally the 'Idiot' wouldn't stand it any longer, and went to Mrs. S., telling her she did not like the work and was going away. Mrs. S., who liked Miss Beauchamp very much, said she was very sorry, and tried to persuade her to stay—but not being able to do so, told her if she would wait till Mr. S. returned, he would pay her. But the 'Idiot' wouldn't; she said she didn't want the money anyway, and left then and there. . . . At the station, after paying for the carriage, she found herself with only a little silver, less than a dollar, in her pocket, not enough to pay her fare. . . . She pawned her watch for four dollars, and returned to Boston.

"When Miss Beauchamp (B I) later found her watch gone, she was much distressed, because it belonged to Miss Z. Now, in addition to the loss of her money, she had lost another person's watch. . . . Thanks to Sally, the watch was located in the pawnbroker's shop, and later I redeemed it. It is only fair to the 'Idiot' to say that she had a right to keep the watch if she so chose, having, unknown to Miss Beauchamp, exchanged her own for it, and further she had the pawnbroker's card carefully preserved. After the return of the family to Boston, Miss Beauchamp (B I) in her turn waked up to find herself in a strange lodging house on —— Street, which Sally claimed the honor of selecting. . . .

"Miss Beauchamp, harrowed and worried by it all, was ready to give up . . . One night, soon after returning to Boston, she had closed tight the windows of her room, turned on the gas and got into bed, but Sally—again a guardian angel—immediately got up, turned off the gas, opened the windows, and thus saved her life. The attempt at suicide evidently impressed Sally, who pondered upon it awhile and then asked me whether, if Miss Beauchamp killed herself, she, Sally, would be dead too. On learning that this would be the case, she shuddered, and said, 'I shouldn't like that.'"

During the autumn and winter (1899-1900), the vicissitudes of a triple personality were going on. Sally had largely transferred her

* Sally's epithet for B IV.—A. K.

interests from B I to B IV, whom she liked better. Leaving B I, whom she regarded as a weakling, a sentimentalist, to go her own way alone, she expended her energy on B IV, whom she persisted in hazing as she used to haze B I. . . . The outdoor sports, the adventures, and the strenuous life which Sally loved were impossible for Miss Beauchamp. One can imagine the difficulty of providing three kinds of lives, for one and the same individual, to be pursued at different hours, and even the same hour of the same day. The result was that Sally, having nothing to do, found her enjoyment in teasing the others. She did not hate IV as she hated B I; with IV it was more the excitement of playing the game. Then too, IV took it all differently from what B I did. B I was terrorized by Sally. IV was unterrified, defiant, determined to be mistress of herself. . . .

It was now April, 1900. During the last ten months the Beauchamp family[*] had worried through life after a fashion. It had attended lectures in a local college, had performed a certain amount of outside duties, not perhaps very systematically, and had attended to the daily routine of its own life; for, like other families, the Beauchamps required three meals a day, a proper amount of dressmaking, a reasonable amount of household duties, and the maintenance of a certain degree of social intercourse with its friends. Most of Sally's autobiography was written during the winter and spring. This was slow work, subject to many interruptions, and, as we know, it had to be almost entirely rewritten once and partly rewritten twice. All these duties had to be done, and were done, even if in an eccentric way; the surprising thing is that they were all done without exciting the suspicions of those not in the secret of the case. Miss Beauchamp was known to be a semi-invalid, liable to periodical break-downs—and that is all. . . .

The home life was probably the most trying to B I and B IV. To begin with, dressing was a labor. It was apt to mean two or more baths, for IV would never believe she had had one unless she took it herself. This may seem a trivial matter, but what answer was she to make to the other inmates of the house when she was reminded that she had just taken one bath? Then the afternoon bath was likely to be similarly duplicated and similarly commented upon. She did manage to give apparently satisfactory answers and avert suspicion, but it was trying. B I, too, was often in the same predicament.

[*] The various personalities of the corporeally single Sally Beauchamp.—A. K.

Then, after the bath, came dressing. Suppose it was B I who began, and suppose Sally had not hidden some of the most important articles. When nearly dressed, B IV as likely as not would come and then off would come everything, to be replaced by clothes of B IV's liking, and the hair would be done all over again another way. Lucky it was if B I did not come again before finishing, and all did not have to be done over again for a third time. Then came the family breakfast involving new difficulties; and then the family papers, exercises, and letters had to be found. Where were they? Had Sally destroyed them, or IV, or B I? . . . And so it went on during the day. . . .

It would seem at first sight to have been impossible for Miss Beauchamp to successfully disguise her infirmity from her friends, and maintain her social relations; but a little consideration will show that although difficult it was not impossible. Both B I and B IV were unusually reticent about themselves, having the faculty of keeping people at a distance. . . . The former always tried to conceal her anxieties, her depression, and, we may say, her morbid sorrows. The latter did the same for her peculiar troubles . . . Sally was only too anxious to be thought Miss Beauchamp to disclose the secret of her own existence. While the varying moods, therefore, of the three personalities made Miss Beauchamp appear a "strange, incomprehensible" character, no one suspected that they represented alteration of personality.

As to the amnesia, even this was not as difficult a matter to conceal as would seem at first. . . . At any given time of the day we do not keep in mind many of the preceding events of the day; we recall them only when required. When B I or B IV could not do this, an evasive reply, an inference, or a guess would answer the purpose. . . .

Miss Beauchamp's life was not all trial and tribulation. Through treatment she was given many peaceful days, and often rather long periods of comparative mental and physical health. The difficulty was that these results did not last, roughly speaking, over two or three days. . . .

Sally had often attempted to get hold of IV's thoughts, but without success. At last her efforts were rewarded. By an ingenious artifice, after first "rattling" IV, she penetrated within the secret chamber of her mind, and on several occasions became conscious of what IV was thinking. But—*horrible dictu*—like Bluebeard's wife, after that lady had unlocked the forbidden door, she was astounded by what she learned.

"Why, she is not at all what I thought she was," Sally often said. "She is a terrible person. I never dreamed she was like that." . . .

The fact is that Sally was not only frightened but astounded when she found that IV was in dead earnest when she fought. It was a game only, just fun for Sally, that meant nothing more than is meant by children's "scrapping" with one another. But now Sally . . . discovered that her other hot-tempered self really was angry and meant to destroy her if she could and that she would let nothing, not even her own comfort, stand in the way of accomplishing her ends. . . .

One great grievance of which IV complained was Sally's choice of friends. These people were very objectionable to her. "I must be allowed to choose my own friends," she insisted. How could she if Sally was free to hob-nob with anybody? On waking up (that is, coming to herself) she found herself constantly and unexpectedly in friendly relations with people whose personality was distasteful, and in situations where she was obliged to play parts foreign to her own character. For instance, there was some friend of somebody's—to be sure she did not know positively whether of Sally or B I (but presumably of Sally)—named Miss Lamartine, a French woman, whom she seemed to see very frequently. This woman's personality and foreign point of view were distasteful to IV.

Then there were two art students, girls, whom she knew very slightly, but with whom Sally was on intimate terms. She disliked their attitude towards her. They expected her to be always amusing, in high spirits, gay, and frivolous—ways which were not natural to her own disposition. . . .

Then, equally uncomfortable were the occasions when others, like the Reverend Mr. C., who knew her only as Miss Beauchamp, spoke to her and treated her as morbidly conscientious and unhappy; whereas, she, B IV, is not so at all, and finds it difficult to live up to any such lofty part. In fact, she cannot attain to the high ideals of Miss Beauchamp. She finds it as difficult to live up to the standard of this other self as to come down to the standard of Sally. Then Miss Beauchamp's friends bored her as much as Sally's offended her. B I had a lot of old lady friends whom she liked to visit and to whom she was very kind. They were "awfully stupid, and bored" B IV. . . .

And so it went on. . . .

THE CASE OF ROMAN MALINOVSKY

by Bertram D. Wolfe

*From about 1900 on the Russian revolutionary movement be-
came heavily infiltrated with police spies, some of whom held high
Party posts and were quite close to Lenin. In 1913, Vladimir Burtsev, a sort of self-appointed revolutionary counterespionage agent,
informed Lenin that he now had collected considerable evidence
that Dr. Jacob Zhitomirsky, one of Lenin's confidential aides—
about whom Burtsev had previously expressed suspicion—was a
Tsarist spy. In this excerpt from his* Three Who Made A Revolution, *Bertram D. Wolfe relates how the Zhitomirsky investigation
meshed with the even more dramatic career of Roman Malinovsky.
In this edited version much of the documentation and political
detail have been deleted so that the main lines of this remarkable
story can be more clearly followed.*

Alarmed at last, Lenin sent another "man of confidence" to take up
the Zhitomirsky matter with Burtsev, and, at the same time, to discuss
the whole problem of combatting the spies with which the Bolshevik
movement was now obviously infested. The man whom Lenin sent
was Roman Malinovsky!

Malinovsky questioned Burtsev with strained interest. Who in the
police or the government was giving him his secret tips? what reasons
had he for suspecting Dr. Zhitomirsky? how could the Bolsheviks
judge the reliability of such grave charges unless they were given the
sources? what other Bolsheviks did he suspect? Insistently, Malinovsky pleaded that Burtsev communicate "in strict confidence" his
sources in the government. For his part, Burtsev had not the slightest
reason to suspect his interlocutor, whom he knew as a prominent
trade unionist, as a member of the Central Committee which the
Bolsheviks had just set up allegedly as the Central Committee of the
entire Party, and as the newly chosen chairman of the Bolshevik

81

fraction in the Fourth Imperial Duma. Yet an old habit of caution and a respect for confidences caused him to withhold the names of the officials.

In 1917, when the Tsar fell and the Provisional Government opened up the police archives, they found proof that Zhitomirsky had been a spy during all the years he enjoyed Lenin's confidence. This, of course, was no surprise to Burtsev. But what did startle him was the realization that Malinovsky (whom he did not even begin to suspect until the end of 1916) had come to him that day on a double mission, charged simultaneously by Vladimir Ilyich and by the director of the Russian Police, S. P. Beletsky, with the task of finding out which spies Burtsev knew of in the Bolshevik faction, and from what governmental personages he derived his tips concerning these most jealously guarded secrets of the police.

Roman Vatslavovich Malinovsky was a Russified Polish workingman of peasant stock, born in the Plotsk Province of Russian Poland in the year 1878. When he met Lenin at the Prague Conference of 1912, he was thirty-four, robust, ruddy complexioned, vigorous, excitable, a heavy drinker, a rude and eloquent orator, a gifted leader of men. In the closing years of the preceding century he had been convicted several times of common crimes, the third offense being that of burglary, for which he had served a prison term from 1899 to 1902. The police noted that he was a heavy spender. Though he earned a living first as tailor and then as metal turner, his wages were never sufficient for his expensive tastes. In his youth he had worked for a while in Germany, then returned to Saint Petersburg. Here he entered the labor movement, probably in 1902, with a perfect background for the role of police informer.

How early he became a regular agent is unclear. For years his chief source of income was his wages as a metal worker, while he used his police connections only to pick up a bit of extra cash. When he thought he had something which would interest them, he would telephone, or send in a written report signed *Portnoi(Tailor)*, for which he would be paid a sum like twenty-five or fifty rubles. Even after he became a professional agent with a regular salary, he did not become a "professional revolutionist"—his usefulness consisted in his continuing to be a worker at the bench. He himself was to confess to the Bolsheviks, and the police confirm it, that one of his motives was always the ambition to rise to a place of prominence in the revolutionary movement. This ambition felt a double spur: the higher his advancement, the more he meant to the police and the higher the sum they set on the value of his services.

In 1906 he was one of the founders of the Petersburg Metal Workers Union. In 1907 he became its secretary, serving till the end of 1909. Here he steered a careful course between Bolsheviks and Mensheviks. The former were more interested in control and political leadership of the union, the latter in the preservation of its autonomy. Therefore, as an active unionist, he inclined to the Mensheviks. In 1908 he successfully resisted an attempt of the Bolsheviks to capture his union, but, after he went over to them completely, he helped them to win control.

Five times he was arrested for his activities, either by police who had no inkling of his role, or because he was at a meeting which he himself had betrayed, where everybody had to be taken in. His early reappearance on the scene after each arrest was so managed as not to excite suspicion. A typical arrest was that of late November, 1909. He had tipped off a secret caucus of the labor delegates to an impending anti-alcoholic congress and was present when it was raided. Released in January, 1910, he was exiled from Saint Petersburg to avert suspicion from him. This ended his secretaryship of the Petersburg union, but he immediately turned up in Moscow in the spring of 1910, where he was welcomed by the entire labor movement and was able to report to the police on every phase of it. On the rolls of the Moscow Okhrana he appears as of March, 1910, no longer as a "piece worker," but with the regular salary of fifty rubles a month, plus expenses. In addition, of course, to his wages as a metal turner.

The police had come to the conclusion that the chief danger to the régime was the possible unification of all opposition forces. Since the political aim of deepening the Party split coincided in an essential respect with that of Lenin, Malinovsky was now instructed to take the earliest possible opportunity to come out as a Bolshevik and to attach himself as closely as possible to the Bolshevik leader. Police Director Beletsky testified that, in view of this important mission, he freed his agent at this time from the further necessity of betraying individuals or meetings (though not from reporting on them), as arrests traceable to Malinovsky might endanger his position for the more highly political task. It was the easier for the police to make this exemption since they had by now advanced their men to a number of key posts in the Bolshevik underground, including the headship of the Moscow organization itself, which had just been taken over by agent Kukushkin, aided by the spies Romanov, Poskrebuchin and Marakushev. The agents ascended quickly in the Party hierarchy by the simple expedient of arranging the arrest of incumbents, persons who suspected them, and others who stood in their way.

But Malinovsky seemed to enjoy denunciatory work, and, despite the exemption, continued it. Indeed, he could not resist one more grand coup before he went to the Bolsheviks. As a leading official of a legal trade union, he was highly regarded by the Liquidators, who set all their hopes on legal unions and a legal labor party and found the underground party a handicap. He joined with them in planning a conference at which they hoped to launch their broad legal party. Then, on Malinovsky's suggestion, according to the testimony of Beletsky, the preliminary planning conference was raided and most of the leading Liquidators were bagged. Thus their hopes were ended for some time to come.

About the same time, Malinovsky learned that Lenin was summoning a Party conference too, at which he was to "remove" the Central Committee regularly elected by the last united Party congress, and set up in its place a Bolshevik-dominated Central Committee. The conference was held in Prague in January, 1912. Malinovsky appeared as the representative of the Moscow trade unions and of the Bolshevik underground political organization, of which his fellow-agent Kukushkin was the head. Lenin had of course heard of this well-known trade unionist, newly won from menshevism. He was so taken with the convert that Malinovsky was elected to the new Central Committee, and was urged to become the Party's standard-bearer in the contest for the Moscow deputyship.

A police spy with a record of convictions for common crimes as a Duma Deputy—the idea was so audacious that the highest authorities had to be consulted. From now on, Police Chief Beletsky met with his agent only in private rooms of the most fashionable restaurants. He took him in person to see the Minister of the Interior. He consulted with the Assistant Police Chief, the Assistant Minister of the Interior, and the head of the Moscow Okhrana.

Both police and Bolsheviks set to work with great energy to secure their candidate's nomination and election. The newly founded daily *Pravda*, the Bolshevik apparatus, and—what proved more important— the whole machinery of the Department of the Interior and its police were mobilized to further Malinovsky's fortunes. The first hurdle was his criminal record. The Ministry saw to it that he got the necessary "certificate of good repute" from local authorities in his native province. Next, all the more popular of his possible rivals were eliminated by the simple expedient of throwing them into jail. This included the most likely candidate of the Moscow workers, Krivov.

As election day approached, Malinovsky reported that a hostile foreman was planning to fire him from his factory. And no working-man was eligible to vote or to be chosen as delegate, elector, or Deputy unless he had worked in the given factory for the six months preceding the election. The Police Department came to their candidate's rescue once more by throwing the astonished foreman into jail, releasing him after the elections with the explanation that the arrest had been "an unfortunate mistake." Aided by such campaign methods, the Bolshevik and police joint candidate swept all before him. The Department showed its appreciation of his advancement in the secular world by raising his salary from fifty rubles a month to five hundred. It was the first time that any police spy ever got such princely salary. And this was now supplemented not by a metalworker's wage but by a Duma Deputy's. *"For the first time* among ours in the Duma"—wrote Lenin in a letter full of the underscorings with which he showed his excitement. . . . "there is an *outstanding* worker-*leader*. And the results—perhaps not immediately—will be *great.* . . ."

The Fourth Imperial Duma, to which Malinovsky was elected, began its term in late November, 1912. It was to be a long Duma, destined to continue in being until the Revolution of 1917 thrust power into its reluctant hands. Its thirteen Social Democratic Deputies (seven Mensheviks and six Bolsheviks) formed a single Fraction, for the split which Lenin had started abroad at the Prague Conference at the beginning of that year had not yet taken effect inside Russia.

Lenin was highly displeased with this unity in the Duma Fraction, for, as long as it endured, here was an authoritative and conspicuously public leading body around which the longing for unity inside Russia might crystallize, as against the Prague (Bolshevik) Central Committee. So strong was "conciliationism," i.e. the mood for unity, that the six Bolsheviks had gotten elected only by pledging themselves to work for a united Party. Thus the entire bloc of Deputies lent their names as contributing editors both to the Bolshevik legal daily, *Pravda*, and the Menshevik daily, *Luch*, and even unanimously adopted a resolution calling for the fusion of the two papers. *Pravda* went so far as to censor, mutilate, or suppress Lenin's articles where they sought to sharpen the fight against Mensheviks, Liquidators, Bundists and Vperyodists.

Finding Malinovsky able and willing, Lenin left to him the task of finding pretexts for leading the Bolshevik Duma group toward an open break with the Mensheviks, while he himself turned his attention to *Pravda*. He called Stalin to Cracow to instruct him on the matter, and sent Jacob Sverdlov, his best organizer, to Saint Petersburg to whip the editors into line.

Malinovsky dutifully reported the arrival of Sverdlov. He hid in Duma Deputy Petrovsky's home, but was arrested when he left there to "move to a safer place" (Feb. 10, 1913). Thereupon Lenin dispatched Stalin to Saint Petersburg, now fully prepared to carry out the splitting or "irreconcilable" line. On March 13, after confiding his plans for that night to Malinovsky, Stalin went to a concert for the benefit of *Pravda*, where he too was arrested. Both Sverdlov and Stalin were sent to Siberia. This time they stayed, all through the war, until released by the Revolution of February, 1917.

Next Kamenev was sent to take charge.

As early as December 18, 1912, that is to say a few days after the Duma Fraction was organized, the astute Malinovsky was able to report to his superiors the news that he would be able to split the Fraction and would have Lenin's support for this purpose. Unexpectedly, Kamenev's stay was made legal by an act of the government: an amnesty for all "literary political" offenders, decreed to celebrate the three hundredth anniversary of the founding of the Romanov dynasty. So, instead of turning Kamenev in, Malinovsky provided him with excellent copy by fiery denunciation of his Menshevik fellow-Deputies. The new line found a willing supporter in the new editor-in-chief of *Pravda*, Miron Chernomazov, another police agent.

The police, too, were satisfied. Yet this business of having the Bolshevik leader of the Duma on their payroll was bringing its complications. First, there were his speeches. He was undeniably eloquent and forceful. Sometimes Malinovsky wrote them himself and sent them to his two chiefs, Lenin and Beletsky, for approval. At other times Lenin or Zinoviev or Kamenev drafted them, or even wrote out whole speeches in detail. These, too, were sent to Police Chief Beletsky for his opinion. In the police files were found drafts in Malinovsky's hand, with amendments in the handwriting of both Lenin and Beletsky, as well as drafts by Lenin, Zinoviev and Kamenev. Realizing how popular their Deputy was, the police tried to cut out some of the most "subversive" passages. But Malinovsky had difficulty following instructions. In reading the first declaration of the Fraction, he managed to eliminate an offending passage on "sovereignty of the people" by pretending to get rattled and skipping an entire page of his manuscript. But *Pravda* and *Luch* next day followed his original script. When his speeches were attacks on the Liberals, Constitutional Democrats (Kadets), or Mensheviks, the police were glad to give him full rein. Sometimes he tried to substitute a belligerent "revolutionary" fight with Duma Chairman Rodzyanko for the delivery of the speech itself, thus managing to get himself interrupted and denied the right to continue. Yet, on the whole, the Leninist régime so closely limited the autonomy of a Deputy and of the Duma Fraction that the police had little success in modifying his speeches.

Without doubt he enjoyed both roles and there must have been moments when he thought of himself as a Bolshevik doublecrossing the police rather then a police agent spying on the Bolsheviks.

Another complication was the danger of exposure. Some official high in the Ministry of the Interior or the Police was privy to the arrangement and did not like it. From the outset, this still today unknown personage tried to communicate with the socialist "underworld" without revealing his identity. When Malinovsky was elected, *Luch* received an anonymous warning on his role. A year later the wife of Theodor Dan received a letter telling her that a high police official wanted to see her in confidence, and that she could signify acceptance of the appointment by a code advertisement in a stipulated newspaper. Both warnings were ignored.

When Bukharin, living in Vienna, learned of Malinovsky's election, he wrote to Lenin that he had escaped from exile in 1910 only to be seized again in Moscow, suspiciously, right after a meeting with Malinovsky. He was puzzled by the angry tone of Lenin's answer: there was a dark campaign of slander being waged against this wonderful Bolshevik; if Bukharin joined it, Lenin would brand him publicly as a traitor. He desisted.

Then there were the February and March, 1913, arrests of Elena Rozmirovich (Mrs. Troyanovsky), Sverdlov and Stalin. Acting on a hunch, Troyanovsky wrote from abroad in a "shot-in-the-dark" letter to his wife's relatives in which he said that he knew who had caused her arrest: "a man playing a double role." If she were not freed, he would make an exposure which would "stagger society." As Troyanovsky had calculated, the police opened the letter. Director Beletsky testified in 1917 that when he had shown the letter to Malinovsky the latter had "become hysterical" and demanded her release as a condition for serving the Department further. She was released.

To ward off suspicion, Malinovsky declared at a meeting of the Central Committee that "someone close to the Duma Six was a person who had police connections." The axe fell on agent Miron Chernomazov, already under investigation, and in May, 1914, he was quietly removed from the editorial board of *Pravda*. He had been its editor-in-chief while Malinovsky was its treasurer. The latter position enabled the Duma Deputy to turn in copies of the paper's balance sheet, and a complete list of the names and addresses of all who contributed money. On the other hand, he held meetings, raised funds for the paper, contributed himself from time to time—amounts which he always added to his Police Department expense accounts. These sums the police more than recouped when they levied fines on the paper, in one case a fine of five hundred rubles for an article written by none other than Duma Deputy Malinovsky.

During all this time he was practically a commuter between Cracow and Petersburg. Aided both by police and Bolshevik underground, it was easy for him to cross the frontier. Lenin summoned him at every important juncture, giving him entry into the most highly confidential meetings, when the only other persons present were Lenin and Krupskaya, Zinoviev, and Kamenev. The Police Department received full transcripts of the decisions taken, all Lenin's most secret acts and plans. Malinovsky went on joint lecture tours with Lenin to all the Russian colonies in emigration. Together they attended a secret congress of the Lettish Social Democrats and another of the Finns. He was entrusted with setting up a secret printing plant inside Russia, which naturally did not remain secret for long. Together with Yakovlev he "helped" start a Bolshevik paper in Moscow. It, too, ended promptly with the arrest of the editor. Inside Russia, the popular Duma Deputy traveled to all centers. Arrests took place sufficiently later to avert suspicion from him. Thus a Bolshevik "Conciliator" group headed by Miliutin disappeared, as did the regular Bolshevik organization in Tula and other local bodies. The police raised his wage from five hundred to six hundred, and then to seven hundred rubles a month.

On the eighth of May, 1914, Roman Malinovsky handed in his resignation to the Chairman of the Duma, Rodzyanko, "for reasons of health," and the same day left the country. He had notified neither Central Committee nor Duma Fraction nor constituents. The amazement at this inexplicable action was enormous.

That same day, Chairman Rodzyanko received a visit from Assistant Minister of the Interior Junkovsky, who informed him, "in strict confidence," that the departed Deputy had been a police agent and had been ordered to resign to avoid a possible scandal. Rodzyanko was told that he might inform the Presidium of the Duma, but that the secret should go no farther, or the good name of the Duma itself would be compromised. The last police entry on Malinovsky was a dismissal bonus of six thousand rubles to start life anew abroad.

Now *Luch* remembered its old anonymous letter. Rumors swirled around the corridors of the Tauride Palace and soon the entire press was speaking of "dark police complications." But when Lenin's friend Bonch-Bruevich, as correspondent of the Kharkov daily *Utro*, sent a dispatch of the same tenor to his paper, he received a sharp telegram from Lenin categorically denying the allegation. For the ever reckless Malinovsky, despite the peril of his situation, had gone straight to Lenin in Cracow!

There he had given several contradictory "political" and "personal" versions of his flight. Then, on closer questioning, he had "confessed" that in his youth he had been sentenced for an attempt at rape, which fact the police now threatened to expose if the most useful of the Bolshevik Deputies did not resign from the Duma. While Lenin was pondering this, the Menshevik and Liquidator press arrived with their reports of rumors that the Bolshevik leader had been a police spy. Martov and Dan demanded a non-factional or multi-factional Party tribunal to investigate the case, political and personal, of Roman Malinovsky. To accept the proposal of Martov and Dan was to recognize that the "expelled" Mensheviks were still part of the Social Democratic Party. And what a weapon against bolshevism would be provided by the thought that its outstanding spokesman, its leader inside Russia, the driving force of its campaign to split the Duma Fraction, was a police agent!

In the name of the Party (i.e. the Bolshevik) Central Committee, an investigating commission was immediately set up. It consisted of Lenin, Zinoviev, and Hanecki, a Polish Social Democrat of the Warsaw Opposition and a close supporter of Lenin's. No Mensheviks were included. This commission heard testimony from Malinovsky, from Bukharin, who reiterated his old charges, from Mrs. Troyanovsky, who told the circumstances of her arrest and release, and testified that her interlocutors had shown knowledge of matters which, in her judgment, only Malinovsky could have told them. Burtsev was asked his opinion. He answered that he thought the Duma Deputy a "dirty fellow but not a police agent." It is possible that Lenin knowingly decided to defend a police spy and attack his accusers out of cold factional calculation. But a careful weighing of the evidence leaves no doubt in our minds but that Lenin believed Malinovsky's story of his early conviction for attempted rape, and resignation of his mandate under threat of exposure. "One feels ashamed for mankind"—wrote Lenin on June 4, 1914—"when one sees how a man's personal misfortune is utilized for a struggle against an opposing political tendency."

That was a little over a month before the war began. Lenin's treatment of Malinovsky during the war, when the latter was an obscure prisoner in a German prison camp, demonstrates his conviction of the ex-Deputy's innocence of the spy charge. Lenin sent him reading matter and material for agitation among the other Russian prisoners. Krupskaya sent him food parcels, took care of his laundry and clothes and performed other services that had no political meaning beyond that of personal comradeship. Late in 1916 (two or three months before his exposure) the Bolshevik paper *Sotsial Demokrat* publicly stated that Malinovsky had been "fully rehabilitated" by his subsequent conduct, for his past crime of "desertion of his post."

The last act in this strange drama of Roman Malinovsky occurred in November, 1918, when Lenin had been in power for a full year. On November 2, reckless adventurer to the end, Malinovsky, aware that the Bolsheviks had seized police archives, crossed the Russian border and turned up in Petrograd. For three successive days he visited the Smolny Institute (Bolshevik headquarters), demanding either to be arrested or taken to see Lenin. On the third day, Zinoviev saw him and ordered his arrest. He was taken to Moscow for trial. The Bolshevik Krylenko, who was later to conduct so many prosecutions until he himself disappeared in a purge, was appointed as prosecutor. He knew the defendant well since he too had reason to believe that one of his arrests by the Tsarist police was Malinovsky's work. The trial was swift and secret.

Malinovsky's bearing was proud and challenging. Repeatedly he demanded that Lenin be summoned, but his request was refused.

Lenin, he asserted, must have known of his role after his resignation from the Duma. He had often tried to tell Lenin that his past was "filled with abominations," but Lenin refused to listen, saying that for Bolsheviks these personal misdeeds of his youth had no meaning. Did not Lenin know that the police had a hold on him, yet had permitted him to rise to prominence? Did not Lenin know of the charges against him by Bukharin, Rozmirovich, Krylenko, Petrovsky? Still Lenin had permitted him to rehabilitate himself in a German prison camp by making propaganda for bolshevism among Russian prisoners. Had not the Bolshevik organ, *Sotsial Demokrat*, in December, 1916, declared that Malinovsky had been "fully rehabilitated" for, his past indiscipline by his present services?

According to Badaev, "He alleged that he was forced to become an *agent provocateur* because he was already completely in the hands of the police. He represented his career as a long martyrdom, accompanied by suffering and remorse from which he could not escape. . . . He tried to prove that he left the Duma of his own free will because of personal unhappiness, and that he obtained permission from the police to quit politics. . . . He adopted a pose of sincere repentance while admitting the gravity of his crimes."

A notable procession of witnesses testified in the trial: ex-Police Chief Beletsky; ex-Assistant Chief Vissarionov, ex-Minister Makarov, ex-Assistant Minister Junkovsky, former Deputies Badaev and Petrovsky, and many of the men and women he had betrayed. Both Junkovsky, and Beletsky were asked leading questions tending to prove that his activities had benefited the Bolsheviks more than the police. Beletsky agreed to this, but Junkovsky declared that he was "an honest monarchist and that he could not enter into a discussion of that question."

His closing words, according to Badaev, were a profession of sincere repentance and a reminder that he had returned voluntarily to Bolshevik Russia knowing that he could expect nothing but the death penalty.

The verdict was the firing squad. At 2 A.M. of the very morning after the trial ended, he was shot. Not long thereafter, his former chief, the ex-Police Director Beletsky, and that other chief who had forced his resignation from the Duma, the ex-Assistant Minister of the Interior Junkovsky, met the same end. Burtsev was released from jail and fled beyond the frontier of Soviet Russia.

II

HOAXING THE EXPERTS

VAN MEEGEREN: ART'S MASTER FORGER

by Klaus Mann

After a delay of more than two years, Hans van Meegeren, the Dutch artist who made millions by painting magnificent pictures and palming them off as Vermeers, was brought to trial in 1947 and sent to jail. Almost immediately a movement was afoot to have him pardoned. Almost immediately, too, his genuinely own mediocre paintings, which previously had been admired most by Nazi chieftains, began to command high prices. The principal mystery was not the delay, the light punishment, or the sudden popularity of van Meegeren's "own" work; it was the fact that the man who could paint those "Vermeers" could also paint those van Meegerens. The mystery remained when he died in December.

It was in the summer of 1945, soon after the liberation of the Netherlands, that van Meegeren volunteered his sensational confession, claiming the authorship of certain paintings which had been attributed to old Dutch masters—notably the great Jan Vermeer of Delft (1632-1675)—and sold, as outstanding samples of seventeenth-century artistry, to leading museums and collectors.

Clearly, Dutch authorities were in no particular hurry to have "*L'affaire van Meegeren*" discussed in public—a reluctance which could not but cause suspicious rumors. Were there any prominent figures involved in the fraudulent plot, men of such wealth and influence that the police would prefer to spare them?

If Dutch officials had been surprisingly slow in conducting the preparatory examination, they seemed all the more eager to do a speedy job once the trial proper had started. The whole affair was rushed through in a few hours. Even conservative Dutch papers, like the *Haagsche Post*—usually rather inclined to be lenient with "collaborators"—appeared to be mildly shocked by the at once perfunctory and diplomatic way in which the matter was handled. Would it not have been interesting to go into certain questions of political significance? Did the public not have a right to be fully informed about van Meegeren's dealings with German occupation czars and Dutch quislings? But, for one reason or other, the police chose to drop the charge of collaboration on which the painter had originally been arrested. Now he found himself prosecuted for "deception" only —an offense for which the Dutch law reserves a maximum penalty of two years' imprisonment. The sentence was one year.

But if the trial failed to shed new light on the political aspects of van Meegeren's case, the story of the counterfeit masterpieces remains amazing enough—psychologically as well as from a purely criminologic point of view. Here are the basic facts:

Back in 1937, a lawyer from Amsterdam discovered a dusty canvas, stored away in the Paris apartment of a Dutch businessman who had recently died. The heirs did not think much of the painting—a fairly large composition showing Christ and the Disciples at Emmaus. But the lawyer rather liked it: in fact, liked it so much that he took the next train to Monte Carlo to have the picture examined by the noted art expert and collector, Abraham Bredius. Dr. Bredius (who, incidentally, died in 1946, at the venerable age of ninety-one) looked at the painting, was struck by the superb quality of the workmanship; had another look, and recognized—one can imagine with what delight!—the familiar monogram, *I.V.M.*, standing for I. V. Meer.

A few weeks later, the discovery of "a new Vermeer" was enthusiastically announced by Bredius in the columns of the highly respected English art review, *Burlington Magazine*. "It is a wonderful moment in the life of a lover of art," he wrote, "when he finds himself suddenly confronted with a hitherto unknown painting by a great master, untouched, on the original canvas and without any restoration, just as it left the painter's studio! Neither the beautiful signature . . . nor the *pointillé* on the bread which Christ is blessing, is necessary to convince us that we have here a—I am inclined to say—*the* masterpiece of Johannes Vermeer of Delft, and, moreover, one of his largest works (1.20 by 1.17 m.), quite different from all his other paintings and yet *every inch a Vermeer*. . . ." And so forth, in the same rhapsodical vein.

In the meantime, other connoisseurs had rushed to Paris to admire the new-found treasure. It is true that some of them—notably the director of Amsterdam's Rijksmuseum, Dr. Schmidt-Degener, and the distinguished historian and philosopher, Jan Huizinga of Leyden University—voiced certain doubts as to the authenticity of the chef-d'oeuvre; the majority, however, agreed with Bredius' verdict (every inch a Vermeer!), and shared his enthusiasm. Director Hannema of Boymans Museum in Rotterdam was pleased to buy the masterwork for the trifle of 540,000 Dutch guilders, or about $270,000.

"De Emmausgangers," as the picture is called in Dutch, was the main attraction of an art show, "Masterpieces of Four Centuries," presented at Boymans Museum in 1938. Although works by Rembrandt, Frans Hals, Matthias Gruenewald, and other giants of art were displayed at the same exhibition, the "new Vermeer" stole the show and aroused more curiosity, more enthusiasm than all the genuine masterpieces together. The art critics—not only in the Netherlands but also in France, Belgium, Germany, and other countries—raved about the magnificent, incomparable, typically seventeenth-century, unmistakably Vermeerish painting which, as one of the experts put it, "came to light recently, as if to show that we have until now underrated Vermeer most of all as a religious painter." The lay public seemed at least as deeply impressed as the high priesthood of art criticism. A few weeks after the opening of the Boymans show, "De Emmausgangers," reproduced in millions of copies, had found their way to churches, hospitals, school buildings, farmhouses, patrician mansions, and proletarian tenements all over the country.

In the course of the following years, some more unknown Vermeers and two pictures by another master of that period, Pieter de Hooch, were discovered—allegedly in the possession of a noble but impoverished family. While the De Hoochs seemed pleasantly typical samples of genre painting, a gaily realistic style in which that artist had successfully specialized, the Vermeers appeared less characteristic. The Master of Delft—hitherto famed for the serene lucidity of his portraits, landscapes, and domestic scenes—now showed himself as an accomplished mystic, concentrating exclusively on biblical subjects. But however strange and puzzling this unexpected predilection in Vermeer may have been, the more recently found paintings, in contrast to the Emmaus composition, failed to cause much of a hullabaloo. There was little publicity. The new discoveries were handled, quietly and competently, by two of Holland's major art dealers, P. de

Boer and D. A. Hoogendijk, who offered the masterpieces to their choice clientele. A "Last Supper" went to a private collector for 1,600,000 guilders (about $800,000, at that time); another well-to-do art lover paid 1,275,000 guilders for "The Blessing of Isaac." In 1943, the Netherlands Government bought one of the finest "new Vermeers," "Christ's Ablution," for the exclusive Rijksmuseum in Amsterdam.

All those transactions took place while the country was occupied by the German army. Nazi chieftains bought (or stole) Dutch masterpieces on the largest possible scale. One of their main agents and purchasers was a German banker by the name of Miedl, who had taken over the well-known Goudstikker gallery in Amsterdam. It was Herr Miedl to whom an impoverished, anonymous family entrusted one of their precious Vermeers, "Christ and the Adulteress." The picture was bought, for the rather impressive price of 1,650,000 guilders, by a collector of almost unlimited means and insatiable appetite—that famous patron of art and lover of all things beautiful, Hermann Goering.

The van Meegeren scandal might never have exploded if it had not been for this particular deal of the jolly Reich Marshal's. For no sooner had the Netherlands been liberated than Dutch authorities detected the illegal, immoral transaction. A national treasure, one of Vermeer's splendid works, had been sold to a foreigner, an enemy, a notorious ringleader of the Nazi gang! The man responsible for the crime, Banker Miedl, was not available for punishment; he had already left the country, taking along a fortune in jewelry on which he would be able to live in style as an honored guest in the Spain of Generalissimo Franco. But what about Herr Miedl's agents and associates?

In the course of investigations, a certain name came up repeatedly —Hans van Meegeren. No doubt there had been a connection of some sort between the fugitive German financier and that Dutch artist— rather a mediocre artist, by the way, not very highly thought of by local critics, but comparatively successful under the Nazi regime. Van Meegeren had been in touch with Miedl, had received payments from him. As police went on investigating, they soon had enough evidence for the painter's complicity to justify his arrest.

He did not take to jail very well. A nervous, delicate man in his late fifties—chain smoker, used to sleeping tablets and considerable quantities of strong liquor—he felt incapable of facing the hardships of life in a prison cell. After a fortnight or so he seemed about to collapse. It was at that point that he announced his willingness to make "a complete confession."

Those much-vaunted Vermeers Mynheer van Meegeren claimed, were his own work. He whom ignorant critics had brushed off as a second-rater, had produced—not just copied, mind you, but actually produced!—all those glorious paintings, including "Christ and the Disciples of Emmaus."

The "Emmausgangers" a forgery? It sounded like a blasphemous joke and the officials refused to believe it. Obviously that queer little van Meegeren was a neurotic, a pathological liar trying to pull a trick.

But, amazingly, the queer little man was able to prove his assertion. First of all, he proposed to paint another "Vermeer" in the presence and under the strict control of police officers. So he did, having been released from jail and allowed to return to his studio. The subject authorities had picked for him was "Young Jesus Teaching in the Temple." Mynheer van Meegeren sat down and, under the unbelieving eyes of professors and commissaries, completed another masterly composition à la Jan Vermeer—an exquisite piece of work (technically at least) which would have delighted Dr. Bredius and other infallible experts.

Was that sufficient proof? The master forger had more to offer. He produced some of the rare and precious colors he had used, in strict accordance with seventeenth-century methods—a mellow ultramarine made of genuine lapis lazuli, a radiant crimson consisting of the dried bodies of a scale insect (cochineal) native to Mexico, white lead to form a basic ingredient of the bright hues, dark pigments containing earth. Moreover, he presented various objects—dishes, weapons, articles of clothing, pieces of furniture—which had served him as models for certain details in the Emmaus tableau and other "classical" paintings. Investigators were shown the places where he had hidden while doing his stealthy job—Rocquebrune, in the South of France, and the village of Laren near Amsterdam.

For those who still remained unconvinced, van Meegeren had additional evidence that verified his claim beyond any question. The seventeenth-century canvas on which "Christ at Emmaus" was painted showed originally a "Resurrection of Lazarus," the work of a minor artist of that period. The forger, while removing most of that original composition, left certain parts of it intact, using them as a base for his own effects. Experts, having examined the picture by means of X-rays and various chemical tests, were familiar with the contours of the half vanished Lazarus group. Was Mynheer van Meegeren able, by any chance, to oblige the investigating commission with some information about that invisible painting?

He was indeed. Not only did he know, and disclose, the general subject of the original, but he also recalled the position of the major figure, the distribution of colors, and other particulars. To the astonishment of all, the artist jotted down a few lines indicating with remarkable accuracy the composition of the Resurrection scene—quite a stunt, considering the fact that almost ten years had elapsed since he had seen the picture.

Now even the skeptics were compelled to admit that van Meegeren had proved his authorship of the "Emmausgangers" and the other discoveries. Where was the money museums and collectors had paid for six phony Vermeers and two equally spurious De Hoochs? Van Meegeren was asked to refund something like eight million guilders to the outraged buyers, including the Netherlands Government.

Being unable to satisfy his creditors, van Meegeren was judicially declared a bankrupt. Authorities permitted him, however, to stay in his beautiful home, a large eighteenth-century mansion in the center of Amsterdam, where he enjoyed complete freedom while preparations for his trial were dragging on.

It was there, in his private residence, that I called on Mynheer van Meegeren a few weeks before his trial. . . . Mutual friends introduced me to the man whom some people considered a genius, and others a clever, unscrupulous crook.

He seemed delighted to see us, almost pathetically eager to talk, to make an impression, to explain his case. "Why did I do it?" he cried, pacing the room with frantic restlessness, his face twisted to a wry grimace. "The critics, my dear sir! Don't you see? The critics made me do it! 'No talent,' that's what they said about me! 'No imagination!' 'No personality!' "—He shook his fists furiously, then rattled on: "I had to teach them a lesson; had to prove, once and for all, their utter incompetence, their shocking lack of knowledge and understanding. . . ."

Drinking and smoking, he continued his breathless talk. "Besides, is there anything immoral about producing a work of art in the style of a great master?" he demanded, somewhat aggressively. "If the so-called experts are not smart enough to see the difference—that's too bad! I am not the first one to fool them. Others did it before. The great Michelangelo sold some of his works as newly excavated antique sculptures, just to get better prices. And then, in the nineteenth century, that incredible fellow, Bastianini—you surely remember him, Giovanni Bastianini of Florence?—his statues and busts were admired all over the world as the most wonderful artistic monuments of the Renaissance period. And even though Bastianini's success should have made the critics a little cautious, they allowed themselves to be duped again, just a few years later, by another Italian of stupendous versatility, Alceo Dossena. What a craftsman! He mastered all the different styles of the past three thousand years—Greek, Etruscan, Roman, Gothic, Renaissance, Baroque. But all the great exploits of forgery were accomplished in the field of sculpture. It was my ambition to prove that the same thing could be done in painting."

Of course, in reality plagiarism has by no means been limited to the particular sphere of sculpture: the *chronique scandaleuse* of art records numerous cases of forgers successfully imitating the mannerisms and signatures of illustrious painters. . . . But it would have been tactless, indeed cruel, to remind van Meegeren of those facts, since it obviously flattered his ego to think of himself as the first and only large-scale plagiarist in the history of painting.

Clearly, he was a man of unusually strong emotions—tormented by ambition, haunted by doubts and fears. What bitterness, what fierce resentment in his voice whenever he referred to his archenemies, those despicable scoundrels, the critics! And what profound joy, what passion, as he described those wonderful, exciting weeks he spent in the solitude of his Rocquebrune studio, working on "Christ and the Disciples at Emmaus"!

"It was the most thrilling, the most inspiring experience of my whole life!" he said, his eyes alight with real enthusiasm. "There were so many things to consider, so many traps to avoid. It took me about seven months—seven months of constant solitude, of frantic labor, of unending delight! I was happy because I felt, yes, I was positive, that good old Vermeer would be satisfied with my job. He was keeping me company, you know. He was always with me, during that whole period. I sensed his presence; he encouraged me. He liked what I was doing. Yes, he really did."

It was strange to watch this little wizard—his shifty eyes, the expressive play of his dexterous, fidgety hands. There was something queer, something disquieting about his smile as he paused from time to time, absorbed in memories. If you were a believer in occultism, you might suspect some kind of mysterious contact to have existed between the immortal Vermeer and this frustrated, harassed mortal. But why should the dematerialized genius have employed such a rickety material tool? . . .

The room where we were sitting, a large, paneled hall on the ground floor of the fine old mansion, was lavishly decorated with "real van Meegerens": huge black-and-white compositions showing lasciviously ecstatic nudes, torture scenes, skeletons, angry-looking soldiers, musicians with sheepishly transfigured faces over stiff white collars and neatly tied white ties. Of course, all these drawings and paintings are the work of an experienced craftsman; they testify to an accomplished technique, even to a certain virtuosity. Some of them are not without charm, especially a few likenesses of wide-eyed and graceful deer. But on the whole, what an array of macabre grimaces! What poor taste!

It is no wonder that the Nazis had a penchant for Mynheer van Meegeren's products. . . . How Hitler must have loved this conspicuously Germanic-looking pianist surrounded by the ghosts of Bach, Mozart, Beethoven, Chopin, Schubert, Schumann, and Brahms! How this cheap and showy mysticism must have appealed to the Fuehrer's poetic heart! Don't I recall having heard rather unpleasant stories about the pianist, one Theo van der Pas, portrayed here in such illustrious company? The Dutch virtuoso on whose shoulder van Meegeren placed Chopin's spooky hand was in fact such an ardent "collaborationist" that his compatriots, after the liberation, banned him for two years from the concert halls. Van Meegeren, however, did not deem it necessary to remove his friend Theo from the wall of his drawing room. It was not without pride that he showed us a large, pompously presented book containing, among scores of other "real van Meegerens," a full-page reproduction of the Pas portrait. The book, which offers also some rhapsodical articles on van Meegeren's art and personality, was printed in the Netherlands at the time of the German occupation. A copy of it was found in Hitler's personal library, adorned with the artist's autographed dedication to the Fuehrer.

The longer I look at van Meegeren's graphic nightmares, the more I am perplexed. Where is the affinity between these grotesque, sultry hallucinations and the sublime discretion of Vermeer's mastership? If the profound persuasion of Vermeer's art lies mostly in its natural and effortless *nobility*, it is the complete absence of anything noble or harmonious which makes van Meegeren's work so repulsive. How could an artist, a man so utterly devoid of greatness, produce a great picture like "Emmaus?"

There is something fascinating and disturbing about this strange contradiction, as there is something fascinating and disturbing about the phenomenon of split personality in general. No doubt van Meegeren ceased to be himself while composing his masterpieces *à la* Vermeer. . . . This was more than just a case of extreme adaptability; rather, it had to do with metamorphosis in the old, mythological sense—meaning a permanent or temporary change of substance and structure, presumably by witchcraft.

But Black Magic and Art are irreconcilable contrasts. By stooping to the dubious tricks of sorcery, the artist betrayed his real mission and polluted the pure sphere of the creative genius. The Dutch prosecutor, H. A. Wassenbergh, was right, in a sense, in telling the Court that Hans van Meegeren had "insulted the great masters of our nation" whose style and spirit he copied with such terrifying skill.

Hans van Meegeren died in 1947 shortly after he was sentenced to one year's imprisonment. A brief review of the main facts of his life may help place his fantastic feat in clearer perspective.

Van Meegeren was born in Holland in 1889. As a child, he was ambitious but felt inferior about his small size, expressing fear that it would keep him from achieving greatness. Van Meegeren studied architecture at the Institute of Technology at Delft, the birthplace of Vermeer. His interest, however, soon shifted to painting. In 1912 he was appointed an assistant at Delft to teach drawing and art history. He married. Soon his oils, watercolors and drawings won first prizes and gold medals at several exhibitions. The paintings he had not been able to sell before he won any prizes now found ready purchasers. Friends recall his reaction. "Why?" he asked. "I'm no better now."

Despite his growing reputation, van Meegeren had difficulty in making a living. He soon discovered that by painting pictures he didn't give a hoot about, but which the public seemed to prefer, he could do a lot better financially. At first he resisted this temptation, but he soon succumbed; he needed the money to indulge in the pleasures of the rather loose and wild life he had begun to lead. The critics, however, attacked this superficial work he was turning out. In his exhibitions van Meegeren would generally include a few paintings into which he had put the best of himself, but these were largely overlooked.

By 1930 van Meegeren was making a fair amount of money from his commercialized paintings and his portraits of nobility, not only in Holland but in London and on the Riviera, as well. One day a friend told him of having fooled an expert with a Rembrandt he had copied—and then watched the expert writhe when he revealed the hoax. This incident was the trigger that set van Meegeren off on his fabulous imposture.

He considered painting da Vincis and Rembrandts first, but finally picked Vermeer, partly because less was known about his life, partly because Vermeer, although a prosperous artist, had also been mistreated by the critics and been forgotten for almost two hundred years after his death because a major contemporary art historian disliked him and made no mention of him in his books. Van Meegeren studied every available Vermeer and practiced duplicating the technique. Then he prepared himself to create paintings that would appear 250 years old to every expert test—infra-red and X-rays, quartz lamps, chemical analysis and so on. In seventeenth-century accounts he learned what materials Vermeer used and he scoured around for them; in one instance he paid $2,000 for a single tube of lapis lazuli.

Then, in 1936, van Meegeren left Holland for a long stay on the Riviera. There, without using living models, he painted most of his "original" Vermeers and De Hoochs, in a special locked room, where no one was allowed, not even his wife. He told her he was struggling with some difficult conception and she—knowing the ways of artists—did not pry. When each painting was finished, van Meegeren had to maneuver his wife out of the house for a day so he could bake the picture to complete the effect of age. Then he disposed of the painting through an attorney who was told that van Meegeren was acting as agent for a famous Italian family who insisted on remaining anonymous because they did not want word to get around that they had fallen on hard times and were forced to sell precious heirlooms.

To account for the huge funds he obtained for his paintings and his luxurious mode of life, van Meegeren claimed, several times, that he had won a huge prize in the Lotterie Nationale, for which he religiously purchased tickets. Originally van Meegeren had intended to paint one Vermeer, then expose the hoax publicly and turn the tables on the critics who, he felt, had so maligned him. But the opportunity to reap a continuing harvest proved irresistible. He took the cash and let Vermeer and the anonymous Italian family take the credit. In 1939, wealthy and nursing a secret feeling of great power, van Meegeren returned to Holland, where the rest of his incredible drama played itself out.

LIFE AMONG THE AUSTRALIAN CANNIBALS

by Edith Sitwell

Monsieur Louis de Rougemont, and his adventures, narrated as they were in the *Wide World Magazine* for August, 1898, caused a stir throughout the whole of our Empire. I find myself obliged to turn to *Sober Truth,* the authors of which have with the utmost industry and sympathy dug up and reproduced for us Monsieur de Rougemont's history.

The *Wide World Magazine's* announcement of Monsieur de Rougemont's narrative of his adventures begins thus:

"We now commence what may truly be described as the most amazing story a man ever tried to tell. In all the annals of geographical science there is practically but one case that can be compared for a moment with M. de Rougemont's, but in that instance the man returned to civilization a hopeless idiot, having lost his reason years before, amidst his appalling surroundings. Quite apart from the world-wide interest of M. de Rougemont's narrative of adventure, it will be obvious that after his thirty years' experience as a cannibal chief in the wilds of unexplored Australia, his contribution to science will be simply above all price. He has already appeared before such eminent geographical authorities as Dr. G. Scott Keltie, and Dr. Hugh R. Mill, who have heard his story and checked it by means of their unrivalled collection of latest reports, charts, and works of travel. These well-known experts are quite satisfied that not only is M. de Rougemont's narrative perfectly accurate, but that it is of the very highest scientific value. We also have much pleasure in announcing that arrangements are being made for M. de Rougemont to read an important paper before that great scientific body, the British Association for the Advancement of Science, at their next Congress, which will be held in September at Bristol.". . .

Life among the cannibals had, it seemed, taught M. de Rougemont to "size up" human nature fairly accurately; and none knew better than he the value of the Dog-the-Friend-of-Man theme as a softening

factor. No head so soft, no heart so soft, that these could not be molli-
fied still further by a really good story about a virtuous and courageous dog. M. de Rougemont's history therefore ran thus. In the early
'sixties he was engaged in pearl-fishing off the South coast of New
Guinea, and in the course of this industry, and in mid-ocean, he found
himself alone save for the Captain's dog. A storm arose. Where was
the Captain? Where was the ship's Company? Where was M. de
Rougemont's partner? They had vanished, leaving M. de Rougemont
in charge of the Dog. For a fortnight these two inseparable companions navigated the ship, drifting hither and thither, and sharing each
other's joys and sorrows, and then—probably just as M. de Rougemont
was telling the Dog some simple poignant story—the ship struck a reef
and was seen to be sinking, Man and Dog sprang into the sea, and began to swim towards a small island; but the tide was too strong for M.
de Rougemont, and he, like the ship, was seen to be sinking. Then it
was that the Friend of Man, sagacious and faithful, held out his tail
to the drowning M. de Rougemont, who with a last effort seized it
between his teeth, and in this manner was towed ashore. The companions found themselves on a small island one hundred yards long, ten
yards wide and eight feet above the sea-level. Here they made themselves as comfortable as they could, by means of the furniture from
the wreck, and settled down to a life of work and of thought, and of
such sports as turtle-riding, and deep-sea diving on the backs of the
turtles. "I used," he tells us, "to wade out to where the turtles were
and, on catching a big six-hundred pounder, would calmly sit astride
on his back.

"Away would swim the startled creature mostly a foot or so below
the surface. When he dived deeper I simply sat back on the shell, and
then he was forced to come up. I steered my queer steeds in a curious
way. When I wanted my turtle to turn to the left, I simply thrust my
foot into his right eye and vice versa for the contrary direction. My
two big toes placed simultaneously over both his optics caused a halt
so abrupt as almost to unseat me."

Here they remained for two years, undisturbed, and then four
naked savages, a man, a woman, and their two children, were blown
up to the island by another gale. The savages were friendly, especially
the woman; they seemed pleased to see Monsieur de Rougemont, and
he learned their language, and was informed by them that they were
Australian aborigines. The woman, whose name was Yamba, was pe-
culiarly intelligent, and taught him many things about the customs

and language of the Australian Negroes, which proved invaluable to him when he came to reign over them.

It may be said that Monsieur de Rougemont had, by this time, discarded all clothing, in preparation for his future state.

These inseparable friends at last decided that they would try to reach the mainland in a boat they had constructed, so, after full preparations, they set out on their journey. A few days passed, land appeared on the horizon, and Yamba and her husband and children proclaimed joyfully that it was their native country. They decided, however, that the joy of arriving there immediately after such an arduous journey would be too much for them, and they therefore landed on an island, in the mouth of a large bay, and here Yamba lit fires which were to serve as a signal to her friends on the mainland. The result was that when, after a few days' complete rest, they arrived in sight of Yamba's native country, Monsieur de Rougemont was much impressed by the sight of a huge shouting crowd of Negroes, excited, singing, and gesticulating, pouring down to the shore to welcome them. The enthusiasm, the friendliness, the respect of this simple people knew no bounds. They insisted indeed that Monsieur de Rougemont must make his home with them, and to this he agreed. . . . His new friends then insisted on finding a wife for him, but the faithful M. de Rougemont would look at nobody but Yamba, and so, after some amount of amicable bargaining with her former husband, he married her. The marriage was a happy one, for M. de Rougemont had high ideals of womanhood, and Yamba fulfilled these to a remarkable degree. Her husband tells us, "Often has that heroic creature *tramped on foot a hundred miles* to get me a few sprigs of saline herbs; she had heard me say I wanted salt." And later, as we shall see, she proved her devotion in a manner even more striking and even more grateful to the masculine belief in that wise predilection of Providence for the heavier battalions. "The battle goes to the strong," cries heaven. And heaven may not easily be put in the wrong.

Life amongst the subjects of M. de Rougemont was extremely simple. We are assured that, "Every morning I was astir by sunrise, and, hope springing eternal, I at once searched for the faintest indication of a passing sail. Next I would bathe in a lagoon protected from sharks, drying myself by a run on the beach. Meanwhile, Yamba would have gone out searching for roots for breakfast, and seldom returned without a supply of my favourite water-lily roots. . . . The natives themselves had but two meals a day—breakfast, between eight and nine o'clock, and then an enormous feast in the late afternoon, their ordinary food consisting of kangaroo, emu, snakes, rats, and fish, an especial dainty being a worm found in the black avia tree, or in any decaying trunk.

"These worms were generally grilled on hot stones, and eaten several at a time like small whitebait. I often ate them myself, and found them most palatable."

At this point, the readers of the *Wide World Magazine* became so violently excited by the prospect of seeing the hero of these adventures face to face, that the Editor inserted this notice: He was receiving, we are informed, "shoals of letters daily from all quarters asking whether M. de Rougemont is likely to afford the British Public an opportunity of seeing him in the flesh. To these correspondents we can only say that it is very probable M. de Rougemont may shortly be induced to lecture in the principal towns and cities in the United Kingdom. Moreover, he at present is sitting to that well-known artist Mr. John Tussaud, who is preparing a portrait-model of this marvellous man. . . ."

The duties of a prospective Cannibal Chief were as painful, at moments, as they were arduous, and M. de Rougemont gave the appalled readers of the *Wide World Magazine* this description of the sequel to a battle. Having explained that the dead were placed on litters made out of spears and grass and carried into the camp, he tells us that "the chiefs decked themselves with gorgeous cockatoo feathers, and painted their bodies in stripes with red and yellow ochre, and other glaring pigments." The narrative continues:

"There were so many signs to presage what was coming, that I knew a cannibal feast was about to take place; but for obvious reasons I did not protest against it, nor did I take any notice whatever. The women (who do all the real work) fell on their knees, and with their fingers scraped three long trenches in the sand, each about 7 feet long and 3 feet deep. Into each of these ovens was placed one of the bodies of the fallen warriors, and then the trench was filled up—firstly with stones, and then with sand. On top of all a huge fire was built and maintained with great fierceness for about two hours. There was great rejoicing during the period of cooking, and apparently much pleasurable anticipation among the triumphant blacks. In due time the signal was given, and the ovens laid open once more. I looked in and saw that the bodies were very much burnt. The skin was cracked in places and liquid fat was issuing forth. . . . But perhaps the less said about this horrible spectacle the better. With a yell, several warriors leapt into each trench and struck spears into the big 'joints.' At the moment the roasted carcases were taken out of the trenches the whole tribe literally fell upon them and tore them limb from limb. I saw mothers with a leg or an arm surrounded by plaintive children, who were crying for their portion of the toothsome dainty . . . !"

At this point, M. de Rougemont narrates a discovery which must have roused a kind of furore of excitement amongst natural-history societies. For he tells us that, "One day I decided to go and explore one of the islands in search of wombats, whose skins I wanted to make into sandals for myself. I knew that wombats haunted the islands in countless thousands, because I had seen them rising in clouds every evening at sunset. As usual, Yamba was my only companion.

Miss Barton and Mr. Sitwell, in a note, remark, with justice and admiration, that "A wombat is an animal closely resembling a small bear. The existence of flying wombats, it may readily be imagined, caused a stir among naturalists." Whilst engaged in the search for this volatile quadruped M. de Rougemont met with an adventure which would have ended badly for any man less intrepid than this great traveller.

He explains that, "I had not gone many yards along this track (in the forest) when I was horrified to see, right in front of me, an enormous alligator. The great reptile was shuffling along down the path towards me, evidently making for the water, and not only blocked my advance, but also necessitated my immediate retreat. The moment the brute caught sight of me, he stopped, and began snapping his jaws viciously. . . . I decided, however, to make a bold dash for victory, having always in mind the prestige that was so necessary to my existence amongst the blacks. I therefore walked straight up to the evil-looking monster, and then, taking a short run, I leaped high into the air, shot over his head, and landed on his scaly back, at the same time giving a tremendous yell in order to attract Yamba, whom I had left in charge of the boat.

"The moment I landed on his back I struck the alligator with all my force with my tomahawk, on what I considered the most vulnerable part of his head. So powerful was my stroke, that I found to my dismay that I could not get the weapon out of his head again. While I was in this extraordinary situation—standing on the back of an enormous alligator, and tugging at my tomahawk embedded in its head—Yamba came rushing up the path, carrying one of the paddles, which, without a moment's hesitation, she thrust down the alligator's throat as he turned to snap at her. In this way the monster was prevented from moving his head either backward or forward, and then, drawing my stiletto I blinded him in both eyes, afterwards finishing him leisurely with my tomahawk, when at length I managed to release it. Yamba was enormously proud of me after this achievement, and when we returned to the mainland she gave her tribesmen a graphic account of my gallantry and bravery. After the encounter with the alligator, they looked upon me as a very great and powerful personage indeed."

Great and powerful, however, as was Monsieur de Rougemont, he decided that it was, by now, time that he should shine once more in the outer world, and as he had given up hope of being rescued by any passing ship, he decided to make a journey overland, accompanied by the faithful Yamba. With him he took, not only Yamba, but a "native passport—a kind of masonic mystic stick, inscribed with certain cabalistic characters. Every chief carried one of these sticks, stuck through his nose. I, however, invariably carried the passport in my long luxuriant hair, which I wore 'bun' fashion, held in a net of opossum hair. This passport stick proved invaluable as a means of putting us on good terms with the different tribes we encountered."

Here the Editor of the *Wide World Magazine*, stirred to the foundation of his being by the events narrated by Monsieur de Rougemont and by those which followed, explains that "The publication of the preceding instalments have, we may say, caused some truly amazing developments of the story, people having turned up here long since believed to be dead. We cannot say much about these developments, but we earnestly advise our readers to follow the story with the closest interest. Arrangements are already being made for its translation into several European languages from Spain to Sweden. . . ."

And now, quietly and soberly, the idealistic M. de Rougemont gives us the most amazing instance of the devotion of Woman, "before it was corrupted and turned selfish by civilization." For M. de Rougemont, attacked by malarial fever in its most terrible form, and nursed night and day by Yamba, when he came round a little, fancied he noticed a great change in Yamba. "I asked her if anything had occurred to her during my illness. I then learned something which will haunt me to my dying day. There is perhaps no more extraordinary instance of womanly devotion recorded in the annals of the human race. To my unspeakable horror, Yamba quietly told me that she had recently

given birth to a child, *which she had killed and eaten*. It took me some
time to realize a thing so ghastly and so horrible, and when I asked
why she had done it, she pleaded: 'I was afraid that you were going
to die—going to leave me; and besides, you know that I could not
have nursed both you and the baby, so I did what I considered best.'
She saw I was perfectly horror-struck, but she altogether failed to
understand my point of view. For a long time after this incident, however, Yamba carried a little parcel in bark round her neck, and this
she appeared to treasure very much.

"One day when I had recovered, she told me that the little packet
contained some of the small bones of the infant, which she was pre-
serving out of love for its memory."

I do not think it is possible to deny that, from a man's point of view,
Yamba was the Ideal Woman, combining as she did in one person the
virtues of an overwhelming understanding of the importance of man,
strong practical common sense, and mother love.

However, to continue our narrative, Monsieur de Rougemont now
underwent a most remarkable and efficacious cure for the chilly feeling by which he was beset as a result of his illness. Having killed a big
bull, "I determined to test the efficacy of a very popular native remedy for fever—for shivering fits still continued to come upon me at
most abnormal times—usually late in the day. No matter how much
grass poor Yamba brought me, I never could get warm, and so now I
thought I would try some animal heat.

"Scarce had the life left the body before I ripped the buffalo open
between the fore and hind legs, and then crawled into the interior,
fairly burying myself in a deluge of warm blood and intestines. My
head, however, was protruding from the animal's chest. . . . Next
morning, to my amazement, I found I was a prisoner, the carcase
having got cold and frigid, so that I had literally to be dug out. As
.I emerged I presented a most ghastly and horrifying spectacle. My
body was covered with congealed blood, and even my long hair was
all matted and stiffened with it. But never can I forget the feeling of
exhilaration and strength that took possession of me as I stood there
looking at my faithful companion. *I was absolutely cured*—a new
man, a giant of strength."

Alas, this story, and others, equally remarkable, proved too much
for certain members of the public, and these persons (as I think, very
unkindly) set about exposing this poor harmless creature, who had
injured nobody, and whose worst crime was that he had given a little

innocent amusement to others, brought a little harmless romance into his own threadbare life. Letter after letter appeared in the *Daily Chronicle* challenging the Cannibal Chief to prove the truth of his statements, to appear in person. Naively and courageously, he agreed to appear at the offices of the *Daily Chronicle* in order that he might be asked questions, and his persecutors were surprised to see "an elderly man, slightly built, with a tanned, wrinkled face, the upper part of which bore obvious signs of marked intellectual power. In a pleasant, cultured voice, he gave such ready replies to the questions that were put to him that his examiners were disconcerted." . . .

But the *Daily Chronicle* was determined on his ruin, and, after having made the most exhaustive enquiries, it published the true story of poor M. de Rougemont's uneventful threadbare life.

He had never been a cannibal chief, though he had, once, risen to the position of being butler to a Lady Robinson in Australia. His real name was not de Rougemont, but Grin; he was a native of Switzerland, and had once been footman and courier to Fanny Kemble. In the early 'seventies, he led a wandering life in Australia, and then, in 1898, enlivened our shores with his presence. The Library of the British Museum may, or may not, have inspired in him the desire to be known as a cannibal chief, for it is certain that he spent many weeks in that haunt of learning before appearing in the presence of the awestruck Editor of the *Wide World Magazine* in the character of Monsieur Louis de Rougemont. I am glad to think that he enjoyed fame and prosperity, even for such a short time, but his subsequent fate is cruel and undeserved. Mr. Osbert Sitwell, in his preface to the book from which I have culled this narrative, tells us that the writer remembers so well and for so many years seeing a tall bearded figure, lank and stooping, selling matches in Shaftesbury Avenue or Piccadilly. This ghost of the streets was dressed in an old ragged overcoat, over the top of which the thin hair fell, and showed above it a calm, philosophical, curiously intelligent face. He was told repeatedly that this man was Louis de Rougemont. . . .

I wonder if the persecutors of this harmless creature ever passed the man they had so wantonly ruined, and, if so, if they felt ashamed before that mild and uncomplaining gaze.

THE WONDROUS BOX OF DR. ABRAMS

by Robert Yoder

Doctor Abrams was perhaps the greatest medicine man of modern times. The particular charm of his story lies in the fact that he rose to fame and fortune selling a sealed box. How much he believed in its efficacy it is impossible to say.

Doctor Abrams was a California physician who had taken his degree in Heidelberg in 1882 and settled down to peaceful anonymity. Apparently he prescribed the time-honored remedies, used the time-honored methods and instruments. There seems to have been nothing whatsoever in his early days to indicate that here was a white swan or, more specifically, to suggest that he was to become a serious threat to established medical practice, as he did.

The doc did nothing to attract much notice until 1910, when he went out lecturing on something he called "spondylotherapy," the "spondyl" part referring to the spine. Fellow-physicians who went to hear him said there was nothing much new in this—just a mixture of the ideas of chiropractic and osteopathy. The American Medical Association remarked sourly, however, that Abrams' followers included "many of the outstanding faddists and quacks of the country."

Doctor Abrams' first big splash as an innovator came when he announced the invention of an exceedingly handy machine which enabled him, he said, to sit in California and diagnose for patients anywhere in the world. All he needed was a drop of the patient's blood on blotting paper, sent to him by mail. He could do this because every ailment, he explained, had its distinctive "vibratory rate" somewhat as every radio station has its wave length. His machine would somehow identify this vibratory rate from the blotting paper. . . .

The nice thing about Abrams' machine was that the doc himself still played an important and colorful part. His machine did not simply light up like a pinball game and spell out Mumps, High Blood Pressure or Bad Hang-over. On the contrary, there was a ceremony, as Abrams described his procedure, of considerable style.

A wire extended from Doctor Abrams' device, ending in a metal plate. When the blotting paper had been inserted in the machine, a stooge was called forth. This stooge was the patient's proxy and local representative. The machine would transmit to him the symptoms of the patient so far away, and the patient would get the benefit of Doctor Abrams' knowledge at a great saving in carfare.

The records do not make it clear just why the stand-in faced west in a dim light, but he did. Now the machine was turned on and Abrams diagnosed. He did not use such prosy methods as taking this substitute patient's pulse or listening to his innards with a stethoscope. The doc diagnosed by tapping the stooge on the tummy, as if looking for a joist to hang a picture or rapping a melon to see if it is ripe.

The doc must have been doing a considerable business in this long-distance transcontinental diagnosing, and the American Medical Association had its skeptical eye on him, but orthodox physicians are always hesitant about dignifying such things with an investigation. So it appears that no standard medical man ever examined one of Doc Abrams' stooges, which is a pity. For if Abrams was right, this proxy must have gone through the most remarkable experience in medical history. No one seems to have asked why—with a second-hand case of measles in the morning, with perhaps jaundice, kidney trouble and asthma in the afternoon—this poor wight wasn't a complete wreck within a week.

The diagnosing device undoubtedly made its inventor a good deal of money, but it was a mere toy compared to the machine Abrams was to come up with next. About 1920 he announced the discovery of E.R.A., the initials standing for "the electronic reaction of Abrams," and began to speak a mixture of electrical and medical terms that had reputable physicians baffled and wondering if here was something new, strange and rich. And Abrams also announced the perfection of what became known as his "magic box." There was a more formal name for it—the "occilloclast." It was a machine so entrancing, with such a pleasing air of science about it, that it threatened for a time to starve reputable physicians out of business. This was no mere diagnoser. This machine, Abrams announced, would treat. It would—if it did what he claimed—make taking medicine, in most cases, a thing of the crude, unscientific past.

His reasoning went as follows: There are specific drugs which cure.

Quinine for malaria is an example. Now Abrams reverted to his theory about those mystical vibratory rates. "Specific drugs," he said, "must have the same vibratory rate as the diseases against which they are effective. That is why they cure." This new machine of his was a kind of superscientific short cut. It put out some kind of wave which, as he explained it, did the same work as the drugs, and without need for the drugs themselves.

Here was something sensational and of tremendous value, though no joy to the drugstores. True or false, the idea had a great appeal to the suffering public—just getting used to the radio, which was a magic box itself—and to that sizable number of men and women who like going to doctors' offices the way others like to go bowling, shopping or to the movies. By 1922, conventional physicians were saying glumly that, although not every man who had one of Abrams' sealed boxes in his office was a quack, certainly every quack had one. There were quacks who had eight or ten of them, as a saloon might have a battery of slot machines. It was customary to charge around $200 for a course of treatments, which consisted of having one of these machines buzz at you, and many a slightly phony doctor took in $50,000 to $75,000 a year while honest physicians bit their nails in wonderment and frustration.

By 1923 there were hundreds of oscilloclasts in doctors' offices here and abroad, but none had ever been sold. Abrams leased them, asking a deposit of $250 and $200 more for a course of instructions.

Abrams added a nice touch of mystery by swearing the lessees never to look inside. The cabinet was tightly sealed, presumably to guard some tremendous secret.

It was clear enough to reputable physicians that this gadget was capable of great harm, for quacks were promising to cure anything, including tuberculosis and cancer. It was not clear just whether the inventor himself was a faker of considerable genius, a nut of the nuttiest or had, in this mumbo-jumbo about wave lengths, the vague shadow of something real and important. Abrams was working in a field of knowledge that was misty at best, and just what role some form of electricity plays in the operation and failure of the body is a large question. There were men of good reputation who studied Abrams' assertions seriously. The *Journal of the American Medical Association* decided, however, that things were getting out of hand. Fakers equipped with one of these boxes were declaring they could cure nine out of ten cases of anything and everything. By holding up such hopes as that, it was not difficult to get ten to twenty-five dollars a consultation, and all the treatment cost the quack was a little electricity. The *Journal* took Doctor Abrams under fire.

If Doctor Abrams' calm claims of being able to make transcontinental diagnoses infuriated the conservative physicians who worked somewhat closer to the patient, a further claim he made must have burned them to a crisp. The buoyant Californian announced one day that with his remarkable diagnosing machine—not the later, greater machine, but his first effort—he really did not need a sample of the patient's blood at all. His machine would work very well, he said, from the patient's handwriting.

The idea struck Doctor Abrams that it would be possible to diagnose the ailments of persons long dead—the great of centuries past. He announced that he had experimented with the signature of the great Dr. Samuel Johnson, and had found that Doctor Johnson had suffered from syphilis. He announced the same findings from the signature of Edgar Allan Poe, and from the signature of Sam Pepys. The machine seemed to have a single-track mind. Even those who were willing to believe the worst of Poe and Pepys must have balked when Doctor Abrams tested the signature of Henry Wadsworth Longfellow, and made his customary finding.

Of all the statements Doctor Abrams made about his machines, perhaps the blandest was his reply to those who scoffed at the diagnosing machine. Abrams replied cheerfully that the machine would, of course, fail in the presence of doubt; it just wouldn't work when there were skeptics around. Quacks who possessed the curing or treating machine had a fine array of excuses for failure. The whole technique was delicate in the extreme, they could explain, and was easily upset by radio broadcasts, the weather or the steel in buildings.

For a long time there was little the reputable physicians could do about this except to smolder. But Doc Abrams loved to diagnose by mail, and this proved the chink in his armor. In a journal he published, Abrams had said he and his diagnosing machine not only could diagnose ailments but could diagnose religion. When he drummed on his stooge, he found "areas of sensitivity" which differed, he explained, in the case of Protestant, Catholic and Jew.

More importantly, he said he could ascertain the unseen patient's sex. From a physician in Chesaning, Michigan, there came one day a drop of blood on blotting paper, and a request that Doctor Abrams make a diagnosis. The patient, Doctor Abrams reported, had diabetes, malaria, cancer and two social diseases. The doc was reassuring about it. "This may look like a formidable array of diseases," he wrote the

Michigan medico, "but it isn't bad from an Electronic standpoint." The Chesaning physician had been setting a trap. He sent this diagnosis on to the American Medical Association, with a note of explanation. The blood in question was that of a young Plymouth Rock rooster of impeccable virtue, who had not been out of his cage since birth, and was in robust health.

About this time a Miss Bell wrote to an Abrams disciple in Albuquerque, New Mexico, for a diagnosis. She was informed she had "cancer to the amount of six ohms." Miss Bell was told, in addition, that she had many ailments distinctively feminine and an infection of the left frontal sinus. Now the crafty physician who had posed as Miss Bell disclosed that the blood sample in question had come from a healthy guinea pig, and a male guinea pig at that. He had sent another drop of blood from the same guinea pig, using the name of "Mrs. Jones," and had been told that Mrs. Jones had a skin ailment and stomach trouble. "What Abrams needs now," the doctors jeered, "is a machine that will tell the blood of humans from the blood of healthy roosters and guinea pigs."

Finally a formal, though unofficial, investigation was launched. The magazine *Scientific American* commissioned a panel of experts to study the occilloclast. In this group were two doctors of high standing, a civil engineer, a radio expert, and because thought waves seemed somehow to be mixed up in the Abrams theories, the investigators included a man who had delved into spiritualism and telepathy. In the fall of 1923, this group opened one of the sealed boxes which had made Abrams between $1,500,000 and $2,000,000.

What they found inside left the investigators completely at sea. There was a condenser, a rheostat, an ohmmeter and a magnetic interrupter. They were neatly wired together, but seemed completely without meaning. As near as the investigators could tell, the famous magic box was nothing and did nothing.

"At its best," the investigators concluded, "it is all an illusion. At worst, it is a colossal fraud."

A few months after the committee's findings were published, Abrams fell ill. The man who had treated thousands was now in need of medical help himself. The malady was pneumonia, and paid no heed either to the Abrams diagnosing machine or to the Abrams treating machine. Fate being an inexorable satirist, the outcome was never in doubt. The man who almost upset standard medical practice died in complete accordance with the rules of conventional medicine.

THE BOY WHO WROTE A PLAY BY SHAKESPEARE

by William Henry Ireland

Chatterton and Macpherson, perhaps the two most famous literary forgers, are well-known chiefly because the creations they produced under the guise of newly discovered, ancient manuscripts had sufficient merit to become accepted, if minor, items in the history of English literature. The story of Ireland's great forgery is less familiar, because what he created was less durable as literature. But as a hoax it was far bolder and appeared under far more auspicious circumstances.

Most forgers of Shakespeare have produced chiefly little tidbits, such as letters, autographs on deeds, and the like. Ireland, a youth of eighteen, after some initial trials boldly came up not only with some locks of Shakespeare's hair, but with a complete play by the great poet, a play which, on the evening of April 2, 1796, was produced by Sheridan at the Drury Lane Theatre, with the famed Kemble in the lead role.

William Henry Ireland was the son of a bibliophile, Samuel Ireland, but he received a meagre education and, apparently, showed no signs of special talent. In his early teens William was taken to Shakespeare's birthplace and was greatly moved. Some time later he met and talked with Chatterton's sister, querying her with considerable interest about her late brother's activities.

William Henry began his forgeries by obtaining from booksellers blank sheets of ancient paper taken from folios and quartos of the Elizabethan period. From a chemist he purchased some special ink which had been treated to simulate age. Ireland never fully explained under what pretenses he obtained the ink and paper; perhaps his money was good and that was all that mattered.

Ireland's first Shakespeare forgery was an autograph on a lease. He brought it to his father and explained that he had discovered it while going through some papers in the home of a gentleman he had met. His father was delighted with the find. William said he'd rummage some more. He soon came up with several smaller items and then hit on the idea of once for all proving that Shakespeare was not a Roman Catholic, as had been claimed on the basis of a profession of faith said to have been written by John Shakespeare, the poet's father, and internal evidence from Shakespeare's work, particularly the language in which the Ghost in Hamlet *refers to purgatory.*

The boy sat down and, according to his later Confession, *"without any previous transcript or subsequent alteration" composed and simultaneously wrote in a hand modeled on Shakespeare's autograph, a "Protestant Profession of Faith by William Shakespeare," running over three hundred words. Despite basic anachronisms, the document was accepted by Shakespeare experts. A leading clergyman, moved, no doubt, by the source and the sentiment, declared: "We have many fine passages in our Church Service and our litany abounds in beauty, but here, Sir, is a man who outdistanced us all."*

Much encouraged, William quickly discovered the complete original manuscript of Lear *and portions of the original* Hamlet *manuscript, as well as a box with some locks of Shakespeare's hair.*

The Irelands became outstanding celebrities. There were, of course, skeptics. But the list of believers in the genuineness of the relics included most of the leading experts and critics. Boswell knelt before the locks of hair and the Lear *and* Hamlet *manuscripts and declaimed: "I now kiss the invaluable relics of our bard, and thanks to God that I have lived to see them." The Prince of Wales was another distinguished visitor who made the pilgrimage to the Ireland house to view the treasures.*

Thus seventeen-year-old William Henry Ireland had made his father a very happy and proud man and had made an invaluable contribution to England's historical and literary archives. The persons from whom he had bought the paper and ink, and to whom he had to return from time to time for more supplies, must have heard about the great discoveries, but they kept silent. But how did the boy explain the circumstances of his discoveries? The answer, which follows in his own words, describes a landmark in human credulity. These excerpts from Ireland's Confession *(1805) also detail the composition of his original Shakespeare play, his inner feelings at certain crucial moments, and the great plans he had for nearly doubling William Shakespeare's output.*

After the production of the profession of faith, I was much questioned as to the source from whence the manuscripts were drawn; and it was then for the first time I began to discover the unpleasant predicament in which I had involved myself by the production of the papers; for to screen a falsehood it was absolutely necessary to have recourse to a second duplicity: in consequence of which the following story was framed, which was invariably told to every individual who requested satisfaction on that head.

I informed the public, that, having made an acquaintance at a coffeehouse with a gentleman of fortune, who was from my conversation given to understand that I had a great predilection for every thing like antiquity, he had in consequence requested that I would pay him a visit; stating at the same time that he had many old papers, which had descended to him from his ancestors, who had practised the law, among which some might in all probability be found worthy my notice, in which case he would willingly make me a present of them. . . . Upon paying my friend a visit, he desired me to go into an adjoining apartment, where I observed a vast collection of old deeds and papers tied up in bundles and numbered, which I instantly began to inspect, when, after having looked over some parcels, I discovered, to my utter astonishment, the deed between our bard and Michael Fraser, bearing the signature of Shakespeare. I then proceeded to state, that, my first surprise having subsided, I took the above-mentioned deed to my friend, who also appeared much astonished, not conceiving any such document had been in his possession; that he remarked it was certainly a very curious instrument, but that having promised me every thing I should find worthy my notice, he would not be worse than his word. . . .

As the manuscripts became rather voluminous, great stress was laid upon their value, and it was thought a matter of astonishment how any man in his proper senses could think of giving away such a treasure. I stated that during my research among the deeds of my friend I had discovered one which established his right to certain property that had long been a subject of litigation; on which account he conceived the giving me the Shaksperian manuscripts no other than a just recompense for the service I had thus rendered him.

As every individual inspecting the papers remarked that it would have been his pride to be known as the original possessor of the documents produced, I was in consequence questioned as to the name of the donor: my reply to which was that the gentleman being possessed of a large fortune, and being well aware of the inquiries which must take place on the production of the papers, did not think fit to subject himself to the impertinent questionings of every individual who conceived himself licensed to demand an explanation concerning them; that he in consequence gave me the documents as mere curiosities, exacting from me at the same time a most solemn asseveration that I would keep his name for ever concealed.

When the idea of writing a play first took possession of my mind, I continued for some days undecided as to the subject most appropriate to the purpose; when a large drawing executed by Mr. S. Ireland representing Rowena in the act of presenting wine to Vortigern, and which hung over the chimneypiece in Mr. Ireland's study, suddenly attracted my attention. In consequence, when alone I took down Mr. Ireland's edition of *Holinshed's Chronicle*, and referred to the story of Vortigern as related by that historian; when, conceiving it apt to my purpose, I immediately planned the outline of the play; and with my usual impetuosity made known to Mr. Ireland the discovery of such a piece, before a single line was really executed.

In consequence of which I was unceasingly tormented for the manuscript; which I brought forward in small portions, as I found time to compose it, in my own hand-writing, pretending to have copied it from the original: and I believe I may with safety aver, that the play, though procrastinated in the delivery, did not actually occupy more than two months' time in the composing; notwithstanding the inconveniences I had to surmount from Mr. Ireland's unceasing applications, from the questionings of the numerous persons who inspected the papers, and the difficulty I found in snatching opportunities to proceed with the manuscript.

It is extraordinary to observe how willingly persons will blind themselves on any point interesting to their feelings. When it was known that a play on the subject of Vortigern was coming forward, every person who inspected the manuscripts admired the strange coincidence of Mr. Ireland's having so long possessed a drawing on the very subject of that drama; yet do I not recollect, even in one instance, that the drawing in question excited the smallest suspicion.

Being considerably under the age of eighteen when I wrote the play of *Vortigern*, the following fact will not appear singular. I was really so unacquainted with the proper length of a drama as to be compelled to count the number of lines in one of Shakspeare's plays, and on that standard to frame the *Vortigern;* and the play I had chosen happening to be uncommonly long, mine consequently became so: when completed, it contained, to the best of my recollection, two thousand eight hundred lines and upwards. Upon observing this, Mr. Sh*r*d*n remarked, that "the purchase of the play was at any rate a good one, as there were two plays and a half, instead of one." Having perused several pages, Mr. Sh*r*d*n came to one line which was not strictly poetic; upon which, turning to Mr. Ireland, he remarked —"This is rather strange; for though you are acquainted with my opinion as to Shakspeare, yet, be it as it may, he certainly always wrote poetry."—Having perused a few pages further, Mr. Sh*r*d*n again paused, and, laying down the manuscript, spoke to the following effect: "There are certainly some bold ideas, but they are crude and undigested. It is very odd: one would be led to think that Shakspeare must have been very young when he wrote the play. As to the doubting whether it be really his or not, who can possibly look at the papers, and not believe them ancient?"

After the most unaccountable procrastination, the terms of the deed, as to the purchase of the *Vortigern* by Mr. Sh*r*d*n, were agreed upon, and the papers drawn up by Mr. Albany Wallis of Norfolk Street; Mr. S. Ireland being made trustee for me, as I was then under age. The terms of the agreement were, that Mr. Sh*r*d*n should pay down three hundred pounds, and that the profits of the performance for the first sixty nights should be equally divided between Mr. Samuel Ireland and Mr. Sh*r*d*n, after deducting the necessary expenses of the theatre.

The three hundred pounds was paid in notes of hand, at short dates, drawn upon Mr. H*mm*rsly the banker, out of which I received sixty pounds. I have thought it necessary to mention this circumstance, that the charge of avarice may not be attributed to me; such an idea having never once entered my mind. . . .

For some weeks previous to the performance of the play of *Vortigern,* Mr. Malone had daily given intimation that his *Inquiry* into the Validity of the Papers attributed to Shakspeare was on the eve of publication. The volume, however, did not appear until after the representation of the piece. . . .

It is almost impossible to convey an adequate idea of the influx of persons who came to behold the representation of *Vortigern.* Every seat in the boxes had been previously taken; and so eager were the public to witness the fate of the play, that numerous persons paid the box prices, not being able to pass the pit door with sufficient expedition; after which, finding all the places in the boxes in keeping for the various parties who had bespoken them for weeks previous, they dropped down from the lower tier of boxes into the pit, in order to procure seats.

I did not enter the theatre till a very short period previous to the rising of the curtain; and the box being so very conspicuous, I soon retired from observation behind the scenes.

There is something so appalling in the conviction that a man does not stand upon the basis of truth, that he shrinks with terror when circumstances appear most favourable to his wishes. On the important night which was to seal the fate of my long-expected *Vortigern and Rowena,* I spent the greater part of the time of its representation in the green-room of the theatre; where I conversed for the most part with Mrs. Jordan*; who, at the commencement of the third act (at which period not a dissenting voice had been heard) congratulated me on the success of the piece, and gave it as her opinion that it would succeed. I am by no means superstitious, but a presentiment had taken possession of my mind which led me to augur very differently: and I then returned for answer, "That, notwithstanding appearances were auspicious to the success of the play, I felt a full conviction that it would not be a second time represented."

I do not mean to detract from the merits of Mr. Dignum as a vocal performer; but the idea of beholding that gentleman strut forth in tragedy is quite sufficient to excite risibility even in Melpomene herself. I have no doubt that that circumstance was justly appreciated by the acting manager of the day, who in consequence suffered Mr. Dignum to *"bellow on";* which he did so effectually, by his guttural pronunciation, as to set the whole house in a convulsive peal of laughter—a circumstance highly conducive to the success of a tragedy! !

The late facetious Mr. Phillimore, of *large-nosed* memory, was also placed by the manager in a prominent point of view, having, if I recollect aright, to perform the part of the Saxon general Horsus, whom I unfortunately killed in combat. That gentleman, on receiving the deadly wound (which proved, indeed, a *deadly blow* to my play), either from prior tuition or chance (I will not pretend to de-

* A singer who appeared only briefly.—A. K.

cide which) so placed his unfortunate carcass that on the falling of
the drop-curtain he was literally divided between the audience and
his brethren of the sock and buskin; his legs, &c., being towards the
spectators, and his head, &c., inside the curtain, which concealed
them from observation. This, however, was not the only calamity:
for as the wooden roller at the bottom of the curtain was rather
ponderous, Mr. Phillimore groaned beneath the unwelcome burden;
and finding his brethren somewhat dilatory in extricating him, he
adopted the more natural expedient of extricating himself; which,
for a *dead man*, was something in the style of Mr. Bannister, jun., in
the *Critic*, who tells Mr. Puff "that he cannot stay there *dying* all
day.". . .

I had almost forgot to mention the conduct of Ch*rl*s St*rt, esq.,
M.P., who was seated in a private box even with the stage, and who
was so exasperated at the pointed ill conduct and buffoonery of Mr.
Phillimore, as to make several attempts to seize him by the robe. . . .

I must, however, remark, that the particular line on which Mr.
Kemble laid such a peculiar stress was in my humble opinion the
watchword agreed upon by the Malone faction for the general howl.
The speech alluded to ran as follows; the line in Italics being that so
particularly noticed by Mr. Kemble—

> . . . O sov'reign Death!
> Who hast for thy domain this world immense.
> Churchyards and charnel-houses are thy haunts,
> And hospitals thy sumptuous palaces.
> And when thou wouldst be merry, thou dost choose
> The gaudy chamber of a dying king.
> O then thou dost ope wide thy hideous jaws,
> And with rude laughter and fantastic tricks
> Thou clapp'st thy rattling fingers to thy sides.
> *And when this solemn mockery is o'er,*
> With icy hand thou tak'st him by the feet,
> And upward, so, till thou dost reach the heart,
> And wrap him in the cloak of 'lasting night.

No sooner was the above line uttered in the most sepulchral tone
of voice possible than the most discordant howl echoed from the pit
that ever assailed the organs of hearing. After the lapse of ten minutes, the clamour subsided; when Mr. Kemble, having again obtained
a hearing, instead of proceeding with the speech at the ensuing line,

very politely, and in order to amuse the audience still more, redelivered the very line above quoted with even more solemn grimace. . . .

As in case the play of *Vortigern* had met with success a very considerable profit must have accrued to the managers, Mr. Sh*r*d*n was much displeased at the conduct of the gentleman mentioned in the preceding paragraph. . . .

When the fate of *Vortigern* was decided, I returned, in company with Mr. S. Ireland, to Norfolk Street, where a few gentlemen shortly after arrived to converse on the events of the evening. As I found it more than probable that they would remain in conversation till a late hour, I retired to bed, more easy in my mind than I had been for a great length of time, as the load was removed which had oppressed me. I that night slept most profoundly, and even awoke in the morning much later than usual. . . .

On applying to the treasurer of Drury Lane theatre, the morning after the fate of the *Vortigern* had been decided, Mr. S. Ireland was given to understand that there were two hundred and six pounds in the treasury, after the payment of all expenses: consequently the division of that sum took place between the manager and Mr. S. Ireland, who received one hundred and three pounds; out of which I had the sum of thirty pounds. . . .

Having heard with attention the diversity of opinions which had been given respecting the play of *Vortigern,* I conceived that I might profit by the information thus acquired, and therefore determined on writing another drama, which I planned from the story of Henry the Second and fair Rosamond; a subject that appeared to me amply stored with incident for the structure of a dramatic performance: and to the selection of that monarch's reign I was the more incited, as the genius of William Shakspeare had been so amply displayed in dramatising the histories of our Henries—the Fourth, Fifth, and Sixth. On the completion of this play, it was by all allowed to be a more finished composition than the *Vortigern;* and the only regret was that I had not brought it forward prior to that play. . . .

The plan of the play of *Henry the Second* I formed from a thin folio containing the life and reign of that monarch: and I was about ten weeks occupied in its composition. It was delivered to Mr. Samuel Ireland in my own hand-writing: nor was I ever at the trouble of reproducing it in the disguised hand, upon old paper, as my confession of the transaction intervened, and thus prevented my being put to that unnecessary trouble. . . .

Had the play of *Vortigern* succeeded with the public, and the manuscripts been acknowledged as genuine, it was my intention to have completed a series of plays from the reign of William the Conqueror to that of queen Elizabeth; that is to say, I should have planned a drama on every reign the subject of which had not been treated of by Shakspeare. . . .

I shall now pass over a considerable period of time, during which my mind was unceasingly harassed by the constant reproaches of Mr. Ireland (who was then regarded in the light of the fabricator of the papers), and the importunate interrogatories of his friends; who stated, that it was a duty incumbent on me to give up the name of any unknown friend, in order to clear my father's character from the odium which was so unjustly heaped upon it.

Having no name to bring forward, I of course evaded these reiterated entreaties by a statement of the grounds upon which the papers had originally fallen into my hands, and the manner in which Mr. Samuel Ireland had embarked in the publication of them. This, however, was not sufficient: the clamour increased daily; and a committee of several gentlemen was called to investigate the matter. . . .

The investigations eventually led William Henry Ireland to confess the forgery, chiefly in order to exonerate his father who was accused of being the architect of the whole scheme. But many people still found it impossible to believe that a young boy of seemingly no superior abilities had been the sole creator of the hoax. Ireland's father also felt that his son had made a false confession to shield him from further attack. All his life the elder Ireland preferred to believe the authentication he had originally received from numerous authorities.

William Henry Ireland later wrote a number of novels and other prose works which were published but were considered quite undistinguished. He died in 1835.

THE REAL STORY OF THE CARDIFF GIANT

by Alan Hynd

Scientific hoaxes, such as the recently exposed Piltdown Man, often serve as obstacles in man's struggle for knowledge, without providing much entertainment by way of compensation. The Cardiff Giant is a happy exception.

In Binghamton, New York, back in the 1860s, there lived a bluff and well-nourished big man of middle age by the name of George Hull who, although lucratively engaged in the manufacture of cheap cigars, had the instincts of a confidence man.

Hull was out in Ackley, Iowa, visiting a sister, in the spring of 1868 when he heard about a Methodist evangelist named Turk who was burning up the prairies with fire and brimstone. The cigar manufacturer decided to audition the Reverend Turk. The evangelist's favorite passage in the Bible was the fourth verse of the sixth chapter of Genesis, which speaks of giants having walked the earth. On the night that Hull caught the Reverend Turk, in a tent near Fort Dodge, the evangelist referred to the giants not once but several times. Hull finally got to his feet and, removing an unlighted cigar from his mouth, inquired, "How *big* were those giants?"

The Reverend Turk paused in mid-syllable, smiled briskly, and replied, without the slightest hesitation, that the giants had probably been anywhere from ten to twelve feet in height. Hull, who knew the Bible, inquired as to just where the height of the giants was specified. The evangelist roared something about just *knowing* that the giants had been twice as big as modern man.

Hull, by his later admission, lay awake all that night. His con man's instincts told him that he had collided head-on with his big opportunity. By daybreak, he had evolved a scheme for monetizing the public's belief in giants.

Hull hung around the stone quarries near Fort Dodge, on the hinge

126

for a piece of good hard stone about twelve feet long, four feet wide and two feet thick. He located just what he wanted in a gypsum bed and paid for it with a barrel of lager for the quarry workers.

The block of gypsum weighed five tons. The nearest railroad was forty miles away. The gypsum broke down several wagons and a couple of small bridges during the journey. This attracted much attention. Hull dealt an explanation off the cuff: he was a government agent, touring the country to collect mineral specimens from every state which were to be placed on exhibition in Washington.

Hull and the block of gypsum eventually landed in Chicago. There he deposited it in a barn owned by an old friend in the 900 block on North Clark Street. He hired an artist and a stonecutter. His basic instructions were simple. "Make me," he said, "a naked giant."

The artist and the stonecutter began work on a bald-headed male giant with Caucasian features. The giant was complete with eyes, nose, mouth, fingers, toes, nails, orifices and more personal equipment in proportion to his jumbo size. "Make him," Hull instructed as the work progressed, "like he died in great agony." Thus the entire figure was slightly twisted to the right. The left foot was somewhat turned up; the right arm lay across the abdomen and the left arm was drawn up under the back. The muscles of the legs were slightly contracted.

At the end of four months, the boys had a figure ten feet four and a half inches tall, weighing 2,990 pounds. The effect of skin pores was achieved by going over the entire surface with needle-pointed mallets. The gypsum itself bore dark streaks that looked like human veins.

The problem of endowing the giant with great age was a difficult one. Sulphuric acid finally turned the trick; it imparted a dingy brown that might have come from many centuries in the earth. Two small grooves were cut in the underside of the figure. These were to be palmed off as having been made by the action of water in the ground through the ages.

Hull paid the artist and the stonecutter several hundred dollars each, which was a bundle back in the Sixties, handsomely reimbursed his friend for the use of the barn, swore the three to secrecy, then took off for the East with the giant. The gypsum man traveled in a copper-coopered box under the alias of a piece of machinery. He and his creator landed in Union, New York, near Binghamton, in the late fall of 1868. The giant hung around a freight station while Hull hustled up a spot to plant him.

Hull had a cousin, a farmer named William Newell, who had for years fought a standoff battle with some belligerent acreage outside the hamlet of Cardiff, in the Onondaga Valley thirteen miles south of Syracuse. Stubby Newell, as the agriculturist was called because of certain anatomical dimensions, was a pious-looking, bearded character of middle age with elastic ethics. Newell had but one question to ask. Did the scheme entail the risk of jail? Not the slightest. "I just want to bury something on your farm," said Hull, "and leave it laying there for maybe a year."

The box containing the giant, drawn by a four-horse wagon, proceeded by easy stages to a point near Cardiff. There, Hull, Newell, a son of Newell's, and a trusted neighbor named Amesbury transported the giant to Newell's farm. Its arrival was timed for the dead of night. As an added precaution, Hull had arranged for Newell to send his family, with the exception of the son who was in on the scheme, away to visit relatives.

The conspirators dug a grave behind the barn, interred the gypsum man three feet down and face up, covered him over, and seeded the ground for clover. It was now October. Six months had elapsed since George Hull had heard the Reverend Turk speak of giants walking the earth. Hull's giant had, up to this point, set him back exactly $2,200.

If ever a man was festooned with horseshoes, it was George Hull. The following spring, a farmer less than a mile from the planted giant came upon some bones while plowing. Scientists from Cornell University at Ithaca pronounced them genuine fossil bones. This genuine find would pave the way for acceptance of the fake.

Hull knew that the successful perpetration of a fraud was contingent upon the proper conditioning of the victims. The discovery of his giant must come about *naturally*. Hull decided to construct his build-up out of equal parts of Newell's talents as an amateur actor and the man's constant struggle with the wolf at the door. He met Newell surreptitiously in the spring and early summer of 1869 and carefully coached him in what he was to do.

Newell began to go around complaining that the well on his farm was beginning to run dry and that he would be forced to go to the expense of digging for a new one. The whole region was aware that any sizable expense would plunge the farmer into a state of fiscal emergency. Newell moaned about his approaching crisis throughout the summer.

The giant had been stashed under the clover for about a year when, on the afternoon of Friday, October 15, 1869, Stubby Newell summoned two welldiggers to his broken-down land. The diggers followed Newell as he zigzagged over his property holding a dowser's two-pronged hazel stick, the while wailing about the expense of a new well. Finally the prongs of the stick pointed downward—guess where!

"All right," said Newell, marking the spot. "You can start diggin' here in the mornin'." Newell wasn't on the premises when the digging started. Hull had him away in Syracuse, developing frostbite from shaking hands with bankers he tried to put the slug on for a loan to pay for the well.

When Stubby Newell returned to his farm in the middle of the afternoon, as short at the pockets as when he had left, he saw a crowd of people gathered around the spot where his dowser's stick had pointed downward the previous afternoon. Newell's big moment, rehearsed many times for Hull, was at hand.

"What's the matter!" Newell started yelling as he broke into a run toward the crowd. "What's the *matter!* Is somebody hurt?"

The welldiggers had, early that morning, come upon something hard three feet down. By noon, the welldiggers had uncovered the complete surface of George Hull's gypsum man. Overwhelmed, they had gone running from the Newell property, shouting the news. Residents of the region had abandoned their chores to go and see for themselves. The whole country was jumping.

Newell, impecunious as he was, was able somehow to scrape up enough money, on a Saturday afternoon, to drive into the general store in Cardiff and purchase a large white canvas tent. He pitched the tent over the open grave of the giant. On Sunday morning, he began to charge people half a dollar to pass under the canvas and behold what was presently to be known as the eighth wonder of the world.

By Monday, Newell was really in business. A ticket booth was up at the entrance of the tent. Workmen had cut a trench around the giant. Eyewitness reports are agreed that the gypsum man was a remarkable sight. Lying there in the trench, under the subdued light of the tent, he impressed viewers as an ancient human being who had fallen where he died, become covered by the shifting sands of antiquity, and then turned to stone.

Reporters from Syracuse and Binghamton, the first of the press to view the giant, posed the question: was the giant an ancient statue or a petrified man? In Binghamton, George Hull, located inside a cloud of cigar smoke, was asked by a neighbor if he had seen the story in the papers about the great discovery on his cousin's farm. Hull said he had been too busy in his cigar factory to read the papers. When the neighbor filled him in with the details, Hull regarded the man suspiciously. "Go on," he said. "I don't believe it!"

Four regional preachers presented themselves in a body and inquired of Stubby Newell, still charging fifty cents a look, if there were special rates for the clergy. Newell let the divines in for two bits a head. When they came out, they made a joint pronouncement: the man in the grave was unquestionably a real human being going back to Biblical days; here, at long last, was irrefutable proof that the Bible was literally true.

Up to the time of the clerical pronouncement the fame of the giant had been strictly local. Now that the clergy had labeled the giant a petrified man—a real human being—the thing in the ground began to attract wide attention. On the first week end after the pronouncement, more than a thousand of the curious, many of them coming a considerable distance, beat a path to the farm.

Hull, the master mind, made his first visit to his cousin's place over that first big week end, to stare in unbelieving wonder into the grave. Then, after counting the house, he drew Newell aside. "Take down that sign that says fifty cents," he whispered, "and put up one that says a dollar."

The renown of the giant continued to build. Peasants and the intelligentsia were equally fascinated. Four-horse stages began to make round trips from Syracuse. Railroads started excursions from as far away as New York City, hours to the south. Seeing the giant carried a certain snob appeal; it was the thing to do.

Stubby Newell, the impecunious farmer, was taking in an average of twenty-six dollars an hour. He carted the cash into a Syracuse bank. But the stuff was just passing through his hands. Newell kept ten per cent and sent the rest to George Hull by draft.

Although there were several men in on the secret—the three in Chicago who had been in on the giant's creation, and the son and the neighbor of Newell who had buried it—keeping the secret was advantageous to them. Hull was declaring them in for a small percentage of the take.

Stubby Newell had meantime climbed out of his overalls and into a pair of striped pants, a cutaway, and a boiled shirt. He was delivering a little lecture in the tent, ghost-written by Hull, about how the giant had been discovered. At first, Newell's tale was simple. Then it began to take on flourishes. Eventually, he was claiming that God had guided him to the Biblical man.

Early in November, the snows came and made travel to Newell's farm difficult. The giant was disinterred by an elaborate system of cables, pulleys, and scaffolding, and moved to an exhibition hall in Syracuse. By now, its reputation had penetrated the sanctums of the scientists . . .

The scientists came to look, to ponder. Two Yale professors—Othniel G. Marsh, an internationally recognized authority on fossils, and Benjamin Silliman, a celebrated chemist—spearheaded a school of thought that maintained that the giant was a true fossil. A delegation of archeologists, sparked by Professor James H. Drator of the New York State Museum, who was perhaps the most distinguished paleontologist of the era, were of the opinion that the giant was an ancient statue. Professor Drater went so far as to call it "the most remarkable object yet brought to light in this country."

But now an iconoclast walked into the scene. He was Doctor Andrew D. White, the first president of Cornell University, later to become Minister to Russia and Ambassador to Germany. A friend of Dr. White somehow managed to chip off a piece of the giant in Syracuse and turn it over to the educator. The Cornell president had the piece analyzed; it was pronounced plain gypsum. Dr. White took a scientific friend to examine the giant. The friend detected what he thought were chisel marks.

Dr. White didn't make a public pronouncement. But he did summon scientist friends and caution them not to stick their necks out any further.

The first discordant note was publicly sounded when New York's most famous sculptor, Erastus Dow Palmer, went up to Syracuse, examined the gypsum man, and started to yell "Fraud!" The giant, said Palmer, was neither a fossil nor an ancient statue. It was something that had been planted, perhaps not more than a year previously, for commercial purposes. Palmer, being a man of stature, was widely quoted. He gave the papers scientific and technical arguments to buttress his stand. Among those who chewed over the sculptor's conclusions was Phineas Taylor Barnum. The Connecticut showman, although sixty years of age, was not to found the Barnum circus for two years yet; he was, at the moment, running a museum and menagerie on New York's Broadway. Barnum had naturally been interested in the giant since its discovery; now, however, that Palmer called it a fake, he was fascinated.

The showman dispatched a representative to Syracuse to size things up. Barnum's man happened to hit town on a Sunday when, in the six-hour period between 10 A.M. and 4 P.M., three thousand people paid a dollar apiece to look at the giant.

Barnum authorized his man to sound Newell out on leasing or buying the giant. Newell had been told by Hull just what to say to any offer. Newell said no.

Barnum sent for a Syracuse sculptor named Fox, who had done some work for his museum. "Make me," said Barnum to Fox, "an exact replica of that giant."

Early in December, when the giant had been on exhibition less than two months, a syndicate of three regional citizens of stature approached Newell with $37,500 in cash for a three-quarter share in the giant. This was handsome money eighty years ago.

Hull, operating through Newell, grabbed it. One of the syndicate men was a dentist named Amos Westcott. He was the father of the Edward Westcott who, nineteen years later, wrote the American classic, *David Harum*. Another member of the syndicate was a sharp, middle-aged, small-town banker and horse trader named David Hannum, who later became the David Harum character in the book by Dr. Westcott's son.

Hannum arrived in New York with his gypsum charge the third week in December. The idea was to put the giant in a museum and catch the Christmas shopping crowds. Hannum was startled to find that P. T. Barnum had just installed a duplicate giant in his museum on Broadway. Barnum was advertising his giant, at half a dollar a look, as the one, the only, the original Cardiff giant.

The Cardiff syndicate applied for a court injunction against Barnum. They didn't get it. The judge who denied the injunction had apparently heard the cry of fraud raised by Palmer, the sculptor, and couldn't see any harm in Barnum exhibiting a fake fake. The Hannum syndicate thereupon installed the original giant in a museum only two blocks from Barnum's fake giant. Barnum, flushed with his court victory over Hannum, began to incorporate in his advertising matter the charge that the other giant was fraudulent.

Everybody benefited. The public began to patronize *both* giants.

The charges and countercharges between Barnum and the Hannum group, carried daily in the press, were good for business. The public was curious to see what all the shouting was about. . . .

The authentic fake giant remained in the Broadway museum for about a month. In that time, the Hannum syndicate recouped its investment; after that, everything was nectar.

The scientific controversy over the giant now raged on both sides of the Atlantic. It had also become incredibly involved. One school of thought continued to insist that the Hannum giant was a fossil. Another school continued to insist that it was a piece of ancient sculpture. A third school held that it was a hoax. A fourth school started all over again by beginning on the premise that the Barnum giant was the one that had been found near Cardiff and that the Hannum giant was the replica.

Late in January, business began to diminish. Barnum's giant continued at its original stand. The original giant moved up to Boston. There it did a fine business. Ralph Waldo Emerson, the essayist, pronounced it "astonishing." The giant was, Emerson continued, beyond his depth. "But it is undoubtedly a bona fide, petrified human being." The Emerson statement gave the giant a second wind.

Cyrus Cobb, a noted artist and sculptor, looked long and soberly at the fake. "Any man calling this thing a humbug," he said, "brands himself a fool."

It remained for Doctor Oliver Wendell Holmes, the celebrated anatomist, to do something that none among the scores of scientific men who had examined the giant had even thought of doing. Doctor Holmes bored a hole in the giant's head, behind his left ear. Dr. Holmes found the interior of the head quite solid; this indicated to him the absence of a fossilized brain. The giant was, however, in the opinion of Holmes, a statue, "probably of great antiquity."

Although the admission price to see the giant in Boston was lowered from a dollar to four bits after Doctor Holmes' explorations into the giant's head, George Hull's creation attracted several hundred people a day. Even those who were now inclined to believe that the giant was a hoax of some kind, or at most a statue, were willing to part with half a dollar to see what all the noise was about. The giant became grist for the mills of the wits. Since he was now exposed as having a head of solid stone, he was compared to political candidates and officeholders throughout the East.

After his stand in the nation's first citadel of culture, the giant hit the road. David Hannum and his associates traveled with the stone man to various cities and towns in Massachusetts, New York, New Hampshire, Connecticut, and Pennsylvania. By now, practically nobody who pretended to know about such matters thought the giant was a fossil, but few dared call it a fraud. Scientific opinion had solidly crystallized into the belief that the giant was an ancient statue.

It was the press, the good old Fourth Estate, that finally decided to put the blast on the giant. Barnum's fake giant, still drawing 'em in on Broadway, but at cut rates, was proof to the skeptics of the press that an authentic-looking giant could be faked. Some unsung reporter, perhaps from a New York newspaper, began to take George Hull's hoax apart at the seams by poking around Cardiff.

This scribe learned that while the giant had first been discovered as a result of Stubby Newell's search for a much-needed well, Newell had never gone ahead with his search for water. His old one had never, as he had loudly claimed prior to the discovery of the giant, begun to dry up. With the whole premise of the discovery now open to suspicion, the boys from the city rooms really fell to their tasks. One of them got next to a clerk in the Syracuse bank and learned about those drafts that Newell had made payable to George Hull of Binghamton.

Now the reporters learned that George Hull had, a year before the giant's discovery on his cousin's farm, arrived in Union, New York, with a large box marked machinery. Hull attempted to explain this by saying the box had contained new machinery for his cigar factory. Employes of the factory told the newshounds the place hadn't seen a piece of new machinery in years.

Next, the press learned that Hull had made a visit to Ackley, Iowa, to see a sister, some months prior to his appearance in upper New York state with the big unexplained box. Reporters in Iowa took it from there. Hull's name was dug up in the register of a Fort Dodge hotel. A man answering his description had acquired a large block of gypsum in exchange for a barrel of beer.

Since the block of gypsum had broken down several wagons and bridges, tracing it was comparatively easy. It was traced to a railhead. Railroad records disclosed that George Hull had shipped a piece of machinery, weighing exactly what the gypsum weighed, to Chicago.

Windy City reporters examined drayage records. They wound up at the barn in the 900 block of North Clark Street. The man who owned the barn thought George Hull had committed a crime of some kind with the giant, instead of a hoax. He confessed his part in the deception. He named the stonecutter and the artist. They, too, spilled their tales.

When George Hull was confronted with the unearthed facts, he laughed and admitted the whole story. Every paper in the country, and the important ones in Europe, printed Hull's story. *That* should have finished Old Hoaxey, as some reporters were now calling the giant. Instead Old Hoaxey, who had, after making a profit of $100,000 for his backers, begun to lay eggs at the box office, became a red-hot attraction again.

Old Hoaxey went out every spring, appearing at fairs and carnivals. As the Eighties approached, he went into decline.

Old Hoaxey emerged for an appearance in 1901 at the Pan American Exposition in Buffalo, where President McKinley was assassinated. Then he went back into storage.

The giant passed into several hands. In 1934, he appeared at the New York State Fair at Syracuse. Then he came into the possession of Gardner Cowles, Jr., of the Iowa publishing family. Cowles lent him to the Iowa State Fair in 1935.

In 1939 the New York State Educational Department put up markers in the vicinity of Cardiff, pointing the way to the scene of the giant's first public appearance seventy years before. The New York State Historical Association acquired Old Hoaxey from Cowles in 1948 and placed him on view in the Farmers' Museum, lying in an open grave, just the way he was "discovered" eighty-one years before. There, secure in the knowledge that he is the most unique fraud of modern times, he rests.

Well, not exactly rests. There are those who profess to have seen Old Hoaxey trying to turn in his grave for that fake fake—Barnum's replica of Old Hoaxey—is still around, palming himself off as the one, the only, the original Cardiff Giant.

THE GREAT FRITZ KREISLER HOAX

by Louis Biancolli

Some years ago, while serving as annotator of the New York Philharmonic Symphony, I was obliged to write a program note about a Concerto in G major by Fritz Kreisler. Now when this same concerto was first published in Mainz in 1912, Antonio Vivaldi was billed as the composer, with Kreisler credited only as arranger and editor. The 1912 score, however, did carry a tell-tale inscription—in German, French and English—which included the following: "This concerto is freely treated from old manuscripts and constitutes an original work. . . . When the concerto is played in public Fritz Kreisler's name must be mentioned in the program."

Several previous "arrangements" by Kreisler, from "classical manuscripts" carried similar statements. Even with so many clues lying around, it was not till February, 1935, on his sixtieth birthday that Kreisler's secret finally leaked out. It was then discovered that all but one of the pieces "edited" by Kreisler and ascribed to Vivaldi, Pugnani, Couperin, Francoeur, Porpora and Padre Martini were Kreisleriana, pure and simple. The music world promptly split into two camps—those charging Kreisler with having played cheat, as opposed to those applauding the supreme mastery involved in carrying off the hoax and successfully concealing it for so many years. To get the full story I went to the best authority on the subject—Fritz Kreisler himself.

"I was at the beginning of my career when it all started," Mr. Kreisler said. "For a while I wasn't sure what I wanted to be. I had studied medicine and art. I also wanted to be an army officer and had entered training. But the violin was really my first love. I had begun to study it when I was four. I entered the Vienna Conservatory when I was seven and finished at ten with first prize. Then came the Paris Conservatory and the French gold medal at twelve. At fourteen I was already touring America."

"What made you undecided about continuing as a violinist?"

"My father was a medical doctor, and at the time I thought of becoming one, too. He himself had wanted to be a violinist, but his parents wouldn't let him. Being a violinist then was like going around in the streets with a hurdy-gurdy, unless, of course, you were a Wilhelmj, a Sarasate, or a Joachim. Well, in spite of the risks, I decided to remain a violinist."

"I suppose by 'risks' you mean more than the dangers of bucking competition with the spectacular personalities of that time."

"Well, there was the problem of programs. . . . The violinist's recital repertory was then very small."

"I don't follow you," I interrupted. "How about all the standard violin concertos?"

"Anybody playing a violin concerto with piano accompaniment at that time would have been laughed off the stage."

"How about Bach's unaccompanied sonatas?"

"They were not very popular."

"Beethoven and Schubert?"

"There were some sonatas by Schubert, but Beethoven's sonatas were out of the question. You had to be big to do them and you needed a big pianist to collaborate with you, a combination, let us say, equal to Horowitz and Elman or Rubinstein and Heifetz today."

"Couldn't you hire an orchestra to play the concerto accompaniments?" I asked.

"Scarcely, if you were poor and unknown. The result was that if you were a concert beginner you never played a concerto. And if you were poor and unknown, no great pianist would appear with you. Therefore, no Beethoven sonatas."

"I begin to see why medicine and a military career seemed more attractive to you than music."

"So what did you do if you began to give concerts?" Mr. Kreisler went on. "You fiddled around with Bach's Chaconne or the 'Devil's Trill' of Tartini or sonatas by Corelli, Veracini and Geminiani. The rest of the program was made up of smaller pieces, like Ernst's 'Elegie,' Raff's 'Cavatina,' Wieniawski's 'Mazurka' and 'Polonaise,' and Vieuxtemps' 'Ballade.' They were all good pieces as far as they went, but I wanted to play other things. And there just weren't any."

"How about arrangements of compositions originally written for voice or piano, which is such a growing practice today?" I asked.

"That wasn't done then," replied Mr. Kreisler. "The great exception was Chopin's E-flat Major Nocturne, which was called 'The Virgin's Prayer' in the violin version."

"That left you with repertory enough for about one concert-size program, complete with encores."

"That was why I resolved to create a repertory of my own." Mr. Kreisler leaned forward, his brow furrowed. . . . "I then began to write music under other composers' names. I took the names of little known composers like Pugnani and Louis Couperin, the grandfather of François Couperin.

"Not a single composition of Couperin's was known. Maybe in far-away libraries there were pieces by him, on yellow illegible manuscripts. You had to rummage around to find them. So with Padre Martini. Naturally, Vivaldi was a bit different. Bach had made arrangements and transcriptions and even borrowed ideas from him. So had others. And his music was scattered around everywhere."

"Was it ever your idea to imitate the style of these composers?"

"Not for one moment. I could have done a better job of copying their style if I had intended it. That wasn't my plan at all. I just wanted some pieces for myself . . . and I wrote them. I was eighteen then and I wanted to be a violinist, not a composer. I wanted to give recitals and I couldn't put several pieces on the program and sign them all 'Kreisler.' It would have looked arrogant.

"So I took those old forgotten names. First I brought out a piece by Pugnani. There is extant only one little piece by Pugnani."

"Was there anything in the composition that might have given you away?"

"A child could have seen Pugnani never wrote it. There was a semi-cadenza in the middle of it completely out of style with Pugnani's period. I played it and it was a huge success."

"What did you answer when people began to ask you where you had found these little pieces?"

"I was stumped. I didn't want to be known as a composer. Finally I said: 'I found them in libraries and monasteries while visiting Rome, Florence, Venice, and Paris. They were in dusty old manuscripts. I copied them.' "

"Didn't they ask you to name the libraries and monasteries?"

"Oh, yes, but I told them to go around and find out for themselves. I assured them there was plenty of material to choose from."

"Were you the only violinist to play these pieces of yours?"

"For a couple of years I was. Then a colleague of mine asked, 'Can

I have that Pugnani piece to play?' I made a copy and let him have it. Others began asking for copies. I asked nothing in return except mention in the program that the piece was brought out from manuscript and edited by Fritz Kreisler, with bowing and fingering."

"How about the critics?"

"They were calling them 'little masterpieces,' worthy of Bach, and so forth."

"You must have been really stumped when the publishers approached you." . . .

"I told Schott, the publisher in Mainz, the whole truth. The pieces were all mine, I said, but I didn't want my name appearing on them. Schott agreed."

"Were you paid very much for them?"

"He bought the whole set of twenty-five pieces at ten dollars each, bringing me exactly $250. That was all the revenue I ever derived from them in Europe. Later I sold them to Carl Fischer's in America and earned some money on them."

"Did Schott profit from the deal?"

"Did he? Hundreds of thousands of copies were sold."

"You must have had lots of fun reading what the critics had to say about these 'old and forgotten' composers."

"I remember one German reviewer in particular. He once wrote as follows about me: 'We heard Fritz Kreisler again last night. He played beautifully, but naturally his temperament lacks the strength and maturity to reach the heights of the Pugnani music.'"

"You didn't write him a little love note telling him the truth?"

"No, but I did tell Eugene Ysaye, the great violinist, one day that the pieces were all mine."

"What was his reaction?"

"He smiled and said, 'You pig, so you wrote all these things? Then why do you let these fellows run around playing your music without mentioning your name? I'd give them hell if I were you.'"

"I'd like to hear more about the music critics, being one myself. I feel that there but for the grace of God, write I."

"Let me tell you the most beautiful instance of all. Once I wrote a few special pieces for a Viennese recital. I called them 'Posthumous Waltzes' by 'Joseph Lanner.' The following day Leopold Schmidt, the critic of the *Berliner Tageblatt*, accused me of tactlessness. He raved about the Lanner waltzes. They were worthy of Schubert, he said. How dared I bracket my own little salon piece, 'Caprice Viennois' with such gems?

"I wrote to Dr. Schmidt. I said I was pained, but I felt compelled, for once, to say that he was 'not devoid of tactlessness' himself. I was terribly sorry, but if the Lanner pieces were 'worthy of Schubert,' then I was Schubert, because I had written them! The letter was reprinted everywhere.

"Now don't you suppose critics and musicians who saw that letter would have said to themselves: 'If this is so, then the same thing must be true of the Francoeur, Couperin, Vivaldi, and Pugnani pieces.' All they had to do was look at the pieces themselves and read the inscription, which almost gave the whole thing away."

"Did no one ever ask you point-blank whether you had composed those pieces yourself?"

"Not until my sixtieth birthday. I was in Vienna. Yehudi Menuhin was playing at the Brooklyn Academy of Music. Olin Downes, the critic of the New York *Times*, was on the program as lecturer and commentator. Mr. Menuhin was paying me a tribute by including several of my pieces. Mr. Downes wanted material for his talk. He came to see my publisher Fischer.

"Fischer hemmed and hawed. He told him he wasn't a hundred per cent sure himself. Mr. Downes immediately smelled a story. He cabled me in Vienna for the information.

"That was really the very first time I was ever asked directly. I did not want to lie. So I cabled back: 'I composed them all myself,' and gave my reason: I had needed program material and thought it unwise to use my own name. The story appeared in the New York *Times*. That started the avalanche."

Mr. Kreisler picked up a copy of his Concerto in G and signalled me to come over and inspect it with him. He conceded that the themes of the first and third movements might be rightly termed "Vivaldian" in style. Then he pointed to the sudden harmonic changes in the second movement. These, he said, were strictly Schubertian and Berliozian.

"It should have been obvious to anyone studying the score carefully that the rest is Kreisler," he remarked.

"You may be right," I said, "but on behalf of my fellow-critics and musicians I like to feel that even Antonio Vivaldi might have been fooled."

"Or Fritz Kreisler himself," he replied smiling, "that is, if someone else had discovered the concerto among 'classic manuscripts' in a monastery."

ATOMIC ENERGY, 1872-1899: R.I.P.

by Alexander Klein

During the last quarter of the nineteenth century, while Edison was dabbling around with electricity and various individuals of equally limited vision, such as the brothers Wright, were attempting to conquer the air, a man named John Worrell Keely was devoting all his energies and scientific acumen and millions of dollars invested by thousands of people to the much more fundamental problem of creating a technological millennium by developing a revolutionary motor to harness the basic "etheric force" in which, Keely had discovered, the universe abounded. All the miracles of power and performance which atomic energy promises to deliver some day, Keely was on the brink of creating for mankind three-quarters of a century ago. What's more, his etheric force did not snobbishly inhabit some rare and expensive substance like uranium; the great, newly discovered force was there, for the taking, in every drop of water that dripped from the faucet.

Etheric force, harnessed and channelled by the Keely motor, would —Keely confidently predicted in talks before scientific groups—in the near future enable an entire railroad train to run from Philadelphia to San Francisco using only a quart of water as fuel; to propel a steamship from New York to Liverpool would require at most a gallon.

For some twenty-seven years, between 1872 and 1899, while the civilized world was poised for the millennium, Keely occasionally took time out from his labors to give some demonstrations that hinted at the great things to come. Early in 1890, for example, Keely—a carpenter by training, and quondam conductor of a small, obscure orchestra —invited a group of scientists, journalists and some of the leading stockholders in the Keely Motor Company to his laboratory workshop at 1420 North Twentieth Street in Philadelphia. Standing in front of an enlarged copy of the physico-musical chart by means of which he had first discovered etheric force eighteen years previously, Keely picked up a violin and played a few notes to set in motion the har-

monic vibrations which, he explained, triggered the "liberator." The
liberator consisted of a series of ultra-sensitive tuning forks whose
vibrations, in turn, disintegrated air and water and, in the process,
released etheric force of cyclonic proportions. By way of demonstration Keely poured a glass of water into the cylinder of the "hydro-
pneumatic, pulsating vacuum engine." Within a few seconds the indi-
cator of the gauge attached to the cylinder leaped to record a pressure
of 50,000 pounds per square inch. Before the visitors' eyes etheric
force tore apart great cables as if they were wisps of straw, twisted
iron bars in two and sent bullets crashing clean through twelve-inch
planks.

This same etheric vapor or force, Keely told his audience, would,
via his motor, finally make the dream of human flight a reality; and
the Pneumatic Keely Gun, utilizing etheric force, would be the dead-
liest weapon in the nation's arsenal of defense. Sprinkled liberally in
Keely's discourse, as he continued, were technical terms the visiting
scientists found familiar, as well as many revolutionary ones, such as
"quadruple negative harmonics," "etheric disintegration," and "atomic
triplets." Some of the newspapermen present were freely skeptical in
their accounts, others simply reported what they had seen and let the
public judge. Most of the stockholders were impressed—as they had
been on other occasions—new funds were subscribed and the development and research continued. So did Keely's opulent mode of life.

Although the headquarters of the Keely Motor Company was in
Philadelphia, the firm was originally founded in New York, in 1872.
Keely, within a few months after discovering his force, had generated
enough enthusiasm for it to make possible a meeting at the Fifth Avenue Hotel of a group of bankers, merchants, scientists and engineers
to discuss practical measures for getting to work in earnest. Edward
B. Collier, one of the nation's leading patent attorneys, presided, but
most of the talking was done by Keely. Unlike most inventors, such as
the creator of Fulton's Folly, for example, Keely had no trouble raising
capital. The day after that first meeting he was handed a token check
for ten thousand dollars, with ample funds pledged to assure him the
solid support he knew he would need. Keely immediately established
his Philadelphia workshop, and went on the prowl for the universal
etheric force which had eluded mankind for countless centuries.

Like all great developments in science, the Keely motor was a slow
and expensive affair. About two years after the Fifth Avenue Hotel
meeting, on November 10, 1874, Keely demonstrated his first "vibra-

tory generator" to his leading backers. This precursor of the more advanced harmonic vibration liberator (which took another fourteen years to develop) operated, according to the newspaper reports, "out of a bath tub from which a stream of water, passing through a goose-quill sets the entire contrivance in motion."

From time to time, when funds were dangerously low, Keely called a meeting of the Board of Directors, and gave them a progress report, replete with portentous terms they had heard before and did not understand, plus some new ones, equally enticing and mysterious. These meetings generally brought in the needed funds, from the directors themselves, from other old investors, or from new ones. Many of the investors were medical men, who found Keely's vivid demonstrations irresistible. Discussions of etheric force and the Keely motor appeared frequently in both popular and scientific journals. For twenty years, whenever a noted scientist was interviewed by the press, he was invariably asked his opinion of the Keely motor. A few scientists scoffed openly. Many indicated an open mind on the subject and an eager interest in seeing further developments.

Visitors to his workshop always found Keely at his labors. Coatless, his hands grimy, his brow deeply furrowed, Keely would glance up from the experiment in progress, greet the newcomer with a smile and, apologetically, say he would have to finish what he was doing before spending any time with his guest. "But," Keely would usually add, "you can watch, if you're interested. It won't disturb me." And soon the visitor would see some startling examples of the etheric force's great power, usually of the cable-snapping variety.

Keely's most frequent visitor was Mrs. Bloomfield Moore, a wealthy widow who invested heavily in the Keely motor. In later years when Keely was under attack from many sources, Mrs. Moore also wrote impassioned pseudo-scientific defenses of etheric force in *Lippincott's* and many other widely read periodicals.

All the while Keely was both a struggling inventor-scientist and the President of the Keely Motor Company. He styled his manner of living wholly in conformity with his latter role, explaining to the Board of Directors that this was essential in order to attract new capital.

As the years went by many Keely stockholders began to exhibit a deplorable lack of patience. Keely tolerantly suggested they bone up on the history of science so they could see, for themselves, that, in comparison with other major scientific developments, their great pioneering enterprise was moving along at meteoric speed. As a matter of fact, Keely had come a long way from the old goose-quill days. Improved models of his experimental motor came forth almost with the precision regularity of today's new automobile models.

The basic constituents were the motor proper, the transmitter and a hollow brass sphere, all resting on a heavy metal base. Between the engine and the transmitter ran a series of wires, and along the base of the transmitter an array of steel rods bristled like so many fixed bayonets to repel the attacks of unbelievers. The sphere enclosed a complex mass of wires, tubes, and adhesive plates; Keely termed this the shifting resonator. At this point, revolutionary though his discovery was, Keely made a concession to conventional mythology, in which the number seven has played so prominent a role. His resonator carried seven different kinds of vibrations, each, however, "being capable of infinitesimal division." The motor itself consisted of a heavy iron hoop, inside which ran a drum with eight spokes. When etheric force set the motor going, the rapid movements of the heavy drum rarely failed to impress onlookers. Keely used various triggers to start the motor. Sometimes it was the violin; at other times a zither, a harmonica, or an ordinary tuning fork wooed etheric force into impressive activity.

Despite these entertaining concert-demonstrations, Keely stockholders were frequently dissatisfied. They suggested that the least Keely could do was obtain some patents as tangible assets. This Keely refused to do. The secret of etheric force was so staggering in its potentials, he said, that he did not dare reveal any part of it publicly until he had solved the entire mystery. Suppose, that, based on the information his patent application revealed, some other company put scientists to work and succeeded in filling in the missing elements? Then, all his own years of toil and all the dollars invested by stockholders would be lost. No, the only course was fortitude and patience, and in these qualities Keely set his investors a remarkable example.

In 1884, twelve years after Keely had first begun his heavily endowed research project, *Scientific American* magazine sponsored a series of experiments which proved to the satisfaction of its editors that everything Keely had demonstrated could be performed with nothing more wondrous in the way of force than compressed air. A complete description of these experiments, amounting to a devastating attack on the Keely motor, appeared in the pages of the magazine. But Keely, with an I-told-you-so smile, pointed out to his alarmed backers that practically all great scientific developments had to be carried out in the face of attacks from vested interests based on established prejudices. It would be naive, he said, not to expect such a revolutionary discovery as etheric force—which would necessitate a complete revision of physical theory—to be vigorously opposed. In fact, Keely predicted, the closer he came to complete success, the more virulent would the attacks become.

During all this time Keely had never revealed the secret of etheric force to a living soul. Mrs. Moore, his staunchest supporter, pleaded with him now to call in Thomas Edison and share the secret with the great wonder-worker in the field of electricity, so that Keely's detractors could be silenced by Edison's benediction. Surely, Mrs. Moore argued, Edison could be trusted to keep the matter confidential; perhaps he might join forces with Keely to speed the development of Keely's motor. Keely refused even to comment on these suggestions. Instead he labored on with renewed zeal and in a short time came up with another improved version of his demonstration-motor. This, combined with his complete imperturbability and unfailing charm convinced most of the backers to stay with it. And new investors continued to flock to the Keely standard.

One female stockholder, who admitted that scientific theories were beyond her, based her faith chiefly on the beauty and symmetry of Keely's musical chart, of which Keely had given her and various other backers handsomely framed reproductions. This musical chart consisted of a series of overlapping circles, cones of radiating lines, a generous sprinkling of asymetrical forms and—presumably most important—a series of musical notations. After Keely's death, a newspaper account said of this chart: "It may mean something to the men who employ the compass and the square. To others it merely illustrates a trend into domains where mortals should not venture." Apparently even the author of that debunking report was not free of the Keely influence, for, to an unbelieving observer the musical chart appears a harmless simple pattern, hardly intricate enough to be considered mysterious. Physicists today find no meaning whatsoever in the chart, and an attempt by a pianist, at the present writer's request, to play the notes resulted, disappointingly, neither in some haunting melody nor in a jarring bedlam, but rather a weak and vapid disconnectedness. Failing examination by modern psychologists, who seem to have enough on their hands with current phenomena, the mystery of the Keely musical chart will probably never be solved. For, after some twenty-six years of hard experimentation and high living, Keely died in 1898, without divulging the secret of the musical chart or the etheric force which he discovered thereby. Keely did, however, set a record that has never been matched: in all those twenty-six years the Keely Motor Company, avowedly formed as a profit-making concern, sold not a single item of any sort, not even at a loss, obtained not a single patent, and operated in the red at all times.

Mrs. Bloomfield Moore, Keely's embattled supporter, died a few months later. Her son, Clarence B. Moore, who had consistently opposed her interest in the Keely motor, then rented the building which had housed the Keely workshop. Moore asked several professors from the engineering, physics and psychology departments of the University of Pennsylvania to aid him in finding out just how Keely had produced his phenomena. The Keely apparatus had been removed by the inventor's friends. But the investigators soon found the answers —in the walls, the floors and underneath the building.

In the cellar, embedded in the earth, they discovered an immense steel globe, which weighed three tons. It had a hole at the top. Nearby lay varieties of piping and tubing, suitable for conducting compressed air. Keely had demonstrated all his puzzling and impressive phenomena in a rear room, curiously raised above the others. When the investigators had the flooring of this room torn up, they found brass tubes running through holes specially cut in the joists, and leading down to the giant globe in the cellar. The scientists surmised that every time Keely played his fiddle or harmonica or zither for an audience, his foot beat time to the music, at least once, to operate the real trigger, a foot-controlled spring valve that allowed the compressed air to do its yeoman work.

Thus, the quarter-century hoax of John Worrell Keely had finally been exposed for all who were willing to see. Many Keely supporters were not willing to do anything of the sort. In their own way, they turned over a new leaf. They made up for their uncritical belief in scientist Keely's etheric force by subjecting the Keely exposé to the most critical and skeptical attacks. This time they would not believe what any scientist told them, not so long as a shadow of a doubt remained. Controversy raged for years, but it was an academic debate at best, for no enterprising wooer of the etheric force came forward to assume the mantle of its original discoverer and lead the world to the technological millennium. That is until some four decades later when the men in the thick lead suits came on the scene.

PSALMANAZAR: THE MAN WHO INVENTED FORMOSA

by J. A. Farrar

Many impostors have created complete fictional personal his-tories. George Psalmanazar went far beyond this. In the early part of the eighteenth century, when he was barely twenty years old, Psalmanazar hoaxed his way to fame by the fantastic expedient of inventing a new country. Admittedly, he started with a grain of reality, but thereafter it was sheer inspired creation. If he were around today, Psalmanazar would certainly be giving our top-ranking science-fiction writers a hard run for their money.

Remarkable from first to last was George Psalmanazar, still of un-known birth and origin, who made his first appearance in London early in the eighteenth century.

When Dr. Johnson knew him Psalmanazar was about eighty; a man who earned a livelihood from his work for the booksellers, but a man who enjoyed a somewhat wide notoriety for the earnestness of his piety and the regularity of his devotions.

Yet George Psalmanazar is connected with one of the most astonish-ing frauds in the history of literature. Coming to England from the Continent, under the auspices of the Reverend W. Innes, an army chaplain, he at once interested the religious world in his favour, by claiming to be a native of Formosa, who had been converted from an appalling heathenism to the truths and practices of Christianity. No one ever guessed rightly of what country he was a native, but there was nothing Oriental about his skin or hair. This, however, stood very little in his way.

He found an easy introduction to Compton, Bishop of London, on whom he palmed off the English Catechism translated into Formosan. Not only did bishops and the clergy receive him gladly, but even some men of learning declared his Formosan language to be a real one because it was so regular and grammatical "and so different from all they knew both with respect to words and idioms." This interesting proselyte, who had trained himself to eat raw flesh the better to support his character as an Oriental, was introduced to all men of distinction in Church and State, and we find him dining on 9th February, 1704, with Sir Hans Sloane, and eating his meat raw in the company of two noblemen and the Prussian Ambassador. A week before at the Royal Institution he had held a public discussion with Father Fontenay, who had been for eighteen years a missionary in China, and he had responded without loss of credit to the searching questions put to him by that doubting Father.

Psalmanazar's story was that he had left Formosa six years earlier, when he was nineteen. This would have made him twenty-five at the time of his coming to London, but he added some years to his real age in order to make his story more credible. For a youth of twenty he had some right to be regarded as a marvel. He had more than a smattering of six languages, and wrote and spoke Latin fluently. It was in Latin that he conversed with Archbishop Tenison, Innes acting as interpreter, and it was in Latin that he originally wrote his *Description of Formosa*.

The book was a reproduction of the many marvellous things about Formosa he had propounded in conversation, but not of everything. Asked, for instance, about longevity in the island, he replied that 120 was accounted a common age, and 100 a very moderate one; his own grandfather had lived to 117, and was then as fresh and vigorous as a young man, owing to his habit of sucking the blood of a viper warm every morning! There seems to have been no limit to British credulity in the early years of Queen Anne. Good people subscribed for the support of this marvellous proselyte, and the Bishop of London had him sent to study at Christ Church, Oxford, in the pious hope that he would in return instruct in Formosan some future missionaries to that promising island.

An exceedingly curious book is the *Historical and Geographical Description of Formosa, an Island subject to the Emperor of Japan*, published in 1704, and dedicated to the Bishop of London.

According to Psalmanazar, the Emperor of Japan conquered Formosa in a strange manner. Under the pretext of religion, of offering sacrifices in Formosa to the God of Formosa, he sent a great army into the country. Thirty or forty soldiers were placed in large litters, drawn by two elephants, and at the windows of these litters, were placed the heads of oxen or rams, which removed all suspicion from the minds of natives. Then the soldiers jumped out, and by threatening death to the natives secured their acceptance of the yoke of Japan without bloodshed or difficulty.

The Formosans were represented as having worshipped the heavenly bodies till two philosophers appeared, who bade them turn from this worship to that of one Supreme God. To Him they were bidden to raise a temple, and on an altar therein to burn the hearts of 20,000 boys under the age of nine. The indignant Formosans pursued these philosophers into a desert, but their persecution of them being avenged by eclipses, storms and earthquakes, the Formosans became penitent, and accepted a prophet, by name Psalmanazar, or "the author of peace," so called because he was to declare a new peace between the Deity and the Formosans. In the book this other Psalmanazar plays the part assigned to Moses in the Old Testament, as the mouthpiece of the Divine commands. Most striking of these was the command that on a given annual festival 18,000 boys under nine should have their hearts burnt upon an altar. This festival was the anniversary of the day on which the Deity first appeared in the tabernacle in the form of an ox, when for nine days in succession 2,000 children were thus sacrificed daily.

To overcome the difficulty of the depopulation consequent on such a system of religion the author made the Formosans polygamous, and the eldest son exempt from liability to sacrifice. Psalmanazar, the author, was as bold as his namesake, the prophet. He cared nothing for existing authentic accounts of Formosa; for why should a real Formosan adjust his narrative to that of a Dutch missionary like George Candidius? If Candidius, who had some years previously visited Formosa and written about it, had confined the sacrifices of the Formosans to such offerings as rice and fruits, that was all very well; the British public needed stronger fare, and would be pleased with nothing short of 18,000 infants annually.

The Dutch writer had said that there was no regular government in the island, but that at most each village was governed by twelve men of the same age, not under forty; Psalmanazar declared for an elaborate hierarchy of ministers, of whose very dress he described and depicted the minutest details. Candidius had described the laws as so lenient as to be almost non-existent; robbery was barely punished at all, and a present of a few hogs was ample compensation for murder or adultery. According to Psalmanazar, robbers and murderers were hanged head downwards and shot to death with arrows, whilst other offences entailed burning alive, the cutting off of legs and arms, tearing in pieces by dogs, or the boring of the tongue with a hot iron.

Candidius also had denied the existence of gold or silver mines in the country; Psalmanazar made "the great quantity of gold and silver" the Formosans' chief source of profit, and located three gold and three silver mines in the several islands. Nor was this enough for British consumption, for "their temples and houses were often covered with gold, both in cities and villages."

The Formosans were said to look upon serpents as affording "very good meat and very savoury"; but how did they extract the poison? Catching the serpents alive, they would irritate them by beating them with rods; the consequent furious passion of the serpent would cause all its venom to ascend to its head, so that when this part of the body was cut off there would be no poison left in the remainder.

More wonderful even than the description of Formosa were the drawings in illustration. There was the temple, with the altar and gridiron whereon the children's hearts were burnt; the different altars to the sun, moon and stars; the funeral processions; the dresses of every class and kind from the king and queen downwards to a country woman or a country bumpkin; the floating villages; the coins with their names; and above all the marvellous alphabet of twenty letters, with the names of some of them, like Lamdo and epsi, for "l" and "e," so strangely similar to the Greek Lambda and epsilon. But then they taught the Greek tongue in the academies of Formosa!

From the first Psalmanazar had certain sceptics to deal with. Father Fontenay pointed out that Formosa was a dependency of China, not of Japan, as Psalmanazar declared; whilst Dr. Halley, the astronomer, asked the writer some unanswerable questions. Still the book had so large a sale that a second edition was published the year following, in 1705. In the preface to this edition Psalmanazar boldly replies to twenty-five objections "of the first magnitude" which had been raised by various critics. On no point would he give way. At most he would say about the annual sacrifice of the 18,000 boys that such was the number laid down by the law; in practice the law might be evaded. As for the "forgeries" of Candidius, why should they be believed against the word of a native? And as to his differences from Candidius, what could more completely prove his own veracity? For surely a forger would have taken care that his statements should conform to those of previous writers.

The secret of Psalmanazar's success lay in the fact that he not only tickled that love for the marvellous in the British people but also pandered to the strong feeling against the Jesuits then prevalent in England. He concluded his amazing *Description* with a sketch of the history of the Jesuits' mission to Japan, which he made the vehicle of a strong attack upon that society, whose pupil he had been in earlier years.

This made it difficult for Psalmanazar to clear himself of the imposture, when he came to entertain a genuine wish to set himself right with the public. But a serious illness in 1728 vanquished his irresolution, and he at once began the composition of his *Memoirs*. He took his leisure over it, for it seems to have occupied him for twenty-five years. It was finished before 1752, when he made his first will with directions for its posthumous publication, but it did not reach the public till 1765. But long before that there had been a semi-public recantation. To Bowen's *Complete System of Geography*, published in 1747 in two large folio volumes, Psalmanazar contributed the chapters on China and Japan, and therein he dealt again with Formosa, giving an account avowedly from Candidius, with whose account some forty years before he had deliberately made his own to clash!

Psalmanazar's repentance for his fraud amounted to remorse, and his self-humiliation bordered on the abject. Henceforth he would pay by voluntary self-effacement and obscurity for his earlier wicked love for notoriety. If he writes a most meritorious *History of Printing* for Palmer, the printer, it is published under Palmer's name as the author. If he publishes (1753) five *Essays on Miracles*, the work is attributed on the title-page to "an obscure layman in town." This is in keeping with his curious will prefixed to his *Memoirs*, which directs that his body may be buried in some obscure corner of the common burying-ground, and unindosed in any kind of coffin, save a shell of the lowest value, without lid or other covering to hinder the natural earth from entirely surrounding it.

Withal, a life that started on a fair course to the tree at Tyburn ended with the esteem of all men and the friendship of Dr. Johnson.

THE ROYAL CANADIAN NAVY'S MYSTERY SURGEON

by Joseph McCarthy

Many impostors have posed as doctors. Only a few have dared to undertake surgery. In 1952, during the Korean War, Ferdinand Waldo Demara, posing as a surgeon, successfully performed a number of major operations under trying battle conditions; this was the climax of one of the most varied and startling careers of imposture on record. The original title of this account was "Master Impostor: An Incredible Tale"; it is all of that.

Ferdinand Waldo Demara, Jr., is a bright and lively young man who usually seems to enjoy life. He has a crew haircut and the build of a lineman on a professional football team and he knows how to make a bored and indifferent hat-check girl crumple with laughter.

But Demara has also been revealed as the central figure in one of the most intriguing impostor stories since the tale of Huckleberry Finn's encounter with the Duke and the Dauphin.

Ferdinand Waldo Demara is the Royal Canadian Navy's "Mystery Surgeon." Using the name and credentials of Dr. Joseph C. Cyr of Grand Falls, New Brunswick, he was commissioned as a surgeon-lieutenant by naval authorities in St. John. Some months later when the press and radio praised some remarkable chest and lung surgery that he performed in combat in Korea, the real Dr. Cyr came forward in New Brunswick and revealed him as an impostor. The Canadian Navy's Dr. Cyr was actually Demara, a thirty-year-old American who not only had never attended medical school but had never even finished high school.

Subsequent research on Demara's past uncovered other colorful episodes. Despite his lack of schooling, he had posed successfully as a doctor of philosophy named Robert Linton French and had taught college classes in psychology. He also passed himself off as Cecil Boyce Hamann, a Ph.D. in zoology, and had been a law student,

Trappist monk, American soldier and sailor, hospital orderly, twice a "convert" to Catholicism (although he was born a Roman Catholic) and a deputy sheriff.

The story as he tells it begins one winter day in Lawrence about twenty years ago when he was a youngster on his way home from school. In a trash can he found a pair of artificial legs, the kind that are used in store windows for displaying ladies' stockings. Fred stuck the two legs in a snowbank beside a fairly busy thoroughfare and hid nearby to watch the results. Alarmed motorists leaped from their cars to pull the legs from the snow. As they drove on, cursing, Fred replaced the legs and enjoyed the confusion of the next victim. He has been confusing people, especially his parents, ever since.

Big for his age, Fred was playing football at fourteen at Lawrence's Central Catholic High School. He never made the starting lineup because he refused to take Coach Jim Jordan's orders seriously. He never studied his lessons, but he read extensively and deeply and he was an entertaining talker. When he was sixteen he ran away from home and joined the Cistercian monks, an order of meditative farm workers, at Valley Falls, Rhode Island. A year later the abbot of the monastery convinced him that he would be better suited for teaching than for a life of contemplation and he transferred to the Brothers of Charity. In 1941 he left the Brothers of Charity to enlist in the U.S. Army. But he promptly went AWOL and, without bothering to notify the Army, enlisted in the U.S. Navy a week after Pearl Harbor.

In the Navy, Demara was assigned as a seaman to the U.S.S. *Ellis*, a destroyer on the North Atlantic patrol, and then sent to hospital school at Norfolk. "That was my first taste of medicine." Shortly afterward he made his first attempt at dissembling. He had been assigned as a medical corpsman with an amphibious invasion force and there were certain aspects of landing on a beach that he did not relish. He decided to give himself a college background so that he could apply for Officer Candidate School.

"As I recall, I picked Iowa State College," Demara says. "For good measure, I also threw in a letter from Senator Capper of Kansas, praising my character. But I made the mistake of not including enough mathematics and the application was turned down. So I made up another transcript of credits with more math. It was a pretty crude job—I was strictly an amateur in those days—and the Navy caught wise. I decided to leave the service temporarily."

Demara went to Kentucky and joined the Trappists at the Abbey

of Our Lady of Gethsemani near Louisville, the retreat of silence
described by Thomas Merton in the best-selling book, *The Seven
Storey Mountain.* Demara presented himself at the monastery as
Robert L. French, a graduate of the University of Michigan, with a
Ph.D. in psychology from Stanford, and a Sterling Research Fellowship at Yale. He obtained the background of French (who is now
doing psychological research for the Air Force) from the catalog of
a college where French had served on the faculty.

After a short stay with the Trappists, Demara, still masquerading
as French, entered the Clerics of St. Viator, an order of Catholic teachers, and studied scholastic philosophy and ethics at De Paul University. The records of the university show that he received straight A's
in rational psychology, metaphysics, cosmology, epistemology, ethics
and natural theology. "Maybe the instructors were impressed by my
Ph.D.," Demara says with a depreciative shrug.

He had only one scare while he was in Chicago. One day, wearing
his black suit and Roman collar, he was parking his superior's automobile at a railroad station. Out of the station marched a group of sailors,
carrying duffel bags. He says they were members of his beach battalion at Norfolk. He was afraid that one of them might recognize
him but nobody did.

"In this little game I was playing," Demara says, "there always
comes a time when you find yourself getting in too deep. You've made
good friends who believe in you, and you don't want them to get hurt
and disillusioned. You begin to worry about what they'll think if
somebody exposes you as a phony."

That time of uneasiness came in Chicago when Demara found
himself facing serious preparation for ordination as a Viatorian priest.
"There was nothing I would have liked more," he says now. "I thought
at the time that I had a true religious vocation. But I couldn't go
ahead without telling those men the truth about myself. So I disappeared. No explanations. I just disappeared."

At each stop on his route Demara was careful to save a small
emergency fund of cash so that he would have traveling expenses
when it seemed advisable to move on. "My mad money," he calls it.
He had enough mad money in Chicago to take him to Erie, Pennsylvania, where he turned up a year later, teaching psychology at
Gannon College. He showed up next in Los Angeles, where he says
he served as an orderly at a sanitarium of the Brothers of St. John of
God. Then he ventured north into Washington. French's credentials

brought him a position as instructor of psychology at St. Martin's College in Lacey, near Olympia. When he is asked if he had any qualms about teaching such a subject to college students, Demara blandly registers mild surprise. "Why?" he asks. "I just kept ahead of the class. The best way to learn anything is to teach it."

In Washington, for the first time since he left the Navy, Demara felt safe. He decided to settle there permanently. He was popular at the college and he made influential friends in Olympia and Seattle. Sheriff Frank Tamblin of Thurston County made him a special deputy so that he could enforce the law around the college campus and Demara, in turn, made speeches for Tamblin when the sheriff ran for re-election. One day Tamblin appeared at the college with a warrant for Demara's arrest. In the sheriff's office Demara found two strangers. One of them looked Demara over and said, "Hello, Ferdinand."

The two men were FBI agents. They wanted him as a deserter from the Navy.

Demara says he conducted his own defense at the Navy court-martial, but the case was hopeless. He served a year and a half at the U.S. Disciplinary Barracks in San Pedro, California, during which time the Army caught up with him and discharged him too. He then came home to Lawrence to see his parents and think things over. With the help of his reliable collection of college catalogs he decided to take the identity of Cecil Hamann, a biologist on the faculty of Ashbury College, Wilmore, Kentucky, who has master's and doctor's degrees from Purdue. Through a method which he refuses to divulge, Demara acquired records of Hamann's academic background from colleges and universities where he studied and taught.

Demara went so far as to equip himself with Hamann's birth certificate, although he did not know the name of the town where Hamann was born.

"I only knew Hamann came from New York State," Demara explains. "I wrote a tearful letter, a real sob story, to the vital statistics office at the state capital in Albany. I told them I'd been abandoned by my parents as an infant and I wanted to know where I was born. I gave them my age. That and my name, Cecil Boyce Hamann, was all they had to go by. But back came the information: Hamann was born in Shelby, Orleans County, New York. Then I wrote to Shelby and got his birth certificate."

As Hamann, Demara enrolled in night law school at Northeastern

University in Boston and took a job as an orderly at the Massachusetts Eye and Ear Infirmary. After a year of law Demara decided he had had enough. He has a scornful opinion of the value of any kind of formal schooling, and besides he had no intention of becoming a lawyer. "I just wanted a knowledge of torts, procedure and criminal law," he says. He left Boston and entered the seminary of the Brothers of Christian Instruction, a French teaching order, at Alfred, Maine.

He may have been motivated by the fact that his own origin was French-Canadian. Besides, "I had heard that these French-Canadian brothers in Maine were having a hard time," Demara says. "I decided they could use a man with, shall we say, my peculiar talents."

The Brothers of Christian Instruction supply teachers to parochial schools, and most of the novices they receive are young farm boys. When Demara introduced himself as Dr. Cecil B. Hamann, an eminent Boston physician with a magnificent array of college degrees, the brothers were overjoyed.

"I was regarded as a windfall," Demara says. "They rolled out the red carpet and all the bells in the place began to ring. Now that they have read about me, I imagine the good brothers have changed their opinion. If a legitimate college graduate went there now and knocked on the door, they would probably punch him on the nose."

A story was published in the press about the arrival of Dr. Hamann at Alfred. A scientist in Oak Ridge who was a former pupil of the real Hamann received a package from Boston that was padded with newspapers and, while unpacking it, came across an account of how somebody with the Hamann name and background had renounced the medical world to join the Brothers of Christian Instruction. He mailed the story to Kentucky. The real Hamann was determined to take action, but he never actually got around to doing anything about it.

By that time the bogus Dr. Hamann had the situation at the seminary in Alfred well in hand. He took the religious name of Brother John. He fascinated his fellow brothers with tales of mythical adventures in India, Japan and Tibet. He helped the seminary in its efforts to obtain a college charter so that the young men of the order would not have to go to the University of Montreal to obtain credits that would qualify them as teachers.

Demara says his path crossed that of the real Dr. Hamann a few months later while he and two other brothers were attending an educational convention in Chicago. He recalls that he was standing at the desk in the lobby of his hotel when he heard a man beside him asking the clerk if there was any mail for Cecil B. Hamann. "There was no danger of his discovering me," Demara says. "I was registered as Brother John, my religious name. Nevertheless, it gave me quite a turn."

To prepare Demara for his solemn vows the brothers at Alfred sent him to Grand Falls, New Brunswick, to study theology under Brother Boniface, an older man who managed a farm there. Here his time was pretty much his own. He was becoming deeply interested in medicine and he spent hours in the company of Dr. Joseph C. Cyr, a local general practitioner. Demara first met Dr. Cyr, a young man fresh out of the medical school at Quebec's Laval University, when the doctor was treating Brother Boniface for rheumatoid arthritis. As Demara tells it, Dr. Cyr, hearing that Demara had been a physician before joining the order, turned to him for advice. Demara suggested bee venom. He had read about its use in treating arthritis in one of the many medical journals to which he subscribed.

"The bee venom cost plenty," Demara says, "but it worked like a charm."

From then on, according to Demara, Dr. Cyr's admiration for Brother John, the former Dr. Hamann, knew no bounds. Newspaper reports on the Demara-Cyr hoax have intimated that Demara stole Dr. Cyr's credentials. Demara denies this firmly. "I don't stoop to larceny," he says with a certain pride. "Joe Cyr told me he wanted a license in Maine so he could practice medicine on both sides of the border. I was due to go back to Alfred shortly and I told him that I'd be only too glad to present his credentials to the Maine medical board. That's how it happened. I didn't steal his papers. He *gave* them to me."

When Demara returned to Maine he was too busy with other things to present Dr. Cyr's case to the state medical board. He felt that the Brothers of Christian Instruction no longer needed him; the college charter for the seminary was secured. To his surprise and disappointment another brother had been selected to head the institution. So Demara departed for Boston in one of the order's automobiles. He abandoned the car in Boston, then doubled back by bus to New Brunswick where he offered his services, as Dr. Cyr, to the Royal Canadian Navy at St. John. He was given a warm welcome. Doctors who are willing to serve overseas are just as eagerly accepted in Canada as they are by the U.S. armed forces.

"I told them that if they didn't take me in a hurry I'd join the Canadian Army," Demara says. "That did it. Within two hours they had me on a train to Ottawa and I was commissioned there the next day. I passed the physical exam without taking off my clothes and they never even bothered to take my fingerprints. One of the admirals on the selection board told me the processing that I went through in a day usually takes ten weeks. I guess they wish now they hadn't been so quick about cutting off that red tape."

As a surgeon-lieutenant Demara was first assigned for two months last spring to the sick bay at the naval hospital in Halifax. His medical cases were routine ones and he handled them with ease and confidence. He claims he also treated a few psychiatric patients. Demara's conversation shows an intimate knowledge of the writings of Freud and Jung, but he takes a light view of the professionals in the field. "There's no mystery about psychiatry," he says. "Anybody with common sense could practice it." While he was in Halifax, Demara also made what he considers the greatest mistake of his whole checkered career. He fell in love.

"I had always kept myself from getting involved with a girl," he says. "I'm a phony and you can't be a phony and really fall in love. But this time in Canada I couldn't help it. I kept telling myself it would work out all right. We planned to get married this coming June and I was going to finish my time in the Navy and then settle down in Canada and practice. I never thought it would turn out the way it did."

In June, Demara sailed to Korea on the *Cayuga*, a destroyer with a complement of twelve officers and 280 enlisted men. His first official task as medical officer of the *Cayuga* presented a challenge that might have shaken a lesser impostor. He was obliged to pull a tooth from the mouth of the captain, Commander James Plomer. "He came to me and asked me to pull it," Demara says. "I told him to wait until morning. That night I stayed in my cabin, reading up on dentistry, which was all new to me. In the morning I shot the skipper's jaw full of novocain and out came the tooth; no trouble at all."

While he was in the Far East, Demara decided to branch out and had himself enrolled in the General Medical Council of the United Kingdom. "I don't know whether Joe Cyr realizes it," he said recently, "but he is now licensed to practice medicine and surgery not only in Canada but also in England, Wales, Scotland and Northern Ireland, thanks to me. I ought to ask him for the $30.80 it cost me to get into the United Kingdom council."

The *Cayuga's* Surgeon-Lieutenant Cyr removed a few tonsils and treated colds and infections. His first really serious case came one day when the *Cayuga* was bombarding enemy shore positions near Chinnampo. A junk carrying three wounded South Korean soldiers came alongside. One of the soldiers had a bullet near his heart. As Demara tells it, he had the man brought to the captain's cabin and prepared to operate.

"I couldn't have been nervous, even if I felt like it," Demara says. "Practically everybody on the bloody ship was standing there, watching me."

Conditions for such a risky job of surgery were far from ideal. Demara's equipment was limited and he had no autoclave in which to sterilize it. His only assistant, the ship's sick-bay attendant, was too nervous to find the vein for the injection of Pentothal Sodium that Demara used as an anesthetic. But, says Demara, he worked swiftly, as though he had been performing surgery for years. He opened the chest with incisions above the heart and along the sternum, or breastbone. "I kept one basic principle in my mind," he says. "The less cutting you do, the less patching up you have to do afterwards." Cutting and bending back a slightly splintered rib, he found the bullet wound within a fraction of an inch from the heart.

"I was afraid he'd hemorrhage when I took out the bullet," Demara says. "But he didn't. I pulled it out and slipped some Gelfoam, a coagulating agent, into the wound and it clotted almost immediately."

A small cheer went up from the fascinated spectators. Demara replaced the rib, sewed the incisions, wrapped the chest tightly in an immobile bandage with the left arm folded across the heart, and gave the man an injection of a million and a half units of penicillin to ward off infection. In a few hours the soldier was sipping beef broth. His pulse and blood pressure were normal and his temperature was one hundred. Twelve hours later, before the *Cayuga* left the area to return to Japan, he walked off the ship.

When the *Cayuga* came back to the same part of the Korean coast a week or so later, Demara went ashore to look up his patient. He found him in a native hut that the South Koreans were using as an aid station. The man was feeling fine, but Demara was appalled by the lack of medical care among the South Korean troops that were fighting in the sector. He obtained permission to go ashore daily and spend a few hours taking care of casualties. Working alone—his attendant had to remain at the *Cayuga's* sick bay—he claims to have performed countless operations and amputations.

One of the officers aboard the *Cayuga*, Lieutenant R. A. V. Jenkins, was the public-information officer for the Canadian Navy in the Far East. Jenkins heard one day that the local South Korean military commander, a Captain Kim, had walked seventeen miles to thank Demara personally for his services. He decided to prepare a story about the unusual Surgeon-Lieutenant Cyr for release to the press and radio.

"I couldn't talk Jenkins out of it, but I knew that a story in the papers would finish me," Demara says. "When Jenkins asked me about my operations, I tried to make them sound dull, hoping that the correspondents would ignore what he wrote. And I told him my home town was Halifax. I figured that might keep me from being linked up with the other Doctor Cyr in Grand Falls."

However, Jenkins turned out a dramatic news release with a detailed account of the surgery Demara had done ashore and a description of the chest operation on the *Cayuga*. He also credited Demara with saving a South Korean soldier's life by collapsing his lung, a feat that Demara does not recollect. As a matter of fact the one operation in Korea that Demara remembers with satisfaction was not mentioned in his press clippings. It was, he says, a resection, or removal of a lung.

"Just like that operation on the King of England," Demara says. "Except that the king's surgeon had an army of assistants and nurses to help him. I was alone. I kept quiet about it at the time because I didn't want any more publicity."

As Demara tells it, he found one day at the South Korean aid station a soldier who had been hit in the chest by a dumdum bullet. There was a small hole in the front of the chest, but a gaping wound in the back showed that most of the right lung had been destroyed. The man was dying. A few days before, Demara had read about King George's operation in *The Lancet*, a British medical journal.

Demara felt that a lung resection was the Korean's only chance and began the operation. It was hard work. After cutting an L-shaped incision and exposing the back of the damaged lung, he reached into his bag for the clippers that he used to cut ribs. They were not there. He had to saw six ribs with an amputation saw, pausing every eight or ten minutes, when the patient became restless, to administer a small dose of Pentothal Sodium. The anesthetic could be injected only in small amounts, which wore off quickly. He removed the lung, dusted the inside of the cavity with sulfa powder and closed the incision.

"Then I wrapped him like a mummy," Demara says. "The guy had lost a lot of blood. He'd been wounded about eight hours when I got him. I wished I had some plasma, but I had none. I fed him a lot of glucose intravenously and shot over a million units of penicillin into him. I hated to take him off the portable operating table because there was no other place for him to lie except on a grass mat in one of the mud huts. But I had to move him to make room for other casualties."

The *Cayuga* was sailing for Japan the next day to take on supplies. Ten days later she returned to the same area. Demara could not wait to get ashore. He rushed to the hut, but the Korean was gone. "I decided he was dead," Demara says. An interpreter told him that he was needed at a schoolhouse three miles up the road where a number of casualties were waiting for attention. Demara and the interpreter began to walk along the road. When they had gone half a mile, they noticed some farmers in a field, harvesting grain. Beside the field a number of women were sifting chaff from the grain and among them, still wearing the bandage, was Demara's patient.

"There he was, as big as life, working," Demara says. "When he saw me he broke into a big grin and, with his free hand, he reached under his shirt and tried to give me about a dollar in Korean money. I stuck a thermometer in his mouth. He had a fever, but it was only a hundred. I don't mind saying it made me feel good."

Less than a week later, Demara says, he was summoned to the captain's cabin. He found Commander Plomer seated at his desk, frowning at a radio message. Demara knew immediately what was in the message.

"Joe, I've got something here about you," Commander Plomer said. "It's a lot of rot. Somebody in Canada made a mistake. It's so embarrassing I'm not going to read it to you."

Demara urged the captain to read the message to him. He still remembers its text word for word. It said, "We have information that Joseph C. Cyr, surgeon-lieutenant, O-17669, is an impostor. Remove from active duty immediately repeat immediately conduct investigation and report facts to Chief of Naval Staff Ottawa."

When Commander Plomer finished the radio message, he shook his head and sighed. "I told you it was a lot of rot, Joe," he said. "Carry on with your duty and I'll set them straight about this." Demara thanked him and left the cabin. But in a few days he was ordered to return to Canada.

"He was a remarkable personality," Commander Plomer said about Demara a few weeks ago. "He had a warm, sympathetic regard for all the officers and men on the ship and a high perception of human character. As a layman I cannot judge, but to my knowledge he performed his duties with considerable skill. The outcome of the whole affair was one of the greatest individual tragedies I've ever encountered." The men of the *Cayuga* even sent their former shipmate a Christmas card from Korea. Enclosed with the card were some lines of verse, entitled "Because He's Our Friend," written by one of the officers on the *Cayuga*. The verse reads, in part:

> He may be six kinds of a liar,
> He may be ten kinds of a fool;
> He may have faults that are dire,
> And seem without reason or rule. . . .
> But we don't analyze, we just love him,
> Because—well, because he's our friend.

As he started back to Canada, Demara knew nothing about how he had been exposed or how much had been found out about his past. He felt certain that he was on his way to prison. "But all I could think of was the girl," he says. "I knew that I would never be able to face her after all this and I imagined what she was thinking about me. It just about killed me."

To make matters worse, an accumulation of mail was delivered to him on a hospital ship in Japan while he was awaiting air transportation to Victoria. In it was a package of food for Thanksgiving from his girl and several long letters from her, discussing plans for their approaching wedding. One of the letters announced that she was sending him a Christmas tree for the *Cayuga's* wardroom.

On the plane that took him to Victoria he was shown a news story about his case. As he suspected, Jenkins' release had been published in New Brunswick and Dr. Cyr had identified the Navy surgeon's photograph as that of the man he had known as Dr. Cecil B. Hamann and Brother John. Mail addressed to Dr. Hamann was awaiting him at the seminary of the Brothers of Christian Instruction in Alfred, Maine. And the Brothers of St. John of God in Los Angeles thought that they remembered the mystery man as Dr. Robert L. French. To make matters more complicated, the real Dr. Hamann in Kentucky said that the Navy surgeon sounded like a fellow who had been kicked out of St. Louis University for cheating. Demara noted, however, that his true identity had not yet been discovered.

To his surprise Demara found no serious charges awaiting him when he reported to the naval authorities in Victoria. The Canadian Navy accepted the fact that he had enlisted under a false name but it assumed that he was a doctor. Demara did nothing to change their opinion. His fingerprints were taken in Victoria. A check in Washington with his U.S. Navy fingerprints finally revealed that he was Ferdinand W. Demara. He was released from the Canadian service with the pay that was due him and politely asked to leave the country.

That night Demara took a plane from Seattle to Chicago, where he spent the next three weeks. "I guess I did a little drinking," he says. "I couldn't get that girl out of my head. And I kept thinking about how happy I was in the Canadian Navy. I guess I was happier there than I had been anywhere in my life. If only that story hadn't gotten into the newspapers, everything would have been all right."

Since that time, at his home in Lawrence, Demara has been trying to decide his future. His parents have offered to finance his way through college and medical school, but he shows little enthusiasm for this: it would impose considerable hardship on them—not to mention a tediously conventional way of life on himself. Thinking about the future demands making some sense out of the past, and here Demara has not been conspicuously successful. Vaguely he seems aware that his huge contempt for convention has stemmed from an' unbridled ambition, yet an ambition (he thinks) redeemed by an anxiety to do good. "I guess I've always wanted short cuts," he said recently. "And being an impostor is a tough habit to break. . . .

"I guess you can say I don't know exactly what I'm going to do next," he added. "But I have a few things in mind."

III

FOR THE DEVIL OF IT

THE ABYSSINIAN PRINCES WHO OUTWITTED
THE BRITISH NAVY

by Joseph M. Hone

This is the famous Dreadnought *Hoax in which Virginia Woolf, the novelist, participated. Joseph Hone, the Irish writer, recalls it with proper gusto and appreciativeness.*

In a picture paper of February 16, 1910, which I have by me, is a photograph of four Abyssinian princes. Profoundly impressive they look. Behind them is their German interpreter, and beside them, debonair in morning clothes, completely unembarrassed, a gentleman described as Mr. Herbert Cholmondeley of the Foreign Office. Mr. Herbert Cholmondeley had just conducted the princes to Weymouth, where, amid the pomp of a large part of the British Navy, the visitors had been shown over the mightiest battleship of those days—H.M.S. *Dreadnought*. Beneath the vast bushy moustaches of this Mr. Herbert Cholmondeley not even the smallest smile is to be seen, and it was typical of Horace Cole, otherwise Mr. Herbert Cholmondeley of the Foreign Office, that he should have been unruffled even by laughter at a moment when he had set all England laughing, set Europe laughing, and nearly set the House of Commons, the Admiralty and the Government by the ears. For that photograph is a picture of an enormous hoax which had driven a coach-and-four through all the formality which Horace Cole in his actions mocked at—at heart perhaps respected.

Horace Cole's jokes were probably the most serious things in a life which, it is right to say, found time for the cultivation of the things of the mind—art and poetry in particular.

London, Dublin and Paris were the scenes of his amazing hoaxes. There was the London prank Cole played on a Member of Parliament, so young, so handsome, so complacently respectable. This young politician had been boasting that a Member of Parliament could never be arrested. That very evening Horace had the M.P. himself arrested!

Strolling along Piccadilly with the M.P. and a friend, Horace slipped his gold watch into the M.P.'s pocket, then brightly proposed a race as far as Jermyn Street. Off they dashed, the M.P. well ahead, and when half-way across the street Horace began to shout "Stop thief! Stop thief!" The public responded gallantly, the running M.P. was chased, collared and Cole declared that his watch had been stolen. He then wished to put an end to the joke, but the police, justifiably annoyed, hauled them all off to Vine Street, and though Cole tried hard to keep the next morning's police-court proceedings out of the papers, he failed to do so and the unfortunate M.P. almost had to resign, only saving himself by a two-hour speech of contrition to his constituents.

But the most famous hoax of all was that visit to H.M.S. *Dreadnought* in February, 1910. At that time both the Home and Atlantic Fleets were concentrated in Weymouth Bay—a striking spectacle for the world—and Cole decided that the Fleet must receive the Princes of Abyssinia. For his "princes" he had available a tall athlete, Anthony Buxton, who had twice helped Harrow to beat Eton at Lord's, secondly Duncan Grant, the artist, thirdly Guy Ridley, the son of a judge, and lastly a beautiful young woman known to you as Virginia Woolf, the renowned author. Virginia Woolf's brother was the other member of the party—he posed as the interpreter to the Abyssinian princes—and pretended to be a German. Early on in the plannings the participants began to weary of studying the Abyssinian language and costumes at the British Museum, so cards were engraved in Swahili which was unlikely to be known to any Navy. Then Horace discovered that only one man in the Fleet knew Abyssinian, and so, by choosing a day when this officer would be absent, they themselves could talk a fictitious language. Meanwhile, Horace, by experiment, had found that at one West End Post Office, staffed only by women, the maddest telegram would be accepted with a smile.

Early on the chosen morning Willy Clarkson's make-up men began to turn three young men and one beautiful young woman into formidable-looking Abyssinians and the lady's brother into a somewhat dusky German interpreter. Here one mistake was made—the princes had not had breakfast and once disguised, their false complexions would have been ruined by eating, so they had to face a hungry and thirsty day. Then at the last moment, all learned with dismay that the Chief Staff Officer of the Fleet was a first cousin of the lady and her thinly disguised brother, the interpreter. It was too late by then to make plans against this considerable danger and Cole, quite unembarrassed, went off in his morning things to Paddington Station where the stationmaster, though astonished that the Government had not given him the customary advance warning to expect royalty, hurriedly arranged for a reception committee, special carriages and so on. On to the platform strode the dusky princes, the reception committee bowed and did the honors. It wasn't until the train had left that a fellow-conspirator who has never been convicted, dashed off to send to the Admiral at Weymouth a telegram signed in the name of Hardinge, the Permanent Under-Secretary at the Foreign Office.

On the train Cole and the poorly-disguised interpreter had luncheon in almost regal style, but the unfortunate princes, starving in their reserved carriage, nearly mutinied until finally Cole bought four bath buns at Reading and, behind drawn blinds, the "princes" munched their buns. And then the express steamed into Weymouth where beside a red carpet stood the Commander in Chief's Flag Lieutenant with cocked hat and sword.

The Admiral's launch took the party out to the flagship, where the Admiral, Commanders, Staff and a guard of honor of bluejackets were all drawn up with the band ready to play the Abyssinian National Anthem. But the band did not know the Abyssinian Anthem, nor was there an Abyssinian flag to be found, and by an extraordinary coincidence the anthem played and the flag flown from the flagship were the anthem and flag of Zanzibar, whose "princes" Cole had previously impersonated in another hoax at Cambridge. Utterly bursting with delight at this fine coincidence, Cole solemnly introduced the "Ras el Sabganya," "Ras el Mendax"—his only regret being that he had failed to bring the official coffee-maker who was to have made coffee on the deck of the flagship and also stop the sun from setting too soon. Most courteously and laboriously the officers showed their guests around. The really remarkable part of the story, so typical of the man, is that Cole did not once laugh during the long tour of H.M.S. *Dreadnought*—not even when the ship's guns and instruments were explained to the "princes" and the four of them threw up their arms admiringly and exclaimed each time "Bunga-Bunga."

When it came to tea-time Cole saw to it that he himself had a good tuck in, but said that in Abyssinia princes took food only twice a day. So Cole had a good tea, while up on deck the "princes" went on saying more and more hungrily "Bunga-Bunga!" And then the blow fell! For just then there appeared the Chief Staff Officer, own first cousin of the lady prince and the poorly disguised interpreter. To Cole's horror, the officer's eyes centered at once on the interpreter and he quickly demanded: "Who is that fellow there?" Desperately Horace answered "Their Royal Highnesses' German interpreter." "What!" exclaimed the officer angrily, "a German! But we oughtn't to have Germans on board the *Dreadnought*." And Cole breathed again.

When it was time to go, the guns were manned for a royal salute, but etiquette demanded that a request must be made for a salute, and just as the interpreter was about to make the request, the band struck up "God Save the King" and the interpreter was afraid to speak for fear of exploding into laughter. So, with "Zank oo ver mooch" and many "Bunga-Bungas" the party went off amid naval cheers. Now, with the whole plot almost successful, disaster once again seemed to swoop down, for barely had the Chief Prince stepped from the red carpet and the cheering crowds into the train than half his false moustache fell off. He had a cold and had sneezed it off. He glued his face to the window on the off-side and sat with twisted neck and jammed nose until the train left the station.

Even now, Horace had not finished. When the starving "princes" clamored for food, Horace secretly told the train attendants that their "Highnesses" could receive food only from people wearing gray kid gloves, and in the dusk of that February evening, the express was stopped at Reading while the town was searched for two pairs of gray kid gloves.

Back in London, Horace quickly arranged that the press should have photographs and a full story, and then he sat back to enjoy the fruits of his day's labor. Questions were asked in the House of Commons, Scotland Yard hummed; the Admiralty hummed wildly; a book was written about the occurrence; but the crown of Cole's delight was when he learned that a Royal Prince, one of Prince Louis of Battenberg's sons, had while returning to his ship crossed the bows of the launch bearing Cole's party and had been severely reprimanded for crossing the bows of royalty.

Thus ended the greatest of Cole's practical jokes. In his last years, spent in France—he died in 1936—Cole developed the more contemplative side of his nature, although friends who saw him noticed little decline in his old high spirits.

THE SAWING-OFF OF MANHATTAN ISLAND

by Herbert Asbury

One of the most extraordinary hoaxes ever perpetrated in New York originated a little more than a hundred years ago in the fertile imagination of a little dried-up old man named Lozier, who had amassed a competence as a carpenter and contractor and had then retired to enjoy life. For almost two months during the summer of 1824 Lozier's fantastic activities, which he carried on with the enthusiastic assistance of John DeVoe, a retired butcher better known as Uncle John, kept a considerable portion of middle- and lower-class New York in a veritable frenzy of excitement. In later years Uncle John's nephew, Thomas F. DeVoe, an honored member of the New York Historical Society and himself a prosperous butcher of Civil War days, incorporated an account of the hoax in his two-volume work: *The Market Book, Containing a Historical Account of the Public Markets in the Cities of New York, Boston, Philadelphia, and Brooklyn, With a Brief Description of Every Article of Human Food Sold Therein, the Introduction of Cattle in America and Notices of Many Remarkable Specimens, et cetera, et cetera, et cetera.*

In those early days, when the Present American metropolis was a comparatively small city of not more than 150,000 population, a favorite loafing-place was the old Centre Market at Grand, Baxter, and Centre Streets. A dozen long benches lined the Grand Street side of the Market, and every afternoon from spring to winter they were filled with amateur statesmen, principally retired butchers and other such small business men, most of whom combined scant knowledge with excessive gullibility. Chief among them were Lozier and Uncle John DeVoe, and of these two venerable jokesters, Lozier was the leader. He did most of the talking at the daily forums in front of the Market and was invariably able to produce a definite and apparently practicable remedy for every conceivable financial, political, or economic ill. He was always listened to with enormous respect, for he was wealthy, he possessed more education than his fellows and was there-

171

fore better able to express himself, and he was a recognized traveler, having made several voyages to Europe as a ship's carpenter. There was no lack of subjects to talk about, for those were wondrous times. The first great wave of Irish immigration had begun to beat against American shores as a result of the potato famine of 1822; Brazil and Mexico had thrown off the shackles of Portugal and Spain; the first steamship had crossed the Atlantic only a few years before; President James Monroe had just promulgated the Monroe Doctrine; and Mrs. Monroe had almost precipitated a revolution in New York and Washington society by announcing that as the First Lady of the Land she would no longer return social calls. The gifted Lozier professed to know the inside stories of all these momentous events, and so convincing was he that there were many who believed that he was high in the confidence not only of the President, but of foreign potentates as well.

Early in July, 1824, Lozier was absent from his accustomed bench for several days, an unparalleled occurrence which aroused much comment. When he returned, he refused to join in the flow of conversation and even declined to settle arguments. He talked only to Uncle John DeVoe, and for the most part sat alone, brooding, obviously concerned with weighty matters. When his friends asked where he had been, and sought diligently to learn what mighty thoughts troubled his mind, he would at first divulge no information. At length, however, he admitted that he had been at City Hall in consultation with Mayor Stephen Allen. No one doubted the truth of this statement, which caused even more talk than had his absence. In those days the Mayor of New York was a personage of impressive dignity; he was not so approachable as now, and a man who had been summoned by His Honor automatically became a person of considerable importance. For almost a week Lozier kept his friends and admirers on tenterhooks of curiosity. Finally, on a day when all the Market benches were occupied and he was thus assured of an audience worthy of his talents, he made a full and complete explanation.

It appeared that Lozier and Mayor Allen had had a long conversation about Manhattan Island and had reached the conclusion that it was much too heavy on the Battery end, because of the many large buildings. The situation was rapidly becoming dangerous. Already the island had begun to sag, as was plain from the fact that it was all downhill from City Hall, and there were numerous and alarming indications that it might break off and sink into the sea, with appalling

losses of life and property. Lozier and the Mayor had decided, therefore, that the island must be sawed off at Kingsbridge, at the northern
end, and turned around, so that the Kingsbridge end would be where
the Battery end had been for ages. The Battery end, of course, if it
did not fall off in transit, would take the place of the Kingsbridge end.
Once the turn had been made, the weaker end of the island would be
anchored to the mainland, thus averting the danger of collapse.

When the conferences at City Hall began, it further appeared,
Lozier and Mayor Allen were not in complete agreement as to the
best method of accomplishing the mighty task. The Mayor thought
that before Manhattan could be turned around it would be necessary
to detach Long Island from its moorings and tow it out of the way,
returning it later to its proper place. Lozier finally convinced him,
however, that there was ample space in the harbor and the bay. It
was at length decided, therefore, simply to saw Manhattan Island off,
float it down past Governors and Ellis Islands, turn it around, and
then float it back to its new position. For political reasons Mayor Allen
wished the job to appear as a private undertaking and had turned the
whole project over to Lozier, instructing him to employ the necessary
labor and to superintend the work.

Such were the force of Lozier's personality, the power of his reputation, and the credulity of his generation that practically none who
heard him thought of questioning the feasibility of the scheme. The
few who were inclined to scoff were soon silenced, if not actually convinced, by his earnestness, and by the acclaim which had greeted the
announcement of the project. Everyone realized at once that it was
truly a gigantic plan, but they had Lozier's word for it that it could
be accomplished. Moreover, as Lozier pointed out, the construction of
the famous Erie Canal, which was then nearing completion, had once
been called impossible even by competent engineers, and much deri-
sion had greeted the prediction that steam ships would one day cross
the ocean. If man could run a river through the very heart of a mountain, and if he could cause a simple steam engine to propel a gigantic
boat, why couldn't he saw off an island? Nobody knew the answer,
and Lozier's story was swallowed *in toto,* hook, line, and sinker.

Sawing Manhattan Island off soon became the principal subject of
argument and conversation at Centre Market, and elsewhere as news
of the great project spread. Neither then nor later, however, did the
few newspapers of the period pay any attention to Lozier's activities.
It is doubtful if the editors ever heard of him, for in those days the

only way of transmitting intelligence was by word of mouth, or by letter, which was even more uncertain. Important happenings in one part of the city did not become generally known for weeks or months, and frequently not at all. And Grand Street then was as far uptown as the farthest reaches of the Bronx are today.

·   A few days after he had started the ball rolling Lozier appeared at Centre Market with a huge ledger, in which he proposed to record the names of all applicants for jobs, pending an examination to determine their fitness. This and other clerical work which developed during the progress of the hoax was the special care of Uncle John DeVoe, who ceremoniously set down the names, ages, and places of residence of all who applied. Work was none too plentiful that year, and laborers, many of them recently-arrived Irishmen, answered Lozier's call in such numbers that the big ledger soon bore the names of some three hundred men, all eager to begin the great work of sawing off Manhattan Island.

·   Lozier further aroused confidence in his scheme by notifying various butchers of his acquaintance to begin assembling the enormous herds of cattle, droves of hogs, and flocks of chickens which would be necessary to feed his army of workmen. He estimated that he would require at once five hundred head of cattle, an equal number of hogs, and at least three thousand chickens. He was especially anxious to obtain as many fowls as possible, for he had definitely promised that all who obtained jobs would have chicken dinners twice a week. There was great excitement among the butchers, the immediate effect of which was an increase in the prices of all sorts of meat. One enterprising butcher had in his pens fifty fat hogs awaiting slaughter, and to make certain of a sale to Lozier he drove them north and penned them near Kingsbridge, where he fed them for almost a month at considerable expense.

With his food-supply assured, Lozier engaged a score of small contractors and carpenters to furnish lumber and to superintend, under his direction, the building of the great barracks which were to house the workmen during the sawing operations. A separate building, to be constructed of the best materials, was ordered for the convenience of the twenty or thirty women, wives of laborers, who had been employed to cook and wash for the entire crew. Several of these contractors let their enthusiasm get the better of their judgment and actually hauled a dozen loads of lumber to the northern end of the island and dumped them near Kingsbridge. They implored Lozier to let them begin building, but he said that actual construction must wait until he had engaged all the men he would need and had assembled all his materials. It was his intention, he announced, to muster his workmen at a central meeting-place when everything was ready and march them in a body to Kingsbridge. He assured the contractors that by using a new method of building which he had devised, but which he declined to disclose in advance, they could easily erect the necessary buildings within a few hours.

The excitement was now at fever heat, and Lozier added fuel to the flame by producing elaborate plans for the various appliances which were to be used in the project. First, there were the great saws with which Manhattan Island was to be cut loose from the mainland. Each was to be one hundred feet long, with teeth three feet high. Fifty men would be required to manipulate one of these giant tools, and Lozier estimated that he would need at least a score. Then there were twenty-four huge oars, each two hundred and fifty feet long; and twenty-four great cast-iron towers, or oar-locks, in which the oars were to be mounted, twelve on the Hudson River shore and twelve on the East River. A hundred men would bend their backs at each oar, and row Manhattan Island down the bay after the sawyers had finished their work, then sweep it around and row it back. Great chains and anchors were to be provided to keep the island from being carried out to sea in the event that a storm arose. Lozier gave the plans and specifications of these Gargantuan implements to a score of blacksmiths, carpenters, and mechanics, who retired forthwith to their shops and feverishly began to estimate the cost, and the quantities of material that must go into their manufacture.

Lozier now turned his attention to the unskilled laborers whose names Uncle John DeVoe had set down as potential sawyers and rowers. He sent word for them to report at Centre Market for examination and announced that he would pay triple wages to those who performed the hazardous work of sawing off that part of the island which lay under water. The longest-winded men would be awarded these dangerous but desirable jobs. Laborers swarmed to the market, and every day for a week Lozier sat enthroned on a bench while man after man stepped forward and held his breath. As each displayed his prowess, Uncle John DeVoe timed them and entered the result in his ledger.

Lozier kept delaying the commencement of actual work by professing dissatisfaction with the estimates on the oars and towers and by insisting that he had not hired nearly enough men to do the job properly. At last, however, "the numbers became so thick and pressing," as DeVoe put it in *The Market Book*, that Lozier was compelled to fix a date for the grand trek northward. He hurriedly awarded the contracts for manufacturing the saws, oars, and towers and ordered them rushed to completion. He then instructed all who were to have a hand in the great work to report at the Bowery and Spring Street, where they would be met by a fife and drum corps which he had thoughtfully engaged to lead the march to Kingsbridge. The exact number who appeared at the rendezvous is unknown, of course, but DeVoe says that "great numbers presented themselves," and there were probably between five hundred and a thousand persons. Laborers were there by the score, many accompanied by their wives and children; the contractors and carpenters drove up in style, escorting wagons laden with lumber and tools; the butchers were on hand with cattle and hogs, and carts loaded with crated chickens. Practically everyone who had ever heard of the project was there, in fact, excepting Lozier and Uncle John DeVoe. When several hours had elapsed and they still had failed to appear, a volunteer delegation went to Centre Market in search of them. They found a message that both Lozier and Uncle John had left town on account of their health.

The crowd at Bowery and Spring Street milled about uncertainly for another hour or two, while the hogs grunted, the cattle mooed, the chickens cackled, the children squalled, and the fife and drum corps industriously dispensed martial music. At length, for the first time in weeks, if not in years, some of the more intelligent of Lozier's victims began to think, and the more they thought, the less likely it appeared that Manhattan Island would ever be sawed off. Gradually this conviction spread, and after a while the crowd began shamefacedly to disperse. A few of the more hot-headed went looking for Lozier, vowing that if they couldn't saw Manhattan off they could at least saw Lozier off, but they never found him. Lozier and Uncle John DeVoe had fled to Brooklyn as soon as Lozier had issued his final instructions, and had sought refuge in the home of a friend. There was much talk of having them arrested, but no one seemed willing to make a complaint to the authorities and so admit that he had been duped, and both Lozier and Uncle John went scot-free. However, it was several months before they again appeared at Centre Market, and when they did, Lozier found himself an oracle without a temple. The Centre Market statesmen had had enough.

THE MASKED MEDIUM SPOOF

by Bernard O'Donnell

I was just sauntering past the London Pavilion one day when I happened on a very old friend, the late P. T. Selbit, the most amazing and amusing stage illusionist I have ever known.

We drifted into the Café Monico, Piccadilly, for a drink and a chat; over a couple of double Scotches, P.T. remarked with a twinkle in his eye, raising his glass, "Bernard, I am about to raise a spirit of even greater interest than this in the very near future."

"Impossible," I muttered with feeling.

"You know the *Sunday Express?*"

"I have heard of it," I said.

"Well—the editor is offering five hundred pounds to any medium who can produce a spirit form under strict test conditions imposed by its own appointed committee," Selbit went on.

"So what?" I inquired.

He took another sip of spirit.

Then, "I've accepted the challenge," he said. "And I'm producing a medium who will do just that; materialise a spirit form."

"Genuine stuff?" I asked, for I knew Selbit's aptitude for showmanship. He shrugged his shoulders.

"Come along and see for yourself," was all he said.

That is how I came to be in on what I have always regarded as one of the most daring and flagrant "spoofs" ever perpetrated in connection with a supposed spiritualistic séance.

There was nothing lacking in showmanship where Selbit was concerned. And it was showmanship plus a perverse sense of humour which prompted him to stage the séance that took place on March 21, 1919, in Selbit's own flat in Bloomsbury. The séance room was situated on the third floor, its four windows looking out on to the square where stands the Princes' Theatre, Shaftesbury Avenue.

It was a long wide room, one end of which had been heavily draped with black curtains. Into this room were ushered the members of a committee of investigation appointed by the editor of the *Sunday Express*. Chief among them was Sir Arthur Conan Doyle. Then came Lady Glenconner, afterwards the wife of Viscount Grey of Fallodon, Sir Henry Lunn, Dr. Wynn Westcott, the well-known coroner and expert on things occult, Dr. Edwin Smith, lecturer in Forensic Medicine at St. Thomas' Hospital, Superintendent Thomas of Scotland Yard, Mr. Stuart Cumberland, an authority on thought transference, Mr. David Gow, Editor of *Light*, the spiritualist journal, and Mr. Ralph Shirley, Editor of the *Occult Review*. In addition there was Sydney A. Moseley, the well-known author.

Before the medium was introduced, the committee made an exhaustive search of the room, lifting up the carpets to see there were no trapdoors or other trick apparatus. They examined the walls and the windows, tested the floor for electric wires, and made sure that the lighting arrangements were not rigged in any way.

Mr. Selbit of course was there, looking as sardonic as ever, and with true showman instinct making his visitors feel that they were at liberty to impose the sternest of conditions in order to ensure there should be no trickery. He produced a small black cigar-box to which a lock was attached. This he handed to the investigators to examine thoroughly. They did so! He next produced a small silk bag which was likewise examined. The visitors were then invited to place any articles connected with either the living or the dead, into the bag which reposed in the box, what time Selbit impressed upon them to observe closely that the box was *never out of their sight*.

It was then that he introduced the medium. He opened the door of the room and there entered a slender young woman clad in white evening dress which stood out in strong contrast to the black hair and gleaming dark eyes which gazed out at the assembly over a yashmak. She was shown to a seat at the curtained end of the room, and Selbit placed the box upon her knees. The lights were dimmed. At the request of the committee the illusionist took a seat at the opposite end of the room as far away from the medium as possible.

In a few moments there was the sound of a cough and a sigh followed by a little moaning, and then the medium began to speak. Amidst pauses as though groping for the right words, she mentioned first a surname, and then a Christian name. It turned out to be the name of a member of the staff of the newspaper who had been sent along with a sealed letter which was a special test devised by the editor of the paper.

"I see machinery—cotton mills—something suggesting machinery," she went on, "cotton mills in the North—Yorkshire. They are at Halifax . . . I see words . . . German words . . . but they are not real German . . . only German in a jocular mood I see the word *Ober-intellect* . . ."

You will note the amount of detail in the revelations of the medium concerning a letter which she had never seen. A letter which it was afterwards revealed was enclosed first in a thick blue cover, which was then placed in an envelope sealed with wax, and then stamped with a private device.

But perhaps her most remarkable performance, for it *was* that as you will presently see, was her deciphering of the cryptic message in the letter which in fact read: "Liebe Ober-intellect, Ich habe until January 10 ein extension gewangled!"

This was a faithful and sensational rendering of the exact words in the letter, and a most convincing proof of mediumistic phenomena.

Having thus gained the confidence of the committee, the Masked Medium, as she became known, simply went on from success to success. She described a medal which had belonged to the dead son of Sir Arthur Conan Doyle. Stuart Cumberland agreed with her description of a bit of broken stud which he had dropped into the bag. Dr. Wynn Westcott deposited a strange medallion bearing the insignia of the occult society of which he was the President. This was a symbol containing triangles with his initials W.W.W. interlaced with the letters Q.S.N. The medium described this object with uncanny precision. . . .

She appeared to experience some difficulty with one object, and it is a tribute to her showmanship that her failure to give a detailed description was even more convincing than if she had been completely successful.

"I see a swan . . ." she said hesitantly, "I see something black . . . yes a swan . . . it is something to do with correspondence. I am sorry I cannot tell you any more."

In fact it was a black *Swan fountain pen,* and the owner of it was absolutely convinced of her psychic powers.

How did she do it? How could she possibly know what was contained in the box?

You will remember that just before Selbit introduced the medium he drew attention to the fact that the box *never left their sight.* He then opened the door and the medium, wearing a mask in the form of a yashmak, entered the room. Every eye was naturally turned upon *her* and in that moment Selbit switched the box which he held, to an assistant behind the door, receiving in its place a duplicate box, which the medium subsequently held in her lap. It was done so quickly and with such dexterity that nobody noticed the exchange. I was as completely fooled as the others.

The real box was taken to a room where it was unlocked with a duplicate key, and where a wireless installation had been set up. The mask of the medium concealed two tiny ear-pieces acting as a receiving set. Meanwhile assistants were making notes of the articles in the box which had been opened with a duplicate key. They unsealed the test letter by means of a hot knife to melt the wax, and copied word for word its contents.

The transmission of the messages was made by means of a large induction coil, the man in charge of this part of the show literally *telling* the medium what to say. While she was reeling off the various descriptions given, the back room boys were resealing the letter and replacing the articles in the box.

Presently when the medium said she felt tired and would like to rest for a few minutes. Selbit suggested that Lady Glenconner should retire with the medium and carry out a search of her person in accordance with the terms of the test. Just across the passage was a small room. A maid held the door open, and the medium with a polite "After your Ladyship," ushered Lady Glenconner into the room, the maid seizing this moment to change the box carried by the medium for the original box containing the objects she had just described.

At once the medium handed this box to Lady Glenconner asking her to retain possession of it so that she could assure the committee that it had not been changed. Then throwing aside her yashmak mask—and thus cunningly discarding her receiving set—she submitted to the search.

But the séance was not yet over. There was to be a materialising test, and once more the medium, now minus ear-pieces which had been adroitly whisked away by the maid when readjusting the mask, took her seat. Those present indulged in a little hymn singing to encourage favourable conditions. Very soon in the shadowy darkness there appeared to come from the side of the medium a sort of vapoury figure bearing some resemblance to the human form. It grew and grew, and the silence was intense as it took a roughly human shape and then gradually disappeared.

This phenomenon was as daringly produced as had been the previous psychometric demonstration. For the purpose of the materialisation Selbit engaged an acrobat who, when the room had been sufficiently darkened, slipped out of a window in the next door flat, and crept along a narrow coping to a window at the curtained end of the séance room where the medium was sitting. He was clad from head to foot in black tights. Under cover of the hymn singing, he gently raised the window, stole in behind the black curtains and made his way to the side of the medium. Once there, from a pocket concealed in the front of his tights, he produced some phosphorescent butter muslin which he gradually formed into something resembling a human form. Having produced his ghost he made the muslin vanish into his pocket and made his way back to the next door flat via the windows through which he had entered the séance room.

How convincing this séance must have been may be gathered from the fact that Sydney Moseley wrote a book on it titled *An Amazing Séance*. Lady Glenconner in writing a comment on the demonstration declared, "The medium possesses remarkable powers, and deserves, and has, our gratitude for placing them before our circle of investigators in so generous a manner." Sir Arthur Conan Doyle was a bit sceptical of the ghostly apparition but expressed his firm belief in the clairvoyant manifestations.

Selbit said nothing, but thought a lot. He refused to accept the five hundred pounds offered by the *Sunday Express*, realising that if he did so it would savour of obtaining money by false pretences. When, however, he was approached by several city men to give public performances of a similar nature, he agreed to do so and in due course appeared with his now famous Masked Medium at the Victoria Hall, Criterion Restaurant, Piccadilly. And there he met his Waterloo.

Incidentally so did I, for I had arranged with Selbit that, later on, when he felt that the moment was ripe for disclosing that the whole manifestations had been produced by trickery, I should have the story exclusively. Selbit's object in carrying out his spoof was to show that the physical manifestations of the séance room, purporting to be produced by spirits could be produced by trickery. Of course it would have been an intriguing story when, as I put it, the moment was ripe. Unfortunately for me it became overripe.

At the Victoria Hall the objects to be described were collected in little bags which were then dropped through a hole in the top of a box standing on a sheet of plate glass on the stage. "To prevent any trickery," Selbit explained. The box was then attached to two cords hanging from the flies and drawn up so that it hung in mid-air in full view of the audience. On this occasion you will notice there was no substitution of the box as before, but the same means was used to obtain knowledge of the contents, this knowledge also being conveyed by wireless telephony as at the séance in Selbit's flat. As the objects were dropped into the box at the Victoria Hall, an assistant reached up through a trapdoor in the stage, and putting his hand through a cunningly concealed trap in the back of the box, withdrew the various articles from it.

The real difficulty came when the bags had to be returned to the box after they had been duly described. To achieve this, when the box was lowered from the flies it descended into the arms of an assistant gorgeously attired in the roomy black knee-breeches so beloved of illusionists on the stage. The concealed trap door in the box reached to just about his waistline. Having completed the examination of the contents of the bags so that the medium could give her description, while they were still—apparently—in the box suspended in mid-air, they were tucked into the waistband of the assistant deputed to hold the box at the conclusion of the séance.

It was then Selbit's job to reach through the hole in the top of the box, grope through the trapdoor near the waist of his confederate, and withdraw one by one the bags containing the objects from their place of concealment. Actually it would appear as though they were being produced from the box which had never been out of sight.

Unfortunately for him, instead of getting hold of a bag he seized the top of the man's trousers and tugged. He told me later that it seemed as though those bags were glued to his assistant's body for, in spite of giving several more tugs he couldn't get the bag away.

Suddenly there came a disconcerting cry from a member of the audience.

"You're pulling his trousers off," someone shouted, and sure enough, when Selbit looked down he realised that he had tugged so hard that one leg of his assistant's trousers had been pulled up to such an extent that a large expanse of white leg was showing.

The Masked Medium spoof was over. And so was my story. The exposure was already complete.

OUTER BALDONIA VS. SOVIET RUSSIA

by William Bancroft Mellor

Many of Washington's keenest political observers have seen fit to ignore the mounting tension between the Soviet Union and the Principality of Outer Baldonia. But those in the know are waiting with bated breath and expectant chuckles for the next move of the Kremlin in its propaganda war with a "nation" which exists only in the engagingly whimsical mind of Russell M. Arundel, a Washington businessman and sportsman.

Arundel, an ardent tuna fisherman, invented "Outer Baldonia" over a bottle of bourbon one bitterly cold day in 1949, while he and a couple of companions were out after blue fins in the Atlantic off the Nova Scotia coast. He had just purchased an uninhabited island—a barren, 40-acre mass of rock jutting out of the sea 16 miles southwest of Wedgeport, in the middle of some of the best tuna waters in the world—and built a one-room fishing lodge on it. On your map, if it is a very large one, you will find the island listed as Outer Bald Tusket, one of a group of tiny dots scattered below the southernmost tip of Nova Scotia.

On that day in 1949, Arundel and his companions, casting about for a diversion to make them forget the chill winds which whistled through their fishing boat's drafty cabin, decided to create on the island a new and independent state—the Principality of Outer Baldonia —a nation peopled by fishermen alone, and only *tuna* fishermen, at that. Braced in the heaving cabin of their fishing boat, they drew up their first state document: a Declaration of Independence. It proclaimed for the citizens of the new principality the right to swear, lie, drink and gamble, and guaranteed them freedom forever from nagging, shaving, women, taxes, politics, war, cant and inhibitions.

Arundel is mild-mannered, slight of build, and wears horn-rimmed spectacles secured by a broad black ribbon looped around the back of his neck. Seeing him sitting in his deeply carpeted Washington office, one would hardly envision him on the plunging deck of a fishing boat or astride a galloping hunter behind the foxhounds, of which he is master at Warrenton, Virginia. And certainly he is not the princely type. But beneath his proclamation, in a bold scrawl, Arundel signed himself "Russell, Rex," and proclaimed himself "Prince of Princes." Beneath his signature went those of Prew Savoy, a Washington attorney and business associate of Arundel's, who was named Prince Regent and Minister of State, and Captain Elson Boudreau, skipper of the fishing boat, who became Chancellor of the Principality.

Back in his Washington office, the Prince of Princes next ordered stationery with a gold-embossed letterhead bearing the Great Seal of Outer Baldonia; had the new nation listed on the directory of tenants in the lobby of the World Centre Building where his offices are; and then hied himself to the Chesapeake & Potomac Telephone Company. Presently in the Washington telephone book there appeared a listing for "Outer Baldonia, Principality of" (DI 7-2463)—a listing which subsequently was to occasion no little embarrassment for certain State Department fledglings who, told to make routine calls to "all foreign diplomatic missions," included Outer Baldonia on their lists.

Arundel is a busy man. His interests include a number of enterprises which allow him little time for whimsy. His spur-of-the-moment gag, however, developed such fascinating possibilities that he couldn't let go of it, and for days he devoted all his time to "affairs of state." He drew up an impressive Constitution, plastered with seals and ribbons and vesting all powers in himself—but recognizing, "for international amity," the laws of the Dominion of Canada. The document also provided that the citizenry of Outer Baldonia should consist entirely of "Princes," and of "Admirals of a rank no lower than six-star."

Each of the sixty-nine members of the Wedgeport Tuna Guides' Association received a formal commission as a "six-star admiral," together with notification that thenceforth his boat was to be considered a unit of the Outer Baldonian Navy. To a few tuna-fishing cronies, Prince Arundel also sent embossed scrolls creating them Knights of the Order of Blue Fin and Hereditary Princes of the Realm.

To insure the fullest possible diplomatic acceptance, the Prince of Princes appointed both an ambassador *and* a minister to Canada (Dr. Ronald Wallace, of Halifax, and Harold Lohnes, of Louisville, Kentucky), while to William DeGarthe, also of Halifax, went the post of Naval Attaché.

Arundel also designed passport forms, "valid forever and a day and until revoked," and had dies manufactured in preparation for the coining of his own money (the basic unit of which was to be the "tunar") and his own stamps.

Negotiations were then opened with Rand McNally & Co., the map people, and with the Interior Department's Board on Geographic Names to have Outer Baldonia shown on all future maps and charts of the Atlantic. Both requests were made on Outer Baldonian stationery over the signature of "Russell, Rex," and were phrased as royal commands.

It wasn't long before some of the Canadian newspapers blossomed out with feature stories about Outer Baldonia. The Provincial Government of Nova Scotia went along with the gag and announced to the press that it was "still undecided about recognition of the new kingdom." One of the Canadian papers, carrying a deadpan treatment of the yarn, found its way into Germany, where the trade journal, *Industrikurier,* picked it up and printed it as a serious news dispatch. And so it got to Moscow.

On October 25, 1952, a vehement denunciation of Outer Baldonia appeared in the pages of the *Literary Gazette,* a state-controlled publication in the Russian capital. Quoting the Baldonian's constitutional right to lie, swear and otherwise misbehave, the article unleashed a bitter tirade at the "führer" of Baldonia and declared he had "set himself the aim of turning his subjects into savages."

"In a word," the *Gazette* said, Prince Arundel had given them "the 'right' not to adhere to the ethical and moral laws which have been established by mankind."

It was several months before the *Gazette* reached the western hemisphere and was reprinted, tongue-in-cheek and in translation, in a Canadian Government publication.

Deeply hurt, the Prince of Princes brooded in his Washington "chancery" over this breach of diplomatic etiquette by the Russians. Then he took pen in hand.

Presently a messenger was on his way up Sixteenth Street, bearing a formal protest to the Soviet Embassy—a note which threatened severance of diplomatic relations unless amends were quickly forthcoming. Thus far there have been no further moves on either side, but Russell, Rex, and the Outer Baldonian Navy are ready.

It's your move, Malenkov.

UNDEFEATED AND UNDETECTED

by Lloyd Mann

As the autumn of 1941 punted and plunged its way through the sports columns, bewildered stockbroker Morris Newburger of Newburger, Loeb & Company, New York, pondered on how the exploits of such teams as Slippery Rock, for example, rated weekly coverage in the local press. Where were these obscure schools—and how many people were there in New York who cared what happened to their football teams?

The dilemma so tortured his imagination that one frosty Saturday evening he rose from his table at the Bird and Bottle at Garrison, New York, and telephoned the sports departments of the New York *Times* and the *Herald Tribune*. He would like to report, he reported, that Plainfield Teachers in New Jersey—an institution as authentic as the School of Hard Knocks—had just walloped the equally mythical Scott by a score of 12 to 0. Furthermore, Plainfield's offense had been sparked by a triple-threat Chinese quarterback named Johnny Chung, the "Celestial Comet," who had darted all over the field like a chickaree.

Unsuspecting and swamped with scores from all over the country, the papers swallowed the story, cleats and all, and printed it. It was a delight to Newburger to pick up the New York *Times* the next morning and skip airily from the war in Europe to the account of Plainfield Teachers' smashing victory over Scott, complete with the line-ups which included Morris Newburger at right tackle for the Teachers and a smattering of his business partners and relatives in other key spots.

The newspaper accounts the next week were even better. Plainfield Teachers, inspired by Johnny Chung, bowled over Chesterton 24 to 0. Newburger was still at right tackle, fighting alongside his senior partner and his uncle. But aside from Johnny Chung—who, by the way, consumed a crock of rice between halves and came out for the kickoff like a wildcat—there were other interesting features of the Teachers'

187

attack. Most unusual was coach Ralph "Hurry Up" Hoblitzel's new "W" formation in which the ends faced the backs and generally accounted for a fifth man in the backfield. It was sensational, so the papers commented, and opened great holes for lightning, snake-hipped Chung, the Celestial Comet. Herbert Allan of the New York *Post* warned that if Hoblitzel didn't watch out, Chiang Kai-shek would grab Chung for his own offensive. Within a week, Chung's name came up for more man-in-the-street comment than all the Chinese generals combined.

Succeeding weeks brought triumphs over such fantastic opposition as Winona, 27 to 3 (the only points ever scored against the Teachers); Randolph Tech, 35 to 0; Ingersoll, 13 to 0 (Chung scored on a 47-yard run for the first tally and dragged five tacklers with him for the second); St. Joseph's, 6 to 0. There remained only games with Appalachian Tech and Harmony Teachers.

The *Times* as well as the *Tribune* listed Plainfield Teachers among the unbeaten, untied teams in the country. The Monday morning quarterbacks spent a great many happy hours comparing Chung's playing with that of his brothers in the better publicized and larger Eastern colleges, and there was considerable speculation as to which of the pro teams would be lucky enough to sign him up.

By this time Newburger had fallen in love with his own creation and was going all out. His team had gained a reputation beyond his wildest expectations and he now had an accomplice in Philadelphia who fed the Philadelphia *Record* with stories of Plainfield Teachers and the Celestial Comet. In New York, Newburger installed a one-way telephone through which a character known as Jerry Croyden, the publicity agent for the Plainfield Teachers Athletic Association, fed juicy morsels to the press. Releases went out on the Athletic Association's new stationery, usually date-lined Newark, New Jersey, and bearing a telephone number that didn't work for incoming calls. On outgoing calls, the agent's voice resembled that of right-tackle Morris Newburger.

At this point Johnny Chung's meteoric career blew up in his face. The story was too good to keep within a small group. It passed from office to office, from luncheon table to luncheon table, and from club to club, and the weekly accounts of the Plainfield Teachers' games had an evergrowing and always eager group of readers who enjoyed the stories all the more because they happened to be in on the hoax. It was inevitable that somebody would blab to an editor of *Time*

Magazine; and *Time* takes delight in exposing hoaxes. When Newburger got wind of the treachery he rushed, headguard in hand, to *Time's* offices. Please, he begged, let Plainfield Teachers finish her season unbeaten and head for the grand finale—the Blackboard Bowl championship. He'd give *Time* the advance scores right then if it wanted them.

But *Time* was adamant. Disconsolate, right-tackle Newburger shuffled back to the bench. But he fired one last release. It announced that so many of Teachers' stars, including Johnny Chung, had flunked their exams and become ineligible for athletics that heartbroken "Hurry Up" Hoblitzel had decided to cancel the remaining games with Appalachian Tech and Harmony Teachers.

Even trusting sports writers suspected that one. The *Tribune's* ferret-minded Caswell Adams found the genuine Chamber of Commerce of New Jersey's genuine city of Plainfield ignorant of any such institution as Plainfield Teachers. Then, behind perfect blocking by the telephone company, he overtook Newburger in his office and brought him down viciously on top of his one-way telephone, his athletic association stationery, and a bundle of releases on the Blackboard Bowl game. At the bottom of the heap lay the ephemeral Celestial Comet, never to rise again. At that very moment on the newsstands, *Time* Magazine was serving its scoop to an astounded and delighted public. The *Tribune* took time out to laugh, but the stately *Times* remained mum.

We resurrect the ghost of galloping Johnny Chung only because information reaching this writer indicates that another group of financiers, not including Mr. Newburger, anticipating an unprecedented volume of football claptrap this coming fall, hopes to sponsor a new athlete who will make the Celestial Comet look chickenhearted and muddy-footed. We understand that the current prospect has an athletic scholarship at a seat of learning that, as we heard it, sounded like Crandon College—in the State of Pennsylvania, we believe. Maybe you've never heard of it.

WHO'S WHO AND WHY: A FLORENTINE HOAX

Anonymous

The Renaissance, which produced the Borgias and that classic treatise on diplomatic deceit, Machiavelli's The Prince, *was, of course, the age of the hoaxter, par excellence. Even da Vinci and Michelangelo palmed off some of their creations as antiquities in order to sell them for higher prices, and Cellini's autobiography is replete with deception, as are most of the stories in the* Decameron. *The Florentine hoax described in this anonymous account is of particular interest, for it revolves around the universally puzzling problem of identity, of man's search for himself.*

About the year 1409, a company of young Florentines having met one Sunday evening to sup together at the house of their friend, Tommaso de' Pecori, the whole party began to converse in a pleasant way upon a variety of topics, when one of the guests looking round him, observed, "What can be the reason that we have not the company of Manetto Ammanotini here tonight? Though repeatedly invited, he still refuses to come: it is very strange!" Now, Manetto was by profession a carver in ebony, who had opened a shop in the Piazza San Giovanni, and was considered a very skilful artist in his way; he possessed a very agreeable person and manners, and was about five-and-thirty years of age. Indeed, such was his comfortable appearance that it had acquired for him the name of Grasso Fat, and he was everywhere esteemed one of the most happy, good-tempered fellows in the world. But this time, either from design or caprice, the ingenious carver was wanting to complete the social comfort of the party. As he had sent no message, they felt a little piqued; and the person who had first started the subject said, "I wish we could play him some good trick, were it only to teach him better manners in future."

Now, there was a certain Philip Brunellesco, a man well acquainted with Grasso who, on hearing this, began to ponder a little on the subject. And pondering to some purpose, he at length observed, "If I thought, gentlemen, I were wicked enough to do it, I could tell you how we might have a noble revenge; by passing off a trick upon him that will make us all laugh for an age to come. What do you think? I have not the least doubt we might persuade him that he was actually metamorphosed, and become quite another person." "Nay, that is impossible!" they all cried at once. "I say not," continued Philip, "if you will only listen and let me explain the whole plan." And this he did in so satisfactory a manner that they one and all agreed to join him in persuading Grasso that he was changed into Matteo, a member of the same party.

The ensuing night was accordingly fixed upon for the transformation; when Philip, as being upon the most intimate terms with Grasso, was appointed to go about the time of shutting up shop to visit him. So he went; and after talking with Grasso, as had been agreed upon, for some time, there appeared a little lad running in great haste, who inquired if Signor Brunellesco were there. Philip answered he was, and begged to know what he wanted. "O signor!" said the boy, "you must come immediately, for your mother has met with a sad accident; she is very nearly killed, so you must come home now." With well-feigned grief and alarm, Philip took leave somewhat abruptly of his friend Grasso, who said he would go with him if he thought he could be of any service. Philip thanked him, saying, "No, not now; but if I want you I will make bold to send for you." Then pretending to hasten homewards, Philip turned the corner of a street leading to Grasso's own house, opposite to Santa Reparata, and very unceremoniously picking the lock of the door, he marched in and fastened it behind him so that no one could follow.

Now it happened that Grasso's mother had set off some days before to a little country place at Polerossa and she was expected back again that day. After shutting up his shop, Grasso resolved to go home, but was somewhat puzzled on ascending the steps to find that he could not open the door as usual; and after several vain attempts, he supposed it must be locked in the inside, and knocking pretty sharply, he shouted, "Open the door!" thinking that his mother had returned. But at length a voice answered in Grasso's own tone, "Who is there?" and Grasso, a little startled, said, "It is I; let me in." "No," returned the voice; "and I beg, Matteo, that you will go away. I am in great anxiety about a friend of mine; for as I was just now talking in my shop to Philip, there came a messenger in haste to say that his mother was nearly dead, and I am very sorry for him." Then, as if turning to Grasso's mother, Philip continued, "Pray, good mother, let me have my supper; it is really too bad; you ought to have been back two days since, and you come in just at this time of night"; and he went on grumbling and scolding exactly in Grasso's own voice. Still more surprised at this, Grasso now said, "That is very like my own voice; what the deuce can it all mean? Who is it speaking there upstairs? Can it be I? Have I lost my senses, or what does it mean?" Then he went down the steps again and shouted up at the windows. when there passed by his friend Donatello, the sculptor, who said as he went past, "Good night, Matteo, good night! I am going to call upon your friend Grasso; he is just gone home."

Grasso was now perfectly bewildered on hearing his friend Donatello address him as Matteo; and turning away, he went into the Piazza San Giovanni. There he was met by some officers of police, a bailiff, and a creditor, to whom Matteo owed a sum of money. "This is the man, this is Matteo; take him—he is my debtor. I have watched him closely, and caught him at last!" cried the creditor; and the officers, laying hands on him, led him away. It was in vain that Grasso, turning towards the creditor, exclaimed, "You have mistaken your man! My name is Grasso the carver; I am not Matteo, nor any of his kin: I do not even know him." "You not Matteo?" cried his creditor, surveying him from head to foot; "Do you think I do not know my own debtor Matteo? Yes, too well. Cannot I distinguish him from Grasso the carver, think you? Off with him." They then hurried him in no very gentle way to prison.

Grasso laid himself down to rest, thinking what would become of him if he were really changed into Matteo; "which I fear," he continued, "must in some way be the case; there are so many proofs of it on all sides. Suppose I send home to my mother; but then if Grasso be really in the house they will only laugh at me, and perhaps say I am mad. And yet surely I must be Grasso."

After a sleepless night, he arose and stationed himself at the small grated window, in hopes someone might pass who knew him; and, as chance would have it, Giovanni Rucellai, one of the supper-party when the plot was first hatched, approached. It happened that Grasso was making a dressing-table for Giovanni and the latter had been in his shop the day before pressing him to finish the work in a few days at farthest. Giovanni, going into a shop facing the prison grate on the ground floor where Grasso stood, the prisoner began to smile and make mouths at him; but his friend only stared at him as if he had never seen him in his life before. Grasso next said, "Pray, do you happen to know a person of the name of Grasso, who lives at the back of the Piazza San Giovanni, and makes inlaid work?" "Know him! to be sure I do," replied Giovanni, "and I am going to him directly about a little job he has in hand for me." "Then," said Grasso, "pray be so good as just to say to him, 'A very particular acquaintance of yours, Grasso, has been taken into custody, and would be glad to exchange a word with you!'" "To be sure I will," said the other, "very willingly"; and, taking his leave, pursued his way.

Friend Grasso, remaining at the window of the prison, began to commune with himself, "Well, at last it is clear that I am no longer Grasso, for I am Matteo, and no one else, with a vengeance. The devil give him good of the change! but what a wretched fate is mine! If I say a word about the matter they will think me mad, and the very beggar lads will laugh at me; and if I fail to explain it a thousand mistakes will occur, like that of yesterday, when I was arrested for him. Well, I must wait for Grasso's arrival, and see what he says when I explain the affair to him." After anxiously looking out for his arrival during many hours in vain, he at length retired from his station to make room for other prisoners who wished to look out.

Now, it happened that a certain learned judge had that day been committed to prison for debt, who, though unacquainted with Grasso, observing his forlorn situation, sought to encourage him, saying, "Why, Matteo, you look as melancholy as if you were going to be executed tomorrow, and yet you are only confined for a trifling debt. Send for some of your friends or relatives, and try to accommodate matters so that you may shortly get out, instead of fretting yourself to death." Hearing these consolatory words, Grasso resolved to confide the source of his grievance to so kind an adviser, and, drawing him aside, he proceeded to relate the whole of his adventure.

The worthy judge, having heard him out, came at once to the conclusion that the poor man was either insane or the dupe of some trick. He therefore replied that he had read of many instances of persons being changed in this way. "Then," said Grasso, "pray tell me, in case I am become Matteo, who is Matteo now?" The judge replied, "Of course, he must have become Grasso." The latter rejoined, "Well, I should at least wish to see him in order to put this matter a little to rights."

Near the hour of vespers, Matteo's two brothers came to visit him. Soon after Grasso made his appearance at the grate, and the eldest of the brothers said, "Ah! Matteo, and has all the advice we have given you gone for nothing? How often we have warned you what would be the result, plunging every day deeper and deeper into debt, while your extravagance never admits of your paying anyone! Let me tell you, that were it not in consideration of our own honour and the anxiety of our mother, we would leave you here to pay the penalty of your sins in order that you might learn better for the future. As it is, we have determined to give you one more trial and pay the amount. Be ready, then, when we call for you about vesper-time, when there will be fewer people abroad; as it is not very pleasant to be seen here every day in consequence of your scandalous proceedings." Grasso replied with the utmost humility, promising to abandon the course he had pursued. . . .

Grasso then went back, and thus addressed the judge: "Well, this is strange indeed! Matteo's brothers have just been here to inform me they will come and release me in the evening. But," he continued, very much puzzled, "when they take me hence, where shall I go? Certainly not to my own house, because if Grasso lives there, what can I say? He will assuredly believe me mad; for I am sure he must be there, or my mother would have sent before this to say that I was missing, whereas she now thinks I am at home." The judge replied, "Then do not go there, but accompany your brothers (I mean those who called), wherever they please."

Now they resided at Santa Felicita, near the side of San Giorgio, and when they reached home they took Grasso into a room on the ground floor, and bade him to stay there quietly till supper-time. One of them next went to seek for a priest residing at Santa Felicita to whom he said that he came to consult him in confidence. "You know there are three brothers of us, one of whom is Matteo, who was yesterday arrested for debt. Such is the impression it appears to have made upon him, that he is gone almost beside himself; for he thinks he has become another person, a carver in ebony, of the name of Grasso, who has a shop at Santa Reparata; and there seems to be no way of getting it out of his head. We have taken him out of prison and brought him home, confining him to his chamber, lest he should proclaim his folly to the world. I am come to entreat that you will consent to accompany me back, and try whether there is any chance of restoring him."

The good priest replied that he would cheerfully attend him. On their arrival the priest was instantly introduced to our hero, who rose up on his entrance. "Good evening to you, Matteo," said the former. "Good evening, and good year to you also," said Grasso; "who are you looking for?" The priest answered: "Come, sit down by me, Matteo, and I will tell you what I am thinking of. You must know I have been much concerned to hear that you have been arrested, and have taken the thing so much to heart as almost to lose your wits. I have to entreat you will dismiss these whims altogether from your imagination, and attend to your business like other people. By so doing, you will please your brothers as well as me, besides doing yourself the greatest service in the world; for if you once let people suspect it, they will never give you credit for being in your senses again. Then rouse yourself; be a man, and scorn to indulge such absurdities any longer." Grasso, hearing the kind and encouraging way in which he spoke, declared that he should be glad to obey him as far as lay in his power, and that from that hour he would no longer imagine he was anyone else but Matteo. There was one thing, however, that he particularly desired, which was, to have an interview with the real Grasso, in order to set his mind quite at rest. "What then?" said the priest. "I see it is still running in your head; why do you wish to speak with Grasso? It would only be indulging and proclaiming your folly"; and he said so much that the poor man was content to abandon the idea.

While the priest had been engaged with our hero, came Philip Brunellesco, bringing with him a certain beverage, which he handed to one of the two brothers, saying, "Take care that you give him this to drink while you are at supper, for it will throw him into so sound a slumber, that you might beat him to a mummy during six hours before he would awake." Accordingly the brothers sat down to sup with our hero, and contrived to make him swallow the whole of the mixture without his perceiving it. After supper Grasso turned towards the fire, and the potion very soon began to operate in such a way that he was no longer able to keep his eyes open.

Philip, with three of his companions, then made his appearance, and had him laid upon a litter, with all his clothes, and carried to his own house. No one being within, his mother not having yet returned from the country, they laid him gently upon his bed. Next they took the keys of his shop, which they found hanging on a nail in the wall, and going straight to the place, they took all the instruments of his trade they could find and laid them in different positions. Planes, saws, hammers, rules, and hatchets, all were turned awry, and confused in such sort as if twenty demons had been puzzling their heads how to produce so much disorder. Then shutting up the shop again, they restored the keys to the same place and retired to their own houses to rest.

Grasso continued sunk in profound repose the whole night, nor awoke until after matins the next morning. Directly recognizing his old spot at Santa Reparata, he gazed through the window and felt the utmost astonishment at finding himself in his own house, considering where he lay down the preceding evening. "The Lord help me!" he exclaimed as he dressed himself, and took down the keys, proceeding with all haste to inspect his shop. "The Lord help me! what a sight is here!" he continued, as he beheld everything out of its place and foresaw the herculean task of readjusting his different articles in the manner he had left them. With this he seized his cloak, and closing his shop, began to walk about in great wrath, until he happened to be joined by one of his companions, formerly his fellow-labourer in the same trade of inlaid work under Maestro Pellegrino, a native of Terma. This youth had for some time been settled in Hungary, and managed his affairs so well that he had often returned to Florence in order to obtain assistance to execute the numerous commissions he received. The moment Grasso cast his eyes upon him, he resolved to avail himself of the offer. Hastening towards him, he said, "You have more than once asked me to go with you into Hungary, and I have hitherto refused; but now, from some particular circumstances, as well as a little dispute with my mother, I shall be very happy to return with you." The young man received this proposal with great joy, Grasso accordingly hired a horse and set out, having first left a letter for his mother, informing her of his departure and desiring her to take possession of his property in Florence. The undertakings of the two friends in Hungary prospered so well that they acquired considerable fortunes, and Grasso more than once returned to his native place, and diverted his friends by relating the mysterious adventure of his earlier years.

If the entire tale is not apocryphal, surely the anonymous author is hoaxing us here when he pretends that all the perpetrators of the jest were able to resist the impulse to tell Grasso how thoroughly he had been fooled.

THE LEGENDARY MIZNERS *

by Alva Johnston

The brothers Mizner—particularly Wilson—lived fantastic, adventurous lives, in which deception was almost as much a matter of course as dinner. These excerpts, from Alva Johnston's full-length chronicle, describe some of the feats of Jefferson Randolph "Soapy" Smith, Wilson Mizner's master, as well as samples of his pupil's achievements, including his leadership of the parade of con men during the Florida boom of the twenties.

Soapy Smith

Always looking for a new spot to establish a little monarchy, Soapy hurried north soon after the Klondike strike. Skagway was the ideal location for a new storybook kingdom. It was full of bewildered men with ready money concealed about their persons. Two tides of population—northbound gold-seekers and southbound gold-finders—were flowing through the bottleneck at Skagway, and Smith clipped them going and coming. When Mizner arrived in Skagway, Soapy had a saloon and gambling joint called Jeff's Place, which had become the seat of government. Mizner attracted attention almost immediately as one of Soapy's bright young men. Mizner admired Soapy's imagination and mental rapidity. Jefferson Randolph Smith certainly did have a gift for figuring out how to make any situation pay dividends. Most of the newcomers in Skagway wanted to get in touch with the home folks, so Soapy had a large sign saying "Telegraph Office" painted, and hung it on a log cabin. He charged five dollars for a telegram to any place. Within two or three hours, a five-dollar collect reply was always delivered to the sender. What the newcomers didn't know was that there was no telegraph line out of Skagway. Nearly every stranger was in dire need of information, so Soapy hung a sign saying "Information Office" on another cabin. His men imparted much

* From articles originally published in *The New Yorker*.

197

information and they also acquired much information. The burglars
and holdup men of Skagway became famous for clairvoyance in sens-
ing where money was hidden. The San Francisco papers reported
that there had been twelve holdups in Skagway in one night. James
Wickersham, Alaska historian and federal judge, wrote that Soapy's
gang had been unequalled anywhere since the palmy days of Virginia
City, forty years earlier.

One of Mizner's stories throws light on Soapy's business methods.
Skagway had a young clergyman who thundered against Soapy's rule.
His church was a tent and he needed a log tabernacle for the winter.
The tradition of the West was that bad men always have a soft spot
in their hearts for the church, and the clergyman went to Soapy
with his project. Mizner said that Soapy instantly put his name down
for a thousand dollars and handed over that amount in gold. With
Soapy's prestige behind him, the young cleric collected thirty-six thousand dollars in one day. Unfortunately, he was held up that night
and robbed of the entire amount. Here Mizner paused in his tale, and
then added, "Thirty-six for one is pretty good odds."

Assorted Coups

Wilson Mizner earned considerable sums by winning ship's pools
with enlightened guesses as to the distance that would be covered by
the ship in each twenty-four-hour period. Because of the generally
high calibre of ships' officers, the steamship pool is usually regarded
as an unfixable form of gambling, but . . . one transatlantic steward
with a private pipeline to the bridge of his ship retired a millionaire
merely by selling inside tips on whether an even or odd number of
miles would be covered in a given day, much of the betting being on
"odd or even." The gifted steward never purported to foresee the total
mileage on a given day, but Mizner and two confederates drew the
lucky number three times in succession. It all started with a ship's
officer who was practically a clotheshorse for medals. His chest, as
Mizner described it, was ablaze with chafing dishes. Mizner couldn't
believe that an honest heart beat beneath a whole showcaseful of
jewelry. Standing outside the cabin of the glittering officer, Mizner
mentioned to a confederate the number he had drawn in the pool for
the next twenty-four hours, and added in a loud voice, "You know
what I would do to show my gratitude if I won? I'd stick a thousand
dollars under the right officer's pillow." Somehow or other, the day's
run came out exactly right for Mizner, and a thousand dollars of his

winnings turned up under the medal collector's pillow. There were two more conversations outside the cabin and two more miraculous strokes of luck for Mizner and his confederate. The fourth time they approached the cabin, however, a hoarse voice growled through the door, "Get out of here, you bastards. I'm four hundred miles off my course now."

He won a roll of bills at Atlantic City once by a game that was halfway between a lucrative practical joke and a crooked gamble. He and some other sports were lounging along the boardwalk betting on anything in which they could find an element of chance, such as which of two sunbathers would be the first to go into the water or which of two swimmers would be the first to come out of it. One of the party noticed a pair of gigantic feet sticking out of a window on the first floor of a boardwalk hotel. The owner of the feet was out of sight, apparently lying back in a chair. Mizner and his friends began to guess how tall the man was, from the evidence of his feet. Finally, they backed their guesses with money. Most of the bettors placed the man's height at well over six feet. Mizner made the lowest estimate. With a curious disregard of the principles of human symmetry, he guessed five feet one. When the money was up, they called on the man in the hotel room. He was a dwarf, four feet six inches tall, with No. 11 shoes. Mizner had brought him from New York and planted him there, figuring he could probably win a few bets on the man's paradoxical physique.

Men who were in Wilson's confidence tell of the wide range of devices by which he raised money. A rich young man of Seattle, on a visit to New York, complained to Mizner of a hangover and a complete inability to remember the events of the preceding night. Mizner hopped over to confer with the maître d'hôtel of a reigning lobster palace, concocted an itemized bill for nearly two thousand dollars, to be split two ways, and had it collected from the Westerner, who was informed that during the period about which his mind was a blank he had thrown one of the biggest and wildest parties of the season. Once, on a visit to a prosperous underworld establishment, Mizner faked the symptoms of scarlet fever. A confederate, masquerading as a physician, notified the proprietress that he would have to quarantine the place for a month. He settled, however, for a thousand dollars. On one occasion, Mizner sold a selling-plater for ten times its value by the simple device of moving back the six-furlong post in an early-morning workout, thereby shortening the course so that a stopwatch indicated the horse had broken the six-furlong record.

He was twenty-five or twenty-six when he executed one of the most profitable of his coups. A close pal of his was a member of a San Francisco family that had gained enormous wealth in Nevada silver mines. Mizner took the young scion of the Comstock Lode to New Orleans; their mission was to clean out a poolroom with the help of inside racing information. What the young silver millionaire didn't know was that the poolroom, with its entire personnel, customers and all, had been organized by Mizner solely for the purpose of getting a slice of the silver millions. Mizner's net profit at the expense of his bosom friend was more than $100,000, and in those simple days it lasted him more than a year. Mizner never had the slightest compunction about this informal method of redistributing the wealth. On their return to San Francisco, the young silver millionaire became suspicious and accused Mizner of fraud. Mizner gave him a beating, after which they became comrades again.

EL CAMINO REAL

Addison and Wilson Mizner built the broadest highway in the world during the Florida boom of the early twenties. This was El Camino Real, or the King's Highway, which led to the Mizner principality of Boca Raton, the most snobbish of all the Florida real estate subdivisions. El Camino Real was two hundred and nineteen feet wide and had twenty traffic lanes, or enough to deliver several hundred thousand people a day to the most exclusive spot on earth. Harry Reichenbach, the highest-paid publicity man on earth, exhausted the national bank of superlatives in describing the widest road on the planet. He found that the Mizner highway took first place in seven or eight respects among the world's arteries of traffic. It was, for example, the most extravagantly landscaped. The parks and gardens and promenades of El Camino Real were patterned after those of Avenida Beira Mar, which stretches around Botafogo Bay, in Rio de Janeiro, but the Mizner boulevard was broader and better. One of the novelties of El Camino Real was indirect illumination. Drawing on his experience as a Broadway playwright, Wilson Mizner lit the road from the wings, using concealed lights in the curbs in place of lampposts. El Camino Real was waterscaped as well as landscaped. Down the middle ran the Grand Canal of Venice, with Rialtos, ornamental landings, and electrically driven gondolas. These romantic vehicles were actually made in Venice. The great Florida boom had touched off many minor booms, one of them being a burst of activity in gondola-making circles on the Adriatic. At a meeting of the Boca Raton directors, Wilson Mizner, a fanatical perfectionist, fought for an appropriation to import Venetian gondoliers, in costume, to sing and play on guitars. An economy-minded director objected that a genuine gondolier was superfluous in a gondola that had batteries and a propeller. He argued also that the gondolier might cause accidents by poling it in one direction while the man at the wheel tried to steer in another. "We'll have him use a fake oar," said Wilson. "Then the son of a bitch can't do any harm."

El Camino Real had certain defects. Addison had set his heart on having beautiful blue water in the Grand Canal, but it persisted in being muddy. The architect was furious. No man was ever so exasperated with a body of water since Xerxes scourged the Hellespont. Addison kept scores of workmen busy cleaning out mud and silt, but more kept seeping in. The harder they tried to make the canal blue, the muddier it got. The trouble was that, the canal being at sea level, the tides kept bringing soil in. Addison was fighting the Atlantic Ocean, and he was as badly overmatched as the Mrs. Partington who fought a tidal wave with a mop. Another trouble was that automobiles kept diving into the canal. But the chief defect of the commodious thoroughfare was its length. While it was the widest road in the world, it was also the shortest. The great boulevard ran from the Dixie Highway to Lake Boca Raton, a distance of slightly less than half a mile. Also, whereas El Camino Real was twenty lanes wide on the east side of the Dixie Highway, it was hardly two lanes wide on the west. All the world-beating effects disappeared on the west side, El Camino Real becoming a mere trail in the sand. Two cars could barely pass without becoming entangled in the branches of the scrub pines on either side. In boom maps and blueprints, El Camino Real rolled its twenty traffic lanes past a series of colossal nonexistent cities. In real life, it died away in brambles and swamps.

El Camino Real was not of much use as an artery of traffic, but it had a vast power of suggestion. The two million lot-buyers in Florida were all seeking clues to the subdivision that had the most sensational future. El Camino Real was a startling piece of evidence. Just as a scientist can reconstruct dinosaurs from one giant fragment of bone, so the Florida sucker was able to forecast the tremendous future of

Boca Raton from the giant fragment of road. London had no twenty-lane highway; Paris, Rome, New York, and Chicago had no twenty-lane highways. As investors studied the implications of El Camino Real, the corner lots in Boca Raton jumped in value from a few hundred dollars to a hundred thousand dollars. When enthusiasm was running wild, Wilson Mizner offered fifty thousand dollars for a choice Boca Raton lot owned by Lytle Hull, the well-known society man. Hull was insulted. He wouldn't talk to Wilson for two weeks. He hung on to the lot until after the Florida bubble had exploded, and then found that it was worth about two hundred dollars by the new scale of prices.

"Proposed"

Almost anything—a nearby city, a new hotel, a civic center, a mountain, a bay, a lake, or an ocean—became a talking point for a development. A resourceful promoter could make almost anything do for a landmark. Charles Ort, a promoter known as the King of the Keys, was sold a tract on Key Largo by a realtor who didn't mention that it had been a quarry and was full of deep holes. Ort looked ruefully at the hollows and chasms, but then snapped his fingers and danced wildly about, shouting, "Sunken Gardens! Sunken Gardens!" He doubled the price of the lots with the deepest abysses. The promoters of Wyldewood Park, near Fort Lauderdale, had difficulty finding a talking point to wrap their subdivision around. There were no startling geographical features, no skyscrapers, coliseums, or campaniles. But there was an interesting tree—a large banyan, which had dropped branches into the ground to become new roots, until the tree was beginning to look like a small forest. A big sign, "$2,000,000 Tree," was hung on it, and it became the logical argument for buying homesites in Wyldewood, the claim being made that a banyan-crazy Yankee had once offered two million dollars for the tree if it could be moved to his home up north. . . .

Promoters who couldn't find even a tree or a quarry to rave about took refuge in the word "proposed." A newspaper advertisement or a sign was the only immediate expense required for a "proposed" improvement. Kenneth Roberts has told of a group of capitalists who hired a painter to do a sign reading, "A Million-Dollar Hotel Will Be Erected Here," but the capitalists couldn't raise the eighteen dollars to pay for the sign, so the painter sold it to another group of capitalists. . . . The word "proposed" was considered important enough to carry whole cities on its coattails in the last stages of the bubble. Billions and billions of dollars' worth of "proposed" architectural and engineering feats were placed before the investor. "All of these here lots," said Will Rogers, plugging for his own imaginary world capital, "are by our Proposed Ocean." The humorist's Proposed Ocean was outdone by reality.

The ocean was not only proposed, it was built into dozens of subdivisions. "The sea is actually being brought back into the heart of the pine woods," wrote Rex Beach in "The Miracle of Coral Gables." Coral Gables, which is several miles inland, advertised "Forty Miles of Waterfront," but the forty miles bordered on canals cut through to the ocean. The idea of working a synthetic coastline into the subdivisions came from the brain of a resourceful realtor named C. G. Rodes. He was shaking his head mournfully over an unlovely drainage ditch when an idea came to him. "The Grand Canal of Venice!" he exclaimed. He beautified the drainage ditch, added a network of ditches to it, and gave the name of Venice to the subdivision, which is on the Gulf Coast of Florida. The idea of gliding along on canals had a mysterious appeal to railroad men, and the Brotherhood of Locomotive Engineers threw away more than ten million dollars on the Florida Venice. After Rodes made his historic discovery, nearly every slough and open sewer in Florida became a romantic piece of water. Islands were popular with the suckers, and the promoters found that, instead of paying millions to build islands by pumping sand, they could produce cheap ones by digging ditches around low-lying properties. The banks of any ditch that held a few gallons of brine became "waterfront" or "oceanfront" property, and the postal authorities, no matter how fervently they tried to prevent fraudulent advertising from going through the mails, couldn't do anything about it. Some buyers of ocean frontage were astonished to learn that the Atlantic was hardly big enough for a duck to turn around in. Abandoned canals, choked with vegetation and lined by decaying little Rialtos, are still to be found in the old boom country.

Ben Hecht and Fellow-Buccaneers

The oddest of the new industries was digging for doubloons, moidores, louis d'ors, pieces of eight, and just plain bars of bullion. Somebody had dreamed of buried treasure, and the state was swept with an epidemic of "pirate gold." . . . The Mizners claimed that their Boca Raton was the ancient headquarters of Captain Teach, or

Blackbeard, a formidable old scourge who was credited with having mastered the difficult art of mounting lighted candles in his beard to scare coastal towns at night. Harry Reichenbach and Wilson Mizner buried some doubloons and some fake relics of Blackbeard in Boca Raton Inlet, and they were disinterred amid wild excitement. The Mizners had no monopoly on buried treasure. A big haul of ancient Mexican money was announced at Grassy Key. A Portuguese fisherman broke into print with a report that he had fished up near Miami an iron chest weighing a couple of hundred pounds, but the fishing line had broken and he could never find the old chest again. Captain Kidd was dragged in to boost the new industry. So were Sir Henry Morgan, the Laffite brothers, Black Caesar, Gasparilla, and Sir Francis Drake. The greatest center of pirate legend was Key Largo. Seventeen galleons with cash and jewels were sunk off Key Largo in one sentence by one Florida writer.

National interest was excited in the finds of pirate gold in the Key Largo City subdivision of Charles Ort, one of the most brilliant shooting stars of the boom. Ort, who arrived broke in Miami when the boom was already approaching a climax, took options on a city dump. Covering the ashes, tin cans, broken bottles, old kitchen sinks, and rusty bedsprings with blazing tropical flowers, he sold the enchanted oasis for millions and then poured his wealth into Key Largo City, a combination of Tahiti and Newport. No ordinary press agent was good enough for Ort. He hired the famous novelist Ben Hecht and the Broadway author J. P. McEvoy to handle his public relations. Their imagination was promptly captured by pirate gold when two ancient crocks filled with doubloons were dug up in the sands of Key Largo. Hecht telegraphed accounts of the discovery to hundreds of newspapers. Herbert Bayard Swope, of the New York *World*, who won the Pulitzer Prize for his reporting of the First World War, wired that he planned to hurry down to chronicle the amazing discovery himself, but he demanded Hecht's guarantee that the thing was on the level, and his telegram was ignored. Hundreds of people poured into Key Largo to dig for treasure. The two crocks of doubloons had been dug up by a fisherman named Captain Chester, and Hecht then spent a week helping the Captain find adequate words to describe his discovery to newspaper reporters. The Captain became the worst victim of the pirate fever. Calling in his thirteen grandchildren, he kept them digging for weeks after the other treasure hunters had departed.

TWO SHORT TAKES FROM HOLLYWOOD

THE NEXT NOEL COWARD

by Joseph McCarthy

Hollywood is always well stocked with impostors. Artfully helped by Charles MacArthur, the playwright, one of them managed to secure a job as a screen writer at $1,500 a week. He held it for more than a year. "If he'd followed my instructions more carefully, he would have been able to land two thousand a week," MacArthur says. "And if he hadn't been so greedy, he'd still be on the studio pay roll." The principal in the case was a young Englishman with no literary background, and no writing ability. "He couldn't even write a check," MacArthur recalls. MacArthur was a screen writer himself at the time, but he was spending more hours playing tennis than devising scenarios. The young Englishman also frequented the tennis courts, and they began to meet for singles in the early morning. The Englishman, whom we shall call Basil, had a job at an oil company, and he was always worrying about being late for work. So he developed a habit of glancing frequently at his wrist watch during a match. This disconcerted MacArthur.

"I was willing to do anything to stop that business of his looking at his watch," MacArthur says. "It got me nervous, and it threw me off my game. I asked him how much he made at the oil company. He said sixty-five a week. I told him if he'd promise to quit looking at his watch while we played tennis, I'd get him a job as a writer at my studio for two thousand a week."

MacArthur began to bring Basil along to story conferences at the studio. The movie producers eyed the stranger curiously, and finally asked MacArthur who he was. "Brilliant young British dramatist," MacArthur confided. "The next Noel Coward. Just out here for a rest and not interested in working for pictures. I wouldn't make a move on a story line unless I asked his advice." Finally the head of the studio asked MacArthur if Basil could be hired. "Not a chance,"

MacArthur said. Behind MacArthur's back, a meeting was arranged with Basil. Disregarding the coaching MacArthur had given him, Basil gave in when the bidding came up to $1,500 a week, instead of holding out for $2,000.

Basil held his position as a screen writer by following the line of MacArthur strategy. When he was given a story to work on, he sent it back untouched, saying simply that it was not his type. Eventually, the studio sent him to the frozen wastes of northern Canada to look into the possibilities of a picture about the Hudson's Bay Company. "Even in Hollywood he had never spent a dime," MacArthur says. "Up there in the Arctic, still drawing fifteen hundred a week, he was able to save a fortune. He came back feeling very cocky." But it turned out that Basil, either through miserliness or love of security, had never resigned from his sixty-five-dollar-a-week job with the oil company. There was a mix-up about his Social Security deductions, the studio learned of his other job, and all was lost.

JOHN BARRYMORE HYDE

by Gene Fowler

In September, 1927, Dolores' father obtained an uncontested divorce. The papers had been filed in June of that year, charging incompatability. Dolores Costello now leased a new home for her mother, Helene, and herself at No. 1388 Schuyler Road, Beverly Hills. Barrymore began to visit Dolores more frequently than when her father had been on the premises. Mr. Costello had not regarded Jack as the village paragon.

The housekeeping activities of the Costellos in their new and splendid abode revived in Jack a longing for a place to live other than in a hotel. One morning in September he telephoned Hotchener: "Clementine spoke to me in my dreams last night. She wants a home in the country, where she can play."

Jack's manager inquired: "Is it to be a bachelor's house or a—?"

Barrymore interrupted him: "A house for two, meaning Clementine and myself, of course. The imp has persuaded me that a reconnaissance in Beverly Hills is indicated. All the swells live there. Why should Clementine reside in a lower social environment?"

Manager Hotchener, upon calling at Jack's hotel, suggested that property owners might "raise the price" when it became known that Barrymore was house hunting.

"We'll fix that," the actor said.

Jack turned, while speaking, to open a chest of drawers. Hotchener naturally thought that he was looking for a bottle. The manager was hardly prepared for what followed. Barrymore wheeled about suddenly, to present a face of horrible contours. Fangs protruded from his lips. Talon-like nails curled from his fingers. He was wearing part of the make-up once used by him in *Dr. Jekyll and Mr. Hyde.*

After Hotchener's pulse again became normal, Jack drew on a wig and a battered hat. "I don't think the real estate harpies will mistake Mr. Hyde for a man of means," he said.

They set out among the hills north of Beverly. Clementine, after becoming somewhat accustomed to Mr. Hyde's demoniacal phiz, went along.

Jack now remembered having visited a Spanish type dwelling, a hilltop home belonging to King Vidor, the Hollywood director. He had seen a "For Sale" sign there. Jack didn't remember the address. They cruised among the hills for more than two hours. Jack finally located the Vidor house on a private drive off Tower Road.

"That's the place," he said. "Buy it instantly!"

Hotchener decided against stopping to inspect the estate at close range. As Mr. Hyde, the actor might invite a shot from the house. Barrymore agreed to crouch low in the car while his manager consulted the agent on the premises, some thirty yards from the road. The prospective buyer and the broker, after a tour of inspection, stood in the Spanish garden to "talk terms." The agent for the owner placed a "fancy price" on the property, almost $60,000.

The agent caught a glimpse of the crouching Mr. Hyde. The hat and wig and one malevolent eye could be seen above the door-level of the automobile. The broker squinted apprehensively.

"A friend," Hotchener explained. The manager touched his forehead momentarily. "A somewhat peculiar fellow. You see, I take care of him."

The agent nodded a little dubiously, then began to explain why such a handsome price had been assigned to the property. "This beautiful place has many advantages. Large acreage, permitting no end of improvements . . ."

"No, no!" Hotchener interrupted. "We don't wish to make any improvements. We lead simple lives."

The agent removed a thousand dollars from the asking-price. Clementine now crawled outside Barrymore's car. She was getting mixed up with her leash. Her jabberings caught the ear of the broker. At this distance he could not be sure whether or not he saw long claws on the hand that reached over the side of the car to seize the little monkey.

Hotchener again explained, nodding toward the automobile, "Have to humor him with pets."

"I see," the agent said worriedly, then returned to his salesmanship. "Think of the beauties of this location. You have an excellent view of the sea, the mountains. At night, millions of lights of Los Angeles twinkling like a jewelry store. You can have, as you see, an extensive tennis court."

"We don't play tennis."

"But," and the agent took another thousand dollars from the price, "that space easily can be turned into a swimming pool."

"Unfortunately, we don't swim."

"Well," and the agent removed a third thousand dollars, "you can have extensive walks, gardens, fountains, even an orchard."

"We have been told," said Hotchener, "that unless one expends a great deal of money on it this is not a favorable district for citrus culture. Also, to bring trees and other supplies up this steep hill and from such a distance would be rather expensive." He nodded toward the automobile, where Mr. Hyde's unwholesome grin now could be seen even at thirty yards. "You see, we entertain *very* seldom. Except for the physicians."

The grimace of Mr. Hyde may have unsettled the agent's judgment. At any rate he now took off three thousand dollars at one slice.

"We do not feel justified," Hotchener told him, "in investing such a great sum. You have been very kind. Good day."

Mr. Hyde could be seen kissing the monkey. "Wait! the agent said. "How about $52,000?"

The purchaser proposed to pay $50,000, no more. The agent cast another glance toward Mr. Hyde, then surrendered. A deposit was given, and the deal closed.

Several days afterward Jack visited his new home. King Vidor now found out that Barrymore had been the real purchaser of the property. Vidor took the matter good-naturedly, but admitted that Barrymore had saved himself at least $10,000 by wearing Mr. Hyde's fangs, talons, and wig.

PHANTOM FAME

by Harry Reichenbach with David Freedman

If any one individual can be called the Father of Ballyhoo, it is the late Harry Reichenbach, the publicity wizard who once over-turned the government of a South American country in a week by devising a provocative coupon-ad that sent the population's blood-pressure soaring. Although Reichenbach's feats of deception were performed for gain—he was paid astronomical fees—they have a delightful, prankish quality that justifies including them with other hoaxes perpetrated for the sheer fun of it.

September Morn

I took a small, one-room office in the Putnam Building and had the sign-man paint in gold letters on the door—"Harry Reichenbach— Publicity"—and nobody came. I was always used to crowds, even in villages, and now in a city of millions I was all alone. I spent much time getting about, becoming acquainted, picking up friends, but no business. I had to give up my room, but I wouldn't give up my office.

I applied for work at a small art shop that had printed a lithograph of a nude girl standing in a quiet pool. The picture sold at ten cents apiece but nobody would buy it. I could earn my month's rent if I had an idea for disposing of the two thousand copies in stock. It occurred to me to introduce the immodest young maiden to Anthony Comstock, head of the Anti-Vice Society and arch-angel of virtue. At first he refused to jump at the opportunity to be shocked. I tele-phoned him several times, protesting against a large display of the picture which I myself had installed in the window of the art shop. Then I arranged for other people to protest and at last I visited him personally. "This picture is an outrage!" I cried. "It's undermining the morals of our city's youth!"

When we arrived in front of the store window, a group of youngsters I had hired especially for this performance at fifty cents apiece, stood pointing at the picture, uttering expressions of unholy glee and making grimaces too sophisticated for their years. Comstock swallowed the scene and almost choked. "Remove that picture!" he fumed, and when the shopkeeper refused, the Anti-Vice Society appealed to the courts. This brought the picture into the newspapers and into fame. Overnight, the lithograph that had been rejected as a brewer's calendar, became a vital national issue. Songs were written about it, actors wise-cracked about it, reformers denounced it, and seven million men and women bought copies of it at a dollar apiece, framed it and hung it on the walls of their homes. The name of the picture was "September Morn." There was no more immorality or suggestiveness to it than sister's photograph as a baby in the family album.

"The Virgin of Stamboul"

In 1919, Universal produced *The Virgin of Stamboul*, a costume picture starring Priscilla Dean. It was the entirely original story of a Turkish maiden abducted by a villain, Wallace Beery, and rescued by a hero, Wheeler Oakman, who off the screen was Miss Dean's husband. Costume pictures at the time had become a serious menace to the box-office and Universal feared that this latest dress parade would never bring back even the cost of the celluloid.

Preparations for the stunt were almost as elaborate as the production of the picture. I befriended an Assyrian, Khalie Ossmun, who promised to dig up eight Turks and he did. They looked as if he had dug them out of sewers. Two of them were ex-dishwashers, one was a pastry cook, another a porter and two sold homemade lemonade out of huge brass tureens strapped to their backs like papooses. The seventh was a fierce-looking Mussulman with an ugly scar that almost cut his face in two, and the eighth was a white-haired old Turk who kept mumbling that his brother was a "pasha."

My Assyrian friend Khalie being the most intelligent and personable, I appointed him chief Sheik Ali Ben Mohamed, ruler of this motley band. The knife-scarred Turk whom we called "Goom" became lord high aide-de-camp and the white-haired old mumbler I turned into the Grand Caliph Shafkrat. The pastry cook became his lordship, the Effendi Houssein, the two ex-dishwashers acquired the titles of Generals Hamedan and Rafkhat respectively and the lemonade pedlars became the grand eunuchs of the Sheik's harem.

A theatrical costumer dressed them in lavish splendor from pompons to aigrets and from sea-green trousers to gold-crescented turbans. The next think was to teach the Turks the manners and customs of their native land. I persuaded a friend of mine, Alexander Brown, who had spent many years in Constantinople as general representative of the American Licorice Company, to show them how to act with true Turkish elegance. For an entire week he drilled them in handling table service. He taught them how to wear their decorations, how to salaam, and how the eunuchs were to taste all food before their masters would take the chance. Another week passed rehearsing the Sheik on the story he would have to tell newspapermen.

We were ready to make our arrival into New York from Turkey. I had my secretary telephone the Hotel Majestic and say, "Montreal is calling." I spoke to the hotel manager, Jack Heath, in a tortured dialect explaining very dimly that, "We are the Turkish mission which comes to your country on a very secret importance. Please reserve for us the best rooms of the suite and protect us please from the newspaper reporting!" Two days later our royal party arrived at the Majestic.

At four o'clock that afternoon the Grandees of the Porte made their first public appearance in full regalia, going to the hotel tea-room in state according to all the rules of Turkish royalty as laid down by the American Licorice Company's manager. Ossmun and Sheik acted as if cameras were turning in all corners.

O. O. McIntyre, the Majestic's press agent, tipped off the newspapers reticently as if they were being let into a secret of international significance. That night the royal suite was a reporters' convention. The next morning the newspapers throughout the country and throughout the world gave many thousands of columns detailing the story of Sheik Ali Ben Mohamed's strange and mysterious mission in America. The hired costumes received the most minute and painstaking description in the press. The New York *Tribune* pictured my Chatham Square Assyrian as follows:

"There was the Sheik Ben Mohamed of Hedjaz, which all students of the League of Nations know to be a newly formed kingdom of Arabia, the subjects of which bear no love for the Turkish Empire, from which it was dismembered.

"A burnous of maroon, margined with a wide band of yellow silk and piped with peagreen, partially hid more gorgeous garments of

the Arab nobleman. His fez lent shape to the white folds of linen
that draped over it and swathed about his neck. The linen was bound
closely about his head by a turban of orange pattern that revealed
the Sheik as a holy man."

Even the Prince of Wales's latest clothes were never more faithfully
reported than these gaudy remnants of a Shubert flop. Then Khalie
Ossmun recited the little speech we had rehearsed.

"Gentlemen, I come to this country, which to my desert-trained
eyes is like the heaven promised in the Koran, to seek the betrothed
of my younger brother. She is Sari, so beautiful that in all Turkey
there was none like her. She was known as the Virgin of Stamboul."

Then he proceeded to give a complete summary of the nine-reel
thriller starring Priscilla Dean.

"Her father was very rich," murmured the Sheik, raising a weary
hand to shield his piercing black eyes. "Her mother too was of royal
blood. Sari had an English governess. The American soldiers came
to Stamboul. They saw Sari. One of them she saw. They spoke together, she proud of her few words of English. Then she disappeared.
That same day the American transport sailed for this country. For
three months we searched Turkey. Sari's mother died of grief. Then
her father. We had established that she was not dead. We knew all
too surely that it was a love affair that had caused the Virgin of Stamboul to disappear."

All this the reporters copied verbatim. Then the Sheik told them
that the Burns and Val O'Farrell Detective Agencies had been retained to aid in the world-wide search. He made them print an offer
of ten thousand dollars reward for information leading to Sari's discovery. He told them that she was heiress to about a hundred million.

Up to this point the Sheik had been doing splendidly. But that
lynx-eyed newspaperman, Boyden Sparkes, detected beneath the
majesty of the Sheik's attire the starched cuffs of a shirt, a bit soiled,
that might have been made in Troy, New York. The starched cuffs
bothered Sparkes. He asked the Turkish lord whether he knew any
Americans and Ossmun promptly answered, "I know your Mr. Henry
Morgenthau very well. I am to have dinner with him." I had anticipated that question and the day before had learned from Morgenthau's secretary that he would be away for the week-end.

When the interview ended the reporters dashed to the nearest
telephones to report the greatest romantic news scoop in years. Only

Boyden Sparkes seemed worried. We heard him call up Morgenthau. To my amazement Morgenthau was in. I vanished.

The next day Sparkes wrote just as elaborate and full an account of his story as all the others, but near the end he added, "Mr. Morgenthau said Sheik Ben Mohamed was a blasted liar, a fake. But that won't interfere with the early release of that thrilling picture, *The Virgin of Stamboul.*"

In view of Morgenthau's statement it seemed that the publicity stunt was killed. But it wasn't. There was that quality of fascination about the incident that made it almost better than truth.

A few days later when Sari was found by Val O'Farrell in a rooming-house on Kenmare Street, the newspapers again covered the story. The reporters swarmed into the royal suite at the Majestic and were treated to a stirring Oriental scene. Through an open door they saw a young hysterical girl tossing in a bed surrounded by the Sheik and five kneeling Turks, while a physician stood near her constantly jabbing hypodermics into the mattress as a nurse anxiously made notes on a chart. The Sheik, deeply touched and distracted, found time however to come out and tell the reporters that Sari had been saved and that the party would sail Saturday on the White Star Line. In everybody's presence he handed ten one-thousand-dollar bills to Val O'Farrell who returned them later on when nobody was around. The Sheik thanked the American press for its co-operation and said that it was no wonder, judging by its press, that the American people were the most enlightened in the world.

The press reported every detail faithfully to the end and *The Virgin of Stamboul* scored a record at the box-office.

Francis X. Bushman and the 2,000 Pennies

The first time I brought Francis X. Bushman to New York to sign a contract with Metro, he had been receiving only $250 a week in Chicago. I wanted to raise his salary to a commanding figure. When we got off at Grand Central I had my coat pockets loaded with two thousand pennies. As Bushman and I walked along Forty-second Street toward the Metro office I dropped handfuls of pennies in our line of march. At first children followed us to pick up the coins, then grown-ups, then everybody grew curious and joined in the parade. By the time we reached Metro, the streets were black with milling crowds, and the police unable to disperse them.

When the officers of Metro looked out of the window they judged Bushman's popularity by the vast throngs that had followed us and he received a thousand dollars a week without any argument. Metro wouldn't think of letting him out of the office before he signed the contract. The fact was not a living soul in the entire mob knew Bushman from Adam then. But they had a natural flair for pennies.

IV

IN THE LINE OF DUTY

THE MERRY PRANKS OF KANONIER SCHMIDT

by Joseph Wechsberg

Blind respect for a uniform, any kind of uniform, is a typical German national trait. But during the Nazi regime there was at least one man who turned the tables on the Nazis and used a uniform to make fun of the Gestapo, the Nazi Party, and the Wehrmacht. His name is Elfried Schmidt, and he is a streetcar conductor in Vienna, Austria. When I was in Vienna recently I heard of Schmidt's incredible experience and called at the modest cold-water flat where he lives with his wife and three children.

A thin, sad-looking man with a boyish face and gentle eyes, Schmidt speaks in a cautious voice, as if he were forever afraid of people. He has an ineradicable air of what he is—a streetcar conductor—and he knows it. Yet this mild and humble Austrian perpetrated a truly fantastic hoax. Using Hitler's own technique—the bigger the lie, the better its chance of being believed—he succeeded in making his victims so ridiculous that when he was finally caught, the authorities' only concern was to hush the story up.

The story begins in 1938 in a village some twenty miles from Vienna that shall be called Rampersdorf. His uncle, Professor Hinner, a noted botanist, was the parish priest of Rampersdorf. Elfried Schmidt and his mother lived at the church house. It was a few months after the Anschluss and the local Nazis were in an exuberant mood. Denunciation and persecution flourished. If you didn't like a man's looks or wanted his shop, all you had to do was denounce him to the Gestapo as an "enemy of the people." The Gestapo took care of the rest. The Nazis hated the village priest, and they didn't like Schmidt's mother, either, who was rumored to have helped refugees across the nearby Hungarian border.

Schmidt, himself an outspoken anti-Nazi, was nineteen years old, working on and off as a locksmith's apprentice. There had been no money to send him to the Technical University in Vienna so that he could become an engineer but he knew a lot more than the average locksmith apprentice. For years he had haunted the streetcar terminals in Vienna studying cars, machines, tracks, switches. A skilled draftsman, he liked to invent things, and in the hall of his uncle's house hung a large technical blueprint of an electric Diesel rail-car he had drawn. Elsa, the girl whom Schmidt hoped to marry some day, often stared at the blueprint and exclaimed, "What a pity, Elfried, that you didn't become an engineer!"

"I guess it was Elsa's remarks that started me off," Schmidt said to me, looking thoughtfully out the window. "Her remarks and my uncle's precarious position. There were rumors that the Nazis were going to send him to a concentration camp. He wouldn't be the first priest to go. I used to sit up nights wondering how I could help him. All kinds of wild ideas occurred to me. It had to be something to make the Gestapo *afraid* of me. But what? I couldn't very well tell them that I had been received by Hitler. Or could I? The more I thought of the crazy scheme, the better I liked it. Suppose I had made an important invention which had come to the ears of important Nazis? Why, I might even be made an engineer—not an ordinary engineer, but a sort of National Socialist engineer who had been decorated by Hitler in person."

The next day Schmidt went to Vienna, carrying with him the blueprint of the Diesel rail-car. He returned a few days later with a brief case containing several rubber stamps and a number of rather astonishing letters. In the first letter, of which there was only the carbon, Schmidt asked the German State Railroad "to consider the enclosed technical drawing." The second letter, from the German State Railroad, informed Schmidt that the drawing had been forwarded with a recommendation to the Transport Ministry in Berlin. The third letter, again from the State Railroad, announced that the blueprint had met with assent in Berlin. "Such gifted young people as you can be sponsored only by our National Socialist regime," the letter said. A final letter from the German State Railroad informed Schmidt that a large factory had been ordered to produce his new

Diesel rail-car, and offered Schmidt a job that would "correspond to your exceptional talents."

"I wrote those letters in Vienna," Schmidt told me. "In our Catholic Youth Organization we'd had correspondence with the Traffic Ministry and used a rubber stamp for the address, *An das Reichsverkehrsministerium, Abwicklungstelle Österreich.* I cut off the words 'An das —to the' and used the rest as letterhead. With this letterhead it wasn't difficult to order rubber stamps, of the State Railroad and of the Technical University. The Nazis were great believers in the 'round stamp,' containing the swastika and eagle, so I ordered one of these from a stamp maker who didn't know me. Everything had to have an air of unchallengeable authenticity."

Back home Schmidt marked his blueprint with several official stamps saying INCOMING, CONSIDERED, and APPROVED, added some illegible signatures, and put it back on the wall. That same afternoon he learned from a friend that two Gestapo men had arrived in the village and that his uncle might be arrested at any moment. Something had to be done right away. The blueprint and the few letters were not sufficient to impress the Gestapo.

Schmidt promptly sat down at his typewriter and wrote a letter in which the University of Berlin informed Elfried Schmidt that he had been awarded by the Führer the title *Ingenieur Honoris Causa.* Herr Engineer Schmidt was ordered to present himself on August 25 at 11 A.M. at the Reich Chancellery in Berlin to be received by the Führer.

"I showed the letter to my mother," Schmidt said to me, "telling her I'd received it in Vienna. I didn't dare look her in the eye, but she was too worried about my uncle to notice anything. Only my uncle, calm as ever, read the letter carefully and gave me a funny look. An hour later the whole village knew of the great honor that had been bestowed upon me. And the two Gestapo men never showed up."

On August 24, Schmidt left for Berlin where he spent a few days sight-seeing and writing postcards home about his visit with the Führer. He took a good look at the Chancellery, from the outside, and also bought a folder with a sketchy description of Hitler's office. Back in Vienna, it occurred to him that he should have a diploma. So he bought a piece of cardboard decorated with a Virgin holding a laurel wreath, surrounded by naked little angels; beneath was printed, in large letters, HONORARY DIPLOMA. Schmidt wrote his name and new title on the diploma, added the round stamp with swastika and eagle, and scribbled several signatures.

Rampersdorf was in an uproar. People who had hardly known Schmidt went out of their way to greet him. Leading Nazis wanted to shake the hand that had touched the Führer's. At a big party given by the Town Council, Schmidt was asked to describe his visit.

"What did you tell them?" I asked.

Schmidt shook his head as if even now it seemed hard to believe. "I said, 'The door was opened and I found myself face to face with our dearly beloved Führer.' I described how Hitler had come toward me, 'smiling benevolently, like a father'; how he had listened to me, his arms folded across his chest, as I had seen in many photographs. I told how he had conferred on me the title of honorary engineer. When they asked me what Hitler looked like, face to face, I looked sort of bewitched and said, 'I suppose he looks just the way you imagine. Just like Hitler.' A few women started to cry and the men blew their noses. They looked at me with such stupid, wide-eyed admiration that I couldn't help adding that the Führer had said to me, 'My dear Schmidt, if you ever need anything, just get in touch with me.' I also implied that Hitler had given me his secret telephone number."

Schmidt shook his head again. "It sounds idiotic, but they swallowed every word of it."

Two days later Schmidt met a classmate, Peter, who asked him how he had addressed the Führer.

Schmidt shrugged. "I said, 'Heil, Herr Reichskanzler.' "

"That's funny," said Peter. "My father once went to a big official reception, and all guests were instructed to say, 'Heil, mein Führer.' "

"Maybe they didn't instruct me because they knew I hadn't been a Nazi before," Schmidt said, trying to look unconcerned.

"Maybe," said Peter, "but it's strange. I must tell my father."

Schmidt went home with wobbly knees. He had to do something quickly. One thing could help: a uniform. A resplendent, fantastic uniform that would convince everybody of his rank and position. The Nazis loved uniforms; they believed in uniforms. Schmidt went to Vienna and bought two shoulder straps corresponding to the rank of major in the German Army. While he was in the shop, a magnificent silver *fourragère* for staff officers took his fancy. The clerk asked whether he had a military purchase permit. Schmidt replied, quite truthfully, that he needed the insignia "for a show." He got the *fourragère,* and also a swastika arm band with silver edge, worn only by very high Party dignitaries. In another shop he purchased a cap with rich silver trimming.

Back home he took out his dinner jacket, sewed the *fourragère* on the wrong (left) side, and put one of the major's shoulder straps on his left shoulder.

"Why only one?" I asked.

"I didn't want to look like a major," Schmidt said. "I wanted to have a uniform such as no one else in Germany wore. Then no one could accuse me of impersonating an officer or an official. I liked myself so much when I looked in the mirror that I had to show off to Mother. I told her the uniform went with the diploma. Mother was overwhelmed and asked about the silver cord. Then I had an idea that could have been Hitler's. I said, 'Mother, this is the silver honor cord of the Third Reich.' My mother gave me a long, sad look and said nothing."

Schmidt walked around just long enough to impress people, and departed for Vienna. At the railroad station a soldier standing with his arm around a girl saw Schmidt, let go of the girl, snapped to attention, and gave Schmidt a smart salute. In Vienna he was respectfully saluted by three colonels and various staff officers. He began to enjoy himself and became bolder.

Two days later he crossed Schwarzenbergplatz to speak to Dr. David Silber, a Jewish lawyer and friend of his uncle's, just as two Gestapo men stopped the lawyer and asked for his papers. While Dr. Silber fumbled in his pockets, Schmidt approached and said arrogantly, "I am Engineer Schmidt, bearer of the silver honorary cord of the Third Reich awarded to me personally by the Führer. This gentleman is my old friend Welfing. I vouch for him." And before the Gestapo men had recovered from their surprise, Schmidt turned to Dr. Silber and said, "Let's go, Joachim. The next time, don't leave your papers at home." Later, Schmidt arranged for the lawyer and his wife to go to Rampersdorf, where Schmidt's mother got them across the Austro-Hungarian border.

A great many of Schmidt's friends seemed to be in trouble and came to see him, having heard of his exalted position. Schmidt did his best for them. He designed a special identity card according to which Engineer Honoris Causa E. Schmidt had been "awarded the silver honor cord by the Führer and Reichskanzler." All subordinate organs of the Party were ordered by the Führer to give Schmidt "all needed aid and assistance." The card never failed him. When he

heard that Herr Huber, a friend of his mother's, had been sent to
Dachau, he walked straight into the office of the Nazi Kreisleiter
of Vienna's Tenth District, threw his card on the table, and glared
at him.

"I assumed a harsh, superior air," Schmidt continued his story,
"and said I wanted to know about Huber—why had he been sent to
Dachau? The Kreisleiter replied meekly that Huber had been arrested
for 'antisocial' behavior. I got very angry. 'I happen to know that
Huber was denounced by a personal enemy who wanted to get hold
of his firm,' I said. 'The Führer told me only last week that he doesn't
approve of such action. Incidentally, I expect to see the Führer in
Berlin on Thursday or Friday. Unless this matter is straightened
out within forty-eight hours, I will have to report you directly to the
Führer.'

"The Kreisleiter's face took on the color of rancid butter. He said
he was very sorry, he hadn't known all the facts. I said, 'I want Huber
to report to my apartment within forty-eight hours.' And I walked
out.

"Well, it's hard to believe, but it worked. A few days later Huber
and his wife safely crossed into Hungary. In all, I sent some forty
people to my mother."

On November 2, 1938, Schmidt was drafted for the Luftwaffe.
He didn't mind. The comedy was beginning to get on his nerves. In
the army he would become an anonymous soldier; people would
forget while he was away. As a recruit, Kanonier Schmidt got the
rough treatment given privates all over the world and spent long
hours shoveling snow.

A few days before Christmas, Schmidt was called into the guard-
room, where his classmate Peter was waiting. Peter's father had become a Nazi official and Peter had come to warn Elfried. "Father
thinks the whole business about the engineer's title and the silver
cord is a swindle. He wants to check up on you in Berlin."

Gripped by cold fear, Schmidt somehow managed to seem un-
perturbed. "Thank you," he said with sarcasm. "If that's why you
came all the way from Rampersdorf, you can go back straight away.
Heil Hitler!" He turned on his heel and walked out.

He didn't sleep that night, though. He had to do something or his
whole family would be in trouble. Something was needed to convince the people back home, once and for all. If, for instance, a newspaper would publish his story . . .

The next day, before going home on Christmas leave, Schmidt called up *Das Kleine Volksblatt,* a widely circulated newspaper, and said he could give them an interesting story. A reporter appeared forthwith and on December 22, 1938, the *Volksblatt* published a sensational article, UNUSUAL CAREER OF A VIENNESE LOCKSMITH APPRENTICE. The story contained details that were new even to Schmidt. The silver honor cord has been bestowed by the Führer "only upon three other persons from the East Mark"; Schmidt's new Diesel rail-car was "twice or three times as fast as older models and was already being used in Hungary."

The article caused a terrific sensation in Rampersdorf. Even Peter's father had no further doubts.

When Schmidt returned to his military unit at the end of the Christmas holiday, he was called into the battery office. There he found himself facing the battery commander and a dozen junior officers. The captain placed his hand on Schmidt's shoulder.

"My *dear* Schmidt," he said. "We are overwhelmed. Why didn't you tell us before?"

Schmidt remained cautiously standing at attention. Maybe this was just a trap. The captain turned toward his officers. "Just as I told you, gentlemen—he's too modest."

Then Schmidt spied a copy of the *Volksblatt* on the captain's desk. So that was it! "I—I wanted no favors, sir. I want to do my duty like any other soldier."

The captain rubbed his hands in delight. "There you are, gentlemen. The true spirit of the good German soldier! Another proof of the fantastic foresight of our Führer, who singled out this simple Kanonier from among millions."

"Heil Hitler!" shouted Schmidt. Everybody clicked heels and saluted.

"At ease!" said the captain. "Kanonier Schmidt, what were your duties up to now?"

"I've been shoveling snow," Schmidt said.

There was a moment of embarrassed silence, then the captain cleared his throat. "Well, that's over now. Kanonier Schmidt, you are freed of all military duties. You'll have a room for your special work. You may come and go as you please. And you will wear the silver honor cord over your uniform." Schmidt thanked them loftily and marched out.

"I didn't bother even to sleep in the barracks," he said to me. "I stayed at our apartment in Vienna and arrived at the barracks after 8 A.M., like a colonel. When I approached the gate, wearing my silver cord, the sentry would call out the guard of honor, which was done only for the garrison commander and all general officers."

A few weeks later Schmidt was transferred to the Luftgaukommando XVII and assigned to the office of Colonel-General Eduard von Löhr. The general, greeting him like a dear old friend, said he had a special job for him. The German secret service had got hold of certain drawings of foreign aircraft engines. General Löhr wanted Schmidt to study the drawings and point out "parts of specific interest."

"I was frightened to death," Schmidt said to me. "I told the general I knew nothing of aircraft engines, being a rail specialist, but he genially patted my back and introduced me to the colonel in charge of Secret Projects. Then came another blow. The general said a man of my abilities couldn't run around as a private; he was going to make me an officer. Now, promotions to officers were handled by Berlin, and if Göring's Air Ministry started to investigate, the bubble would blow up. I tried to play modest but the general said he had already written a memorandum to the authorities. It was this memorandum that later caused my downfall.

"For a while I was a big man at Luftgaukommando headquarters," Schmidt went on. "I had an elegant office with a sergeant as orderly. I set up a model railroad in this office, and the general, the colonel in charge of Secret Projects, and other high officers came to play with it. After a while I realized that I couldn't go around much longer in my private's uniform with the silver *fourragère*. It was asking for trouble. So I bought some black cloth which was reserved exclusively for the SS and explained my wishes to the regimental tailor. The jacket should be like a diplomat's gala tunic. On the lapels I had embroidered a self-designed emblem with the initials of the Technical University. The silver *fourragère* would remain on the left side although the tailor said he'd never heard of anybody wearing it there. I 'improved' the swastika arm band, wore gala infantry trousers and an Air Force cap. No one except Göring could have designed a more beautiful uniform.

"I was quite frightened when I first faced the general in my operetta costume," Schmidt continued, with a chuckle. "But the poor idiot was fascinated and said I could have his private eight-cylinder Mercedes whenever I needed it. I took the car and drove straight out to Rampersdorf. You should have seen the faces of the people as they stared at the car with the general-staff license plate. When my mother saw me, I could stand it no longer. I told her everything. She cried but I assured her that no one would ever dare harm her or my uncle."

The merry life of Kanonier Schmidt came to an end on the morning of February 16, 1939. He had arrived at his office earlier than usual with somehow a strong foreboding of disaster. At 11 A.M., when he was about to leave, a sergeant asked him to wait. "The general wants to talk to you. You're not supposed to leave."

Presently Schmidt was called into the general's conference room Behind a long table sat the general, looking flustered, and several high-ranking officers wearing the red facings of military procurators of the Luftwaffe Court. "Tell us how you got that title of engineer," the general said gruffly.

Schmidt was now convinced they didn't know much. "I'm not used to such treatment," he said arrogantly. "Maybe I'd better telephone the Führer. As you know, he gave me his private phone number."

"You talked with the Führer?"

"Certainly!"

"That's not true! The procurators have checked up on you. You are under arrest. We know you are a spy."

"A spy?" Schmidt said, flabbergasted.

"You'd better confess! But we'll find out soon enough."

Schmidt was taken to the military prison in Floridsdorf, where he was welcomed enthusiastically—his jailers thought he had really pulled a fast one on the big brass. Schmidt didn't share their relish His first reaction had been relief: after seven long months of playing comedy and confiding in no one, he could relax. But now he was frantic. The penalty for espionage was death. Poor Schmidt was in a fearful dilemma. He couldn't tell them the truth—that he had staged his foolhardy masquerade to save his mother and uncle from the Gestapo. That would have been an admission of his family's anti Nazi leanings, which was just as bad as spying.

"I decided that the only way to save my neck was to convince the procurators that a silly love affair was behind the whole business. But how? They wouldn't believe me if I made a confession. Then one night my jailer told me that the prisoner in the next cell was going to be released in the morning. I wrote a passionate letter to Elsa: 'I did it all for you, my beloved. Remember when you said what a pity it was that I wasn't an engineer? And now they say I am a spy. How can I make them believe that all I wanted was to impress you, dearly beloved?'"

The letter was smuggled to the prisoner in the next cell, who was to surrender it to the sentry at the gate, saying that he'd been asked to transmit it to Elsa, but didn't want to become an accomplice to this crime.

Everything worked fine. The letter promptly landed on the desk of the chief procurator.

Schmidt is convinced now that the procurator believed it implicitly. One week later, on May 25, Schmidt appeared before the Luftwaffe Court. It was a strange trial. The judges frequently tittered. Even the chief procurator had trouble keeping a straight face as Schmidt told, with his most honest, dumbest face, how he had in vain tried to impress Elsa, whose father "thought she was too good for an ordinary locksmith apprentice." So he had decided to become an engineer. The diploma was unrolled as exhibit A. The presiding judge burst into laughter.

The trial was over in two hours. The indictment of espionage had been dropped. Schmidt was found guilty of "forging an official diploma" (four weeks of prison), of "unjustified use of an academic title" (four weeks), of "insolently exploiting the name of the Führer and Reichskanzler" (four months). In view of the defendant's good conduct, three months of preliminary arrest would be deducted.

"I suppose they had orders from higher up to kill the affair quickly," Schmidt said to me.

When he was released, he returned to the Luftwaffe and served throughout the war as an ordinary soldier. In 1945 he took a job as motorman with the Municipal Streetcar System in Vienna. His career as motorman was terminated on January 3, 1947, when the brakes of his car failed and it collided with another car, killing three people. Although Schmidt was cleared, he was busted to conductor, a job which bores him to tears.

Between jobs, Schmidt finds time to do some serious inventions. His *Lenkdrehgestell* (self-adjusting truck) for streetcars has received an Austrian patent and has been certified by a commission of Vienna's Technical University as "having excellent running features." Schmidt proudly showed me the certificate.

As Schmidt was finishing his story, his wife entered the room with the baby on her arm. "Elfried!" she said. "If we want to catch a little sunshine, we'd better go."

Schmidt got up at once. "Yes, we'd better go," he said, meekly. He pointed at a wedding picture on the wall which showed him wearing his fantasy uniform, with the silver *fourragère*. "We got married in 1940, a year after I got out of the Army prison," he said. "I hated the very sight of this uniform but the Army forced me to wear it for my wedding so that the people in the village wouldn't get suspicious. They didn't know the truth then."

"Anyway, Elsa did marry you, without an engineer's title?" I said, half jokingly. Frau Schmidt gave me a vexed glance and walked out.

There was an uncomfortable pause. Schmidt cleared his throat. "My wife's name is Helene," he said. "I—I didn't marry Elsa. Shall we go?"

THE INVISIBLE ACCOMPLICE

by E. H. Jones

Stories of escape by prisoners of war are legion. Prisoners have tunneled out, have disguised themselves in camp-made enemy uniforms, have used all sorts of ruses and deceptions. But E. H. Jones literally hoaxed his way out of a Turkish prison in the First World War. His method, to my knowledge, is unique. It required long, sustained mental effort and ingenious invention. Because of special circumstances, his fellow-prisoners had to be hoaxed, too, as well as the enemy. Moreover, a scheme had to be created that would prevent the Commandant from carrying out his threat that if anyone tried to escape he would visit serious reprisals—torture, possibly execution—against the remaining prisoners. How Jones tackled and solved all these problems constitutes a delightful classic in deception.

Yozgad, in Asia Minor, lies in the heart of the rugged mountains of Anatolia, almost due east from Angora. It is over four thousand feet above sea level, and was probably as unaccessible as any prison camp in the world outside Russia. The nearest railhead (Angora) was 120 miles away. The nearest seaport (Samsun, on the Black Sea) was a little farther—about 130 miles. Three hundred miles as the crow flies would have taken us to friendly territory—either to the Crimea or to the Russians at Erzinjan or to Cyprus. But we were not crows.

So far were we from being crows that until August, 1918, not a single attempt at a conventional escape was made from Yozgad. For over two years one hundred British officers and some thirty or forty British rank and file waited patiently for the Armistice. Nobody attempted to run for it.

It was not the difficulty of getting out of the camp. We at Yozgad had no barbed wire, unclimbable fences, electric lights, sentries every few yards, moats, and all the rest of the obstacles which escapers from

German camps had to face. Except for a few middle-aged sentries, armed with old muskets, who dozed in their sentry boxes all day and all night, we had no obstacles to getting away.

The real sentry at Yozgad was the desert, the distance, the mountains, the brigands outside. Every single officer and man in that camp knew he could break out if he wished. But every one of them knew that once he got outside, the chances of final escape were about the same as those of a snowball surviving in the South Sea Islands.

Even so, many would have tried it. The fear of personal punishment would not have stopped them. What really scared them was an official warning by the Turks that if anyone escaped the rest of the camp would be "strafed."

Most of us had been captured at Kut and we knew what the Turk could do in the way of "strafing." I need not enter into details. A single statement will suffice. At Kut 2,680 British officers and men surrendered to the Turks. Two and half years later, at the Armistice, 935 returned from captivity. Two out of every three had disappeared. We in Yozgad knew how and where and when and why many of these men disappeared. Can you blame the prisoners in Yozgad because they weighed in the balance a very slender chance of personal freedom against the safety of their comrades, and found it wanting?

Many of us, probably, thought of trying it. But during the two years I was at Yozgad only one officer, as far as I know, got as far as getting his escaping kit ready. His intention was discovered by his fellow-prisoners, and the senior British officer in the camp put him on parole. The alternative to giving his parole was that the Turks would be informed, for the camp must not be endangered.

I racked my brains for some way of getting out without involving the camp in a "strafe." Very early on I thought of simulating insanity with a view to exchange. But the idea was too dangerous and too difficult. So I discarded it—for the time being.

My chance came in a most unexpected way. A group of us began studying spiritualism early in the spring of 1917, and we took it up for the same reason as we took up philosophy, mathematics, French, Spanish, and a score of other pursuits—to pass the time and to break the hopeless monotony of our days. We commenced very seriously; we made a "Ouija Board," which is a polished board encircled by the letters of the alphabet—a sort of planchette—and night after night we experimented. Two at a time, we would close our eyes, place our forefingers lightly on an inverted tumbler in the centre of the board, ask a question, and wait for the tumbler to move to the letters and spell out the answer. We found the tumbler would move without our consciously pushing it; it even touched letters. But the letters it touched never spelt anything—they were meaningless nonsense.

This went on for a fortnight. We could get no sense. We got disheartened. The group of investigators dwindled till there were only four of us left. We decided to have one more séance and if we got no replies we would give it up.

Then I began to cheat. With my eyes closed, I pushed the glass to the right letters. I invented answers to the questions put, and spelled them out on the board.

It was just mischief. I have always been fond of a leg pull and I fully intended to confess when the séance was over. But the excitement which the answers aroused in my friends amused me too much. Everybody had enjoyed the chat with the spook. So I postponed the confession and carried on for a few evenings, before an ever-increasing audience of prisoners, extracting answers from the Ouija, and inventing a little army of spooks—Sally, Dorothy, Silas P. Warner, and others, each with his own special characteristic.

Then, before I knew where I was, it became impossible to confess without involving others. Another group of spiritualists began to get answers from the Ouija. They didn't know I was fudging. But I knew they were, because they got their answers from the spooks I had invented myself—Silas P. Warner and others.

To salve my conscience, I challenged an investigation. Tests, some very difficult, were set. To my own surprise I got through them all undetected. Half the camp became converted to spiritualism. Séances were held almost nightly. We obtained all sorts of news, including war news. The spook issued a regular war-news bulletin.

Then the Turks came in. First, the interpreter Moise. We called him the "Pimple." He consulted the spook about his love affairs, and he got appropriate answers. Next came an official order from the Turkish Commandant. It forbade us to mention in our letters home "news obtained in a spiritistic state." I questioned the interpreter and discovered that our Commandant, Kiazim Bey, was a confirmed believer in spiritualism.

Have you ever fished for trout with a 3x cast and a light rod, and seen a salmon rise to your fly? That is how I felt when I realized what lay behind Kiazim Bey's official order.

Here was my chance at last. I must get Kiazim into my net. If this Turkish major believed in spooks, then somehow and sometime I would get him where I wanted him—under my thumb. My plan was to make him an unconscious accomplice in my escape. I would implicate him. I would obtain clear proof of that implication. I would place that proof in the hands of the camp before I left. He would not then dare to "strafe" the camp, for the camp could threaten to retaliate by reporting his complicity to the first superior Turkish officer who came round inspecting.

Such was my plan. But I had only risen him. I still had to get him on the hook. How? The answer is obvious to every fisherman. Get the right lure.

We had begun spooking in February. I did not find the lure until September. The Pimple asked me one day if the spook could find buried treasure. My answer was extremely encouraging. Moise asked for a séance. I promised him one. From his talk I learned that the Turks had already been digging for the treasure, but had found nothing. The money they were searching for was the fortune of a rich Armenian in Yozgad—one of the thousands of Armenians in this town who had been massacred by the Turks just before we came. Here was the lure.

Two of the prisoners, Lloyd and Cochrane, had found a useless rusty old revolver buried in our garden. I begged for it. I got it. I buried it again. Then we had the séance. The spook told the interpreter that the treasure was guarded by arms, which must be discovered first. Two Turks were ordered by the spook to be present at the search. I hoped Kiazim, the Commandant, would rise to this fly. He didn't. His bat-man—the lousy villain we knew as "the Cook"—came instead.

This was disappointing. I wanted the big fish, not the small fry, but I carried on. I fell into a trance. The spook then guided us to the spot where the revolver was hidden.

When you are spooking for treasure it does not do to dig it up at once. Ceremony is essential. So over the spot we built up a fire of shavings. And over the fire of shavings we poured water. And in the mingled steam and smoke, standing with outstretched arms, I recited a mystic incantation, necessary for the discovery of all treasures, which I said I had learned from the Head Hunting Waas of Burma.

The incantation was a Welsh love lyric. But it is surprising how effective Welsh can be as an incantation in a leg pull. For example—

"Gwyn fyd na chai Cymru ei diwifr eihun." Yards of this sort of talk make an excellent incantation.

When we dug up the rusty revolver, the Turks were overjoyed. I felt that the discovery would bring out the Commandant. But I waited in vain. Kiazim kept hidden, sheltered behind his subordinates, and for months only the "Pimple" came to question the spook about the treasure. This was no good at all to me. If I was to implicate him, I must have the Commandant himself. So the spook refused to say a word about the treasure and would only curse and threaten the "Pimple."

At last the "Pimple" lost his temper with the spook, and challenged the unseen to *do* something, instead of merely cursing and threatening. The spook at once promised to kill him that night. The "Pimple" begged pardon, frantically, and said, "I only wanted you to take off my hat or my gloves—to move something." "Very good," said the spook, "I shall move something." That night I put six grains of calomel into the "Pimple's" cocoa. He never challenged the spook again. The manifestation of the spook's powers of moving things, next day, did him all the good in the world. Henceforth he was a complete and very obedient convert.

I went on, week after week, trying to build up the prestige of the spook by every trick I could invent. The spook's prestige certainly grew, but it was all no use. The weary days passed on. The Commandant was as far away as ever. I felt pretty certain, but I could not be sure that he was behind the "Pimple" in this treasure hunt.

I made one last effort. Without telling the "Pimple" anything of my suspicion that the Commandant was interested, I managed to convince him that unless everybody concerned with the treasure came forward the medium could never succeed.

A couple of days later a sentry came for me and took me into the Commandant's office. Kiazim and the "Pimple" were there. It was an amazing interview between a junior officer prisoner and the Turkish major in charge. I came away pledged to place my skill as a medium at the service of the Commandant, to try to find the treasure.

What did it matter that I was threatened with death if I sought to betray Kiazim's interest in the treasure to Constantinople? What did it matter that the "Pimple" told me how such things are done—how a prisoner's body is produced with a hole through the back—"shot while attempting to escape." Nothing mattered. The fish was hooked at last.

Hitherto I had kept my own counsel. It had been solitary work this fishing for the Commandant. Now that he was on the hook, I needed a confederate. In my own mind I had chosen him long ago. I went straight to him now. He was C. W. Hill, the Australian flying man. I chose well. He was a companion in a million.

We started at once. Hill made two small tins shaped like shaving soap tins, each with a false bottom. In the false bottom of each we placed a Turkish gold lira, wrapped up in a paper containing directions written by us in Armenian characters. The top part of the tin was filled with ashes. Hill took the tins outside the camp when he went for exercise, and buried them three miles apart. These were clues to the treasure. The spook was going to find these clues later on.

The spook then set about convincing the Commandant that no good results could be obtained so long as the mediums were in camp. They must be confined somewhere by themselves. We convinced him of this easily enough. But to get him to move us was a much more difficult business.

The spook told him how to do it. The Commandant was to accuse Hill and myself of reading the thoughts of the townspeople and obtaining war news in that way. By a conjuring trick of Hill's the spook provided Kiazim with written evidence to support this absurd charge. He was to convict us for it and to sentence us to solitary confinement apart from the camp, whence, of course, we hoped to escape. Kiazim refused to come up to scratch. Fortunately, just then he got a bad attack of colic. Colic is a painful thing. The spook immediately claimed to be the author of this visitation and threatened Kiazim with a worse attack if he did not comply with orders. Remembering the calomel incident, Kiazim gave in at once. The incredible trial was held, in the presence of four British officers, chosen by myself as witnesses because of their honest belief in telepathy. In complete innocence of our scheme these officers testified that thought-reading was possible. Then, to their horror, they found that Hill and I were being charged with thought-reading, and they saw us convicted and sentenced to solitary confinement on this charge of telepathy.

We were confined in a house by ourselves. Within twenty-four hours a letter of mine was on its way to England. The letter seemed quite an innocent affair but it was really a cryptogram that told how we had been imprisoned on an absurd charge of telepathy and asked for an inquiry. We had heard of one case where an officer, unjustly condemned, had been granted a compassionate release from Turkey to make up for it. There was a distant chance the same might happen to us. The letter got home all right, the cryptogram was deciphered; it was placed in the hands of Whitehall. Whitehall did nothing. They said it was dangerous to interfere—for our sakes.

We never placed much reliance on this plan, it was merely an alternative sideline. Hill and I set to work on our main line. The first step in our scheme was to obtain proof that the Commandant was implicated. Our idea was to photograph him digging for the treasure in our company, but without his knowledge. We would give this photograph to our friends in the camp. It would be their safeguard. We had a camera and three films hidden away, ready. The camera had been made by Hill out of a chocolate box.

But before we could get going we had to calm the fears of the Commandant. He wanted to know what he was to report about our trial to Constantinople. The spook board was brought out and the spook dictated the letter he was to send to the War Office. He wrote it, and sent it; and if they keep files in the Turkish War Office, it is there today.

From that time on the spook ran the camp. Every question that arose was submitted by the Commandant to the spook for advice. Thus there was in Yozgad a ski club, originated by Lieutenant Spink. At the end of the skiing season the club gave a dinner to which Kiazim was invited as a guest. The spook wrote Kiazim's speech for him, in which he made promises of new privileges to the prisoners. And Kiazim delivered it. There was a hunt club in the summer months, originated by Holyoake. The Turkish War Office sent a letter to Kiazim telling him such clubs were prohibited. The spook told Kiazim to pay no attention to the letter, and the hunt club continued. Again, the senior British officer had put Hill and myself on parole not to escape from Yozgad. The senior British officer was a member of the hunt club. So the spook told Kiazim to put him on parole when hunting. Kiazim got the parole. It is not often a subaltern gets square with his colonel. I do not think the colonel bears us any grudge.

When these minor problems were out of the way we consulted the spook about the treasure. The story I invented about the treasure was this:

The rich Armenian whose wealth we were seeking had guessed that a massacre was coming. He buried his wealth. At different spots he then buried three clues to where the treasure was. One clue showed the spot from where to measure. The second showed the direction in which to measure and the third showed the distance to be measured. To discover the treasure all the three clues would have to be found.

He did not tell his family where the treasure was because he was afraid they might reveal it to the Turks under torture. But if they happened to escape the coming massacre he wanted them to be provided for. He therefore selected three friends living in different parts of the country. He gave A, B, and C, the three friends, directions for finding one clue each. He also gave them tokens by which to identify one another, and he left instructions that when he died or was killed, friend A was to send for friend B. Friend B, in his turn, knew that he was to send for friend C. The three of them could then go and with their combined knowledge find the clues and dig up the treasure. Friend A and friend B unfortunately had been massacred about the same time as the owner. Friend C was still alive and lived on the sea coast. But the other two being dead he had never been summoned, so the treasure was still intact as he only knew the position of the one clue.

This was the story the spook told to the Turks. We got over the difficulty of giving the names and addresses of the Armenians concerned in a manner too intricate to describe here. But the blame for the spook's failure to give the names was fixed on the "Pimple." When the "Pimple" made his report on this séance to the Commandant, the Commandant smacked his face for him. We avenged the "Pimple" later on, when the spook ordered Kiazim not to kiss his wife for a fortnight.

At the very next séance the spirit of the dead Armenian owner took charge of the board and announced that he was willing to tell us where the treasure was buried on one condition. The condition was that we were friends of the Armenians. He said he was going to test us, and the "Ouija" spelled out a question in the Armenian tongue. The "Pimple" said he did not know Armenian, so our Armenian spook would have nothing more to do with us. He refused to tell where the treasure was and he went further—he organised an opposition party in the spook world to prevent our finding it. It was the "Pimple's" fault again. Because he did not know Armenian we had lost a great chance.

We therefore decided to find the clues. We soon got into touch with the spirits of friend A and friend B. They were most obliging spooks. They were quite willing to lead us to the clues.

On March 31, we unearthed the first clue. Hill succeeded in taking three photographs of the proceedings without the knowledge of the Turks. That night he developed them while I kept guard. They were not perfect, but the Commandant and the rest of us were clearly recognisable in all of them, and considering cameras are forbidden in prison camps, it was not a bad effort. We had got our proof.

Next day we unearthed the second clue. That filthy old rascal, the cook, showed his gratitude by kissing Hill and myself before we could get out of his way. The excitement was prodigious. The Turks had the Armenian messages in the tins translated and now knew the direction in which to measure and the distance to measure. All they needed in order to find the treasure was to know the point from which these valuable measurements were to be taken.

When we came back from the treasure hunt we found that a wire had come from the War Office at Constantinople ordering the Commandant to release us from our imprisonment for telepathy and to send us back to camp. Kiazim consulted the spook. The spook told him not to bother about War Office orders, but to carry on with the treasure hunt. He obeyed the spook.

Hill and I now got into touch with fellow-prisoners whom we could trust. To these we handed the photographs and other proofs of the Commandant's complicity. And in case our documentary evidence was insufficient, we trapped the Commandant irretrievably in a very simple way.

I have mentioned that each of the two clues which we buried contained a gold coin. By the spook's orders each of these coins was cut into three equal parts. I took the third of one coin, Hill took a third of the other. The remaining four portions were given to the "Cook," the "Pimple," the Commandant, and the Commandant's wife. The spook ordered us to wear these little bits of gold, night and day and always until the treasure was found, round our necks and next to our skin. We all did so and I knew I could rely upon the Turks continually doing so. If later on the Turks denied that they were implicated in our scheme the Commandant would find it very difficult to explain how we all came to be wearing pieces of the same coin if there was no understanding between us.

It was easy enough to combine the two objectives. You remember that the holder of the third clue (Mr. C) lived on the sea-coast. He was still alive so we could not talk to his spook. But being thought-readers we could read his thoughts if we could get near enough. Now you can't read thoughts if you are in mountainous country, because thought waves are like wireless waves—mountains stop them. But if you are at sea level you can pick them up from almost any distance.

Naturally the Turks wanted us to read C's thought. They were quite willing to come to the coast to do it. The Commandant at the spook's request agreed to grant leave to the "Cook" and the "Pimple." He himself at the spook's instruction went to the Turkish doctors. The spook told him what to say to get a diagnosis of stone in the hepatic duct. He swung the lead successfully and got a powerful medical certificate. Armed with this certificate, he said, he could get leave by telegram from the War Office at any moment, for he had influential friends there. The Commandant then informed the British senior officer in the camp that he was going to send Hill and myself away from Yozgad. Everything was ready. All we had to do now was to await the arrival of another Commandant to take over charge of the camp from Kiazim. A suitable Turkish officer was actually on his way to Yozgad, in charge of a fresh batch of prisoners. He was due to arrive in a few days and would be available to take Kiazim's place.

Hill and I were also ready. In the handle of my shaving brush I carried enough morphia to put a Turkish battalion to sleep. We had our plans for getting the Turks to supply a boat, for getting them into it, for drugging them with morphia. We had ropes and straps ready to bind them. We had sandbags ready sewn to fill with sand in case the morphia did not work very well. We hoped that when the Turks woke up, we would be half-way to Cyprus, for we intended to kidnap them. We thought that if we succeeded Mr. Lloyd George might give us an O.B.E. each. But even that did not deter us.

Then the crash came. One of our fellow-prisoners warned the Commandant that if he sent us away Hill and I would escape. This prisoner was a friend of mine. He thought perhaps that we were being sent away in order to be put away. At any rate, the Commandant got alarmed. He drew back. He wouldn't come with us. He wouldn't send us to the coast, but he would send us to Constantinople if the spook would show him how. At Constantinople, being on sea level, we could read the thoughts of friend C and send back word where to find the third clue.

It was a pathetic ending to a jolly little scheme. I could have wept. Hill came nearer to losing his temper than I have ever seen him. But there was nothing for it. We gave up the kidnapping plan. The spook proceeded to tell Kiazim how to get us to Constantinople. Kiazim only had to say that Hill and I were mad.

Kiazim said so. Tutored by the spook, he went to the Turkich doctors at Yozgad and pitched a pretty tale about our mad behaviour. He brought the two Turkish doctors to see us. We played our part as lunatics in their presence. They certified us. They called me "a furious, who was suffering from a derangement in his brains." Of Hill they wrote that he was "in a very calm condition. His face is long, not very fat. He is suffering from melancholia."

The spook dictated a wire to the Turkish War Office asking permission to send to Constantinople two British officers who had been certified insane by the local Turkish doctors. A wire came in reply to send us along at once. The Commandant on the spook's instructions ordered the "Pimple" to accompany us.

We had to wait some days for transport. While we waited our own Doctor O'Farrell tutored us. We practised on the sentries, whose lives we made a burden, and on our own fellow-prisoners. We were now all out for repatriation as lunatics.

In a few days we started, under close guard, on our specially conducted tour to Constantinople. On the way, at a town called Mardeen, we pretended to hang ourselves. This part of the scheme was too well acted. Owing to a mistake of the "Pimple's" we were both just about unconscious when we were cut down. Next morning we denied that we had hanged ourselves at all. So the Mayor of Mardeen held an inquiry, and his official (the town clerk we supposed) wrote a report to the Turkish War Office to say that Hill and myself were a pair of liars, and that we had hanged ourselves all right. All the way to Constantinople, a ten days' journey, we behaved like lunatics, to the annoyance of our guards, and tutored the "Pimple" as to what he was to say to the mental specialists.

In this way it came about that an immense volume of evidence proving our insanity was produced by the Turkish officials themselves. There were the certificates of insanity from the Yozgad doctors, the report from Kiazim, the officer in charge of the Yozgad camp, the letter from the mayor and corporation of Mardeen, the evidence of our behaviour en route by the "Pimple" and the sentries, and the marks round our throats of where the rope had cut into our necks. We ourselves denied steadily that we were insane or that we had done the insane acts with which we were charged. We also got O'Farrell, our British camp doctor, to write a letter to say that we were not insane—only a bit eccentric. We thought that the Turkish doctors would naturally delight in a chance to disagree with an English doctor.

With all this official evidence of our insanity at our backs the Turkish mental specialists never had a real chance. All we had to do was to act carefully. In less than a month we were certified for exchange. We now only had to keep it up until the arrangements for exchanging sick prisoners were completed. We did not know that we would have to wait for six months for the exchange ship to arrive, and carry on our acting all that time among crazy men in the mad wards of a Turkish hospital. It nearly killed us. But we did it. Hill left the country with the first boat-load of exchange prisoners. I followed in the second boat a few days later. After all our hard work we had gained only a short fortnight over the prisoners who had sat still and done nothing. For the Armistice arrived within a few days of Hill's leaving Turkey. But we had the satisfaction of having done our best.

THE BIG DEAL

by David Copeland

This is the story of a great spy. But, more than that, it is the story of a man who, not only risked his life for years, but during all that time also sacrificed his private, personal life for an important goal—Allied victory in World War II. For years this man lived a double life—an outcast, cut off from his real friends, despised and reviled by friends and family as a traitor—with only his wife by his side. During those years he was also cut off from his real values, from his belief in democracy and decent human relations. For he had to put on as his "disguise" not only a special identity, but also a new set of values, the values of Nazi totalitarianism.

One of the most amazing and daring, true spy stories to come out of World War II is that of Eric Erickson, an American-born, American-educated Swede, whose super-hoax saved countless American and Allied lives during the climactic Battle of the Rhine.

Eric "Red" Erickson was an international oil salesman, an American citizen, who settled in Sweden after years spent in Europe and the Orient, working for various American oil companies and dealing with English, Dutch and German firms. In Sweden he started his own oil importing business and also became a Swedish citizen. His business prospered. In the summer of 1939 he became engaged to a lovely Swedish girl. The future seemed very bright for Erickson. The only shadow on the horizon was the international situation; the Nazi Panzer divisions invaded Poland that fall and World War II engulfed the Continent. But Sweden was a neutral nation and intended to maintain its neutrality. And Erickson was now a Swedish national. So Erickson and his bride-to-be confidently set a date for their wedding.

A week before that date Allied Intelligence representatives called on Erickson and urged him to make use of his many German contacts to aid the Allies. It would be dangerous work, but it would be extremely valuable to the Allied cause. Erickson could legitimately have chosen to remain safely on the sidelines—and carry on a profitable business.

But, being originally American, and opposed to Nazism, whose brutalities he had observed at first hand, he wanted to serve the Allies.

Erickson asked permission to talk it over with his fiancée. "If you're sure you can trust her, go ahead," the Allied Intelligence agents said.

Erickson's fiancée was, naturally, opposed to the idea. "There are plenty of other people to do this work," she argued. "Besides, perhaps it won't be of much value anyway." Erickson explained that there were not many men who had the basis for potentially valuable espionage that his background provided.

His fiancée finally agreed that he ought to go ahead with it. Erickson suggested that, under the circumstance—much as he loved her— they ought to postpone their marriage. For he would be in constant danger, and, as his wife, she might well be in danger too. Moreover, he would have to play the part of a pro-Nazi; why should the same repugnant role be forced on her.

But the war might last for years, she objected. She would rather share the danger than to be without him. They decided to be married immediately. Erickson then met the Allied Intelligence again and told them he would serve as a spy, starting two weeks from that date, when his honeymoon would be over. He refused any pay for his services. He did suggest that as soon as there was a good reason for it—so that the Nazis would not scent a plan—he be put on the Allied blacklist to help give him status with the Nazis.

Then Erickson proceeded to bait the hook. He drew away from most of his old friends, since they were anti-Nazi. Instead, he joined the German Chamber of Commerce in Sweden, and hobnobbed with German businessmen. The one old friend he did keep on good terms with was Prince Carl Bernadotte, nephew of the King of Sweden, who, at Erickson's request, also began playing ball with the Nazis. Erickson's wife, of course, had to also pretend to be a pro-Nazi. Erickson's best friend, a Jew, was puzzled by the sudden change; he decided that Erickson had hidden his Nazi sentiments until he felt it was safe. The two parted after a sharp verbal exchange.

Erickson pretended to be interested in doing oil business with Germany. He cultivated a certain Herr Finke who was Himmler's top representative in Sweden. Erickson knew that Himmler would have the last word on oil deals. Salesman Erickson's work on his "prospect," Finke, was aided by Erickson's friendship with Prince Carl Bernadotte, for Finke had a weakness for royalty. So Erickson arranged to have Finke and himself entertained frequently at the Prince's country villa.

But a certain Herr Ludwig, commercial attaché of the German Legation in Stockholm, did not seem to care for "the American," Erickson. Erickson wasn't sure whether Ludwig was suspicious or just ornery.

Finally, in the spring of 1941, despite Ludwig's objections, Erickson got permission to go to Germany and try to put over an oil deal. But at the airport, the plane to Berlin was held up, as two men in plain clothes ordered Erickson off. They were Swedish detectives and they made a careful search of him and all his belongings. But they found no legal basis for detaining him.

In Berlin, Erickson was driven to Gestapo headquarters. Two of the men he met in the office to which he was ushered Erickson recognized; they were Gestapo agents who had been on the plane. These agents gave him a clean bill of health. They reported that Erickson had been searched at Bromma airfield, obviously at Allied instigation.

So now Erickson contacted German oil men in Hamburg and a few other cities where he was allowed to travel. He was granted interviews at a number of Hamburg refineries and discussed contract terms with managers. He also kept a weather eye open for any oil men with whom he had dealt in the old days—men who might prove useful to him on his present mission.

The first one he found was Captain von Wunsch, a Junker, who had been associated with one of the big oil companies. Erickson arranged a private rendezvous with Von Wunsch in order to talk over a deal. There Erickson sounded Von Wunsch out and then took the dangerous step of telling him that he was an Allied agent. He proposed that Von Wunsch help him by supplying information from time to time, and by concluding deals with him that would give him legitimate reasons for coming back to Germany on business trips. In return, Von Wunsch would be paid well; more important, if the Allies won the' war, he would have a record of service to the victors. Von Wunsch agreed to co-operate. Erickson, however, could not be sure that the man would not betray him the moment they parted.

The next few hours passed slowly for Erickson; at any moment the Gestapo might come to haul him away to a firing squad. But he was not arrested. Evidently Von Wunsch was really playing ball. Unless Von Wunsch had betrayed him, and the Gestapo was playing a subtle game of letting Erickson continue with his activities for a while so he could lead them to other Allied agents.

Next Erickson made a similar contact with a Herr von Sturker, taking pains that Von Wunsch should not know of the meeting. Again

Erickson took the dangerous step of declaring himself a spy. Von Sturker, too, agreed to play ball.

Later on Von Wunsch came to see Erickson and gave him some information. In return he requested a signed document stating that he, Von Wunsch, was serving as a secret Allied collaborator. After all, he said, Erickson might be put out of commission any day and then what proof would Von Wunsch have that he had helped the Allies.

Erickson was far from eager to sign such a document because it would be, in effect, his own death warrant if it were ever found by the Gestapo. Moreover, once he gave Von Wunsch such a document, the latter could hide it and then turn Erickson over to the Gestapo; in that way Von Wunsch wouldn't have to spy and risk his neck, and he'd still have a paper saying he had helped the Allies. But Erickson gave him the signed document, for it was the only way of getting further information and aid from the man. Shortly thereafter Von Sturker also asked for and received a similar document.

Naturally, Erickson also had to deal with many dyed-in-the-wool Nazis—and he had to play the role of a pro-Nazi to the hilt. There were several occasions when his real views and spontaneous reactions almost gave him away.

Finally, Erickson put over several oil deals and returned to Sweden. Soon he began receiving shipments of German oil in exchange for other items in short supply inside the Reich. Secretly he turned the oil over to the Allies, together with the information he had gathered about the location and layout of certain German oil plants and depots— information that Allied bomber squadrons found most valuable.

Now the Allies put him on their blacklist for trading with the enemy, aiding the Nazi war effort, and consorting with the Gestapo. Erickson's friends all completely shunned him and his wife. Erickson's parents and relatives in America wrote him scathing letters, condemning him as a traitor. When Prince Carl Bernadotte or Erickson and his wife came into a restaurant in Stockholm, their friends would get up and leave to show their disgust at their pro-Nazi activity. And his wife also was forced to entertain Erickson's new Nazi friends.

Erickson made many more trips into Germany. The risk of detection by the Gestapo or betrayal by his co-conspirators was constantly increasing. For he made many more contacts with men and women who agreed to work for him—in return for signed documents saying they were aiding the Allies. Some of these Germans were truly anti-Nazi;

others were simply playing both sides of the fence, or doing it for the high pay Erickson offered. Each new contact was a new danger. Each signed paper was like a sword hanging over his head. And now the danger was further increased by the fact that Erickson was in contact with other Allied agents in Germany passing on information as he got it instead of waiting to report when he returned to Sweden; thus if he were caught, the information would still reach Allied Intelligence. Often, while in Germany, Erickson could hardly sleep at night as he waited tensely for the knock that might mean a speedy funeral.

One morning in Berlin a Gestapo car called for him and two Gestapo officers ordered him to come along. "We are under orders to take you to the Moabit Prison," one of the officers informed him. The dreaded moment had arrived. Erickson was ushered into a room overlooking the prison courtyard and told to wait. Soon he saw a rifle squad marching into position. Were they going to shoot him without even interrogating him?

A moment later two guards led him to the courtyard, to which several other men were escorted by pairs of guards. Then a group of prisoners were led out under guard and marched in front of the firing squad. Erickson immediately recognized one of them, a woman who was one of his German agents, an agent he had grown particularly fond of. But he made no sign of recognition; neither did she. Would he be forced to watch her execution and then be shot himself? Had she been tortured into talking? Or was the Gestapo only suspicious and trying to trap him, perhaps into a start of recognition? Or, on the contrary, had the Gestapo observed his occasional meetings with her—he had never been secretive about them—so that pretending not to recognize her would be the means of betraying himself?

Since there were a number of prisoners lined up for execution, and the woman was dressed in prison clothes, rather than her usual chic garments, Erickson decided to risk not recognizing her. If her name were brought up later by the Gestapo he would freely admit knowing her and express surprise that she had proved a traitor. Steeling himself, he watched the firing squad do its work. As the bodies were being carted away, the prison Commandant came over and introduced himself to Erickson and to the other men the guards had brought in to observe the execution. It had all, apparently, been just a "show," for assorted foreign friends of the Reich, a show, and, possibly, a warning.

Another time Erickson, while in Sweden, learned of the death of one of his German collaborators. This man's wife was a confirmed

Nazi. If she should now discover the document Erickson had given her husband—as proof of the latter's services to the Allied cause— Erickson's usefulness as an agent would be ended, and if he returned to Germany he would be seized at once and executed. Erickson's wife urged that he stop his espionage activities, that he had already done enough. But Erickson argued that, since his work was proving of real value, he ought to make every effort to continue it.

Erickson quickly arranged a business trip to Germany. His wife, who feared the Gestapo might already be waiting for him, wanted to accompany him, but Erickson refused to let her endanger herself, too.

In Germany Erickson visited the agent's widow and children. He managed to get himself invited to stay at the house. The woman was quite attractive and had always been sweet to him; now she evinced a real attraction. This proved useful, but also awkward, for he had to pretend reciprocation. Learning that her husband's papers were to be gone over in the next day or so, Erickson offered to help. Meantime, he examined the soil in the backyard garden, trying to spot any place where a document might have been buried in a tin box. No luck. The next day at Erickson's suggestion, he and the widow began sorting her husband's papers, preparatory to her lawyer's visit. But there was no trace of the document. Erickson asked if there was any other place where her husband had kept papers, adding that there was a certain contract that would bring in some money to her, which apparently had been mislaid.

The widow remembered a small box which her husband had kept in a chest at his bedside. In that box, along with other things, was a bank safe-deposit-box key. Erickson's offer to go and to get the things from the safe-deposit-box was accepted. But, as he was leaving, the widow's young son, a Nazi-Jugend enthusiast who seemed to resent Erickson, asked to go along. Erickson tried to discourage him, but the boy persisted.

The young boy proved a dangerous antagonist. He stuck close to Erickson's heels as he opened the box; and he wanted the envelopes opened at once to see what his father had left inside. Erickson said they'd better wait, and open them in his mother's presence. Minutes later the boy seized the packet of envelopes and ran off. For Erickson it was a deadly game, as he chased the boy and finally retrieved the packet. Later on the way home Erickson suggested they stop for some delicacies at a restaurant. While the boy was busily eating, Erickson went to the washroom, rapidly searched through the papers—and found the damning document.

That evening he pleaded urgent business and disentangled himself from the growingly amorous widow.

So Erickson continued to cultivate Gestapo officials in Germany. Several times he found himself the object of amorous advances by the wives and daughters of Gestapo officials. Once a sympathetic, seemingly anti-Nazi daughter of a Gestapo leader begged him to aid her in arranging for the escape of one of her professors at the University. Erickson had to refuse. He could not be certain she was not working for the Gestapo and trying to trap him. Besides, he had no right to endanger his important espionage mission by engaging in rescue work.

Meantime Erickson was making more deals with German oil men, although as Allied bombings began to hit more punishingly at the Nazi oil industry, it became harder and harder to buy oil from the Germans. For Erickson's spying was paying off. Allied bombers were being informed of the location of every refinery he visited, and of the type of camouflage used, so that they could unerringly smash them.

On one trip to a big refinery, Erickson had to accept the manager's invitation to dinner, served in the latter's private office. Erickson had visited this refinery before and had reported on it to the Allies—so it was surely on the bombing list. Erickson tried to get away early, but it was almost midnight when he finally left. Five minutes later, Allied bombers smashed that plant to smithereens.

All this while Erickson had been permitted to visit only certain specific oil plants in particular cities. Other plants, in fact a substantial portion of the German oil industry, was still kept concealed effectively. And many bombed plants were being repaired more rapidly than the Allies realized. By this time it was the fall of 1944 and the Allies were getting ready for the Rhine offensive. Allied Intelligence agents asked Erickson if it was possible to get additional information, covering more plants. Because if the supply of oil to the Wehrmacht and Luftwaffe could be reduced substantially, it would contribute in a major fashion to Allied victory in the coming months—and it would save many Allied and American lives.

The only way to get that information Erickson said was to make a survey of the entire German oil industry. But in what way could he arrange such a survey? Erickson racked his brain for a method.

Finally, he hit on an idea—a super-hoax, a "Big Deal" of the type only a really high-level salesman would dream of attempting.

Suppose he offered the Germans an opportunity to build a synthetic oil refinery in Sweden, to be financed partly by Swedish and partly by German funds? The idea ought to appeal to the Germans because it would give them a new source of desperately needed oil, a source in a neutral country, safe from Allied bombers. Also it would offer Nazi officials a legitimate means of patriotically investing their funds in a neutral country, where it could come in handy if Germany were defeated and they were forced to flee. The Nazis might well go for the bait. If they did, then Erickson could logically ask to make a survey of the German oil industry, in order to see the techniques and production layouts, so as to set the new plant up with the best operating methods.

Erickson prepared the sales prospectus for his Big Deal with great care, complete with "documents" of Swedish officials' support and the millions Swedish capitalists had promised. (Later when this broke in the press it almost led to the impeachment of several key Swedish officials and the dismissal of a leading bank president.)

Finke thought it was a fine idea. But Herr Ludwig—who had continued to be suspicious of Erickson—was against it. Erickson knew that Ludwig was one of Ribbentrop's boys; and the Ribbentrop faction was more and more at odds with the Himmler faction, the Gestapo. So, taking advantage of the rift, Erickson persisted in selling his deal to the Gestapo big-wigs.

Finally, in October, 1944, Erickson was informed that arrangements had been made for him to see Himmler. Erickson boarded the plane at the Stockholm airfield and was flown across the choppy waters of the Baltic Sea and the gray plains of north Germany to the Templehof airport. Gestapo officials assigned him to a suite at the best unbombed hotel in Berlin. He was treated so royally that he felt like a condemned man on the evening of his execution.

Meantime, Ludwig—still suspicious of Erickson—had gotten in touch with certain friends of his in the Gestapo and put them on Erickson's trail. Thus, there were some members of the Gestapo staff at headquarters who observed Erickson with cold suspicion as he passed them on his way to Himmler's office.

Heinrich Himmler, the Gestapo chief, welcomed Erickson warmly. They talked for quite a while about Erickson's plan for building a synthetic oil refinery in Sweden. Erickson presented all the advantages of the plan—the neutral source of oil, the fine profit opportunities for the investors, the valuable contribution it could make to the Nazi war effort. But, like the good salesman he was, Erickson didn't rush the prospect, didn't try to push the Big Deal over all at once. Instead, he then undersold; he said that in all fairness it might be best if he first surveyed the German plants and saw all types of operations at first hand, so that he'd know just what was required and be sure he could really produce the goods. Himmler thought this a capital idea; he liked a man such as Erickson, he said, a man who did not go off half-cocked and promise things he might not be able to deliver.

At the end of the interview Himmler gave Erickson a special pass which permitted him to travel all over Germany and inspect anything and everything in the oil industry. It also ordered the oil executives to answer all Erickson's questions. And Erickson was assigned a limousine with all the gasoline coupons he needed.

Erickson now toured all the big oil refineries in German hands. He talked with the directors of each plant, found out how much they were producing, how the repairs of the bombed plant were progressing and so on. He gathered every bit of data about the oil industry that could possibly be of use to the Allies—but he had to be careful to try to do it always in a manner that seemed germane to his supposed purpose, the building of a synthetic refinery in Sweden. Himmler might have the Gestapo checking on him—and if Erickson asked too many irrelevant questions they might put two and two together.

Arrangements had been made for Erickson to turn in partial reports, as he went along, to various Allied agents in Germany. Thus, if Erickson were apprehended at any point, the Allies would still get the information he had gathered up to that time. Every effort was made to use the least risky means of passing on the information, such as letters, addressed to his wife or Prince Carl, left at prearranged places where they might carelessly have been forgotten. Nevertheless, such reports increased the risk of detection.

Soon Erickson began to realize that he was being carefully shadowed by the Gestapo. He wasn't sure whether this was being done by Himmler's direction, or whether it was inspired by Ludwig, the Nazi official in Sweden who distrusted him.

In one city Erickson ran into an oil executive, an ardent Nazi, with whom he had several times competed on international business deals in pre-war days. This man knew Erickson as being far from fond of the Nazis. Erickson invited the man for a mug of beer at a tavern and tried to allay the man's suspicions, pretending that with him business was business. The man appeared satisfied, but Erickson felt he was still suspicious. As soon as they parted Erickson managed to throw the Gestapo agent off his trail by mingling with a throng and then cutting away rapidly into another crowd. Then he circled back and tried to pick up the trail of the suspicious executive. At first there was no sign of him. Then Erickson spotted him inside a public phone booth. Erickson edged up and heard him call the Gestapo and arrange for an appointment to give them important information about a man he had just met. Erickson slugged the man with the handle of a heavy jack-knife he carried, before the latter could mention the name "Erickson." As the unconscious man slumped into his arms, a policeman loomed up in the darkness. Erickson laughingly said his pal had a few too many, and dragged the man off. A few minutes later Erickson had to steel himself and, for his own safety and that of his mission, dispose of the would-be informer once and for all.

Erickson resumed his survey, moving along as fast as possible; he had a feeling that his luck might be running out.

Passing through Berlin on his homeward journey, Erickson learned that one of his German collaborators had been arrested by the Gestapo on suspicion; he was probably being tortured to make him talk. Erickson reported on his survey to Himmler and indicated that he believed he could deliver the goods. Then he reserved passage on the next available plane to Stockholm. But Himmler called and suggested Erickson confer with various technical men to clear up some details about the synthetic oil plant deal. Erickson explained that he wanted to reach an important investor now in Stockholm who might leave in the interim, but Himmler said that capital would be no problem.

Erickson had previously arranged to have himself informed by telegram on a certain day that his wife was very ill and would he please return at once. This was to give him good reason for hastening away as soon as his survey was finished. That wire should be arriving in two days. But by then the German collaborator, now being interrogated by the Gestapo, might have talked. Erickson wired his wife telling her he would be home soon and asking her how she was feeling, as a cue to have the pre-planned wire about her illness sent at once.

But his own wire crossed his wife's wire that same day. For, an hour later—two days early—the wire arrived from Dr. Peterson saying his wife was deathly ill. Evidently, Erickson's wife had become apprehensive and jumped the gun.

Erickson was permitted to leave immediately. At the airport, the Gestapo official's daughter who had previously asked Erickson to help her in rescuing her professor, handed him a package which contained a bulky manuscript she wanted him to put into his luggage and take along to Sweden. Her professor had died of natural causes—a heart attack—and had entrusted the manuscript to her. Its title was "Recommendations for the New Dawn of Our Nation." Again Erickson had to refuse. But as he waved good-bye to her, she and the bundle of manuscript under her arm summed up for him the spirit of the new, free Germany which might arise after the war.

Erickson crossed the Baltic Sea for the last time during the war. He turned over his information to Allied Intelligence. Then for several months he pretended to be working on the synthetic oil plant deal in Sweden.

During those few months—preceding the Allies' big offensive—Erickson's information really paid dividends. For our pilots knew the precise location and appearance of every important oil refinery run by the Nazis. No amount of camouflage could hide them; in fact, often the camouflage, reported by Erickson, served as a landmark to help guide our bombers to their targets. The Allies had all the Nazi refineries spotted right on the map, together with the location of the defenses the Germans had set up for the refinery areas: the anti-aircraft batteries, the fighter-plane runways, and so on. What's more, after our bombers put a plant out of commission, Erickson's information made it possible to estimate accurately just when the Nazi would succeed in putting it back into operation, so it could be bombed again.

All this meant that when the Allies' big offensive got underway, large numbers of Nazi tanks, half-tracks and other armored vehicles remained helplessly stalled out in the field; and countless Nazi planes lacked the gas to take off from their airstrips.

After the Nazi surrender, a special victory celebration was held in the American Legation in Stockholm with Erickson and his wife as guests of honor. Erickson's old friends, who had spurned him because of his seeming collaboration with the Nazis, heard the full story from the American Ambassador. Later Herr Ludwig, who had been so suspicious of Erickson, was apprehended and arrested; it's doubtful that he appreciated this confirmation of the excellence of his perceptions.

MASTER OF THE DOUBLE CROSS

by William C. White

In the 1930s, in Berlin, William C. White met an émigré Russian general who told him about this remarkable diplomatic ruse which changed the course of modern history. Whether taken at face value or as itself a hoax, this dramatic tale exemplifies deception carried to its extreme limits.

This is really General Yablonsky's story. He is the old man who sits nightly in a corner of that little Russian café on Nollendorfplatz in Berlin. The rows of medals that blot his blouse will attract your attention. His frayed clothes, uncut hair and his eyes forever fixed on the remotest of shadows will arouse your pity. He asks nothing except a chance for conversation. He accepts graciously an invitation to join in a drink. He will order vodka. The General is a typical Russian *émigré*, poverty-stricken, alive only in his roots which are all buried in the past.

He comes nightly to this café, to talk with anyone who will buy him a small flagon of vodka. He will talk to anyone, but chiefly on one subject, the Japanese. About the Russo-Japanese War he will talk for hours.

Sometimes, when there has been vodka without stint, he tells this story of Captain Tanama.

"One man alone is responsible for the Russian revolution and for all the following filth of the Bolsheviki," he says, leading up to that story. "One man, a Japanese, Captain Tanama. There would be a Tsar in Holy Russia today had it not been for this scoundrel. You see, if we had won that war with Japan in 1905 there would have been no revolution. The Japanese defeated us then and that defeat produced the revolutionary movement in Russia. Did you ever look at things that way?"

An argument usually arises at this point, but the General, intent on his story, carries on.

"And the Japanese would not have won, had it not been for that traitor Tanama. You have never heard of him?"

I had never heard.

This is the story which the old General, once of the Tsar's Intelligence Service, then tells.

Captain Tanama, the General begins, first came to St. Petersburg as military attaché to the Japanese Embassy in 1901. He was of some special breed, I guess, not built like most of his people but nearly six feet tall. His face was the color of bronze and ugly, like some Tibetan devil mask. Ugly, yes, but he looked striking in uniform and women seemed to be attracted to him.

In those days I was a captain, serving as assistant to the chief of the Military Intelligence Division. Tanama was a foreign military attaché, which is a polite way of saying "spy," and it was part of our job to keep both eyes on him. We learned everything that we could about him. He came from one of the oldest families in the country, and his father was one of the Mikado's closest advisers. Thorough breeding and long residence abroad had given Tanama a proud grace and a polish that marked him in any gathering. He spoke perfect French, of course. He went with the fastest set in the diplomatic circle and was popular everywhere. There was no subservient ground-scraping pose about him. He was extremely able. He knew it. He had a marvelous career before him. He knew it. But he made no attempt to impress anyone, either by false pride or, worse, by false modesty.

As a matter of fact, we of the Intelligence Service were more than usually interested in Tanama. Every one of us, on the General Staff, knew that it was only a matter of time before we would have to fight the Japs in the Far East. They knew it, too. That made us pay more than normal attention to things Japanese. Furthermore, we were receiving information from our own agents in Tokio that the Japanese War Office was continually securing our military secrets. In other words, there was a leak somewhere in St. Petersburg.

Tanama had a way of making friends, with officers, actresses, officials—it made no difference. It is not a far step from making friends to using friends. Tanama had a lot of money and he was an inveterate gambler. He almost always lost and always with a smile, and he paid losses of the size which makes smiling difficult.

For a year we put Tanama under the closest observation, but with no results. We watched every Russian officer with whom he was friendly but we found nothing suspicious. Tanama was mixed up with a number of girls around town but these were only the usual sort of liaisons. We knew, because the girls were on our payroll.

Yet every report from our agents in Tokio told us that the leak still existed and was, if anything, growing larger.

There was one thing that we could do and we planned to do it, to drive Tanama out of the country by some means or other, in the hope that his successor would be neither so clever nor so ingratiatingly charming nor so efficient. If we could start some scandal around him he would have to go. No people are as sensitive to disgrace as the Japanese. If the disgrace is awful enough they will commit *hara kiri*, suicide by a sword through the belly.

We planned to threaten Tanama with disgrace hoping that he would either leave or commit suicide.

It was easy to "frame" him. He was most friendly with an actress, Ilyinskaya. They seemed to be attracted to each other. In public they seldom appeared together but in private—! Their relationship was well known in court circles. We went to her and told her what we wanted, but we had to use threats to get her to promise to help us. My God, I think she really loved that scoundrel! She finally promised.

One evening she went to Captain Tanama and said that it was necessary for him to marry her, at once. He refused, like a polished gentleman of course, pointing out that when a Japanese officer marries a non-Japanese, he must leave his country's service. He had his career to think of. Besides, he added, somewhat as an afterthought, he had a wife in Japan. He offered Ilyinskaya money but she would not touch it. It was either marriage—or publicity.

"You can think about it until tomorrow night," she told him. "I will come then for an answer. If you say, 'No,' I shall start a scandal in your apartment."

We sat in our office the next day waiting to hear that Tanama had decided on a sudden departure for Tokio. We could scarcely hope, yet, for suicide. The morning passed and most of the afternoon and there was no news. Ilyinskaya was ready to go to his apartment and there to tear her clothes and to scream for help. We arranged that the first people to break through the door would be newspaper men.

Then my telephone rang. It was Tanama asking to see me alone immediately, "most urgently."

I went to his apartment. I must say that he was frank for he began, in straightforward fashion, "Do you know of this Ilyinskaya affair?"

Unable to return his frankness, I said that I did not.

He explained briefly the situation and said, "You realize what choice is left for me if she carries out her threat?"

I bowed politely. "It is a very nasty situation."

"Very. And awfully awkward. I was a fool to get so involved with her."

There was nothing to indicate that he suspected our part in the affair.

"Could you not help me to change her mind or to stop publicity perhaps?"

I had no answer ready except to mumble, "It would be very difficult."

"I should be very glad to pay—"

"I am afraid that money is of little use here," I said coldly.

"No, no, I could pay in other ways." Before I could guess at what he was trying to say he continued, "Don't think me cowardly. I am not afraid of disgrace nor even of suicide. But my family is a very proud and ancient one and my father, on the Emperor's Privy Council, is a very old man. I should hate to have him know of my disgrace, at the very end of his life. He would think it his duty to follow me in disgraceful death."

He paused, his eyes downcast. Then, abruptly, he stared me in the face and asked, "*Monsieur le capitaine,* you *can* help me if you wish. What are your terms?"

I answered with pretended hesitation, "I am not sure that I can help. In any case you would have to leave Russia."

"Certainly. And what else? In what ways can I—er—serve you?"

I was too confused by the connotation of that question to think clearly but there was no doubt about what it meant.

"I must speak to my superiors about that," I managed to say.

I returned to my office and told my associates of the conversation and of the terms. They laughed loudly at the idea of a Japanese army officer, and one of high caste at that, offering to aid the Intelligence Service of a potential enemy.

"He puts a low value on our intelligence," Major Oblomov, my superior said.

"Anything he would report to us would be specially prepared for us in Tokio, you can be sure of that," I agreed. "If he leaves Russia, that is enough."

"But it would be a shame not to play with him," Oblomov said. "He has been so courteous that we might ask him to supply us with copies of plans for troop movements around Port Arthur and in southern Manchuria. It would be interesting to know just what the Japanese War College would prepare for us. We could be sure that in reality they would carry out just the opposite."

We decided to play Tanama's game. We would insist on his immediate departure and we would ask for copies of vital plans and mobilization orders. Then we would agree to "silence" Ilyinskaya, "difficult" as it might be.

Pretending the greatest seriousness, I gave him our decision on the following day.

"I have already requested my transfer and I shall leave within a week," he replied. "I am grateful for your help. You will have no reason to regret what you have done for me."

He left St. Petersburg on the following day. It was late summer in 1902, the last time that this scoundrel who brought about the Russian revolution of 1917 was in Russia. I was there and we said goodbye most ceremoniously. It would have been better if I had shot him.

Tanama's successor, who turned up a few weeks later, was a little shoat, with no charm and with no great ability.

We were busy thereafter with our own preparations for the war in the Far East that daily appeared more and more inevitable. We forgot Tanama as we concentrated on our own plans. We forgot him, until one day in December, 1902, when a package came to us by diplomatic pouch from our military attaché in Tokio. With it was a note from our attaché saying that it had been left at the Embassy by someone unknown, with instructions to forward it to us unopened. We opened it. It contained plans, to the minutest detail, for Japanese action around Port Arthur, showing where troops would be landed, how they would be distributed, and what the objectives of any drive there would be.

We examined the plans carefully. There were several novelties in proposed tactics which surprised us. Everything had been done with the most meticulous care.

"The Japanese are thorough, even in such imitation works of art as these," said Major Oblomov.

"Perhaps they are genuine," one officer suggested.

"Nonsense. Of course they would do a trick like this with the greatest air of authenticity."

Six months later, in the summer of 1903, another set of plans arrived in just the same way. The same detail, the same meticulousness. These were plans for action on the south Manchurian peninsula in general, focusing on Mukden. The care with which the plans had been prepared increased the number of skeptics in our department. Two or three officers now said that, in the possibility that the plans might be genuine, we should study them carefully and revise our counter-plans accordingly.

"What awful fools we would be if we learned that Tanama was really honest and that these had been made from stolen originals," one commented.

Such work would have called for a complete revision of our own defense tactics and these plans, too, were finally set aside in our archives. But Tanama, at long distance, had been successful in one thing. He had brought ill feeling into our department. Those officers who believed in his good faith, in spite of the ridiculousness of that belief, were on increasingly bad terms with the rest of us.

Late in December of the same year a third set of plans arrived, for action along the Yalu River.

There was no chance for any of the usual discussion this time. A day or so after the arrival of this third package came startling information from Tokio, information almost unbelievable but fully corroborated by our military attaché there: Tanama had been caught stealing plans from the War Office and had been executed as a spy.

We were inclined to scoff at this at first as another Japanese trick. But every source of information that we had supported it as a fact. And whatever doubts may have remained were erased a few days later by a story carried by the press of the world saying that his father, Prince Tanama, of the Privy Council, had committed suicide on hearing of the disgraceful death of his son. They gave the old man quite a spectacular funeral.

War was imminent and we knew it. We went over the plans which Tanama had sent us with all speed. Day and night we worked to correct our own tactics, to take advantage of these mobilization orders. Those officers who had always supported the belief in the authenticity of the plans laughed loud now, when they had time. No one had much time for anything.

Then the war broke out, in February, 1904, the war that was to result eventually in the Revolution of 1905 and the later Revolution of 1917. Our Tsar sent us into battle with his prayers.

In April we fell back on the Chiuliencheng position on the Yalu River. You have never heard of the battle there, on April 30, 1904? It is one of the important battles of the world. There for the first time in modern history an army of yellow men defeated an army of the white race.

We had the plans of the Japanese there. Tanama had given them to us. But, wherever we stationed one regiment to offset the Japs, there were two Japanese regiments waiting. Wherever we had one artillery battery there were two of the Japanese. And the battle ended with our army in flight. There, for the first time, Asia triumphed over Europe. One of every two men in our ranks was killed, and only one of every forty Japanese.

It was too late to revise our general tactics. We were defeated at Nashan, at Mukden, at Port Arthur. Yet history tells you that we lost the war because the Trans-Siberian Railroad could not bring us men and supplies fast enough. Nonsense! We had enough men, and more than the Japanese. But in the wrong place, every time.

I was at the front and in December, 1904, I heard the rest of the story from a captured Japanese officer. I asked him about Tanama.

"He is a great national hero," the prisoner said. "The Emperor has given him and his family the order of the Rising Sun, second class."

"Then he was not really executed?"

"Oh yes, he was executed as a spy and disgraced. But a few months ago there was published the true story, how he had eagerly chosen the privilege of disgrace and of being executed, so that he could completely deceive you Russians. It was a great honor."

"And his father?"

"He committed suicide of course. That was likewise a great honor."

DECEPTION GOES TO COURT

ERLE STANLEY GARDNER

by Alva Johnston

WONG DUCK IS WRONG DUCK

One afternoon in 1913 a cherub-faced boy lawyer was pacing the floor in his office at Oxnard, California. Erle was in his freshman year as a lawyer, but he had already won his spurs in petty-larceny circles in Oxnard. An elderly lawyer, too busy to bother with small fry, had turned over the tag end of his practice to the twenty-four-year-old newcomer. Erle wasn't aware of it in 1913, but the local court was his literary testing laboratory. Every time he thought up a new monkey wrench to throw into the legal machinery at Oxnard, he was thinking up a plot complication for future use in fiction.

Erle paced the floor that afternoon because he was in danger of losing prestige in petty-crimes circles. A brilliant Los Angeles practitioner had just acquitted a Chinese lottery-ticket seller of Oxnard by sheer magic. Then he had gone back to Los Angeles, leaving Erle to defend twenty other Chinese accused of selling lottery tickets. There was no defense. Erle faced the prospect of making a pitiable contrast with the Los Angeles wizard.

The metropolitan courtroom star, Paul Schenck, had won the case by musical-comedy methods. He had a Chinese assistant who suddenly became wildly excited and burst into ear-piercing singsong. Then Schenck became wildly excited and chimed in with shrill singsong of his own. Everybody was as startled as if a crew of bagpipers had opened a serenade in the courtroom. When all eyes were concentrated on him, the Chinese assistant tapped the lottery ticket several times with his index finger and squealed gleefully. Schenck studied the ticket intently and gave a triumphant cackle.

"Now, sir," said Schenck, addressing the prosecution witness, "I ask you to look very carefully at this ticket and tell the jury whether you are quite certain that this is exactly the same ticket that you purchased from the defendant."

The witness was convinced that Schenck and the Chinese had made some big discovery and were about to trap him. He refused to say positively whether the ticket was the right one or not, and the jury brought in a verdict of not guilty.

Schenck couldn't talk Chinese. He had merely given an imitation of it for moral effect on the witness. A perfectionist himself, Erle later mastered the language and learned to stage his own phony-discovery scenes in honest Chinese dialect. But even if he had been able to talk Chinese in 1913, he couldn't have used the Los Angeles lawyer's trick over and over again in the twenty pending cases. Erle paced the floor for four hours in the hope of inventing a legal razzle-dazzle that would save the day.

Suddenly the moon-faced young barrister stopped in his tracks. An idea had popped into his head. He called in the leader of the Oxnard Chinese, unofficially known as the "Mayor of Chinatown," and talked to him for several minutes in pidgin English.

"Got it straight?" asked Erle finally.

The mayor nodded vigorously and hurried away.

Chinatown was a scene of frantic activity that night. It was as peaceful as a Quaker village on the following morning.

At noon an out-of-town detective arrived in Oxnard and picked up a Chinese who was booked as Ah Lee. The prosecutor had twenty cases and planned to bring the defendants into court at his leisure. At the station the Chinese prisoner gave a friendly greeting to a deputy sheriff who was permanently stationed in Oxnard. This deputy was regarded as a mental giant because he could distinguish one Chinese from another, but he had been kept in the background during the anti-lottery crusade because the Chinese could recognize him at a great distance. The deputy was sulky. He felt that the authorities had pointedly gone over his head. When he found that the prisoner had been booked as Ah Lee, he laughed an I-told-you-so sort of a laugh.

"I guess the drinks are on you," he told the out-of-town detective. "That's not Ah Lee."

"That certainly is Ah Lee," said the detective. "I bought a ticket from him a week ago, and I just arrested him at Ah Lee's laundry."

"If that's Ah Lee, I'm your wife's grandmother," said the deputy. "I've known Ah Lee for ten years. He does my Sunday shirts. This is Wong Duck, the butcher."

"But I tell you he was running the laundry," said the detective. "He was bossing the others around. What would a butcher be doing running a laundry?"

"Who knows why a Chinaman does anything" asked the deputy.

The out-of-town detective identified another man, from whom he said he had purchased a lottery ticket the week before, as Ho Ling, the grocer.

"He's Ong Hai Foo, the druggist," said the deputy. "Ong's the biggest dealer in dried-lizard medicine in Southern California."

"But I tell you he was running Ho Ling's grocery when we arrested him," said the out-of-town detective. "He was waiting on customers. Why would a druggist be selling vegetables?"

The deputy grunted contemptuously and went out to look over Chinatown for himself. He found the place all scrambled up. Every Chinese shopkeeper was running some other man's shop. The deputy finally straightened out all the identities, but the prosecuting attorney shook his head.

"There's been a lot of monkey business going on here," he said, "but we can't get convictions when our witness starts by picking out the wrong men. All the cases will have to be dropped."

That was exactly the result Erle had aimed at.

Wong Duck had been booked as Ah Lee. Since the charge was on the record, the case had to be disposed of in court.

The boy lawyer soaked the Chinese the colossal fee of $100, and they paid it without a murmur. They recognized that, in killing twenty cases by a simple memory test, he had outshone the celebrated acquitter from Los Angeles.

Erle didn't realize it at the time, but in his Chinatown shake-up he was salting away thousands of dollars' worth of literature for future consumption. The Chinatown bamboozlement pops up in many disguises in the Erle Stanley Gardner mysteries. It is an instructive example of how big literary crops can be harvested from unimportant-looking seeds of experience.

Bill Fallon

by Avery Hale

HOW DEAF CAN YOU GET?

Sometimes the prosecution had evidence so damaging to Fallon's client that Fallon was obliged to divert attention from it. Once, for example, he was cross-examining a detective who was the state's star witness against a crook client. The questioning began in normal enough fashion, with Fallon speaking in a moderate tone of voice and standing a respectful distance from the witness. As the cross-examination progressed, Fallon's voice grew louder and he inched closer to the witness until he was practically in the man's lap and shouting at the top of his voice.

The district attorney objected to Fallon's tone of voice. Fallon kept right on shouting at the witness. Now the judge banged his gavel so hard he almost broke it and instructed Fallon to stop talking. Fallon, not taking his eyes from the witness, kept right on shouting. Now the judge began to shout at Fallon. Finally Fallon turned to His Honor, cupped a hand to his ear, and inquired if the judge was talking to him.

"*Yes,* I'm talking to you!" shouted the judge.

"What did Your Honor say?" asked Fallon.

"I said I'm talking to you," roared the judge, "and instructing you not to stand so close to the witness and shout at him." Fallon cupped his hand to his ear again and stood there looking puzzled. "What did Your Honor say?" Now the judge began to roar even louder. Fallon looked startled, then hung his head. He couldn't, he said, help it if he had recently suffered an injury that had impaired his hearing. "You mean you are deaf?" asked the judge. Fallon couldn't hear the man. The judge roared a repetition of his question. "Yes, Your Honor," said Fallon, looking at the jury out of the corner of his eye. "I fear that I may never be able to hear normally again."

For the balance of the trial, poor Fallon had to shout at the state's witnesses and practically sit in their laps while the prosecutor and the judge had to interrupt him frequently. "Your Honor," said the prosecutor, "I think counsel is only pretending he is deaf." Fallon asked the judge what the man had said. The judge shouted the information. Fallon looked sad again. "Would that I were but pretending," he said.

The jury was obviously touched by Fallon's plight. Fallon didn't put the defendant on the stand because he, not the crook, had become the defendant. With poor deafened Fallon as his stand-in the crook was acquitted.

Outside the courtroom after the verdict was in, Fallon tapped the prosecutor on the shoulder. "Pardon me, sir," he whispered, "but if I'm not mistaken I heard you drop a pin back there."

THE PROSECUTOR'S WIFE

Fallon was defending a big-time thief down in the Criminal Courts Building one day when the prosecutor appeared with a spanking new briefcase. The briefcase was filled with enough stuff to send Fallon's client up for a couple of hundred years. During the noon recess the prosecutor took the briefcase out to lunch with him. While at lunch, he got a telephone call. He got up from the table to go to the phone, taking the briefcase with him. There was a woman's voice on the other end of the wire. She inquired of the prosecutor if he were aware of the fact that his wife was unfaithful to him. The prosecutor was aware of no such thing but the inquiry startled him. It startled him so much that he forgot all about his briefcase, lying on the floor beside him. When the conversation was over, the briefcase was gone.

When the afternoon court session began, Fallon appeared, immersed in papers, and bathed in innocence. The prosecutor didn't show up. Fallon demanded to know where the man was. The judge explained that the session would have to be adjourned because the prosecutor had lost his briefcase. Fallon seemed shocked. But he quickly recovered from his shock. He demanded that the trial proceed. The judge overruled him. Finally the proceedings were adjourned until next morning while the prosecutor combed lower Manhattan for his briefcase.

Next morning the prosecutor still didn't have his briefcase. He had to admit that all his evidence had vanished. Fallon demanded that the trial proceed. It did. Fallon's client was acquitted.

KEROSENE AND WATER DO MIX

Fallon was once defending a fierce-looking big Russian who was accused of arson. The defendant had a record that was somewhat against him. He had been convicted twice previously of setting fire to furniture stores he had operated and attempting to collect insurance on the fires.

The whole case, by the time Fallon got through twisting it around, revolved around some rags that a fireman had come across in the burning building. A fireman got on the stand and testified that the rags had been soaking wet and that when he had smelled them he had smelled kerosene.

When it came Fallon's time to cross-examine the witness, he

approached the fireman in what seemed to some veteran courtroom attachés as a deceptively friendly manner. "You are, I suppose," Fallon began, "an expert on smells."

"Well," answered the fireman, "I kind of have to be. You got to look out for suspicious smells when you go out on a fire so's to make sure it ain't incendiary."

"And so you picked up these rags and decided they were soaked with kerosene?"

"Right."

"All right," said Fallon, "I'll take your word for it that you are telling the truth. You *look* like a truthful man. But now I want to ask you something else. Are you sure that that was kerosene—and not *water* —that you smelled on those rags?"

The fireman seemed puzzled that Fallon should ask him such a question. He certainly knew the difference between water and kerosene when he smelled the two.

"Then," said Fallon, "you would not object to *proving* to these fine gentlemen here"—Fallon pointed to the jurors—"that you can tell the difference between water and kerosene when you smell them." No, the fireman would not object; he was, in fact, slightly amused.

Fallon went back to counsel table and produced five bottles, each filled with liquid. The bottles were numbered 1, 2, 3, 4 and 5. He took the cork out of bottle No. 1 and handed the bottle to the witness. "Smell that," he said, "and tell me what's in it." The fireman took a smell. "Kerosene," he said. "Take a *good* smell," said Fallon. "I want you to be certain that you do not make a mistake." The fireman took a deep smell. "Kerosene," he repeated.

Now Fallon handed the witness bottle No. 2 and had him repeat the test. "Kerosene," said the fireman. The witness said that bottles 3, 4 and 5 also contained kerosene. When Fallon took bottle No. 5 from the fireman he put it to his lips and took a drink of it. Now he held the bottle to the nose of each juror. "Gentlemen," he said to the jurors, "the contents of this bottle do not taste like kerosene to me. And I am very sure they do not smell like kerosene to you." He paused to savor the drama of the situation. "This bottle—this bottle that the gentleman on the witness stand would have you believe contains kerosene—contains water. When you get into the jury room I wish you would all help yourselves to a taste of its contents. If what you taste in the slightest resembles kerosene I think it is your duty to convict my client. If what you taste is water, then it is your duty to acquit my client."

Of course the client was acquitted. What Fallon had done, simply, was to fill the fireman's smelling apparatus with kerosene fumes by having the man inhale deeply of the first four bottles. Then, when he whiffed the water, the kerosene fumes from the previous four bottles were still in his nostrils and he thought the water was kerosene.

METAMORPHOSIS

The early Twenties in New York was the golden age for the Bucket Boys. They were the fellows who operated bucket shops, or crooked brokerage houses. There was no Securities and Exchange Commission to regulate brokerage houses in the Twenties and the way the boobs were taken by the sharpers was really something awful.

In one typical case, which rotated around a sucker identifying a bucketeer on the witness stand, Fallon simply had his client completely alter his appearance. He put the man on a severe diet and reduced him from two hundred pounds to 140. He changed the color of the defendant's hair from brown to black, mixed with gray. He had the man shave off a naturally imposing moustache and wear needless eyeglasses so thick that they looked like magnifying glasses. To top off everything, he sent the defendant to a dramatic coach and vested him with a Southern accent.

After the sucker had testified for the government, Fallon cross-examined him at length about the appearance of the villain who had bilked him out of his life's savings. The sucker described the villain as a moustached, brown-haired man weighing about two hundred pounds who talked like a typical New Yorker. "And did he wear eyeglasses?" asked Fallon. "No." "You're *sure* about that?" Positively.

When Fallon put the defendant on the stand, the man got up from the counsel table and began to walk toward the witness chair. He walked into the counsel table and fell over it. "Why," said Fallon, "you're so nervous you forgot to put on your glasses. There's nothing to be nervous about. The complainant in this case certainly wasn't talking about *you*."

So the villain put on the thick-lensed glasses and took the stand, and made a categorical denial of the charge against him in moss-and-honeysuckle tones. Then Fallon asked the sucker to stand up. "Is this the man you say took your money?" he asked the sucker, pointing to the defendant. "No," said the sucker.

Acquittal.

V

THE PROFIT MOTIVE

THE AMERICAN GOLCONDA*

by A. J. Liebling

The first and, as far as history records, the last American to salt a diamond mine was a man named Philip Arnold, who died of shotgun slugs as a sequel to a business argument in Elizabethtown, Hardin County, Kentucky, in the year 1873. Arnold was the man who set a limit to American optimism, realistically revising the nation's ideas about its future and its resources, and it is a wonder that historians have not as yet given him his due. Arnold was a banker worth a mere $300,000 when he died, but it was as a creative prospector in the West that he made his impress on his country's imagination. An ordinary prospector merely tries to find deposits of precious minerals; a creative prospector places them in the ground for others to find.

Arnold was born in Hardin County (which gave Abraham Lincoln to the nation) about 1830. When a young man, he inherited a small farm there and married. Shortly before the Civil War, he left his wife and a couple of children on the Hardin County place and went out to California to look for gold. Several times, after making small strikes, he returned to Kentucky. In the early sixties, with a partner named John Slack, he developed a claim near Marysville, California, that the two sold for $50,000. Arnold took most of his share of the money home to Kentucky and placed it in a large safe on his farm. By 1869 he was back in California, looking for something to do. Since no new gold fields had recently been reported, he took a job as assistant book-keeper with the Diamond Drill Company of San Francisco. This firm sold diamond-pointed rock drills to mine-owners. The foundations of the great West Coast mining fortunes had been laid; men like George Hearst, James Fair, Darius Ogden Mills, and William Chapman Ralston, chairman of the board of the Bank of California, controlled the best properties. The haphazard days of Forty-nine were long over, but their tradition lingered in the form of a chronic optimism. An army of disappointed miners was still billeted on the Coast, ready to march at the first report of a new field. In the East and in England, investors, despite a number of unfortunate experiences, were still willing to put money into western mines. The bonanza business needed only a new stimulus. The first hints of what this stimulus was to be came in the form of newspaper stories about the discovery of the diamond fields in South Africa, the third great source of diamonds in the world's history. The mines of Golconda, in India, had supplied most of the world's diamonds until the eighteenth century, when the Portuguese had discovered deposits in Brazil. South Africa eclipsed both these older fields. American prospectors almost immediately began to look for diamonds in Arizona and New Mexico Territories, where there were said to be geological formations like those in the African diamond lands.

Arnold, still at his job with the drill company, displayed great interest in diamonds. He explained to the head bookkeeper, another ex-miner, named Cooper, that he wanted to learn all about precious stones before he began looking for them. The company kept a considerable stock of diamonds on hand, of the flawed or discolored sort used for pointing drills, so Arnold had a chance to handle a variety of the stones and perhaps secrete a few. He used to question Cooper about tests employed to determine if diamonds were genuine and about the differences in appearance of diamonds from the three known fields. When he had pumped Cooper dry, he bought books about diamonds and studied them. By the spring of 1871 he knew as much about diamonds as anybody on the Coast. Reports from South Africa, ever more glowing, maintained the excitement in America. None of the prospectors in America had found any diamonds, but some of them had come back from Arizona with garnets, which they thought were rubies. To doubt the eventual discovery of diamonds here seemed like selling America short. The public was prepared for a diamond rush.

Arnold took a leave of absence early in 1871. He returned to San Francisco two months later, saying he had been into eastern Arizona with his old mining partner John Slack, and he showed Cooper the result of their prospecting: a handful of desert sapphires and rubylike garnets, with a few small uncut diamonds of the type that the Diamond Drill Company used. Arnold said that they had obtained the diamonds by trading with an Indian, to whom they had promised a gallon of whiskey if he would get them some more stones. The two prospectors had then followed the Indian and thus had found where the field was. The field lay within Apache territory, Arnold said, where it would have been dangerous for two white men to remain, so, after killing the Indian, the partners had marked the site of the field and headed back for California, to get help in developing them. Arnold and Slack took their stones to Asbury Harpending, a flamboyant San Franciscan who had once been a filibuster in Nicaragua and was at the time dividing his energies between land speculation and the promotion of wildcat mines. Harpending had known Arnold for a long time, for which reason, perhaps, he took no stock in the story. If the partners returned to their field and found a really impressive lot of stones, he suggested, they would have no trouble getting financial backing. Arnold and Slack then announced they were going back to the Arizona desert, and left town.

The two men reappeared in San Francisco several months later, worn and weatherbeaten. They called on George D. Roberts, another mining promoter, and asked permission to deposit a sack in his office safe, as it was after banking hours and they couldn't place it in the vaults of the Bank of California. This naturally made Roberts curious. He engaged Arnold in conversation—Slack seldom had anything to say—and learned that the sack contained diamonds, rubies, and emeralds, all from a mysterious region that the partners refused to locate specifically. Roberts was in no position to know that Arnold had just made a trip to London, embarking at Halifax, a port where he had been tolerably sure to meet no other Californians, and returning the same way. Arnold had brought back from this expedition about $12,000 worth of imperfect precious stones, uncut. On his return trip, Arnold had been met at St. Louis by Slack, who had remained in this country. They then had traversed the part of Arizona where the Indians traded garnets and had bought a peck or so of the red stones to give their collection bulk and foster the idea that the diamonds and garnets were found in the same general region. The bad feature of their strike, the partners told Roberts, was that it was situated in a section full of hostile Indians. To work it, they would have to organize an expedition strong enough to fight off the redskins, and they hadn't enough money for that.

Arnold and Slack did not ask Roberts to help them; Roberts insisted. Feeling that it would be too big a proposition for one man to swing, he went to the house of William Ralston, the banker, that night and let him in on the secret. Roberts and Ralston sneaked the stones out of Roberts' safe and submitted samples to San Francisco jewelers for appraisal. This was what Arnold had expected them to do, and he had correctly calculated the jewelers' reactions. He knew that there was no jeweler in San Francisco who had any large experience with uncut stones. All of them were familiar with tests by which to prove a stone was genuine; after the tests they could be counted on to set an arbitrary average price per carat, assuming that some of the stones in any given collection were good and others not so good. If they had known that the stones were all malformed culls, they would have named a much lower figure, but they didn't, of course, have that knowledge. The San Francisco jewelers set a value of $100,000 on the prospectors' $12,000 worth of flawed beauties. The stones looked like excellent samples, especially as Arnold and Slack said the lot represented only a few hours' digging. Under no conditions, the partners said when Roberts approached them, would they part with a controlling interest in their claim, but they would sell a good part of it in order to obtain working capital.

Roberts introduced Ralston, who said that he would put in some money if the partners first convinced him by taking a personal representative to the site of the field. Arnold agreed to take a man there on condition that the man should be blindfolded from the moment the party left the railroad. "Otherwise," Arnold said, "our secret is out and he can lead you back to the claim without us." Ralston took command of the promotion. He sent as his agent a satellite named General David D. Colton, a cool, sensible gold miner, not given to enthusiasm. Colton, however, had never seen a diamond field. Arnold and Slack took the agent by train to Rawlins, a station on the Union Pacific, in Wyoming Territory, where the three alighted. This rather surprised Colton, as he had assumed the field was in Arizona. Arnold told him that they had purposely given that impression to throw possible claim-jumpers off the track. Rawlins is not far north of the Colorado line, and the diamond field seems to have been in what is now Jackson County, Colorado. Arnold blindfolded Colton and put him on a horse. The three men rode for four days, the partners taking the hoodwink from Colton's eyes only after sundown, when they encamped. On the fourth day, when Arnold whipped the bandage from Colton's face, the agent found himself blinking on a mesa 7,500 feet high, which he supposed to be deep in the wilderness. The men dismounted and began to walk about the mesa, and before long Colton saw a great anthill sparkling in the sun. Approaching the mound, he found that it was powdered with diamond dust. Arnold came up and dug into the anthill with a knife and soon pulled out a small diamond. Colton then began digging and in a few minutes discovered a diamond for himself. During the day he got forty or fifty diamonds and emeralds, most of them in a gulch which intersected the mesa. Next day, Arnold told Colton they would have to move on, as he feared they had been observed by Indians. After another long, hard journey, during which Colton was blindfolded, they got back to the railroad. The gems which Colton brought in his pocket proved real, like the first batch. They were worth only a few hundred dollars, a jeweler told him, but it seemed a fair assumption that if a man digging with a pocketknife could find that many in a day, the deposits were of unexampled richness.

It appeared to Ralston, after he received Colton's report, that he had stumbled upon a big thing, perhaps the greatest promotion of his life. He believed he might need operating funds of several million dollars, and that meant he would have to enlist Eastern capital. Speed was essential, because some trapper or independent prospector might at any moment find what Ralston was already calling in conversation the American Golconda. Since Ralston's own money was pretty well tied up in investments, he admitted a few more of his West Coast friends to the cabal. One was General G. M. Dodge (the country swarmed with generals for twenty years after the Civil War). Another was a promoter named William M. Lent, and a third was the dashing Asbury Harpending. Each, on being approached, expressed skepticism. Each, on learning of Colton's trip and the high valuation set upon the gems, became convinced. General Dodge, who, Harpending said long afterward, "had a low opinion of his fellow-men," talked to Arnold for a while and then said that he would stake his life on the fellow's integrity.

The promoters decided to go to New York, taking with them Slack, Arnold, and a bag of gems from the American Golconda. On the way East the financiers wrangled a bit with the two discoverers. Arnold and Slack now appeared suspicious and said they wanted some tangible guarantee of the promoters' good faith. Lent gave them $100,000 as earnest money. It was not hard for the Westerners to get a hearing in financial circles, especially as the head of the Bank of California had retained General Samuel L. M. Barlow, the most distinguished New York corporation lawyer of the day, to act as intermediary and legal adviser. General Barlow had engaged as associate General Benjamin F. Butler, an influential congressman. Barlow had bespoken the interest of a group of New York bankers, including August Belmont and Henry Seligman. Before proceeding with the deal, however, the New Yorkers insisted that Charles Tiffany, the founder of the great jewelry house, be permitted to appraise the samples from the diamond field. In the event that Tiffany's appraisal was favorable, Belmont and Seligman wanted a mining expert of national reputation to go out to the site and make a report upon it. Arnold agreed to both tests, but said that his partner and he were not going to lead an expert to the mine until they had some sort of written contract protecting their rights. He signed an agreement with the promoters providing that if Tiffany and the mining expert endorsed the samples and the mine, the promoters would pay to the prospectors $650,000 in cash as the full price of their claim.

It is impossible, in retrospect, not to marvel at Arnold's composure as he went to the meeting with Tiffany, reputed to be America's greatest judge of gems. The rendezvous was at General Barlow's mansion at 1 Madison Avenue. Horace Greeley, the editor of the *Tribune*, soon to be an unsuccessful Presidential candidate, was at the house when the Californian party arrived, as were the Eastern financiers and General George B. McClellan, former Commander in Chief of the Union Armies, who had been an unsuccessful Presidential candidate in 1864. Greeley liked to be in the know even though he had to pledge secrecy. McClellan was slated for a job on the board of directors of the projected mining company. He had a fine mustache and made good window dressing.

Tiffany, as Arnold must have been aware, knew no more about uncut stones than most other American jewelers. He had begun life as a Yankee notion peddler and had never served an apprenticeship on the Continent. He knew that the diamonds before him were real, and that several presumably competent experts on the Coast had made flattering estimates of their value. After a brief glance at the gems, followed by a regal wave of his hand, the whiskery jeweler said, "I cannot fix an exact value until my lapidary has had a chance to inspect each stone, but I can assure you that they are worth at least a hundred and fifty thousand dollars." Arnold, watching him, never blinked.

The meeting, although supposedly secret, was the chief talk of hotel bars and Wall Street offices the next day. That night, Arnold came to the Western promoters and said Slack was fed up with the whole business and would sell his share for $100,000, chargeable against the final purchase price. They got the money for Slack by morning. The two miners now had $200,000 between them. The Easterners who had witnessed the appraisal were feverishly hot on the enterprise and a struggle for the control of the corporation began before it officially came into being. Since it appeared that the financial and technical negotiations, including the selection of a mining expert to examine the property, would take several months, Arnold announced that he and Slack were going back to the West, and that they would leave their precious stones with the promoters as security.

Instead of going West, the prospectors traveled up to Quebec and took ship for London, carrying with them most of their bank roll. They needed more gems with which to resalt the mine. Arnold was not the man to jeopardize a $650,000 deal by skimping on a few quarts of niggerhead diamonds, as the dealers called imperfect South African stones. The pair bought about eleven hundred diamonds in London and then made a business-and-pleasure trip to the Continent, where they bought many of the worst diamonds in Amsterdam and Antwerp. Altogether they spent around $50,000. After their shopping spree in Europe, the partners returned to Colorado and installed the props. The mesa where they had fooled Colton was in fact only about fifteen miles from the Union Pacific railway tracks; they had led him there by a carefully circuitous course. It was near the north end of a pine-clad ridge that ran east and west, to the north of Brown's Hole in Colorado and eight miles below the Wyoming line.

The Eastern and Western promoters in the combination agreed on Henry Janin, the leading mining engineer of his time, to make the inspection. The mine expert's fee was to be $2,500, plus an option on a thousand shares at $10 each. Only a Philip Arnold would have led a Janin to a salted mine. The prospector had the intuition of a great poker player for an opponent's foible. For the fact was that Janin had never in his life seen diamond land, and he was disarmed in advance by the high appraisal of the sample stones. Surely, he must have felt, if a sample from a mine was worth $150,000, the property was bound to be valuable.

Janin went out to the claim in the spring of 1872. Lent, General Dodge, General Colton, and several other Californians who had remained in New York for the winter went out with him. Arnold and Slack met them at Omaha. The party got off the train at a station in

Colorado Territory late one night. Horses were waiting; the men mounted and rode off into the unknown. Arnold and Slack, leading their companions by roundabout trails, made the journey long and difficult, as they had done when they had convoyed Colton. Janin and most of the promoters were physically soft, and the prospectors kept them riding for several days. When the money men got to the mesa they were dead-tired and the provisions were low.

Within a few minutes after their arrival, Colton found the anthill shining with diamond dust he remembered from his first visit. Almost instantly the men started spading into the ground, shouting with pleasure like children at a picnic as they turned up their shining finds. Many of the stones, it appeared, were near the surface. Arnold and Slack pointed out places for their backers to dig, and whenever a promoter followed their advice he found a diamond. The party remained eight days on the ground. During that time, Janin reported, working only with spades and knives, the men turned up 256 carats of large diamonds worth $4,096 at prevailing rates, 568 carats of small ones worth $1,704, and four pounds of rubies worth $2,226. Since the party had dug up what was estimated to be about a ton and a half of rock and dirt, this indicated to Janin that the mesa assayed better than $5,000 to the ton, a figure unparalleled in mining history. He conservatively estimated that the land should yield $5,000,000 an acre. "With a hundred men and proper machinery," he told Lent, "I would guarantee to send out a million dollars in diamonds every thirty days." The mesa contained at least three thousand acres, and Janin said there was no reason the rest of it shouldn't yield as heavily as the spot they had started on. As for the surrounding land, that was of a conspicuously similar geological nature. It might yield billions.

The investigators went on to San Francisco, again led over a circuitous route back to the railroad by Arnold, leaving Slack at the diggings as a guard. Nobody ever reported seeing Slack again. It will never be known whether he lost his nerve and went off with the money he had already made or whether he died by violence. He simply disappeared. Janin sold his thousand-share option to one of the California men at $40 a share, making a profit of $30,000. He said that he did not wish to retain stock in the company, as his report would then be construed as a boost for his own prosperity.

In San Francisco, the promoters organized the San Francisco & New York Mining & Commercial Company, with 100,000 shares of stock. None was offered to the public. The shares were divided among twenty-five leading West Coast mining sharps, men like Ralston, Roberts, Lent, and Harpending. Each of them paid $40,000 into the company's treasury for initial expenses. One of the incorporators, a banker named Gansl, acted as the West Coast representative of Baron Rothschild. Janin released a favorable report and it appeared in the *Mining & Engineering Journal* and in the San Francisco newspapers. It caused a sensation. When Arnold saw the report, he pretended to be very angry. He said he had not realized the property was that good. Roberts and Ralston reminded him of his contract and virtually forced the $450,000 balance of the agreed purchase price upon him. They were glad when he left town. He said he was going back to Kentucky, where he would have a loaded shotgun always ready to welcome any San Francisco mining sharps who came to visit him.

The San Francisco & New York Company opened tremendous offices in the California city, featuring General McClellan and a permanent display of the largest diamonds from the diggings. Would-be investors besieged the place, but the fortunate shareholders would sell no stock. As always on the flanks of a great financial operation, a number of imitations had sprung up. These corporations claimed to have diamond lands of their own, but the public knew that they were only waiting for the big company to reveal the location of its holdings, when they would rush out prospecting gangs and file claims as near the company's diggings as was legally possible. In Paris, Baron Rothschild rejoiced that he had a finger in the pie, even though it was not a controlling interest. "America is a rich land," he sententiously told an interviewer. "It has given us many surprises. It reserves many more."

The exposure came in a curious manner. To explain it requires the introduction of a character who had had no direct connection with the affairs of the San Francisco & New York Mining & Commercial Company. He was a thirty-year-old government geologist named Clarence King, a member of the first class to be graduated from the Sheffield Scientific School at Yale. King is credited with being the founder of the United States Geological Survey; readers of the *Education of Henry Adams* will remember him as one of Adams' closest friends. In 1872, King, with a party of assistants, had completed a survey of the fortieth parallel of latitude in the United States, which had led him through the salted-mine territory. It piqued him that in his painstaking inventory of mineral resources he had come across no trace of diamond lands. Feeling that his pro-

fessional reputation was at stake, King went back over the ground
he had covered to find, if possible, where he had slipped up. Any
party travelling through that country at that time was conspicuous;
King located some sheepherders who had seen the Janin party on the
march. Guided by them, he set out with a small expedition and
found the mesa. The aspect of the place aided him, for Arnold, well
documented in diamond mining, had picked the sort of site where
diamonds might well have been found.

"The section of the geological locality is so astonishingly considered," King reported later to the unhappy directors of the company,
"that I can feel no surprise that even so trustworthy and cautious an
engineer as Mr. Janin should have brought home the belief he did."
This was much kinder to Janin than most of King's statements. Making his way to the top of the mesa, the government geologist
found "in conjunction four kinds of diamonds, Oriental rubies, garnets, spinels, sapphires, emeralds, and amethysts—an association of
minerals impossible of occurrence in nature." "The gems exist in
positions where Nature alone could never have placed them," he
wrote in his report. "They do not exist where, had the occurrence
been genuine, the inevitable laws of Nature must have carried them."
It was a polite way of saying that he found stones which had been
obviously stamped into the ground by a man's boot and others placed
in the crevices of rocks. There was even one in a tree stump. The most
absurd discovery of all was made by a German in charge of King's
pack animals. "Look, Mr. King," the German said, pulling a bright
chip out of the ground near the anthill, "this is the bulliest diamond
field as never was! It not only produces diamonds, it cuts them!"
He had found a cut diamond, one which must have got in among
the rough stones by mistake when a dealer in Antwerp or London was
wrapping Arnold's purchases.

King rode to Laramie, Wyoming Territory, where he sent a telegram to Ralston, the most prominent director of the company, and
then boarded a train for San Francisco. When he arrived in that city
he sent the following note:

To the Board of Directors of the San Francisco & New York Mining &
Commercial Company:
I have hastened to San Francisco to lay before you the startling fact
that the new diamond fields upon which are based such large investment and such brilliant hope are utterly valueless, and yourselves and
your engineer, Mr. Henry Janin, the victims of an unparalleled fraud.

Ralston persuaded him to hold off his announcement while the directors of the company considered what to do. King agreed to wait a fortnight on Ralston's promise to prevent trading in the stock. During this time, King guided a party of the directors back to the site and convinced them that their mine was worthless. Colton was one of the group and so was Janin. The fraud now seemed to them terribly obvious. On November 27, 1872, a long story appeared on the front page of the San Francisco *Bulletin*, embodying the text of King's report to the directors and a statement by Janin admitting he had been deceived. Most of the sharped sharpers felt too foolish to be angry at anybody; Lent was the only one of the crowd who was not ashamed to go after Arnold for his money. He had, it appeared, bought out several of his colleagues, and was hooked for more than $300,000.

Slack had disappeared, but Arnold's whereabouts was no secret. He was home in Kentucky, where, in the short time following his return from California, he had become one of the local nabobs. He had bought himself an $18,000 house on a plot of thirty-two acres near Elizabethtown, moving into it on the day of the purchase and on the next day spending $4,000 for livestock. In the house he had a great safe, and in the safe, according to Elizabethtown gossip, he had at least $500,000 in cash. The late war was a fresh and rankling memory in Hardin County. Most of Arnold's friends were retired Morgan raiders, and indeed he is said to have ridden on a few raids himself during his holidays from the gold fields. Arnold did not fear whatever prosecution might be instituted by Yankees in Hardin County, nor was there any chance that the Governor of Kentucky would allow him to be extradited. The Governor had a prejudice in favor of Kentuckian defendants.

When Lent came to Louisville and instituted a civil suit against Arnold to recover $350,000, the Kentuckian played injured innocence. Arnold's attorney issued a statement that his client would fight the case to the bitter end "for the sake of suffering humanity, which has been robbed and swindled by these California mining sharks for the last twenty-five years." The initial difficulty in Lent's suit was that nobody could be hired to serve the attachment on Arnold. The retired prospector continued to live at Elizabethtown, but Hardin County people insisted he wasn't there. It seemed neither polite nor judicious to contradict them.

Lent and some California friends stayed at the Galt House in Louisville, drinking the wine of the country while they waited for the case to get under way, and every day or so the *Courier-Journal* carried a humorous story on the "search" for Arnold. One day, said the newspaper, a process-server announced that he had got to Arnold by disguising himself as a tramp and had pressed the papers on the miner and escaped before Arnold could get to his shotgun. This was immediately denied by Arnold's friends, whose version was that "a suspicious, seedy-looking man" had been seen by workmen to climb "out of the sewer leading to Arnold's privy." Arnold, they said, was ready with the shotgun and would have fired had not the stranger "dashed through a nearby creek and up the Louisville & Nashville tracks for about two miles" without leaving any papers behind him. The discouraged Lent at last went back to California, but his lawyers kept up such a running fire on Arnold that the former prospector agreed to compromise the case. He might have remained safe in Hardin County for the rest of his life without paying a cent, but he would have risked legal trouble any time he crossed the county line. So he settled Lent's claim with a payment of $150,000.

Of the first $200,000 that Arnold and Slack had received, they had spent about $50,000 on stones for salting and another $10,000 for expenses. If, as seems probable, they divided the rest, Arnold got $70,000, which, with the final payment of $450,000, brought his net receipts from the hoax to $520,000. After disgorging $150,000 to Lent and paying his lawyer $25,000, he remained a very wealthy man for Elizabethtown.

After the settlement, Arnold acquired about five hundred acres of good farming land. He built the first store in Elizabethtown to be equipped with plate-glass windows. He announced that he had discovered a silver deposit in Kentucky worth $9,000,000 and that he would soon start work on it. He also entered the banking business, and that was a mistake. There was another bank in Elizabethtown, managed by two partners. The banks' interests clashed, and the odds, because of the code of Hardin County, were two to one against Arnold. The retired gold miner shot one of his competitors in the arm, but the fellow's partner sneaked up behind Arnold and let him have a charge of buckshot in the back. This was fatal to Arnold, a man who has left his mark on the American psyche. Arnold had found investors willing to believe absolutely anything. He left them willing to believe not quite everything. Their credulity never rebounded to the pre-Arnold level. The Age of Innocence was over.

RIZA BEY, THE PERSIAN ENVOY TO LOUIS XIV

by Phineas T. Barnum

*Barnum, who made a fortune through brash and thorough ex-
ploitation of humbug, also took delight in exposing other humbugs,
at the same time according them their due as masters of deception.
This account is from his book* The Humbugs of the World *(1866).*

"*L'Etat c'est moi*"—"I am the State," was Louis' celebrated and very
significant motto; for in his own hands he had really concentrated
all the powers of the realm, and woe to him who trifled with a majesty
so imperial!

It was toward the close of the year 1667, when Louis, in the pleni-
tude of military success, returned from his campaign in Flanders,
where his invincible troops had proven too much for the broad-
breeched but gallant Dutchmen. In the short space of three months he
had added whole provinces, including some forty or fifty cities and
towns, to his dominions; and his fame was ringing throughout Chris-
tendom. It had even penetrated to the farthest East; and the King of
Siam sent a costly embassy from his remote kingdom, to offer his
congratulations and fraternal greeting.

Louis had already removed the pageantries of his royal household to his magnificent new palace of Versailles, on which the wealth
of conquered kingdoms had been lavished, and there, in the Great
Hall of Mirrors, received the homage of his own nobles and the
ambassadors of foreign powers. The utmost splendor of which
human life was susceptible seemed so common and familiar in those
days, that the train was dazzling indeed that could excite any very
particular attention. But, at length, there came something that made
even the pampered courtiers of the new Babylon stare—a Persian
embassy. Yes, a genuine, actual, living envoy from that wonderful
Empire in the East, which in her time had ruled the whole Oriental
world, and still retained almost fabulous wealth and splendor.

278

It was announced formally, one morning, to Louis, that His Most Serene Excellency, Riza Bey, with an interminable tail of titles, hangers-on and equipages, had reached the port of Marseilles, having journeyed by way of Trebizond and Constantinople, to lay before the great "King of the Franks" brotherly congratulations and gorgeous presents from his own illustrious master, the Shah of Persia.

It would be needless for me to detail the events of the progress of Riza Bey from Marseilles to Paris, by way of Avignon and Lyons. It was certainly in keeping with the pretensions of the Ambassador. From town to town the progress was a continued ovation. Triumphal arches, bonfires, chimes of bells, and hurrahing crowds in their best bibs and tuckers, military parades and civic ceremonies, everywhere awaited the children of the farthest East.

Still Riza Bey and his dozen or two of dusky companions did not, by any means, cut so splendid a figure as had been expected. They had with them some camels, antelopes, bulbuls, and monkeys—like any traveling caravan, and were dressed in the most outrageous and outlandish attire. They jabbered, too, a gibberish utterly incomprehensible to the crowd, and did everything that had never been seen or done before. All this, however, delighted the populace. Had they been similarly transmogrified, or played such queer pranks themselves, it would only have been food for mockery; but the foreign air and fame of the thing made it all wonderful, and, as the chief rogue in the plot had foreseen, blinded the popular eye and made his "embassy" a complete success.

At length, after some four weeks of slow progress, the "Persians" arrived at Paris, where they were received, with tremendous *éclat*. They entered by Barrière du Trône, so styled because it was there that Louis Quatorze himself had been received upon a temporary throne, set up, with splendid decorations and triumphal arches, in the open air, when he returned from his Flanders campaign. Riza Bey was upon this occasion a little more splendid than he had been on his way from the sea-coast, and really loomed up in startling style in his tall, black, rimless hat of wool, shaped precisely like an elongated flower-pot, and his silk robes dangling to his heels and covered with huge painted figures and bright metal decorations of every shape and size unknown, to European man-millinery. A circlet or collar, apparently of gold, set with precious stones (California diamonds!) surrounded his neck, and monstrous glittering rings covered all the fingers, and even the thumbs of both his hands.

Well, after the throng had scampered, crowded, and shouted themselves hoarse, and had straggled to their homes, sufficiently tired and pocket-picked, the Ambassador and his suite were lodged in sumptuous apartments in the old royal residence of the Tuileries, under the care and charge of King Louis' own assistant majordomo and a guard of courtiers and regiments of Royal Swiss. Banqueting and music filled up the first evening; and upon the ensuing day His Majesty, who thus did his visitors especial honor, sent the Duc de Richelieu to announce that he would graciously receive them on the third evening at Versailles.

Meanwhile the most extensive preparations were made for the grand audience thus accorded; and when the appointed occasion had arrived, the entire Gallery of Mirrors with all the adjacent spaces and corridors, were crowded with the beauty, the chivalry, the wit, taste, and intellect of France at that dazzling period. Louis the Great himself never appeared to finer advantage. His truly royal countenance was lighted up with pride and satisfaction as the Envoy of the haughty Oriental king approached the splendid throne on which he sat, and as he descended a step to meet him and stood there in his magnificent robes of state, the Persian envoy bent the knee, and with uncovered head presented the credentials of his mission. . . .

A grand ball and supper concluded this night of splendor, and Riza Bey was fairly launched at the French court; every member of which, to please the King, tried to outvie his compeers in the assiduity of his attentions, and the value of the books, pictures, gems, equipages, arms &c., which they heaped upon the illustrious Persian. The latter gentleman very quietly smoked his pipe and lounged on his divan before company, and diligently packed up the goods when he and his jolly companions were left alone. The presents of the Shah had not yet arrived, but were daily expected via Marseilles, and from time to time the olive-colored suite was diminished by the departure of one of the number with his chest on a special mission to England, Austria, Portugal, Spain, and other European powers.

In the meantime, the Bey was feted in all directions, with every species of entertainment, and it was whispered that the fair ones of that dissolute court were, from the first, eager in the bestowal of their favors. The King favored his Persian pet with numerous personal interviews, at which, in broken French, the Envoy unfolded the most imposing schemes of Oriental conquest and commerce that his master was cordially willing to share with his great brother of France. At

one of these chatty *tête-à-têtes*, the magnificent Riza Bey, upon whom
the King had already conferred his own portrait set in diamonds, and
other gifts worth several millions of francs, placed in the Royal hand
several superb fragments of opal and turquoise said to have been
found in a district of country bordering on the Caspian sea, which
teemed with limitless treasures of the same kind, and which the
Shah of Persia proposed to divide with France for the honor of her
alliance. The King was enchanted.

Thus the great King-fish was fairly hooked, and Riza Bey could
take his time. The golden tide that flowed in to him did not slacken,
and his own expenses were all provided for at the Tuileries. The only
thing remaining to be done was a grand foray on the tradesmen of
Paris, and this was splendidly executed. The most exquisite wares of
all descriptions were gathered in, without mention of payment; and
one by one the Persian phalanx distributed itself through Europe until
only two or three were left with the Ambassador.

At length, word was sent to Versailles that the gifts from the Shah
had come, and a day was appointed for their presentation. The day
arrived, and the Hall of Audience was again thrown open. All was
jubilee; the King and the court waited, but no Persian—no Riza Bey—
no presents from the Shah!

That morning three men, without either caftans or robes, but very
much resembling the blacklegs of the day in their attire and deportment, had left the Tuileries at daylight with a bag and a bundle, and
returned no more. They were Riza Bey and his last bodyguard; the
bag and the bundle were the smallest in bulk but the most precious
in value of a month's successful plunder. The turquoises and opals
left with the King turned out, upon close inspection, to be a new and
very ingenious variety of colored glass.

Of course, a hue and cry was raised in all directions, but totally in
vain. It was afterward believed that a noted barber and suspected
bandit at Leghorn, who had once really traveled in Persia, and there
picked up the knowledge and the ready money that served his turn,
was the perpetrator of this pretty joke and speculation, as he disappeared from his native city about this time.

All Europe laughed heartily at the Grand Monarque and his fair
court-dames, and "An Embassy from Persia" was for many years thereafter an expression similar to "Walker!" in English, or "Buncombe!"
in American conversation, when the party using it seeks to intimate
that the color of his optics is not a distinct pea-green!

ABANDON ALL BEASTS!

by Elmer L. Irey with William J. Slocum

Believe it or not, for many years Ringling Brothers-Barnum and Bailey was guilty of understatement. Their posters billed the show as a three-ring circus, and even the small type failed to list one of their brightest stars, "Honest" John Kelley, who was giving consistently brilliant solo performances in the show's fourth and most profitable ring. Here, Elmer L. Irey, former head of the Internal Revenue Department's enforcement division, gives Kelley his due and reveals the hidden feats ticket-buyers never got to see.

Of all the wonders on display at the Ringling Brothers-Barnum and Bailey Combined Shows, none was comparable to the miracles of gall perpetrated on Uncle Sam for fifteen years by the circus' lawyer, "Honest" John Kelley.

Honest John was a worker of miracles from the day he joined the struggling Ringling Brothers circus enterprises early in the century until the day Uncle Sam accepted $800,000 on a circus tax bill of $3,600,000. The reason for that fiscal defeat for the Government will be explained—rather lamely—in time.

Honest John's earlier miracles were performed in the role of a humble claims adjustor for the circus. Envious associates say Kelley somehow managed to be in attendance whenever an unwary circus customer fell off the top of the bleachers or had half an arm nibbled away by an irritable tiger. As the victim regained consciousness he would find Honest John hovering above him, two tickets for next year's circus clutched in his hand. Before the necessary splints or tourniquets had been fully affixed, the dazed victim would be so impressed by the eloquent claim adjustor that he would be mumbling apologies for upsetting the circus routine. Honest John was never vengeful in the face of this humble apology. He was, in fact, generous, handing over two tickets for next year's stand in return for the autograph of the wounded customer. Honest John carried forms for the purpose of gathering these signatures.

When Uncle Sam passed tax statutes and thereby became a legitimate claimant to circus income in 1918, the job of adjusting these claims was taken over for the circus by Kelley. While John never succeeded in paying Uncle Sam off in circus tickets he did make what might be called a try. From 1918 to 1932 the circus paid taxes on profits of $4,000,000. This would seem a rather conservative estimate by Kelley inasmuch as the various Ringling Brothers connected with the enterprise and their heirs withdrew more than $10,000,000 in that time.

The evidence seemed to show that the brothers and their heirs were unconscious beneficiaries of Honest John's skill with a tax blank. I confess some personal confusion as to how this miracle of mass innocence was affected. None of the brothers was alive when the case was tried. Kelley insisted he was following the orders of the late Charles Ringling, but testimony was introduced and accepted stating that Charles knew nothing of his lawyer's chicanery. It seemed everybody just turned over blank income tax forms with their signatures already affixed and Kelley filled in the detail.

Kelley's reward seems to have been the salary that comes to a good and faithful servant, plus occasional sums of money extracted from the circus coffers to be used, according to Kelley, as bribes for tax examiners. Whether Kelley paid such bribes or not is what is known technically as a "moot point." Kelley had a crack accountant whom he paid $80,000 over a period of years, and then forced the man to return $70,000 of it.

The business of catching up to Kelley deserves no lengthy description. It is simply the routine tale of a discharged employee who became more disgruntled as he became hungrier and walked in and told us Kelley was cheating. This was followed by the equally routine burning of records, minor and major informal perjuries, and the soft sound of clairvoyant mammals abandoning ship. It was all dreadfully routine. The only thing out of the ordinary was Kelley's imaginative and deft hand with a tax blank, and it is because of the macabre humor inherent therein that this case is recorded.

Kelley's main weapon in larceny was depreciation. In 1918 when he had the first inventory made of the circus, it reached $1,800,000 and Honest John was disappointed in the figure. He promptly ordered an inventory to be made of a standard fifty-car circus. This

non-existent circus was added to the true inventory and the value
swelled to $4,000,000 and Honest John was off to the wars against
the tax laws. Kelley kept using the $4,000,000 as the basis for deprecia-
tion charges until he was caught. When the non-existent tents,
wagons, and animals had been fully depreciated, Kelley started all
over again with equally fictional tents, wagons, and animals.

Kelley was deadly with "spectacles." These are the ornate parades
with which the circus traditionally starts its performance. The
parades are always built around a theme, such as "The Burning of
Rome" or "Cleopatra's Barge." Typical of Kelley's use of these ancient
stand-bys was "Joan of Arc," declared a total loss by Kelley after its
use in 1923. Kelley charged $200,000 for this. "Joan of Arc" had cost
nothing like $200,000, but that was academic. What was more to the
point was the fact that "Joan of Arc" had been built in 1911 for use
that year and was dust when Kelley put it on the tax form twelve
years later. Several spectacles that had been the toast of the 1890's
wound up on the books in the 1920's.

The claiming of a deduction such as "Joan of Arc" came under the
head of abandonment. The difference between abandonment and
depreciation can best be described by using the example of a wagon
that costs $100 and can be reasonably expected to be useful for
ten years. If the wagon lasts its full ten years the taxpayer may take
a depreciation of $10 on it annually. If, however, the taxpayer must
burn the wagon or break it up after two years' use, he may claim an
abandonment deduction of $80.

Kelley "abandoned" a rhinoceros which had died a year after it
was purchased. This was a legitimate claim, except that Kelley
claimed the beast had cost $35,000 when it had really been bought for
$3,500. He liked that trick so much he kept "abandoning" the same
dead rhino for three successive years at $35,000 per annum.

The matter of the rhino brought out some strange facets of American life. Did you know that there are men all over the country
who sit by the hour just looking at circus rhinos? They are zoo directors in large cities. The government brought these experts to New
York to testify in rebuttal against Kelley's claims that he had so many
rhinos he lost at least one a year. The zoo experts were able to tell
how many rhinos the circus carried in any one season and name the
season. They could also accurately tell the age, the sex, and the physical characteristics of every rhino that had been with the circus in
thirty years.

The zoologists were as expert about other exotic beasts. There was, for instance, the fearful death rate among circus polar bears and the resultant "abandonment" charges. The solemn experts first ridiculed Kelley's numerical claims anent his stable of polar bears. They then sniffed when it was suggested America was no place for a polar bear. "Polar bears thrive in our climate," they testified. "They like it better than the North Pole."

Death isn't the only reason an animal might be abandoned. It might be "abandoned" in a more literal sense of the word, such as giving a stupid horse away rather than shooting it. Kelley hit a new high in 1927 when the circus moved its winter quarters to Sarasota from Bridgeport. He abandoned madly, leaving behind acres of ground, buildings, and other fixtures which he claimed could not be taken to Sarasota. This was a reasonable claim, except that the circus didn't own any of the things it had "abandoned" in Bridgeport. It rented them.

But Kelley's 1927 exhibition of genius with an "abandonment" was when he took full deductions because it was necessary to leave forty-six elephants behind in Bridgeport, presumably to walk the streets of that factory-filled city until they were taken in by local Yankee mahouts. By a strange twist of fate, Kelley had the poor luck to have a Bridgeport boy as one of the Circuit Court Judges sitting on his appeal trial. The Judge asked for exhaustive details on just how it was possible for forty-six elephants to wander around the streets of his old home town without the matter causing some amount of folk-lore. It seemed the Judge had never heard the matter mentioned in Bridgeport.

The movement to Sarasota and the vast abandonments connected thereto proved fascinating during Kelley's trial, as well as during the appeal. United States Attorney Joseph W. Burns opened his discussion of the case with, "When the circus moved to Sarasota in 1927, Bridgeport must have looked like a jungle." He then touched on the forty-six elephants and went on to point out that Kelley claimed he set loose twenty-three camels, eighteen bears, twenty-three lions, eight hundred horses, and hundreds of monkeys.

Naturally Kelley didn't do all his abandoning in Bridgeport in 1927. He merely did his best work there. He abandoned lions and tigers and other man-eating fauna all over the country.

Except for a few front-office employees, the circus people made excellent witnesses. They would not lie and they had a touch of showmanship that was very helpful to the prosecution. One hardy carpenter insisted that an ornate wagon built in 1898 and depreciated for thousands of dollars had cost $205. The defense was scornful. "How do you know what a wagon built forty years ago cost?"

The witness took the proper pause for effect and drawled, "I know what it cost in 1898 because I built it in 1898."

Kelley not only abandoned horses without number, he also purchased them in unconscionable lots. He was particularly fond of claiming to buy stallions. Stallions are expensive. Kelley claimed the purchase of forty-five stallions in one season. The man in charge of the horses insisted that there were never as many as ten with the show. . . .

"How do you know there weren't forty-five stallions with the show?" demanded the defense.

The horseman looked with pity upon the city-bred lawyer who knew not of the manners and customs of stallions. "Look, mister," explained the patient witness, "we had mares with the circus. If we carried forty-five stallions, too, there wouldn't of been no circus."

John Ringling, the last of the four Ringling brothers who had built up the show, died before the trial. His testimony to the Grand Jury and to us would have made him the Government's strongest witness against Kelley. John Ringling turned over to us all of his books, although he knew their contents were as damaging to him as they were to Kelley. His only stubbornness was about when he would see our agents. John Ringling would do no business with anybody until after midnight. He preferred 3:00 A.M. Intelligence Unit Agent Charles Clarke sat for hours discussing Kelley's claims of abandonments and values of properties with the old man booming "Ridiculous, absolutely ridiculous" into the dawn.

Clarke played Kelley against John Ringling and vice versa. He would sit through the night with Ringling, repeating at strategic intervals, "It's a shame, Mr. Ringling. A great and respected name like yours being sullied by a charlatan like Kelley who abused your honest trust." Ringling would nod agreement and give further evidence of Kelley's unbelievable abuse of trust and friendship.

During the day Clarke would prod Kelley with, "It's a shame, Mr. Kelley. An honest employee like you being used as a cat's-paw by a lot of ungrateful employers who profited by your skill but refuse to help you in your hour of need." Kelley knew a bright, understanding man when he saw one, so he gave Clarke further information.

On April 26, 1938, Kelley was convicted of aiding and assisting the counseling, procuring, and advising the filing of false and fraudulent returns for the Ringlings. He was sentenced to two years in jail and fined $10,000. Two of Kelley's aides received lesser penalties. The Ringlings got a bill for $3,600,000 in additional taxes, penalties, and interest.

That $3,600,000 bill presented many legal problems. The most important problem was the fact that this was our estimate of their taxes and was subject to the Board of Tax Appeals revue. This revue was promptly instituted on appeal from the Ringlings. We were reasonably confident that our figures would stand up, but if they did stand up where were the Ringlings going to get $3,600,000? A forced sale of the circus would bring no such sum. The alternative was for us to take over the circus and run it ourselves until the necessary taxes had been collected. This so horrified the Government that the case was settled for $800,000.

This matter of Uncle Sam shirking his job and not taking over the circus was no capricious decision. We knew when we were overmatched. The Government had once seized a medium-sized circus for taxes and when we got through buying steaks for the lions, hay for the elephants, and ants for the anteaters, the Government found itself in the circus business and losing money. We then sold the circus at a forced sale. With that experience behind us we thought it wise to take the $800,000 and let the Ringlings feed the aardvarks, lions, and elephants. Or abandon them.

BONBONNE D'URANIUM!

by Toni Howard

The atomic age has ushered in many new developments, most of them portentous. Probably only in France could the rise of the atom have produced this hilarious histoire, *complete with high-ranking army officers, American Congressmen, Arabs, Soviet agents, and casks of the newest addition to the list of the world's precious substances, uranium.*

"The baron," said Aimé Gaillard, standing on the beach at Nice and looking out over the blue Mediterranean, "was my pearl. I found him." Gaillard's ugly, flattened face broke in a grin. "And let me tell you, a man's got to crack a lot of oysters before he finds a pearl like that."

Gaillard's pearl was a lustrous one—the young, handsome and wealthy Baron Scipion du Roure de Beruyère. An ardent patriot, the baron wanted to do something for his country. And with the help of Gaillard and his friends, he did. During a summer otherwise notable only for strikes, disorders and the usual government crises, the baron gave France just what it needed—something to laugh about. To do so, he had the help of four of the most rocambolesque scoundrels who ever put a new twist on an old *histoire*.

The baron's adventures began in the spring of 1950, when he drove over to Nice from his villa on the Cap d'Antibes to see Gaillard about a "transaction." Gaillard, a powerful man with the scarred face and broken nose of a thug, listened sympathetically. The baron, it seemed, was extremely worried about the state of the world. He saw the Communist revolution shaping up like a thunderhead over Europe; he saw the Red Army raping and pillaging its way across the blessed soil of France. As Gaillard got it, the baron wanted to clear out with the baroness to America before the shooting started, but first he wanted to make a financial coup.

Being a man of well-rounded interests, most of them concerned

with how to turn an easy franc, Gaillard understood the baron perfectly. In the summer Gaillard runs two beach concessions and an
open-air dance hall in Nice. In the winter, when the supply of fresh
tourist dollars runs low, he engages in "transactions," a form of free
enterprise widely interpreted on the French Riviera.

It so happened that Gaillard had a dear friend named Alberto—
Inspector Jacques Alberto, of the French Border Police—at that
very moment engaged in one of the most delicate operations of French
history—getting uranium out of Germany, out from under the very
noses of the Russians, and into Spain to sell to the Franco government, "last anti-Communist bastion in Europe." The uranium had to
be bought from the Germans at the going price of 50,000 francs—
about $140—the gram. But since the Spanish government was really
hunting for it, anyone who got in on the operation could not only
perform a great service to Western civilization, he could easily double
—or even triple—his investment.

Accordingly, Gaillard took the baron and baroness up to Inspector
Alberto's apartment in Nice, where, behind tightly closed doors, Alberto explained the situation in more detail. Amazingly, the cop and
the aristocrat took to each other immediately. Alberto was a fast-
talking, clean-looking fellow of about thirty-five, as tough as you'd
expect a Corsican police inspector to be. He wore the Croix de Guerre
and the Medal of the Resistance.

The operation, Alberto explained, was a quasi-military one, backed
by the Deuxième Bureau—Secret Police. But since the French parliament had not voted sufficient credits to carry the operation off, the
Deuxième Bureau was looking for a private citizen to put up 10,000,-
000 francs—roughly $28,000—to pay for the first consignment. If the
baron would put up the 10,000,000 and help get the uranium across
the border into Spain, the Spanish would pay him a guaranteed
17,000,000 francs—a neat profit of around $20,000.

There was only one hitch. Soviet agents in Germany and France
had already smelled a nuclear rat and were getting ready to pounce.
Therefore the operation had to be performed in the strictest secrecy.
And therefore, as the baron could well understand, he would have to
be investigated and passed on by the chief of the operation, a Lieutenant Colonel Berthier whose headquarters were in Paris.

Solemn, impressed, the Baron du Roure and his wife agreed. It
was decided to leave for Paris immediately to see the colonel.

Actually, as Alberto told the judge later, there was never too much doubt that Colonel Berthier would accept the baron. The baron had, in effect, everything the colonel liked to see in a man. He was young—twenty-seven—nice-looking, well-educated; member of an old and respected family. He was a conservative in politics, upholder of the good ancient traditions of France, and a stanch anti-Communist. He was married to the attractive brunette, Eléonore Patenôtre, daughter of a former French finance minister, Raymond Patenôtre. In addition, he was rich; his wife was rich, his in-laws were rich. They had two sumptuous villas on the Cap d'Antibes, de luxe apartments in Paris, a family country seat at Bagnols-sur-Cèze in the Gard hunting country —and plenty of folding money as well. And with all that, the baron had managed to remain endearingly naïve. You might almost say he was made for the colonel.

The morning after their arrival the big presentation took place, when Alberto introduced the baron to his chief, "Colonel Jean Berthier of the Counter-intelligence Service." In contrast to the nervousness of the baron, the colonel was very cool and very calm, every inch a colonel. He was young for his rank—only forty—in the French army, a handsome, swarthy man in impeccable uniform, but when du Roure pressed him for more details on the uranium operation, he silenced him so abruptly—"Security!"—that the baron snapped automatically to attention. He questioned the baron sharply on his family, his political ideas and his financial solvency, and finally, reassured, agreed to let the baron finance and handle the first consignment of uranium for Spain.

Next day du Roure went to the Worms Bank in Paris and drew out 10,000,000 francs, which he promptly turned over to Berthier and Alberto. And that night, exactly as agreed, Alberto, Gaillard and the colonel, breathing heavily, struggled up in the typically tiny elevator of the baron's apartment house and lugged in the first case of the precious metal.

It was a beautiful job. From the outside it resembled a giant army foot locker. Inside this was an expensive polished-wood crate with metal hinges and metal seals, and inside this was the "bonbonne d'uranium"—as the French newspapers later called it—an immense lead cask sealed with steel tape and wax and marked: "DANGER! DO NOT OPEN!" Over all, the case measured nearly a cubic yard and weighed about 135 pounds. Turning it over to the baron's custody, Colonel Berthier once more reminded the baron of the heavy trust they had put in him, the dangers of his mission and the need for absolute secrecy. He then handed the baron an envelope marked "TOP SECRET" and stamped military orders for himself and the baroness to get into Spain.

The plans for getting the uranium across the border were carefully laid. The baron and "Nelly"—as the boys were already calling the baroness—were to proceed by auto to St.-Jean-de-Luz on the Bay of Biscay, where they were to hole up and await orders from Paris for the actual crossing of the frontier. Delivery and payment would be made just the other side of the border by General Rodriguez, of the Franquist army. Gaillard, whom the baron was now affectionately calling "Scarface," was to go with them as bodyguard, since at any moment French Communists might get wind of what they were doing and try to ambush them. Feverishly the du Roures made their preparations. They were a little dashed when Gaillard developed a fever and had to take a plane back to Nice instead of going with them.

It was a fine spring day when the baron and baroness set out for St.-Jean-de-Luz, passports and military travel orders all in hand. In the beginning all went well. But at Angoulême, where they spent the night at a hotel under an assumed name, they received a wire from Colonel Berthier saying there would be a slight delay in the plans and adding that he was beginning to have doubts of Gaillard's loyalty.

Somewhat mystified, they went on to St.-Jean-de-Luz. And now everything went wrong. Phone calls and telegrams came flooding in from the colonel in Paris advising one delay after another. By the time they had word to meet Alberto in Bayonne, there, in an army staff car with soldier escort, was not only Alberto but the colonel himself. The colonel's face was a study in grave concern.

Gaillard, the colonel explained, had tipped off the Russians. A Communist attack could be expected any moment. They were to go ahead as planned, but they were to go very cautiously. He asked the baron if he was armed, if the uranium was adequately safeguarded, told him to be ultra-careful, but said that in any case they would have Alberto with them and would be escorted by motorcycles. He himself had to rush back to Paris, from where he would send word as soon as the coast was clear.

For three more days they hung around St.-Jean-de-Luz, waiting. Dutifully the baron reported each morning to the police station to ask if orders had come for him from Paris, but no orders came. Finally, on the fourth day, came a wire: "Too dangerous. Come back."

In whispered conference with Alberto they decided it was too risky to drive back to Paris with the case of uranium with them—better to cut across to the Cap d'Antibes on the Mediterranean.

The trip back was a reactive nightmare. The roads were so poor that it was impossible to keep the uranium from jiggling. The baron began to develop terrible headaches. The motor of the car began to knock and miss. Because of the gamma and other rays, they had to drive with the windows wide open, and the baron and baroness both caught cold. Luckily, the Soviets hadn't yet put up their roadblocks, but even then, it was three in the morning before they reached the baron's villa on the Cap d'Antibes.

Now began a frantic game of cache-cache-the-uranium. First they put it in a cupboard, then in a locked closet. The baron ordered a specially designed asbestos vest and wore it constantly, even in bed; still the radiation was so overpowering it affected his heart. They decided to bury it in the garden, did so, dug it up again, put it back in the closet, changed their minds and buried it again. They bought asbestos gloves to wear when handling it, and moved it only in the dark of night, but in spite of every caution, it seemed to be sapping away their health and ionizing their nervous systems. And then one day Alberto found that the worst had happened—Soviet agents had picked up the radiations with an electroscope and knew now where the uranium was. In haste, he organized and mounted a military guard around the baron's property. The baron breathed easier.

But not for long. On a trip to Paris, he and "Nelly" were invited by Colonel Berthier to lunch at Lapérouse, one of the most expensive restaurants in the city. That lunch cost the colonel 8000 francs— twenty-three dollars—and the baron a diamond necklace. The colonel, a charming and convivial host, explained how narrowly they had missed falling into a Communist trap at St.-Jean-de-Luz as a result of Gaillard's treachery, added parenthetically that unfortunately he had had to have Gaillard bumped off, and then complimented the baron on his loyalty and courage. But since transporting uranium to Spain presented such very real dangers, he advised them now to stock up four or five more cases of the stuff and take it all over at the same time. Could the du Roures finance, say, another 50,000,000 francs' worth?

The baron hesitated. They didn't really have another 50,000,000 they could lay their hands on right this minute, but they did have a magnificent diamond necklace which had been given the baroness by her father and which a noted jeweler valued at fifty-five to sixty-five million. If that would do as collateral, he would get it out of the safety-deposit box and perhaps the colonel could borrow enough on it to finance the operation. The colonel seemed to think that would do all right, and the three parted in excellent spirits. A day or two later the baron turned over the diamond necklace to the colonel and Alberto, and the du Roures then went back to the Cap d'Antibes to look after the uranium.

By this time the uranium was multiplying. When the colonel came down the next week to spend a week end with the du Roures, he and Alberto staggered in with another four cases, plus an enormous cylindrical flask of heavy water. These were all carefully hidden, transferred, rehidden and rerehidden as the first had been. Reporting on the necklace, the colonel said that since they had been able to borrow only 30,000,000 francs on it, he would appreciate it if the baron could now make up the remaining 20,000,000. The baron was happy to, but being a little cramped at the moment, could only give him one million in French francs, "the rest," to quote the baron's testimony, "in dollars and in Swiss gold."

Shortly after this the colonel disappeared—in Spain, Alberto hinted, to arrange for the next delivery. "Scarface" Gaillard had of course reaped the reward of his treachery. So now, for a period of about six months, there was only the faithful Alberto to come and go between the Cap d'Antibes and Nice, fuss over the *bonbonnes* of uranium and heavy water, cart them off for inspection, cart them back again, arrange and rearrange them like a plain-clothes mother hen, and accept the du Roures' hospitality. It was a quiet, uneventful summer and it made the baron restive. He had a lot of money tied up in the Atomic Age now and he wanted to liquidate it and collect his profit. To while away the long afternoons, Alberto helped him write letters of application to the "European Military Counterespionage School" and to the powers behind it—several French and English generals, an American Congressman and one or two big guns of the United States State Department whose names the baron never quite caught. Alberto even addressed and mailed the letters for him.

Still, the plot was thinning out a bit. When the colonel finally turned up again, he and Alberto put their heads together on how to thicken it up again. And a few nights later, in walked a bit of densification in the form of a mysterious and sinister-looking Arab.

The baron had met the Arab before; he had been presented by Alberto as a purchasing agent for the Israeli army—Alberto's usually fertile imagination seems to have given birth to a monstrous hybrid this time. So he let the Arab in and listened to his story. After the usual burnoose-and-scimitar evasion, the Arab came out with it. He was not an Israeli procurement officer at all, but a Soviet agent, and his Russian bosses had authorized him to offer the baron 360,000,000 francs for the original crate of uranium alone! Although flabbergasted at the price—more than $1,000,000—the baron rose to the occasion with manly loyalty, indignantly refused to hear another word and tossed the Arab out.

Confronted with this new example of perfidy and treason, Alberto and Colonel Berthier questioned the baron minutely. What did this Arab look like? Height, coloring, any distinguishing marks or scars? Was he sure this was the same Arab he had met with Alberto?

Late that night the two turned up at the villa again, silently and grimly drove the baron down the coast to the deserted sandy beach of La Garoupe, and there, behind a clump of rushes, asked the baron to identify a blood-spattered, beaten-up corpse.

"The Arab," he whispered.

"Exactly," said the colonel.

Taking the baron's arm, he and Alberto walked the baron back to his car and drove him home to the villa, leaving the poor Arab to wash his face, get rid of his bloody, bullet-spattered jacket and hoof it back to Nice alone.

It was a sobering lesson, but a good one. The baron now knew to what extent the colonel and Alberto meant business. But he also knew now that anything he threw into the enterprise up to 360,000,000 francs was covered by the real value of the uranium casket he was sitting on. With a lighter heart he began scraping the family finances to the bottom of the barrel. With a fortune buried in the garden, why should he quibble about a few million francs? Later that year, when the colonel asked him to make a special effort to help the Counterintelligence track down the Russian agents who had stolen the plans of the super-secret French jet, the Mystère, how could he refuse? All the colonel wanted this time was 30,000,000 francs—only about $85,-000. And in recompense for this and all the other services he had performed, the colonel promised him something he had wanted all his life—the Legion of Honor.

Born healthy, aristocratic and handsome, with an entire set of silverware in his mouth, it was the one thing life had not given the baron. He wanted it passionately. Burbling with excitement, the baron filled out the papers, collected all the documents needed, and handed them to the colonel along with the money to save the Mystère.

But now several disquieting things began to happen. An old friend of the family, a lawyer, called up to say that according to rumors running around Nice the baron was being taken in a radium swindle, and the baron was obliged to deny it vehemently. Then Alberto, too, like the colonel, took to going off on long trips, sometimes for months, leaving the du Roures with no word of what was going on. The four smaller cases of uranium and the flask of heavy water had long since been trundled off for safekeeping to the cellar of the "Paris Military Academy," Alberto had told them, but the big original collateral was still ticking away quietly at the bottom of the garden. The deal with the Spanish was off; the uranium was to be sold any day now to the Americans through the help of Colonel Berthier's brother, an FBI man in New York. But why these prolonged absences?

The du Roures worried it over all winter and up until Easter. Then, one anxious day, they got into their car and drove over toward Marseilles, where Alberto had said his family lived. What they found after much searching was not Alberto, but Alberto's Corsican wife, now the proud proprietress of an imposing new bar, completely remodeled to the tune of six or seven million francs. This upset the baron for several weeks—or until Alberto got back with one of the finest cock-and-bull stories of his entire career.

To explain his long absence, Alberto told the baron that he had been jumped by two Russians and kidnaped in the St. Charles railway station in Marseilles. The Russians had bound and gagged him, tossed him into a German Opel and driven him all the way from Marseilles to Berlin, a distance of about a thousand miles. In Berlin he had been systematically and brutally interrogated on the whereabouts of the uranium case. He showed the baron the terrible welts on his back and arms, the purple bruises on his legs. But—strutting back and forth in front of the du Roures—he was too strong; he had spat at their offer of 600,000,000 francs for the uranium—the price, incidentally, was now sixty times what the baron had paid for it—and he had spat at their threats and tortures. Defeated by his physical courage, they had finally let him go.

It was a superb piece of gaseous diffusion, and it was bolstered up by a series of bruises that Alberto had picked up in what the French underground calls "a settling of accounts." Alberto was, and still is, as proud of that story as a young author of his first fiction sale.

But by now eighteen months had gone by with no sign of a pay-off. And now, for the first time, a splinter of suspicion wedged itself into the baron's head. Remembering the early emphasis on secrecy, it occurred to him that Alberto and Berthier could have stolen the uranium from the Secret Service and could be using him as a fence. He and the baroness talked it over. They decided to use the necklace as a test—they would demand the return of the necklace and see what the colonel answered.

But the colonel was sympathy itself. He understood their impatience. He was getting impatient himself, he said. As for the necklace, that was simple. It was, effectively, in hock with a notary in Dijon for 5,500,000 francs. If the baron would give him the 5,500,000 he would spring it himself. Relieved, the baron gave him the 5,500,000. But no necklace came up.

All the colonel could think to do was to stall for time, and like any good colonel he knew how to do that—kick it upstairs. He told the baron that because of his good work in the cause, the "chief" had asked to see him.

Enter the general. His name was General Combaluzier—an unusual name, but as familiar to Parisians as the name Otis is to New Yorkers, since it stares out at them from the manufacturer's plate of every elevator in Paris—and the minute the baron met him, he forgot about the necklace. Although the general was in civvies, he wore the rosette of the Legion of Honor. He had dignity, a portly military bearing, a massive gray head and a handsome pair of chins.

As is *comme il faut* in the chain of command, he took entire responsibility for everything his subordinates had done; the affair was going along swimmingly and would be totally liquidated by the first of the year, the uranium delivered, the money paid back and the baron's profit assured. In addition, the baron's nomination to the Legion of Honor was being pushed by the Secret Service itself. That, too, would be announced on January first, exactly as promised. Meanwhile, big people in high places were watching the baron for a possible diplomatic post. For proof, the general showed du Roure a letter from the United States Department of State thanking him for the sums he had advanced to so worthy a cause.

Waiting for the first of the year was difficult. The baron had gone to the cleaners for this uranium business. He had sold his Cap d'Antibes villa, he had sold his big American car. He had emptied his bank accounts in Paris and in Switzerland. He had even given his radio and camera to Colonel Berthier for counterespionage use.

New Year's Day dawned gray and dreary. Waking up in his Paris apartment, hung-over, du Roure reached for the *Journal Officiel* and scanned the list of those promoted to the Legion of Honor. No du Roure. No du Roure? But how could that be? Bitterly disappointed, deceived, worried about a measly 100,000 francs—to pay the rent, poor undecorated Baron du Roure threw the *Journal Officiel* at the wall, reached for the phone and called his lawyer.

Four days later, when General Combaluzier waddled up the stairway of the baron's apartment carrying a big box of chocolates for the baroness, there were two cops hidden in the bedroom to listen to the conversation and two more downstairs at the main exit to nab the general on his way out. Mild, pleasant as always, the general sat down and listened to the baron's importunities. His ducats, his diamonds and his decoration—the baron wanted them all. And right now. Ears pressed against the partition, the police heard General Combaluzier calmly explain that by the end of the week everything would be in order. By that time the colonel would be back from the United States with enough money to pay everyone off handsomely; by that time the baroness would have her necklace back; and by that time the error of omitting the baron's name from the roster of the Legion of Honor would be corrected. At the door the general kissed the baroness' hand, clapped du Roure on the shoulder and made his departure, followed by the four cops.

Thus ended the Great Uranium Pipe Dream of 1950-53. When the police came with a special truck to take the uranium *bonbonne* off to the government Atomic Control Center at Châtillon, they packed it in excelsior and treated it as gently as a newborn—and highly explosive—baby. At Châtillon, they tested it with Geiger counters. No reaction. At last, taking every known precaution, they opened it. Sand. Good clean, patriotic French sand, mixed with a judicious amount of heavy water from the Mediterranean and with a stable isotope of rusty lead pipe.

The baron must have felt sad to see it go. It was his baby, his own special personal uranium stockpile, a fissionable dream that had gone "fffsst." For that dream, he was out more than 120,000,000 francs—about a third of a million dollars.

For that dream, too, the prisons of Paris were distinguished by the admission, as non-paying guests, of one general, one colonel and one Secret Service police inspector—all simulated ranks. The colonel turned out to be a wily Niçois toughie named Carlicchi who had done six months in 1947 for theft. General Combaluzier—he of the portly mien and dignified chins—was a just-released jailbird named Gagliardone who had spent his life black-marketing currency and had done five years' hard labor for theft and for fencing stolen goods. "Inspector" Alberto was actually named Alberto, a former Nice cop who had been dropped from the service in 1946 for "irregularities." Gaillard—poor, dead "Scarface" Gaillard—was just what he said he was—a beach concessionaire.

The trial rocked Paris with laughter. Neither the judge on the bench, a twinkly-eyed individual with a reputation as something of a wag, nor the three impenitent rogues who sat in the defendants' box seemed able to take the thing seriously. Neither of course could the courtroom audience, nor the newspapermen. A sample of the courtroom dialogue:

JUDGE (TO GAGLIARDONE): How did you happen to take the name General Combaluzier?

GAGLIARDONE (*scratching his head*): I had to have some name, and I was taking an elevator at the time.

Or this one:

CARLICCHI (*after testifying*): Thank you, M'sieur the Judge.

JUDGE: Thank you, mon colonel.

The jury found the three defendants guilty—of illegal wearing of uniforms, illegal wearing of decorations, abuse of confidence and swindling. The judge sentenced Carlicchi and Alberto to four years each. General Combaluzier, probably because of his rank, got off with eighteen months.

A month or six weeks after the trial, I went to see Gaillard on his beach at Nice. "Listen," said Gaillard. "That baron ought never to have squawked to the cops. He oughta have thanked us. For two years, thanks to Alberto and the rest of us, he lived a real honest-to-God spy thriller—spills, chills, cloaks, daggers and heavy water. Maybe it did cost him a little dough, *d'accord*. But how many people these days can actually live an *histoire* like that?"

Not many, Monsieur Gaillard, not many.

THE 70,000 HEIRS OF SIR FRANCIS DRAKE

by Bill Slocum

Although the prime mover in this drama made the fortune, the stellar performers are unquestionably the seventy thousand rooters for Sir Francis Drake—and, no doubt, other assorted lost causes. That such optimism and romantic faith are still possible in the twentieth century, in a country almost completely yielded to literacy, speaks volumes for the amazing potentials of the human species. To the seventy thousand, then, as editor, I dedicate, affectionately, Bill Slocum's account of their saga. May their means always match their capacity for enthusiasm.

"The Yellow Kid" Weil and the immortal Ponzi are probably the two best-known con men, but there once flourished a little known Iowa plow jockey who was in all ways the superior of his more highly publicized colleagues. He is Oscar Merril Hartzell, out of Madison County, Iowa. Oscar clipped seventy thousand Americans for at least $2,000,000 and the post-office inspectors put him in jail over the screaming protest of all seventy thousand suckers!

Hartzell was the con man supreme. His followers never saw him and got nothing for their money but a succinct demand to keep their mouths shut. They met in semi-religious underground meetings to pour cash into his coffers. Farms were foreclosed and taxes went unpaid in nine states because Hartzell demanded that $2,500 a week be forwarded to him in London for almost fifteen years. Congressmen and state legislators feared him. Presidents and Cabinet members were deluged with demands for his protection and deliverance.

Hartzell first departed the plow in 1913 when he went to Des Moines to join a rather distinguished group of society folk and politicians who were being swindled by a comely widow who called herself Mrs. Sudie B. Whiteaker. Mrs. Whiteaker was indicted for relieving Iowa residents of $65,000, and her scheme was the selling of shares in the estate of Sir Francis Drake!

We next hear from Hartzell in 1921. He sends (not mails) a letter to Iowa friends stating that he has made an extraordinary discovery. He has full proof that Sir Francis Drake had an illegitimate son who was jailed to avoid scandal. The true heir to this son is entitled to $22,000,000,000 and, believe it or not, Hartzell knows the true heir. The problem is to raise money to underwrite the legal fight to restore this heir to his place in the world. He could not now name the heir because he feared the ire of the "Secret Courts of England" but the heir had put Hartzell in charge of the good fight and would pay off at the price of $500 to $1 when the estate was settled. The heir's only stipulation was that contributions would be accepted only from people named Drake or with Drake blood in their veins.

W. H. Shepherd and his wife Adna, née Drake, were made Iowa agents. They mortgaged their homes to collect $5,000, and Iowans tossed in $166,775. There seems no question that Shepherd honestly believed Hartzell, because when the scheme was exposed he suffered a nervous breakdown.

Hartzell soon had more agents. He also persuaded the heir to drop his rule against non-Drake participation, and all were welcomed. Hartzell appointed eleven agents in seven states. He sent encouraging messages and demanded that they send him $2,500 a week. The appointments and the messages came by cablegram. The $2,500 traveled by American Express. Hartzell was having no part of Uncle Sam's mails.

The "donators," as Hartzell called the faithful, signed a note promising "silence, secrecy and nondisturbance." Any violation of this pledge brought a speedy "red-inking" of the culprit. Post-office inspectors, almost immediately aware of this fraud, went slightly mad trying to get somebody to admit he had been bilked. Inspectors got cautious admissions of a "business deal abroad" but when they tried pinning the matter down to Sir Francis Drake the suckers whined, "I can't talk about that. Even to a government man."

Hartzell's followers met in dozens of towns to listen as agents read cables from the master. A settlement was always imminent. Or Hartzell had discovered the birth certificate of the illegitimate heir. Or Hartzell was standing firm against the English government's puny offers to negotiate.

An erudite article on economics printed in a weekly magazine was hailed by the faithful as proof of the imminent disposal of the estate of Sir Francis Drake. Meetings were held to read and discuss this story, not one word of which mentioned the estate. In fact, the author had never heard of it. An innocuous item in the Chicago *Journal of Commerce* about an ever so slight fluctuation of the English pound was accepted as proof of things soon to happen.

Eagerly thousands talked of Hartzell's report that he had proved the estate was now worth $400,000,000,000. They said England's reluctance to pay that sum was responsible for the depression. Those on the inside knew that mighty Albion was soon to be bankrupted. Herbert Hoover's devotion to England, they said, was behind the American depression. Later when Roosevelt was President his every fishing trip or Hyde Park week end was actually a trip to meet with the rulers of England to lay down an ultimatum.

An Iowa minister stood in his pulpit to explain that only fear of scandal kept England from acknowledging its debt to the Drake heir. It seemed that Queen Elizabeth had had a child by Sir Francis.

Not once did anyone ask, "Supposing Drake did have an illegitimate son? How, after all these centuries, could there be but *one* heir to that son?"

Over in England, Hartzell was having a fine old time. He was hitting the high spots seven days a week and came a cropper but once. This was the little matter of an English girl becoming the mother of his child without certain traditional preliminaries. The irate father of the girl called upon Hartzell in his sumptuous quarters and it was touch and go for a while. Father was at last placated when Hartzell permitted him to invest £552 in the Sir Francis Drake Estate.

The great con man, Hartzell himself, became a victim of a somewhat inexact science, crystal-ball reading. The reader was Miss St. John Montague, a prominent South Kensington clairvoyant. Hartzell visited her thrice weekly at enormous fees.

Back in America post-office inspectors had neither complaints nor witnesses. Nevertheless, in 1932, after eleven years of rich, ripe larceny, postal fraud orders were finally issued against several Hartzell agents, for pledges had been going through the mails.

Hartzell kept the cables steaming and agents read them to clandestine meetings of as many as four thousand people. The cables said that the United States was just trying to protect England. Under the threat of "red-inking," the faithful were ordered to write three letters each: one to their congressman, another to the Attorney General and the third to the President of the United States.

In January of 1933 the State Department presented sufficient evidence gathered by the inspectors to have Hartzell deported from England as an undesirable alien. He was arrested in New York and jailed in Iowa. Hartzell told his followers that his deportation from England was all the proof any sane man needed to prove the English were frightened. On the strength of this logic Hartzell got $15,000 to send to lawyers in England, $68,000 for his bond, $50,000 for his personal use plus $2,500 a week until July first, the date he claimed the estate would be settled.

The government had a problem: How was it going to convict a man without the aid of witnesses or at best with hostile witnesses? (The extent of this hostility was proved at the trial when men and women, forced by their oaths to admit they had given thousands and received nothing, were immediately recalled by the defense as enthusiastic character witnesses for Hartzell.)

An inspector was sent to London, and in the Historical Document Room of Somerset House he located Drake's will written in part on paper and in part on parchment. It was written in Elizabethan English and was probated in court Latin. Drake, childless, had left everything to his widow and his brother, Tom. Later Tom and Lady Drake got into a lawsuit which was settled by ecclesiastical court.

An English barrister was imported to Iowa to discuss his specialty, the statutes of limitations. He pointed out that rigid statutes of limitations had been established by Parliament first during the reign of James I. The English barrister was terribly polite, you know, but after all Sir Francis Drake had been gone some 337 years. He made it clear that he thought the whole thing ridiculously American.

In a patriotic effort to save face for America the inspectors allowed the barrister to read a letter they had received from an Englishwoman. She said in part, "I know Hartzell quite well. He swindled me out of most of my jewelry. It was right after Hartzell was made a premier Duke of Buckland in a private investiture by His Majesty."

Having proved that no Sir Francis Drake heir or estate existed, the government then proved that while Hartzell had sent no mail, he "caused to have sent mail to defraud." Hartzell was sentenced to ten years in prison.

The sentencing of Hartzell succeeded only in cementing the faith of his dupes. They were more convinced than ever that the British and the American governments were in cahoots to rob them of their due.

Hartzell entered the penitentiary in January of 1935, and all seemed quiet until April of the same year, when the Chicago police referred a middle-aged man to Chief Inspector Walter Johnson. The man related that his seventy-five-year-old mother had just invested her life savings, $3,500, in a plan to support the heir to the estate of Sir Francis Drake.

Johnson was asked to make a postal case of the affair and he happily offered to try. He discovered the boys had smartened up considerably. Contributions were not accepted unless sent by express. Solicitations were oral. The agents had also spread the word that a speech had been made over a major radio station telling of the expected settlement of the estate. The station had to print a form letter denying that any such speech had been made, and to hire a couple of girls to mail the letter to people requesting copies of the speech.

But some of the suckers did write Yant for information, and to keep them happy and contributing, their letters had been answered. That was enough and the police and Johnson raided Yant's headquarters. They found that business the day of the raid had been $7,500. And in the eighteen months since Hartzell's conviction, at least $350,000 had been contributed. In the three days after the raid $25,000 was accumulated.

Several agents were indicted but meetings continued and donations flowed in. Contributors were assured that the estate would soon be settled and that all the postal inspectors and government lawyers would be fired and thrown in jail. The tale was told, and believed, that Hartzell was *not* in jail but was being protected by the government from the gunmen of the "interests," who were panic-stricken now that they knew the jig was up.

Witnesses remained reluctant. A post-office inspector seeking information in Houston and Galveston was told that a boat lying off Galveston was filled with gold sent from England as first payment. He got half a dozen Hartzell backers to accompany him to the boat to see for themselves that it was loaded with oil-well pipes. They saw and were unimpressed. They knew a government trick when they saw one. The gold must have been removed during the night.

Eight agents followed their leader to jail. Witnesses during the trial, forced to show the receipts they had been given, anxiously watched them being passed around the courtroom, pleading in anguished tones, "Careful of those, please. They are very valuable." To the last they defended the agents and the revered name of Hartzell.

THE MAN WHO TOOK JAY GOULD TO
THE CLEANERS

by Alexander Klein

In July, 1873, a group of Americans, including two future Governors
of Minnesota and three future Congressmen, were arrested by the
Northwest Mounted Police and flung into a Canadian prison for the
very serious crime of kidnaping one of His Majesty's most distinguished subjects, Lord Gordon-Gordon of Edinburgh, Scotland.
Serious international complications resulted. On the advice of a
United States Assistant Secretary of State, an official, armed Minnesota rescue expedition was organized. There was much talk and
printed comment by assorted hot-heads in Canada, England and the
United States about the possibility of war. Eventually, it required the
personal intervention of President Ulysses S. Grant and Canadian
Prime Minister Sir John Macdonald to bring the affair Gordon-
Gordon to an amicable conclusion; although to this day Canadian
and American accounts of the case diverge on certain essential points.

For Lord Gordon-Gordon, this international storm, of which he
was the center, came as the climax to a spectacularly creative career
that had included the honor, at the express request of the Northern
Pacific Railroad, of naming numerous future towns and cities throughout Minnesota, and the task of reorganizing the Erie Railroad in
collaboration with Horace Greeley and Jay Gould. The latter mission
Gordon-Gordon undertook only after the wily financier had handed
him as an inducement and sign of good-faith $500,000 in securities
and cash, with no witnesses present and without so much as a written
receipt to record the transaction.

Apparently, Lord Gordon-Gordon was the illegitimate issue of
an affair between a clergyman's son and the family maid. He first
entered himself in the ranks of royalty around 1868, in Edinburgh
under the name of Lord Glencairn. Dressed in the height of fashion,
he was invariably accompanied by a combination valet and secretary,

customarily called "a gentleman's tiger." Lord Glencairn's gentleman's tiger sported buckskin breeches, long red boots and a blue satin coat with gilt buttons. His hat was topped by an immense cockade which signified that his master held a royal commission.

In the winter of 1868 Lord Glencairn and his colorful gentleman's tiger stopped in at Messers Marshall and Son, Jewelers, of Edinburgh. The gentleman's tiger presented his master's card, and the lord selected several tasteful items, paying with a large check. The check proved as good as gold and Lord Glencairn became a frequent and favorite customer, with an excellent credit standing. By the spring of 1869 Lord Glencairn's account had passed the £25,000-mark. When he did not appear at the shop for some weeks and failed to reply to the bills Marshall and Son had reluctantly sent him, the jewelers turned the case over to the police. There is no further recorded appearance of Lord Glencairn or his gentleman's tiger.

Lord Gordon-Gordon first came to life in the New World, in 1871, not at a port of entry, but in Minneapolis, where he put up at the best hotel. In a local bank he deposited $40,000, the capital he had saved from the Marshall escapade, to draw upon for expenses. Then, armed with fulsome letters of introduction from several famous English noblemen, he met all the prominent officials and citizens and conquered them with his charm, his whimsicality, his titles and his wealth. Tall and slender, Lord Gordon-Gordon dressed immaculately, complete with patent leather gloves and silk hat. He kept his hands exquisitely manicured and was clean shaven except for two tufts of side whiskers à l'anglaise. The deliberateness of his manner and meticulousness of his speech struck Minnesotans as, in their experience, the high-water mark in courtliness. Two days after Lord Gordon-Gordon's arrival, Colonel John S. Lomis, Land Commissioner of the Northern Pacific Railroad, was explaining to acquaintances and associates that the nobleman had arrived from Scotland prepared to invest several million dollars in the railroad lands of Minnesota. Everywhere he went his lordship was introduced as heir of the great Earls of Gordon, cousin of the Campbells, collateral relative of Lord Byron and descendant of the bold Lochinvar and the ancient kings of the Highlanders.

Actually, Lord Gordon-Gordon appeared rather reticent. Showered with invitations, he accepted very few. He did loosen up a bit at a banquet held in his honor by the leading citizens of the state. Expansively, he told his audience that he was in search of immense areas of rich land on which to colonize his overcrowded Scotch tenantry; he could make good use of as much as 500,000 acres.

This was an answer to a railroadman's prayer. The Northern Pacific Railroad, being pushed slowly westward, was badly handicapped by a shortage of capital. Several millions from Scotland would be very helpful. Colonel Loomis set about wooing those millions. He organized a grand buffalo hunt for Lord Gordon-Gordon. He escorted his lordship to a few sample town sites not far from Minneapolis. Finally, Lord Gordon-Gordon said he was ready to begin selecting the lands.

Colonel Loomis proved equal to the occasion. He organized a luxurious expedition, afterwards described by a journalist as "the equal of that Apollodorus planned for Cleopatra." It was all paid for, of course, by the Northern Pacific Railroad. The caravan included fifteen covered wagons, some forty horses, twenty men as Lord Gordon-Gordon's personal retinue, and an American version of the gentleman's tiger, a secretary and valet who shaved the lord, wrote his letters and learned to revel in flourishing the lord's seal decorated with armorial bearings. Wherever rails had been laid, a private railroad car and engine were placed at Lord Gordon-Gordon's disposal, while most of his retainers followed on horseback or in covered wagons. Wherever the expedition camped, they hoisted the historic banner of the Gordons of Scotland, side by side with Stars and Stripes.

For three delightful months in the summer and autumn of 1871, Lord Gordon-Gordon traveled, feasted and hunted in royal style throughout much of Minnesota and Dakota. Carte blanche was the order of the day. To quote from a contemporary account:

"Two palatial wall tents were provided for his exclusive use, in one of them, with silver and the loveliest china, were served to him viands that would have enraptured Epicurus. Fruit was brought from Mexico for him, curaçao from the Spice Islands, dry Monopole from its fragrant home. His table was like Montezuma's."

Business was not neglected, however. A government surveyor whom Lord Gordon-Gordon playfully called "a land-taster," aided his lordship in selecting the choice square miles he desired. Sites for cities were also selected; the surveyor and Colonel Loomis advised, but Lord Gordon-Gordon decided, after which the surveyor stamped them officially as "Sold." The lord proved himself something of a Solomon in naming the towns, for he alternated between Scottish names and typical American ones. Lord Gordon-Gordon appeared as considerate a landlord as he was wealthy. Thus, one of the first things he did at each town site was to select and have marked the location of the church and the school.

Having selected hundreds of thousands of acres and the weather turning quite cold, Lord Gordon-Gordon told Colonel Loomis it was time he went to New York to arrange to have funds transferred from Scotland to pay for his purchases. He returned to Minneapolis, bid his Northern Pacific Railroad retinue a lordly au revoir, attended one more banquet in his honor, withdrew his money from the bank— his original $40,000 had remained almost untouched—and obtained from Colonel Loomis a warm letter of introduction to Horace Greeley, the man whose advice his lordship had, thus far, found so admirable.

Lord Gordon-Gordon traveled East in leisurely style savoring life in America from town to town. He did not arrive in New York until February, 1872. And the visit was perfectly timed for a man of his talents —and wealth. The Erie Railroad war was raging. Jay Gould, much to his and everyone else's astonishment, had momentarily been outmaneuvered. Daniel Drew and Colonel Thomas A. Scott, Vice-President of the Pennsylvania Railroad, were also licking their wounds, while General Dix and General Sickles were fortifying the entrenched positions they had seized. The prize was estimated at some $35,000,-000, with incalculable future potential.

Into the arena stepped slender, silk-hatted Lord Gordon-Gordon, with all of his $40,000 and his Scottish millions. His lordship engaged a magnificent suite of rooms at the elegant Metropolitan Hotel and sent his letter of introduction over to Horace Greeley at the *Tribune* offices. The man who in three months was to become a candidate for the Presidency of the United States found Lord Gordon-Gordon's charm and wit pleasing. His lordship dined at the Greeley home. The two men met frequently for luncheon. They discussed many subjects, including the Erie Railroad battle. As an Erie stockholder, himself, Lord Gordon-Gordon took the liberty of expressing his view; reforms were absolutely necessary. Greeley agreed.

Then, one morning Greeley joined Lord Gordon-Gordon for breakfast in the latter's hotel suite. Special hotel employees detailed to serve his lordship took Greeley's white overcoat and galoshes. Then, at the center table—placed before the fire and spread with white damask—over an omelette eaten with breakfast service of solid silver, bearing the monogram of his lordship, the host told Greeley he had preferred to wait until he was sure of Greeley's sentiments, but that now his lordship felt free to reveal that he held 600,000 shares of

Erie stock. Combining this with the holdings of his English friends, Lord Gordon-Gordon explained, would enable him to control the next election for directors. Greeley congratulated him and immediately dubbed this the "Gordon reform movement." Could he tell Colonel A. K. McClure, editor of the Philadelphia *Times* and Colonel Thomas A. Scott the good news? Lord Gordon-Gordon acquiesced.

Soon the news leaked to some half-dozen financiers that the Right Honorable Lord Gordon-Gordon was interested—provided suitable guarantees of reform were given—in casting his huge bloc of controlling votes of Erie stock shares to enable Jay Gould to retain the presidency and Scott to become one of the directors. Colonel Scott told Greeley he'd like Gordon-Gordon to come and talk things over with him, but Greeley explained that his lordship had made it clear protocol did not permit him to call first upon the Colonel. So Colonel Scott and Horace Greeley called upon Gordon-Gordon at the Hotel Metropolitan.

For nearly an hour the leading editor and the leading railroad operator of the country waited impatiently in the lobby, reading and rereading the posters of Niblo's Theatre on the wall, while upstairs his lordship calmly, deliberately, had his hair oiled and brushed by his valet, his cravat tied to the exact requirements of fashion. Finally Greeley and Scott were admitted.

After the amenities, Scott at once brought up the subject of the Erie's problems and the reforms he would recommend. His lordship listened politely, but, perhaps because the American had tactlessly launched into a business discussion within five minutes of being introduced, seemed disinclined to make any definite commitments.

It took Greeley and Scott another visit, which turned into a long sociable evening, to convince Gordon-Gordon to see Jay Gould about whom, Gordon-Gordon intimated, he had heard some scandalous things. At one o'clock in the morning of March 2, 1872, Gould was awakened by a telegram from Colonel Scott informing him that Lord Gordon-Gordon would see him, and to be at his lordship's suite that morning for breakfast to try to consummate the deal while his lordship was in the mood.

Later in court, Gould described what took place that morning:

> I asked him what his interest in Erie was. He said that individually he owned thirty millions of the stock; his friends, twenty millions more; that he controlled the whole; that he was satisfied that it was best to keep the road under my management, but wanted to put in a new

Board to be selected by himself and Mr. Horace Greeley—all the gentlemen to be approved by me. He told me much about his antecedents, his career and his family; stated that he entered Parliament at the age of twenty-two, and took his seat as the youngest member of the House of Lords; spoke of the great confidence the Queen had in his ability and discretion, and mentioned delicate missions that had been intrusted to him—an important negotiation with the Prussian Government, which he was sent out to attend to as the only man who could cope with Bismarck. Just then there was a knock on the door and in came Mr. Greeley.

In Greeley's presence, his lordship frankly—though graciously—said he did not consider Gould's word sufficient to bind any deal. He would have to think it over and they would have to thrash out all the details of the Erie Railroad reorganization during the week. Lord Gordon-Gordon's court testimony later summarized one phase of these discussions:

> I told him it required more than mere words—that he must show me by satisfactory proofs that what he stated was true. He then said that he would do so, and that if I would aid him he would willingly place his resignation in my hands. He pledged himself repeatedly that he would follow the honest policy I laid down, and I told him that if he did not I could not, under any circumstances, give him my support. Gould urged upon me that we should purchase more stock together; I declined and told him I was not disposed to have my credulity and my pocket tested at the same time. To this he replied: "I don't mean it that way; I will carry the stock for both you and myself."
>
> I thereupon then told Gould that the better way would be to put it in the form of puts and calls, and I would accept them and cooperate with him. Gould said, "with pleasure," and he took the form I handed to him and wrote out and delivered to me calls upon him for 20,000 shares of Erie at $35 per share, good for six months.

His lordship went on to explain to Gould that in making his investigations, in consolidating the stockholders in England and buying out some shareholders, in lobbying at Albany for future favorable legislation he had personally spent a great deal of money. This expenditure, Gordon-Gordon suggested, should legitimately be charged to the reorganized company which would be the ultimate beneficiary of these activities. Gould, hardly the man to be chary with company funds, readily agreed. About how much was involved, anyway, Gould asked?

Now that Gordon had the hook planted, he began to reel in the fish.

He calmly replied that he would estimate his costs in round figures as a million dollars, and that, as guarantee of Gould's promise to have this sum reimbursed to Gordon-Gordon by the Erie, he thought it reasonable for Gould to deposit half that amount with his new partner. According to Gould's later testimony in court:

> In view of the fact, that he had made these advances personally, and that the success of the new plan would depend very much on my good faith and his co-operation, I agreed to deposit with him securities and money to the extent of about one-half of his expenses, or about $500,-000. This pledge was not to be used by him, but was to be returned to me on my carrying out my part of the agreement. . . .
>
> Gordon afterwards wrote me that there was an error in the footing, he thought; and, though there was no error, yet, not wishing to raise any question, and supposing that the money was safe in his hands, I took $40,000 more and deposited with him, making, in all, the securities mentioned and $200,000 cash.

Naturally, Gould asked for a receipt. At this Lord Gordon-Gordon calmly handed back the cash and securities, explaining that *he* never entered into business dealings where his own word was not considered sufficient security. Gould took the package and instinctively headed for the door. But, on second thought, Gordon-Gordon's action appeared so genuine that Gould turned back, laid the parcel of securities and cash back on the table, and said that although he always demanded receipts Lord Gordon-Gordon's word would, of course, be more than adequate.

Gould then told Gordon-Gordon that he expected a big rise in the price of Erie Railroad shares, so that the calls Gould had previously given him on twenty thousand shares of Erie at $35 a share would net his lordship a neat profit of a million dollars in the next six months. Gordon-Gordon deprecated this, adding that he would be glad to sell them to someone for half a million. Gould proved that he believed his own prediction by arranging to buy them himself.

On March 8, Gould delivered payment in cash and securities, totaling half a million. By this time Gordon-Gordon had succeeded in parting one of America's leading robber-barons from a cool million dollars. More important, he had won the complete confidence of the financier, as well as that of Horace Greeley, Thomas A. Scott and Alexander McClure. As a final test of good faith and, as his lordship put it, to be absolutely certain that reorganization of the Erie would in no way reflect on the honor of the Gordon-Gordon family name, he requested and obtained Gould's resignation.

Thus a week after Lord Gordon-Gordon had first laid eyes on Gould, the Scotch nobleman was leading the financier around as effectively as if he had put a ring through his nose.

Instead of carrying on with the reorganization of the Erie or heading for places unknown with the several hundred thousand in cash and the negotiable securities Gould had given him, Lord Gordon-Gordon now began selling some of the securities. First he disposed of six hundred shares of Erie. Then, in Philadelphia, he sold five thousand shares of Oil Creek and Allegheny Valley Railroad. The sale of such a large bloc of shares caused quite a drop in the price of Oil Creek and Allegheny. Gould noticed this and checked up on the transaction. Although his men were unable to trace the sale directly to Gordon-Gordon, they were able to report that no one else known to possess that many shares had put them on the market.

Gould decided that it was Gordon-Gordon selling the shares he was supposed to be holding in escrow. Incensed at having been taken in, Gould personally took charge of the matter. First, he warned all brokers not to handle any large sales of certain shares without checking the share numbers with his office. Then he hired a suite immediately adjoining Lord Gordon-Gordon's and tried to eavesdrop on his lordship's conversations. After several frustrating hours, Gould gave up; the walls were too thick for anything intelligible to get through.

Since the evidence against Gordon-Gordon was hardly conclusive, Gould was persuaded not to have him arrested. Instead, Horace Greeley was dispatched as a friendly intermediary. Greeley appealed to his lordship, as a gentleman of high rank who would hardly wish to become involved in a vulgar controversy over filthy dollars, to return all the money and securities and to desist from any further efforts on behalf of Gould or the Erie Railroad. Greeley added that the return of the money and securities at this point would not prejudice his lordship's rights to recover in court. Gordon-Gordon refused and insisted on seeing Gould and having it out with him. Gould said the only place he'd ever meet Gordon-Gordon again was in court. Greeley returned to Gordon-Gordon's suite and finally persuaded his lordship to give back the cash and securities.

But Gould found that he'd been short-changed by some $150,000. Next day Gould swore out a warrant for Lord Gordon-Gordon's arrest, charging him with obtaining money under false pretenses.

Gould hired Elihu Root and David Dudley Field as his lawyers. Lord Gordon-Gordon was represented by General Dix and General Sickles, Gould's enemies. Horace F. Clark, son-in-law of Commodore Vanderbilt and President of the Union Pacific Railroad, put up the $40,000 set as bail, presumably, not because his lordship could not have provided bail from his own noble coffers, but by way of a hands-across-the-sea gesture of goodwill combined with a bit of nose-thumbing at Gould.

Nearly two months passed before the case came up on the docket. By that time Gould knew he was losing control of the Erie once for all. Naturally he was out for blood. The trial began around the middle of May, 1872. One of the first questions directed at Lord Gordon-Gordon was how it happened that such a large shareholder in Erie as his lordship claimed to be was not listed by name among the stockholders. Lord Gordon-Gordon replied with a query of his own: Wasn't it true that under the American system a man could have complete control of a corporation without having a single share of stock registered in his own name? Score one for his lordship.

Queried about his background, Lord Gordon-Gordon at first protested that his private affairs had nothing to do with the matter at hand. The case, he added magnanimously, should be decided on its merits, without any regard for his own high position and ancestry. But, upon being pressed by Gould's attorneys and the court's directing him to answer, his lordship testified haughtily but with composure and without reticence. He told of his large land purchases in Minnesota, his kinship with the great Scotch Gordons, his friendship with many peers of the realm. Freely and frankly he gave the names and addresses of his Scotch relatives, solicitors and family. In all he testified for three hours, the model witness throughout, legs crossed, thumbs thrust nonchalantly into his waistcoat pocket, the unconcern of innocence marking his every reply and gesture. Once, when one of Gould's lawyers, Dudley Field, went a bit too far in his imputations, his lordship's injured innocence broke through the calm gentlemanly bearing that bespoke an inheritance of centuries of breeding. Lord Gordon-Gordon's outburst moved Presiding Judge John R. Brady to order Field to stop persecuting the witness. "This sort of thing has gone far enough," the Judge cried heatedly, and, out of deference to the distinguished accused, he ordered the session adjourned.

At the end of this first day Gordon-Gordon was definitely ahead on points. Practically everyone, except Gould and his intimates were convinced of his lordship's good faith. But when Gould was out for blood he went right to fundamentals. That afternoon he cabled every single person Lord Gordon-Gordon had mentioned in his testimony; he also cabled inquiries to various official sources. The persons Gordon-Gordon had cited replied separately and unanimously that they had never heard of any such lord; official sources confirmed the imposture.

Next morning Gould came to court early, ready for the kill. Horace Greeley and the confident attorneys for the defense, Generals Dix and Sickles, arrived a few minutes later. But Gordon-Gordon failed to show up. Investigation revealed that his lordship had hopped a quick midnight train to Montreal, taking along $150,000 of Gould's money, and also leaving Horace F. Clark, president of the Union Pacific, in the hole for $40,000 bail. The enraged Gould offered a $25,000 reward for the arrest of Gordon-Gordon and sent agents abroad to get the full facts about his lordship.

Evidently Lord Gordon-Gordon had correctly estimated Gould's thoroughness. He had stayed for the trial, hoping to keep the case strictly to the issues at hand and to bluff it through on breeding, charm, frankness and the high position of the seconds in his corner. But when Gould's attorneys had insisted on delving into his ancestry and title, he had realized the game was up. The free, frank, haughty replies, the citing of names and addresses had been the price he paid to leave court a free man for one more day, long enough for a getaway.

In Canada, Lord Gordon-Gordon rested up for some time. Then, again applying Horace Greeley's maxim, he went west to what is now Winnipeg but what in the spring of 1873 was the Hudson's Bay outpost of Fort Garry, about fifty miles north of the border. Fort Garry's only connection with the outside world was by stage; the nearest railroad station was five hundred miles away. At the hotel he registered as the Right Honorable Lord Gordon-Gordon, a family name he must have found irresistible, and one he may have felt he could allow himself to indulge in because of the limited extradition agreements then in force. His lordship attracted unusual attention, not only because of his title and distinctive bearing, but also because he insisted on a bath every day, an unheard-of-thing in Fort Garry. There was only one tub in the hotel and all the water had to be hauled up specially from the Red River. In a very short time he was moving in the best circles in Fort Garry. He explained that he might decide to settle permanently in the Canadian Northwest and invest in land.

But even in 1873 news of such a distinguished visitor eventually spread. One day it reached Minneapolis. Colonel Loomis, Mayor George Brackett and other prominent citizens had read about the reorganization of the Erie and they had long since given up waiting for Lord Gordon-Gordon to return with his millions of dollars and thousands of Scotch retainers. But their desire for revenge was still strong.

(This is one of the points where Canadian and British accounts of this case diverge from United States records. According to the British and Canadians, the Mayor of Minneapolis, George A. Brackett, had been in New York at the time Gordon-Gordon tangled with Gould, and it was Brackett who put up the $40,000 bail. This version may be charitably meant to provide Minnesotans with a further hard-cash motive for taking the law into their own hands. Or, the Canadian and British chroniclers may simply be unable to believe that Americans would act so boldly and get so worked up generally unless their pocketbooks were directly involved.)

Mayor Brackett immediately sent his chief of police, Captain Mike Hoy, and Sergeant Owen Keega to Fort Garry, to join forces with five Minnesotans who happened to be up in Fort Garry at the time, capture his lordship on British soil and bring him across the border.

In Fort Garry the Minnesotans purchased a light wagon and a fast team of horses, and one evening in July, 1873, they trailed Lord Gordon-Gordon to a friend's cottage, waited until he came out, seized him and raced for the border. A servant noticed the scuffle and gave the alarm. A party of Northwest Mounted Police, augmented by several of Gordon-Gordon's friends, soon set out in pursuit. The following day the Minnesota kidnapers were overtaken near the border, not far from the old Pembina Custom House, now in North Dakota. The Canadian authorities claimed then, and British and Canadian records insist to this day, that the kidnapers were caught on the Canadian side of the border. The Americans were equally certain that they were a quarter mile south of the line.

Chief of Police Michael Hoy produced a document stating that he and his party were acting on behalf of the American bondsman who had put up bail for Gordon-Gordon and that, according to an ancient statute of Great Britain, a bondsman had the authority to arrest a bail-jumper anywhere on British soil. The Mountie in charge said he had never heard of that particular statute, but he could definitely inform the Americans that kidnaping was a serious crime in Canada. The Americans were handcuffed, taken back to Fort Garry, and thrown in jail, charged with conspiring to abduct a British subject from British soil. Gordon-Gordon was, of course, released. And the Canadian authorities refused to grant bail to the Americans, who now telegraphed Mayor Brackett: "We're in a hell of a fix; come at once!"

Mayor Brackett arrived a week later. He told the authorities the facts as he knew them about Lord Gordon-Gordon and he brought along the signed opinions of several distinguished American lawyers, based on an ancient English statute, that the seizure of Gordon-Gordon had been lawful. Attorney-General Clarke of the Province of Manitoba paid no heed to the American lawyers' opinions and Fort Garry citizens refused to believe the canards about the Right Honorable Lord Gordon-Gordon.

The extradition of Lord Gordon-Gordon now became a secondary matter. The chief concern of the Americans now was to get their men out of jail. Minnesotans got quite heated about the matter. So did Manitobans. There were threats and counter-threats. Minneapolis newspapers published reports that the American prisoners were suffering from extreme heat in the airless Fort Garry prison, and were ill fed in the bargain. At a later point Mayor Brackett, in a public statement, claimed that Attorney General Clarke had resorted to blackmail, offering to release the prisoners if Brackett would pay $15,000 for a piece of land Clarke owned. The news was headlined in papers all over the United States and national indignation flared up.

Mayor Brackett had, at the outset, enlisted influence in Washington, and State Department officials had been negotiating for weeks with the British Ambassador. However, late in August, 1873, Mayor Brackett and Governor Austin of Minnesota journeyed to Washington and laid the matter directly before President Ulysses S. Grant and his Secretary of State, Hamilton Fish. Brackett and Austin stated categorically that the capture of the Americans had occurred on American soil. President Grant thereupon instructed his Secretary of State to do everything in his power to effect the release of the prisoners. Weeks later when negotiations were still stalled, Assistant Secretary of State Bancroft-Davis advised the Minnesotans that the only way to settle matters quietly would be for them to go up to the boundary line and seize several Canadian custom house officials and border policemen as hostages. Echoes of the War of Independence and the War of 1812 had, meantime, been evident in the public press in the United States, Canada and England; hot-blooded individuals in all three countries called for war. Governor Austin of Minnesota ordered the state militia to be ready to march at a moment's notice and thousands of Minnesotans volunteered to join the liberating expeditionary force.

Finally Mayor Brackett and Governor Austin decided to make one more diplomatic attempt before militia and volunteers were ordered into action. Brackett and Austin went to Canada and laid their case directly before Sir John Macdonald, the Prime Minister. Sir John insisted that the attempt to kidnap Lord Gordon-Gordon was highly irregular, but agreed, in the interests of international amity, to order an exception and permit bail despite the seriousness of the crime. As a result two future Governors of Minnesota and three future Congressmen and their colleagues in kidnaping, after nearly a half year in prison, got home in time for Christmas dinner, 1873. (American records concede only two months' imprisonment for their martyred heroes, dating their release September 15, 1873.)

Lord Gordon-Gordon remained in Fort Garry, secure in the knowledge that existing extradition agreements did not cover such lesser crimes as embezzlement or larceny. Most citizens of Fort Garry, possibly in a spirit of Empire pride, did not allow their good opinion of Lord Gordon-Gordon to be tarnished by the American accusations. They might have been particularly wary in business dealings with his lordship. But, business apart, Lord Gordon-Gordon became even more of a favorite than before.

At this point American and British-Canadian chroniclers of the affair Gordon-Gordon once again diverge. Each claim that their countrymen were the instruments of the final denouement.

According to Canadian and British accounts one of the Marshalls of Messers Marshall and Son in Edinburgh, still owed £25,000 by Lord Glencairn, read about the Gordon-Gordon case, and decided that, although press reports made no mention whatsoever of any gaily-dressed gentleman's tiger in attendance, the descriptions of the Fort Garry nobleman, and his own memory of Lord Glencairn were similar enough to warrant investigation. Thereupon—so the Canadian chroniclers insist—the Scottish jewelers bet the price of a round-trip ticket to Manitoba that their hunch was right. They dispatched Thomas Smith, the clerk who had most frequently dealt with Lord Glencairn, to Fort Garry. Smith recognized his man. But the Fort Garry police chief refused to believe Smith's story. So Smith went to see Attorney General Clarke, who, as a friend of Gordon-Gordon's called his lordship in and told him about the charge. Lord Gordon-Gordon ridiculed the accusation, but said laughingly that Clarke really ought to issue the warrant in order to stop causing his friends so much trouble. Reluctantly Clarke complied, saying that he was doing so only to make it possible to clear the matter up speedily. Most of Fort Garry, however, did not take the charge seriously. But when Lord Gordon-Gordon asked John F. Bain, a lawyer friend, who had handled some legal affairs for him previously, to defend him, Bain told him he was sorry but he had already been retained as special counsel in the case by the British government. Bain added that Smith's evidence seemed pretty conclusive to him.

Gordon-Gordon, thereupon, told his friends and acquaintances that he had decided to waive the preliminary hearing and return with Smith to clear the matter up in England. A *bon voyage* celebration was held the next night at the house of a friend, out near the old portage trail, some seven miles west of Fort Garry. Gordon-Gordon is said to have scintillated with wit and good humor. When the party broke up about three o'clock, Gordon-Gordon retired to the guestroom, put a revolver to his temple and pulled the trigger.

The American accounts of the end of Gordon-Gordon agree that he committed suicide, but they record an entirely different set of events leading to the suicide. According to these accounts, Lord Gordon-Gordon left Fort Garry shortly after the American kidnapers were released and moved to the suburbs of Toronto. Two Minnesotans tracked him there, and, with an eye on the $25,000-reward offer still outstanding, informed Jay Gould. Special extradition procedures were agreed on by the Canadian and United States governments and two American officers were sent to pick up his lordship. One morning they stole into Gordon-Gordon's cottage and found his lordship still sound asleep. Upon being awakened, Lord Gordon-Gordon is quoted as saying calmly, "Ah, yes; do you want me?" then playfully requesting permission to sleep a couple of hours longer since it was not yet noon, his customary hour of arising. The officers refused to render him this courtesy, but they did grant his next request, permission to consult an attorney. The latter informed him the extradition papers were in order. His lordship then stepped into the other room to pack some things. A moment later the fatal shot rang out.

In any event, Jay Gould never did get his $150,000 back, nor Messers Marshall and Son their £25,000. For none of the money was found, neither by the Canadian police in Fort Garry nor by the American officers in the cottage near Toronto. However, brief though his

New World career was, Gordon-Gordon quondam colonizer of Minnesota and neat decapitator of Jay Gould, did perform a notable educational service for the United States; he caused its citizens rigorously to re-examine their notions about the European nobility.

THE RED BARON OF ARIZONA

by Clarence Buddington Kelland

For persistence, thoroughness, audacity and sheer grandioseness, James Addison Reavis' great land-swindle has had few equals. Clarence Buddington Kelland's thorough account, here somewhat abridged, dramatically recreates every major step of Reavis' incredible odyssey.

On May 9, 1881, a brief, inconspicuous item in the *Gazette,* of Phoenix, Arizona, chronicled the fact that a gentleman named James Addison Reavis was in town as a representative of the San Francisco *Examiner.* His purpose was said to be an investigation of the region and its circulation and business possibilities on behalf of his newspaper.

This is the first recorded appearance in his "barony" of the man who for fifteen years was to menace the prosperity of a region embracing acres of land commencing at a point in New Mexico and extending westward 225 miles, and seventy-five miles from north to south. It was a tract that was approximately half the size of the state of Indiana. It included five counties, and embraced the whole of the city of Phoenix and the towns of Florence, Tempe, Globe, Silver King, Pinal and Casa Grande. It included the right of way of the Southern Pacific Railway. It asserted ownership of the fabulous Silver King mine. It included millions of dollars' worth of unmined ores—copper, gold and silver.

The claim this man was to make was that he owned every foot of the soil in this vast area, every ranch, every building lot, every homestead, every inch of city real estate. It was to cloud every title, hamper every business transaction involving real estate, make dubious the ownership of every ounce of ore mined.

Throughout this region the Government of the United States had granted homesteads to pioneers, who had developed their lands and built homes and established primitive irrigation projects. J. Addison

Reavis was to hold each and every one of these a trespasser and was to demand from the Government in Washington the sum of $50,000,-000 to clear and make good the titles it had granted illegally, and he actually was to negotiate with official Washington the settlement of his claim for $25,000,000.

Great names were to be brought into the dispute and men of nation-wide fame were to take sides with him and support his contentions, even to finance his endeavors to make good his title. Listed among his lawyers and backers were Roscoe Conkling; the great agnostic and orator, Robert Ingersoll; Collis P. Huntington and Charles Crocker, of California, millionaires and empire-builders both, said to have been partial contributors to the great fund that enabled Reavis to prosecute his quest and financed his journeyings about the world in search of supporting historical evidence of the validity of his claim.

It was while he was a Confederate soldier that Reavis made a dis-covery, small and inconsequential at the time, but which was to be the foundation upon which he built his amazing career. He found that he could write the name of his commanding officer so that it would be accepted by sergeants and guards and suchlike people as the veritable signature of the captain. He wrote himself a pass giving him a few days' leave, and presented it, and it was honored without question. He repeated it again and again, and doubtless, for a small consideration, wrote similar passes for friends suffering from boredom. The twig was being inclined.

The most striking of all his attributes, as one delves into his ex-traordinary history, was his grim persistence and his patience and his diligence. James Addison Reavis was not satisfied with a mere rough facsimile of his officer's signature. He aimed at perfection. So, in his dimly lighted tent, he practiced writing that name over and over again until he could almost do it with his eyes shut.

Discharged from the army, he betook himself to St. Louis. Jobs were not too plentiful and the times were troubled. Civil war was still in progress, and business was in a precarious state. But always he was adaptable. He was one of the greatest time-biders in all recorded his-tory. So he took employment as a streetcar conductor. He tried next the work of clerking in a store, but there was not enough scope there, so he went into the real estate business as a broker. Reavis was acting as agent for a man who owned a piece of property whose title was not perfectly clear. There was a good commission in sight if the cloud could be dissipated. So James Addison Reavis took pen in hand again. Not, this time, to forge a mere signature, but to create a complete, spurious document in the nature of a quitclaim deed.

Equipped with this paper, he put through his deal and earned his commission. The quitclaim went on file, and it was a long time before it was questioned. But by that time Reavis was far away in the wild and woolly West, seeking new and fertile fields for his peculiar genius.

The West was really the West. Hostile Indians roamed the plains; the ferocious Apaches were ravaging the Southwest under the leadership of the great Cochise. Great herds of buffaloes roamed the prairies. Immigrants crossed those great wastes in Conestoga wagons instead of in railroad cars, searching for gold or homesteads or a new life far from civilization.

Reavis next emerges into view in the ancient town of Santa Fe, where there were a land office and a bureau for considering and investigating Spanish land claims under the Treaty of Guadalupe Hidalgo, which brought an end to our war with Mexico, and under the subsequent Gadsden Purchase, which added to the territory of the United States all of southern Arizona and certain other lands to the eastward.

Now, under these postwar treaties with our late enemy, Mexico, we Americans guaranteed to recognize and protect Spanish titles to land within the borders of our newly acquired territories. And this guaranty included ancient land grants to individuals from the Spanish crown before Mexico became an independent state.

Clouds of claimants under Spanish grants appeared, and their rights must be investigated and adjudicated. Commissions were erected as quasi-courts to deal with this swarm of locusts. And in the record room of the body functioning in Sante Fe, James Addison Reavis got himself a job. Either by the accident of needing a job and finding one in such a place, or by design and plan, he found himself employed in the one spot in the United States which would furnish the sort of education so necessary to the future Baron de Arizonac and Caballero de los Colorados. For there he was up to his ears in ancient Spanish records and documents, enriched by the penmanship of ancient padres and embellished by enormous and impressive seals—even seals from various monarchs of the Spanish kingdom.

Reavis was an opportunist, but also he planned his opportunities. In Santa Fe, he prepared himself for his profession, which was the creation of the most intricate and firmly based imposture in all the history of chicanery. He worked by day and by night to master the

Spanish language and the writing of that language. But he was not content to know it as it existed in 1866 or 1867. He wanted to know it as it was written 100 or 150 years before. So he studied for his chosen profession as a medical student studies to become a doctor or a young man studies to become a civil engineer.

He whittled out quill pens in order to copy yellowing parchments. He practiced that sort of penmanship. This was far different from forging the signature of his captain to a pass. It required him to learn to take on a state of mind, to put himself in the place of some old padre or state scribe whose lifework it was to put beautiful old letters on parchment. He copied and rejected as imperfect, and copied again and again and again, until he thought he had achieved perfection. He knew well now that it had been the custom of Spanish kings to reward their favorite *caballeros* with vast grants of land—their gifts measured by leagues and not by acres. But the New World was not surveyed with transit and level. The metes and bounds of these princely grants were vague. In some areas, more fertile than others, such as California, long possession and use by Spanish hidalgos had pretty well defined their boundary lines. But in remote and arid Arizona there was no such adverse possession to satisfy the law, and there was only vagueness of extent and location.

When Reavis came to make his claim, he was determined there should be no fog-bank uncertainty about it, but that he should be able to take inspectors to the spot and ride over it and say to them, "It starts here and runs so far in this direction, and comprises exactly so many *varas*, Castilian land measure."

Not many men have been so thorough in their planning of a crime as to resort to forgery in stone, but Reavis accomplished even this. For a dual purpose; first, to show a definite location, and second, to prove that the Spaniard from whom Reavis claimed to derive his title had come to this spot and actually taken possession. So, in a remote desert spot he forged a stone monument with its inscription.

You cannot claim title through a Spanish grandee unless you can produce the bones and history of the grandee. So Reavis, like an efficient novelist, sat down to work out his plot and supply himself with a noble Spaniard who had performed prodigies for his king. Out of whole cloth he invented a warrior and distant kinsman of King Ferdinand of Spain and a very distant relative of the old kings of Navarre, whose name was Miguel de Peralta. This invention of Reavis' was quite a nobleman. He was Gentleman of the King's Bedchamber, Grandee of Spain, Knight of the Military Order of Carlos III, Knight of the Insignia of the Royal College of Our Lady of Guadalupe. The father of this Miguel was none other than José Gaston Gómez de Silva y Montux de Oca de la Cerda y de Caullo de Peralta de los Falces de la Vega. And Miguel's mother was none other than Doña Francesca Ana María, García de la Cordoba y Muniz de Pérez.

But as yet these Peraltas existed nowhere except in Reavis' astute imagination. He had need of historic characters, but he was not so slipshod as to adopt real ones whose history might be traced by scholars. Having thus invented a suitable family, his next labor must be to endow them with historical existence. Reavis had to invent the life story of the original Miguel's son, and he had to invent life stories for subsequent descendants. And all this must be capable of legal and documentary proof to be adduced in court. It seemed an impossible task, yet Reavis accomplished it.

All this invention must have occurred approximately in 1870 and the immediately succeeding years. The making of these nonexistent characters into historical personages occupied the years that followed, and Reavis pursued his purpose doggedly. No records remain of how he earned his living or how he financed himself for the next seven or eight years, when he set out upon a tour of forgery that carried him throughout Mexico, to Portugal and to Spain. He had grown from a youth with a dent in his forehead into a man of distinguished appearance. Though his features had not set in the aristocratic mold which was to be theirs in the days of his greatness, the elements were present. It was a sensitive face with fine eyes and a patrician nose. It was the face of no common person, and later, when he grew splendid side whiskers and was wealthy enough to dress the part, he was an individual to stand out in any company. Tall, imposingly dignified, every inch the Spanish grandee, though he himself never made claim to Spanish blood or nobility.

It is a difficult thing to forge a check so that it will pass the eagle eye of the bank teller: it is a stupendous task to forge a historical document so that it will be convincing to scholars. But it savors of black magic to produce such a document and then to get it into the spot where it will do the most good. The monks and padres who kept so many of the records of old Spain were jealous guardians, watchful that no harm came to the documents under their care. But Reavis managed to elude or evade them in the old provincial capital of Guadalajara, or in Mexico City, or in Sevilla, or in Madrid. He must have spent long hours alone with those precious records, deleting and substituting, forging with skill the script of ancient scribes, inserting in their correct places wholly forged papers. He stuck to it until, spotted all over the Spanish world of Europe and America, were what seemed to be authentic documents providing a legal, historical account of a man and a family who never existed anywhere but inside the inventive head of James Addison Reavis. Out of nothing he had brought to life a family; out of nothing he had provided the members of that family with characters and personalities; he had endowed them with achievements and with friends in high places; he had caused them to emerge from nowhere into documented history. And all with such skill and plausibility that the most famous lawyers in America were taken in by it and passed favorable legal opinions upon the authenticity and incontestability of his spurious claim.

It will be apparent to the least critical, however, that the Peralta family, no matter how efficiently they had been invented and endowed with flesh and blood, were no good to Reavis unless he established some connection between them and himself. He, himself, was a Reavis from Missouri, with traceable antecedents and not a single Spanish grandee in his family tree. Somehow Reavis had to invent a device which would make him the owner of the Peralta Grant. One of his less efficient inventions was devised to fill this need.

Somewhere during his wanderings in the West, Reavis became acquainted with a young man named George Willing. Willing had been educated as a doctor, had married, and then apparently had deserted his family for a nomadic life in the freer and easier atmosphere of the pioneer West. Whether Willing was or hoped to be a confederate in Reavis' plot or whether the Red Baron simply made use of the man without his knowledge, it is impossible to say.

Reavis' story was that Doctor Willing, for $1,000 cash, bought from one Miguel Peralta, a poverty-stricken Mexican, the whole of the enormous Peralta Grant and that Willing resold it to Reavis for some good and valuable consideration, said to be $30,000. So at last James Addison Reavis had legal color of title to his barony in Arizona.

But now and here the one shadow of a crime more serious than fraud or forgery falls upon the record of James Reavis. For upon the very night that the transfer of Willing's title to the grant was made to Reavis, Willing died in a squalid room in a squalid cabin in Prescott. Unofficial records and tradition inform us that Doctor Willing died of poison.

Prescott in those days was a roaring frontier town. Its main street was the famous Whisky Row of border legend. Organized law was negligible, and the quiet death of an inconspicuous citizen, even though there was suspicion of poison, aroused no furor of inquiry.

Reavis was early on the ground after that death. He searched Willing's attic and discovered in a gunny sack under the eaves a number of certified copies of documents bolstering the Peralta claim. Best of all, there was an autographed letter from General Santa Anna to Willing which had accompanied the papers. According to this remarkable letter, the President of Mexico, acting as errand boy for an unknown and impecunious American, had ransacked Mexican records and procured certified copies of important documents. Which, even in this modern and friendly day, was overdoing the Good Neighbor policy. But a dead man can't deny his signature or aver that he never heard of or had dealings with a Miguel Peralta.

Willing died intestate. Reavis overlooked the existence of a wife and father, and especially the dower rights of the wife under the laws of the territory of Arizona, which, as soon as Reavis entered his claim, resulted in legal difficulties. For the widow demanded a half interest. Reavis scampered off and bought her dower rights for a promised sum of $30,000 and made a down payment of a few hundreds. But that was not the end of it, because the good lady persisted in making trouble, claiming she was induced to sell by misrepresentation and fraud. All of which came to nothing but annoyance for the future baron.

Reavis now boldly made public claim to his barony. Armed with certified copies of all the documents in the case, he filed with Royal A. Johnson, surveyor general for the Washington Government, a petition to be declared owner of 10,800,000 acres of Arizona's richest land and of the whole of its most populous city of Phoenix. Having done so, he appeared with some pomp in Phoenix and posted public notices, disturbing and frightening to all citizens, that everybody occupying land under any sort of title must communicate with him at once and make suitable financial arrangements or be ousted from their holdings as trespassers.

This was bold action, for the claim had not yet been passed upon by the courts, but it was a bombshell that hurled the economy of Arizona high into the air. It meant ruin for thousands of citizens who occupied ranches or homes or had constructed stores or business buildings or who ran cattle on range land under grant from the United

States Government. It meant that railroads crossing his barony were trespassers occupying rights of way that belonged to Reavis in fee simple. It meant that rich mines had brought to the surface and smelted millions of dollars' worth of gold and silver and copper that was now the property of James Addison Reavis, and for which they must account. The populace buzzed like a swarm of frightened bees, mobs gathered, threats were uttered, committees were formed for common protection against the usurper. Such great business enterprises as the Southern Pacific Railroad Company, and the Silver King mine, and Wells-Fargo Express, sweating with anxiety, called in their legal counsel in the crisis. Frantic consultations were held at which Reavis obligingly and suavely presented for inspection his whole parade of forged documents. The best legal minds of the nation scrutinized them, and then, it seemed unanimously, gave it as their opinion that the Reavis-Peralta claim was good in law and unassailable! On advice of counsel, the great railroad capitulated and the great Silver King mine capitulated. Strangest of all, overnight some of these men and these interests seem to have become Reavis' allies instead of his opponents. So exact and efficient had been his world-wide forgeries that the most expensive lawyers in the nation advised their clients to settle, to pay up and to get out as cheaply as Reavis would let them. The Southern Pacific actually paid him $50,000, following this advice. The Silver King mine paid an installment of $25,000. . . .

But even with the world by the tail, he seemed to have misgivings as to the impregnability of his claim through purchase from the poisoned Doctor Willing. James Addison Reavis set out in quest of a woman. He was not looking for beauty or for love, but for a dupe. It could not be any woman, no matter how young and desirable she might be. She must be of a certain age, or appear to be of that age —approximately fourteen years old. She must be a waif. She must be Spanish or Mexican, and she must know practically nothing of her origin or who her parents were.

He searched California and he searched Arizona, and at last he found her on a lonely ranch on the edge of the Dragoon Mountains in eastern Arizona—the Six Springs Ranch, whose owner was John Slaughter. John Slaughter had a servant, almost a slave—a little girl who drudged for her board and keep. She worked about the ranch in bare feet with calloused soles, and she was different in nothing from any other halfbreed slavey, except that she had passed from hand to hand since infancy, being taken into various houses by people who pitied her or who could get enough work out of her to pay for her food and the one cheap, flopping dress she wore.

Reavis smelled out this waif and rode to the Slaughter ranch, appearing in the guise of a rescuer and a friend. It was a Cinderella tale he told in that remote ranch house—that the little household drudge was not a household drudge, but was heiress to the wealth and titles of the Peraltas, and that in her veins ran thinly the blood of kings.

As usual, he proved his story with papers. At once he took the child away with him and went to work upon her career with all the patience and thoroughness he had shown in all his other projects. She was without ability even to read or write, which must be altered before she could emerge in society as the Baroness of Arizona, and a great lady worthy of her lineage and title. Reavis took the child to California, declaring her to be his ward, and fitted her out with a wardrobe befitting her rank. The girl began to live a marvelous dream. Reavis turned her over to the good sisters of a convent school and instructed them to educate her and to endow her with all the accomplishments of the most exalted lady.

In vacation times he traveled with her, introducing her as his ward, and in his favor it must be said that always, until the debacle, he treated her with respect and gentleness and kindness, perhaps even with sincere love. She was not an ill-favored child. Expensive dresses and jewels added to her beauty. She was pampered and petted as she learned, and she must have been a child of quality, because she learned well and perfected herself in deportment and social graces, so that she was even unembarrassed to be received by a queen.

Then, when the child was old enough, Reavis, her rescuer and benefactor, made her his wife. It was then that he took upon himself the high-sounding title of Baron of Arizona in his wife's name, and when twin sons were born to them in the Fifth Avenue Hotel in New York, he asserted a secondary and stronger claim to the Peralta grant on behalf of his wife, the direct heir, and his twin sons, who continued the name. The baroness dressed after the fashion of a Spanish lady of high estate; the twins, riding with nurses and entourage, were clad in crimson velvets in the mode of little Spanish princes.

Money was rolling in now from many sources. Reavis was busy with great affairs and important associates. He formed companies in his barony—lumber companies, mining companies, irrigation projects—and a part of his huge income, amounting, it is said, to $300,000 a year, was derived from taking partners into these projects.

He had come to full flower. The young Confederate forger of leaves of absence, the St. Louis streetcar conductor, had now endowed himself with his wife's title. Baron de Arizonac and Caballero de los Colorados. Henceforth to Arizonans he was known as the Red Baron. Little Carmelita, the kitchen drudge, had become Sofía Loreta Micaela, baroness and mistress of 10,800,000 acres of soil.

Reavis did not merely ask the world to accept his word that Carmelita was the last of the Peraltas; he produced ample documents to prove it. The family tree ran something like this: In 1786 a son was born to the original Miguel de Peralta, first Baron de Arizonac, in Guadalajara, and the great bell of the Campanil del Correo told the good tidings to the countryside. The child was named Jesús Miguel de Peralta. Two years later, with Governor Firmin Riestra and an *escribano publico* for witnesses, a will was recorded by the terms of which Miguel left to his son his vast landholdings in Arizona.

But little Jesús, when he came to manhood, did nothing about taking possession of his barony, but grew up slothful and pleasure-loving in Guadalajara, where, according to records discovered by Reavis after a year's delving, he was married and became the father of a child named Carmelita. By the year 1860 the family fortunes had waned and Jesús, now an old man, moved his family to California, where, in San Diego, Reavis unearthed the records of the marriage of Carmelita to one Don José Ramón Carmen y Castillo, a gentleman of Cádiz, who had come to America to make his fortune and had had very little luck in his quest. In fact, his luck had been so bad that, ashamed of bringing disgrace upon his family at home, he had assumed the alias of José Maso.

According to Reavis' evidence, in the year 1862 there arrived at Bandini Ranch, a little settlement near San Bernardino, a party of Spaniards guided by a teamster named Treadway. One of the party was a venerable gentleman named Don Jesús Miguel de Peralta. Also there was a José Maso and his wife Carmelita, daughter of Don Jesús, who was in an interesting condition and far advanced. Here, on this ranch, twins were born, a boy and a girl, who were duly baptized in the ancient church of San Salvador, and here the births were legally registered. Within a week the boy baby died, leaving his twin sister the heir of the Peraltas.

Next the father, José Maso, or Don José Ramón Carmen y Castillo, deserted his American family and returned to Spain. He deserted wife and daughter, but, oddly enough, took his father-in-law along with him—which seems to border upon the eccentric. At any rate, it enabled Jesús Miguel de Peralta to make and file a will in Cadiz leaving his American property to his baby granddaughter. What became of the child's mother is not adduced.

So little Carmelita, or Sofía, became a waif, to be passed from hand to hand carelessly. This was the fairy story Reavis invented, and with which he duped not only the public and Government officials but little Cinderella herself.

However, Reavis' pretensions were not to pass unchallenged. Down in the little town of Florence, Arizona, Tom Weedon girded on his armor and rode into the lists. Tom was a newspaperman, editor and proprietor of the local newspaper. He took pen in hand and belabored Reavis and his pretensions, battling like a paladin, urging the people to courage and to fight for their rights.

The Phoenix *Gazette* also fought the Reavis claims. But the Phoenix editor wrote more courageously than he acted, because he himself was one of the first to go to Reavis and purchase from him a quitclaim deed to his property. A deed from J. A. Reavis to Homer H. McNeil was duly recorded, and it caused an explosion of public sentiment that all but blew the editor out of the state. Advertisers refused to buy space, citizens refused to buy the paper. He was ostracized. Homer was compelled to rush to the recorder's office and withdraw his deed from registry. In his editorial columns he made explanations and pleaded for clemency.

On February 5, 1884, there appeared in the *Gazette* an address to the people, signed by J. T. Alsap, A. D. Lemon, John W. Crenshaw, acting as a committee.

> The pretended land grant known as the Peralta Grant, now claimed by one Reavis, has at length aroused a disposition on the part of some of the people residing within its supposed bounds to look into the claim and see whether there is anything in it. Upon some examination of the papers upon which it is supposed to be founded, it is the opinion of those who have made such examination that the claim is a fraudulent one. . . . Unless some immediate action is taken by you to protect and defend your rights, your interests and your homes from this stupendous fraud, your rights will be overridden, your interests gone, and your homes, which ought to be sacred from all intruders the property of others . . .

There was more of it, impassioned, a bit hysterical. It shows the state of mind of the thousands of men and women living within the limits of the domain of the Red Baron. But nothing was done, nothing but talk and worry and empty threats of action. This was in 1884. Twelve years were to elapse between the appearance of this appeal for united defense and the final settlement of the matter in 1896. During all those years the great valley was blighted, the threat of the Red Baron impended over it like some terrifying storm cloud. And the baron himself went his amazing way, spending with both hands, maintaining a state worthy of a grandee of Spain and the husband of one descended from the Baron de Arizonac and Caballero de los Colorados who also bore the high-sounding titles of Gentleman of the King's Bedchamber, Grandee of Spain, Knight of the Military Order of Carlos III, Knight of the Insignia of the Royal College of Our Lady of Guadalupe.

Reavis traveled the earth with his baroness and twin sons, born in the Fifth Avenue Hotel in New York. In one year he is said to have spent $60,000 in travel alone. He owned a mansion in St. Louis; he occupied for part of the year a sumptuous house in Washington and an extravagantly beautiful palace in Mexico. He had a home in Madrid. Ordinary travel was not good enough for the Red Baron and his family and his liveried entourage. They traveled in private cars. Some tenuous claim that his wife was even of the blood royal seems not to have been ignored at the Spanish court. We are informed that his children knew and played with little Alfonso, the King, and that the baron and baroness were received at court, where they entertained and were entertained by royalty.

Reavis lodged a voluminous petition in the year 1883, praying for full recognition of his rights, and reciting the ancient documents upon which his claim was based. Copies of these documents, certified by Spanish officials, were included as exhibits, a formidable and impressive array, gorgeous with royal insignia and seals and exalted names, well calculated to impress officials of a democratic nation, unused to close contact with royalty. It was received by the surveyor general, and his duty was clear to investigate the matter carefully and to make a prompt report. But he dallied. A storm of criticism grew against his dilatory handling of the matter, but nevertheless it was not until the year 1890, seven years after the filing of Reavis' petition, that Royal A. Johnson made his report.

It was an adverse report, excellently reasoned and showing some skill in deciphering the internal evidence of questioned documents.

It pointed out certain historical discrepancies and broadly suggested forgery.

It had taken the surveyor general's office from 1883 until 1890 to reach this judgment. Adverse though it was, and dangerous, it seems not to have discouraged Reavis. Nor do the legal authorities seem to have done anything about it. Reavis went ahead diligently organizing companies to develop the resources of his barony—lumber companies, irrigation projects. He had battled for his claim with the Department of the Interior and with Congress, and in these arguments he had learned of defects in his chain of title which he had remedied skillfully by new forgeries of old records.

In 1891 the Court of Private Land Grant Claims was established with plenary powers. Before it, for its consideration and adjudication, were filed 301 claims to lands under Spanish grants, and these claims were for a grand total of 36,000,000 acres. Some claims were valid, and of the total number, eighty-seven were found by the judges to be good, and 3,000,000 acres of land were awarded to claimants.

It was an ambulatory court, sitting wherever it desired and wherever it found facts to investigate. It even held sessions in the open air, and took testimony under the light of the moon. It combined in itself the functions of a court of judgment and a detective bureau.

Reavis had little dreamed that any United States judicial officer would have the right or would be endowed with the energy to follow his devious trail all over the world, taking experts along for special assignments and a store of chemicals for the making of tests. But the court, or agents of the court, trailed Reavis through Mexico and even across the ocean to Cadiz and Madrid and the monasteries of Spain which were the repositories of documents in his chain of title.

Among those who served the court well was an able, cultured and persistent gentleman named Mallet Prevost, expert in the Spanish language and able to detect minute flaws in historical accuracy. In Mexico, as he pored over parchments he believed he detected indications of erasure and of substitution of words. The eye of the camera not only demonstrated the erasures but brought to light the words which lay beneath and had been erased. Encouraged by this initial finding, Mallet Prevost persisted. He labored in Guadalajara, in Mexico City, in San Bernardino—wherever Reavis' trail had led in California and Mexico. He took ship and crossed the sea to Spain, where he continued his laborious and skillful detective work until his report was complete.

Chemical examination demonstrated that in certain documents the first page or two were genuine and the last page or two were genuine, but the intervening pages were forgeries, being written upon parchment of a different and more modern sort. The original had been written with iron ink, while the substitutions were written in dogwood ink. Traces of a steel pen were found where the original had been written with a quill. Chemicals were utilized to remove the dogwood ink, and others to restore the iron. In the Guadalajara document appointing Peralta Baron de Arizonac and Caballero de los Colorados, quite another name and quite another title were uncovered.

Mallet Prevost followed two lines: one to discredit the documents creating a Baron de Arizonac and Caballero de los Colorados and the very existence of Miguel de Peralta; the second to demonstrate that the baroness was not, in fact, a lineal descendant of Miguel de Peralta, if facts should demonstrate that he really existed. Sofía, or Carmelita, Maso was alleged to have been one of twins born near San Bernardino in California. The birth of these twins was duly recorded in the church records, meticulously kept by the old padres. The Mission of San Salvador was visited.

It was established that Reavis, in some mysterious and adroit manner, had got access to the records—as, in like mysterious manner, he had got access to archives in Spain. He had removed from the birth register pages containing the births, entered on certain convenient dates. He had procured paper as nearly like the original as possible, and on it had copied truly the list of such births, but had added the names of the Maso twins.

This record of birth, being so skillfully done, must have been accepted, had it not been for the methodical habits of the padres, who indexed their records day by day, and in a separate volume. Reavis was ignorant of this separate index and had not tampered with it. It contained no mention of the names of the Maso twins, but instead the names of two quite other babies.

Excellent detective work also brought to light the perjury contained in affidavits of persons who attended the birth of the twins, and of others who claimed to have known well the Maso family. A large sum of money was said to have been paid to an unscrupulous lawyer for procuring this perjured testimony.

The claim came on at last to be sifted and adjudicated by the Land Grant Court, sitting in Santa Fe. By this time fortune had deserted Reavis. He had spent his last penny in preparing his case and in luxurious living, so that, on the day of trial, he had not a cent to pay for counsel. Reavis sat alone and friendless in the courtroom, save for the sad-eyed and bewildered woman who had lived a fairy story as his wife. She sat there tearless and unbelieving as Government attorneys adduced point after point of evidence to tear down her husband's intricate and incredible pretense. On question from the presiding judge, however, merciful attorneys for the Government declared that, in their opinion, Carmelita was guiltless. They averred that she was a dupe, that from start to finish she had believed Reavis' tale of her ancestry.

Reavis, indicted and brought to trial in January of 1895, was convicted and sentenced to six years in the penitentiary at Santa Fe.

Some years later, the Baroness Sofía Peralta Reavis, taking advantage of the laws governing paupers, sued for divorce from her husband in Denver. She was living in poverty and squalor in a mean boarding house on Larimer Street. And with the record of that divorce proceeding she disappears from visible history. As to the twins, there is evidence that they grew to manhood. It is known that one, at least, served his country well as a member of our armed services.

James Addison Reavis served his term. He emerged a wraith of his old, distinguished self, eyes hollow, cheeks lined with suffering. He returned to Phoenix, which had hated him in the old days and where he had stood in danger from the anger of those he had sought to victimize. He skulked along the streets, hardly noticed. According to Ned Creighton, prominent Phoenix citizen who saw Reavis in those last shadowy days, the great impostor spent his waking hours in the library in the state capitol, reading, reading—reading newspaper stories about himself and the days of his grandeur.

UP AND DOWN WITH SAM INSULL

by John T. Flynn

Ivar Kreuger and Samuel Insull were the two most grandiose false Midases of this century. Although Kreuger operated on an international scale and became for a while the financial savior of various governments, I have selected Insull to represent the genus financier-run-amuck because John T. Flynn's account so clearly reveals the modus operandi. *This is excerpted from a longer study of Insull in which the solid achievements of his earlier years were also outlined.*

About 1912 a certain cocoon burst in Chicago. Insull, the industrial grub, ceased to exist. From it Insull, the beautiful promoter butterfly, emerged, spread his wings and flew over the land.

In those days hundreds of small electric light companies—and big ones too—were losing money in huge gobs. But Sam Insull was making money in Chicago. Insull had the secret. And so, many small proprietors visited his offices and proposed that he go in with them or take over their plants; that he give them the "laying-on of hands" —the Insull hands—and thus cure them of malignant deficits. About 1905 Insull heeded these tempting offers and cast his eyes in the direction of New Albany, near the Ohio Falls. New Albany and its neighbor, Jeffersonville, were located on the Ohio opposite Louisville—two little towns with many factories. Insull took an interest in the electric light and power company there and set about building it up.

Having taken the New Albany and Jeffersonville companies he looked around for others with which to apply his theory of mass production. For several years his operations expanded. They devoured fresh funds—about $60,000 a year which Insull supplied from his slender means. The load became too heavy. His success in the suburban area around Chicago furnished him with a model, and so in 1912 he organized a corporation called the Middle West Utilities Company to which he turned over his Indiana holdings.

This Middle West Utilities Company was a holding company. A holding company is a corporation which is empowered to own the stocks of other corporations. It is usually applied to those corporations which exercise control over the companies whose stocks they hold. It may be employed for perfectly good and legitimate purposes. But it has been made the instrument of abuses so grave that it has become a major issue in American finance and politics.

Insull did not invent the holding company. It began away back in 1832 in Maryland to enable the Baltimore and Ohio Railroad to buy up the stocks of all the numerous little roads it needed to lengthen its system. It was used again in 1868 and 1870 when Pennsylvania went on a holding company spree. The legislature in two years set up forty holding companies. One was the Pennsylvania Company, belonging to the Pennsylvania Railroad, and is still in existence. Another was the South Improvement Company which old John D. Rockefeller used in his first attempt at monopoly in 1872. Another was the Union Company, the first utility holding company, known now by the name to which it changed in 1888—the United Gas Improvement Company. Most of the others were canceled as a result of scandals.

However, the device came into more general use in the nineties when New Jersey went into the charter-mongering business and invited all the big industrial monopolists to "come to Jersey." The Standard Oil Company was one of the first to use it in order to escape the operation of the Sherman anti-trust law and took advantage of it until the Supreme Court declared the practice illegal.

The real use of the holding company did not come until a little later. Men were learning the possibilities of the corporation as a means of making money, not merely out of the business which the corporation carried on, but out of its stocks. And so those promotion giants, John W. Gates and Henry H. Rogers and Thomas F. Ryan and the notorious "Gas" Addicks and Widener roamed the land, gathering up corporations of all sorts, putting them together by means of the holding company, and rolling in wealth through the amazing stock manipulations thus made possible. So in 1912, when Insull organized his little Middle West Utilities Company, these other concerns were extending their operations rapidly. He knew these men well and he had a model ready at hand for his guidance.

In the moment of its birth, Insull delivered to the Middle West

Company a wound—a wound which would be repeated many times. Let us look at Insull delivering this wound as he pulls five million dollars out of a hat, as neatly as a magician extracts a rabbit. Now watch—and remember that the hand is quicker than the eye; the promoter is quicker than the sap.

Sam Insull, individual—and very rugged too—owns stocks in three or four small utility companies. Sam Insull, individual, organizes a corporation—a holding company—called the Middle West. Insull is made its president. Up to this point the Middle West has nothing.

Now Sam Insull, individual, sells to Middle West, represented by Sam Insull, president, his stocks in those little companies. Insull, president, agrees to pay Insull, individual, $330,000 for them. But the Middle West has no money. So Insull, president, tells Insull, individual, that Middle West will pay him when it gets the money.

The next step then is to get the money. Now watch closely. Middle West issues stock. It issues four million dollars of preferred and six million dollars of common. That makes ten million dollars. Samuel Insull, president of Middle West, thereupon sells the whole issue to Sam Insull, individual, for $3,600,000. But Sam has no money either. So he tells Middle West he will pay it when he gets the money.

The next step is for Sam to get the money. He now sells to the public all of the preferred stock—$4,000,000 of it—for $3,600,000. To make the bargain better he throws in a million of the common. Remember, he has six million of that. Now he has $3,600,000 in cash and five million dollars' worth of common stock left.

He turns over the $3,600,000 cash to Middle West, which pays for the 10,000,000 shares he had bought. Middle West can now pay him the $330,000 it owes him. When it is all over things stand thus:

Middle West has Insull's utility stocks—$330,000 worth.

It has the balance of the $3,600,000 cash.

What is humorously referred to as the "public" has all the preferred stock and a million dollars of the common, for which it paid $3,600,000.

Insull has the remaining five million dollars of the common stock, which gives him control of the company and for which he did not pay a red cent. Presto, the trick is done.

Here I must trouble you with one more little trick in bookkeeping. Of course, a promoter offering stock to the public must, ordinarily, show that the company has assets behind the stock. In the operation described above it is apparent there were no real assets to support $10,000,000 of stock. How did Insull show assets? He created them. Very simple! Just call the bookkeeper. The new Middle West Company had as its assets Insull's promise to pay $3,600,000. It also had the securities it bought from him worth $330,000. It needed $6,000,000 more to make up the $10,000,000. Among the securities Insull had transferred to it for $330,000 were several small options to buy other companies. Insull merely arbitrarily put these down as worth $6,000,-000. This is called "writing up" assets. And this practice Insull continued to use until the end of his career.

Mr. Samuel Insull, who performed this little trick, thought to himself that a man was a fool to work for twenty years as he had done, running a tremendous Chicago utility company, for a moderate salary when he could get rich in a few months in this sort of business. Henceforth, Samuel Insull became a promoter. And he would go on expanding the Middle West Utility Company on this pattern until he was worth $170,000,000.

And thus the Middle West started—a small affair with six hundred miles of lines serving 140 small towns in Indiana. It is impossible to follow the whole long, twisting trail, the passing of stocks back and forth, the intricate financing and exchanging of different classes of stock. One little story will suffice:

The Middle West acquired the Central Illinois Public Service Company by buying its common stock. After this the Middle West turned over to the Central a number of small utility properties which it owned in Illinois. Now watch the magician again at work, pulling millions out of the hat.

The Middle West gave to the Central the various small utility companies, which it valued at a little over two million dollars. It gave also a little over $400,000 in cash to help the Central. Altogether it gave a little more than $2,400,000 in property and cash. What did it get in return? The Central gave to the Middle West its own bonds, preferred stocks and common stocks as follows: bonds, $3,000,000; stocks, $4,689,000.

The Middle West then sold the bonds for enough to reimburse it for the $2,400,000 it gave the Central. It had left for itself, without a cent of cost, $4,689,000 worth of stock. Thus the wild game went on.

It must be said for Insull that while he thus built unsoundly—financially—he built well physically. Little by little, he added other utility companies in the Mississippi Valley to the Middle West. He modernized their equipment, applied his principle of mass production, dismantled their old plants and put up new ones.

Up to this Insull continued a very little-known figure in Chicago. He was not a colorful man. He took a grim pride in getting to his office so early that his desk was practically cleared before the rest of the office appeared. And he didn't mind calling attention to his performances before his subordinates. He was not a pleasant man. He was brusque, ruthless with his staff.

A lot of people used to refer to him as a "damned Englishman." He never got over being an Englishman. In later years he professed an intense Americanism. But at this time he made no concealment of his violent preference for all things English. He reminded Chicago bankers that he had been obliged to go to England to get financing for his utilities. He loved to visit London. He loved to stroll around its old streets. He avowed that he was always ready to give a job to an Englishman, particularly if he spoke with a cockney accent.

He had been elected president of the National Electric Light Association but he had refused at first to join the Edison pioneers. Indeed, he sneered at the organization. He was a self-righteous man. He was well satisfied with everything he did. He made countless speeches telling of his own work. He remarked many times that he supposed people noticed that he was always "blowing his own horn." In Chicago he preached that the man to own the utility of a city was the man who used it. Customer ownership had been invented, and he promptly adopted it in Chicago to raise funds there for the Commonwealth Edison. But now that he was down in Indiana and Illinois and neighboring states, buying up other people's utilities, operators and cities criticized him. But the criticism didn't bother him.

When 1917 arrived—and the war with it—Insull's Middle West Company was operating in eleven states. It served 385 communities, 228 of them in Illinois, some as far south as Oklahoma and as far east as New England. The Middle West, a holding company, had come to own other holding companies, some of them quite large, like the Illinois Northern Utilities owning in turn twenty-eight companies, or the Kentucky Utilities Company, controlling nineteen companies. The Insull domain was getting larger and more complicated.

The war brought problems to American communities—problems of fuel, food, economies, labor, the reinforcements behind the lines. To handle these, state councils of defense were organized. In Illinois,

Frank O. Lowden, the war governor, appointed Insull chairman of the Illinois State Council of Defense.

He did an extraordinary job as war council chairman. Possessing the soul of a dictator, it was natural that Insull was the first to suggest rigid food and fuel control later adopted by the President. The vision of a community drastically regimented, perfectly managed, appealed to his imagination.

He bent to his task with appetite. In other states the councils of defense got appropriations ranging from $100,000 to $5,000,000. In Illinois Insull got an appropriation of $50,000 and spent none of it. Instead, he turned it back to the state plus a profit of another $300,-000. People said it was too bad Insull didn't have the management of the war—he could have paid a dividend on it.

When the war was over he was loaded with praises. These were pleasant to his ears. He looked himself over and found that he was good.

One of the casualties of the war was the rich Peoples Gas Light and Coke Company. It had luxuriated in easy profits for decades. It had grown fat, languid and dull. The war sent up the prices of coal and oil and labor. The company clamored for higher rates.

At this point an error, which in the long chronicles of human stupidity must hold a high place, helped to crush it. The $3,000,000 profit of 1915 had become a deficit of $1,366,988 in 1918. But relief was utterly impossible because of the hatred in which the company was held because of one piece of unmitigated folly: Its billing department fell into the slovenly habit of sending out wrong bills—hundreds of thousands of them. Complaints were met with indifference and even insolence. When the company asked for higher rates the Illinois Commission responded by lowering the rates. This meant approaching bankruptcy.

In its desperate plight it appealed to Samuel Insull to assume its management. Insull took the presidency of the $85,000,000 corporation in 1919. He went through it with an axe. He ended the unbelievable era of false billing, restored the company's credit, scrapped its antiquated plants for modern ones, got its rates readjusted, reëstablished it in the good graces of Chicago, and made it prosperous again.

Since 1913 he had dominated the rapid transit situation. The four elevated companies had grave financial difficulties. Each line charged a separate fare. The Lake Street line owed Insull immense sums for electrical interests. Later he brought about a consolidation of the four lines. He put into effect a single fare. He improved service. People praised his management. Thus, by 1919 he was the master—the autocrat of the electric light and power, the gas and the rapid transit facilities of Chicago, and of the light, power, traction and in many cases the water of most of Illinois.

With the war out of the way he resumed building his Middle West Utilities. He began acquiring other holding companies all over the country. In 1919 the Middle West had six thousand stockholders. By 1923 he had increased the number to fifty thousand. In 1919 it was earning around $10,000,000 a year. By 1923 these earnings were $36,000,000. And it was serving 772 communities.

Now came the new era of Calvin Coolidge—that amazing period during which the nation floated upward on a cushion of speculative air. Suddenly the hitherto unsolved mystery of credit seemed to be solved, and America discovered how to tap the golden reservoirs of the future and spend in a single year the income of a dozen years. The whole people—tradesmen and teachers, capitalists and clerks, preachers, politicians, workers, men, women and office boys rushed into the twenty-three stock markets of the country and wagered the savings of the past and the future upon the proposition that prosperity would last forever.

Of course Insull, who had produced five millions from his hat with a few little Indiana utilities in 1912, now a master magician, produced hundreds of millions in stocks and bonds for the infatuated and uninformed investors of America to buy.

By this time Insull had become a god—not a tin god, but a flesh and blood financial deity who sat in isolated grandeur and power remote from the business world of Chicago, which bowed before him. Bankers rubbed their hands with glee when Mr. Insull deigned to borrow money from them. The newspapers vied with one another in proclaiming his story. Nothing had ever appeared in America so much like one of those great earls who ruled in England in the days before the Magna Charta.

Insull was a confirmed prohibitionist. He had gotten his views from his parents with his religion. He boasted that never a drop of intoxicating liquor passed his lips. But he had plenty of liquor available for business conferences, and while with one hand he subscribed a hundred thousand dollars to build a wing in the Temperance Hospital of London, with the other he passed out checks liberally to finance Mayor Thompson, who was proclaiming that he "would make Chicago as wet as the Atlantic Ocean."

Insull became a prodigal giver to all good causes. Does the Cardinal want a new playground? Mr. Insull will arrange it. Does a hospital or asylum or some civic crusade need funds or prestige? Sam Insull will lend his name and his wallet. Chicago's opera falls on evil days. There is no money for the exacting divas and tenors. Insull is appealed to to save the opera. He has always had a weakness for the stage. So he answers the call. Under his inspiration there grew the dream of a great Civic Opera, and in the fullness of time that magnificent building rose on Wacker Drive at a cost of $20,000,000.

Insull himself began to live upon an imperial scale. He had beautiful offices in the Peoples Gas Building where he spent his mornings. He had a magnificent suite of heavily paneled rooms in the Commonwealth Edison Building where he spent his afternoons. After four o'clock he could be found in his suite on the forty-fourth floor of the Opera Building. Private elevators took you to all these chambers. The opera-house suite was apartment as well as office. There were numerous rooms and four baths, all grouped around a spacious central room called the "directors' room" but equipped with a grand piano as well as a directors' table. Here artists from the opera company were received and delightful parties held.

He had, over many years, built up a baronial estate at Libertyville —4,300 acres of park and real farm. There he played out the role of the squire. Libertyville was called a one-man town. As one local commentator observed, the people there "built homes on Insull real estate, sent to an Insull school children born in an Insull hospital, used Insull light, cooked with Insull gas, traveled on an Insull road, saved in an Insull bank and played golf on an Insull golf course."

He liked to go to England. He was a member of several clubs there. It is said he made a number of trips to London just to walk the old streets he had known as a youth. At any rate, he crossed the ocean over seventy times before he made the last gloomy trip to Paris in flight from his crumbling empire. . . .

"I saw him standing at his window one night," said a Chicago banker to me, "looking out over the city as it sank into darkness and the millions of electric lights from his marvelous power stations began to flood the whole scene. Insull was usually in that office as darkness settled on Chicago. As I looked at him I felt sure he chose the evening hour there in order to see this nightly miracle. And when I went home I observed that Sam Insull looked at the moment as if he felt how wonderful it was to have this vast, incredible Chicago in his vest pocket."

Why do not men like Insull pause when they have so much? Because pause is often impossible. In 1925 Insull moved the frontiers of his empire into the East—a dangerous proceeding. Away back in the first year of the Middle West he bought some Illinois properties. To get them he had to take the whole bundle, and in it was a small group in Vermont and New Hampshire called the Twin States Gas and Electric Company. He had no intention of entering New England. But being thus in, he felt it necessary to build up these properties. After a time he had acquired others and soon had enough to form the New England Public Service Company.

As 1929 drew to its close, Insull, a veritable industrial emperor, ruling his domain with an iron hand, controlled not only the light and power and gas and rapid transit facilities of Chicago and Illinois, its politics, its social life, its civic activities, but he dominated the light and power and water and transportation facilities of five thousand American communities. The Middle West and its subsidiaries alone had over 275,000 stockholders and 160,000 bondholders. He ruled properties valued at more than two and one half billion dollars.

As for the people of Chicago, they rushed to put up their money whenever Mr. Insull put out a new issue of stock in any of his great companies. Banking houses sold the bonds. Several financial subsidiaries offered the stock. Stocks were urged upon employees and, while they were not apparently obliged to buy them, they were under an unostentatious pressure which they could not resist. Employees were called upon to sell stocks to their friends and acquaintances. The man who called to inspect your wiring or to fix your gas connections or look over your gas stove tried to sell you a few shares before he left the house.

Then in the summer of 1929 something seemed to infect this high-geared organism with languor. Underneath the hectic and raging surface of speculation certain foci of weakness began to assert their baleful influence. They were not noticed by the men who preferred to be blind. No man shut his eyes to them more resolutely than Samuel Insull, who believed profoundly that the era of prosperity would never halt.

The climax was approaching. But instead of preparing for it, he was making ready for that magnificent and almost barbaric pageantry which, with mock irony, marked the last scene in the gaudy chronicle of the Insull saga. The great Chicago Civic Opera House, built under Insull's direction, costing twenty million dollars, towering forty-five stories above the Chicago River on Wacker Drive, was ready for its opening. It was the last week of October, 1929. The attentive ear might have heard the rustling of the winds of the coming storm stirring through all parts of our rushing business machine.

That week the blow struck Wall Street. The great crash of 1929 sent stocks tumbling in terrifying confusion. But Insull, the prophet of the new era, felt it was just a pause in the long trail up. On the night of November fourth, long lines of limousines rolled up to the colonnaded façade of the Opera House, discharging the ermine- and brocade- and velvet-clad women. The golden horseshoe inside the vast proscenium arch, glittering with jewels, awaited the rising of the curtain. The center of that gala throng, in his box like a monarch, was Samuel Insull. In the fever and rush of that glorious day he had hardly had time to note that a wave of selling had carried his stocks down again that day. It was his hour of triumph, the supreme moment of his life.

It is a far cry from this brilliant scene to the dingy police station of Athens where, after flight from America, from Paris, from Milan, he was finally detained by the police. Oddly enough, Insull hated air flight. He would never get into a plane at home. But with doom at his heels he flew from Chicago to his ship. He flew from Milan to Athens.

To an Athens reporter he said: "I learn for the first time I am accused of breaking the law. I have not stolen any sum. The question which arises is one of civil law."

Insull's real offense was to destroy nearly a billion dollars of investments which represented the savings of some 330,000 stockholders—many of them ruined by the loss.

The point to remember is that most, if not all, of the mortal blows inflicted on his countless companies were delivered by means wholly within the law. Everybody was doing it—or at least almost everybody. The stealing—I mean the plain, old-fashioned, unvarnished taking of money—did not begin until the great companies tottered to their fall. What wrecked them was not stealing, but a form of getting hold of other people's money far more delicate and devious—a form overlaid with so many fictions that even the perpetrator can fool his conscience about it. Insull's great house fell apart because it was built upon sand and because it was full of rotten timbers, corrupt masonry and bungling workmanship.

Just what did happen to Insull's business? All the great plants he built and owned are still in existence, still operating, still making profits. What is it, then, that has failed?

First let me describe briefly the Middle West Utilities group. Imagine some 5,300 towns in thirty-two states, east of the Rockies. They must have light, gas, water, ice. These things are supplied by 524 electric plants, 80 gas plants, 330 ice plants and numerous water and transportation systems. These numerous plants belong to 235 operating companies—separate corporations. Insull's Middle West Utilities Company was a holding company controlling all these corporations.

But the Middle West did not own them directly. It owned the stock in a group of other and smaller holding companies. It owned, in fact, thirteen such holding companies. These holding companies in turn owned other smaller holding companies, which in turn owned the operating companies.

To understand this better let us follow this series of holding companies from the bottom up. The little town of Roxbury in Vermont gets its electric light and gas from the Twin States Gas and Electric Company. The Twin States is owned by the National Light, Heat and Power Company. The stock of this company is owned by the New England Public Service Company. The stock of the latter is owned by the National Electric Power Company and the stock of that is owned by the Middle West.

Thus, starting at Roxbury, Vermont, you must travel through six corporate structures before you come to the ultimate control of that little Roxbury plant—to an old man of seventy-two years, seated behind a broad, cleared desk, in a magnificent office in the Commonwealth Building in Chicago.

He had a board of directors. But they were so much furniture. He was a tyrant—a lone eagle. He shared responsibility with no one. The gray-haired magnate, at a time in life when most men seek repose, was a member of eighty-five directorates. He was chairman of sixty-five and president of eleven.

But just how did he control all these companies? Did he own the stock or a majority of it? He couldn't have that much money. The answer is that he didn't need to. He controlled these vast possessions with other people's money. It is marvelous what you can do with an investment trust if you know how to work it. Insull got his hands on four hundred million dollars in two investment trusts. He worked out a clever scheme by which with twenty million dollars he could control both trusts and, through them, of the whole great utility structure valued at two and a half billions which really belonged to some 330,000 stockholders.

Some spots began to appear on Insull's much glorified name. In 1927 the Senate stopped Frank L. Smith, elected senator from Illinois, at its doors and charged him with having been elected by the use of Insull money. Jim Reed, remorseless prosecutor, then senator from Missouri, handled the case against Smith. The latter was chairman of the Illinois Commerce Commission with power of regulation over Sam Insull's Illinois utilities. Campaign contributions from Sam Insull seemed a shocking thing. Insull dodged and fenced with Reed for hours. Reed slowly drew from him that he had given Smith $125,000. Later he admitted it was $197,000.

During all this time the Federal Trade Commission was bringing out every week its revelations about the attempts of the utility companies under Mr. Insull's sponsorship to poison the press, schools and pulpit of the country with underground propaganda activities. He had gotten control of and dominated the National Electric Light Association. And there a large section of the more reputable utility leaders resented his methods. Altogether, by 1929, when the clouds began to gather over him, his reputation was seriously impaired, though he did not seem to realize it.

Insull, like so many great business promoters, had the usual supply of shirt-stuffers to tell the world what an amazing man he was. One of them wrote how he was "just the public's hired man." Another told in a fulsome tale how "there are no mysteries in Insull's great business structure. Any man of ordinary intelligence can find out as much about what goes on in that business as he wishes." Insull himself began a theatrical stunt of making reports to stockholders by means of the radio. Now here are the things Insull did which gradually weakened his financial structure and brought it to ruin.

Insull sat at his desk in the Commonwealth Edison Building with a great map of his empire spread out on the wall. There were hundreds of plants and corporations all arranged in holding company groups. The master, like a train dispatcher, could move these properties around, from one group to another, as it suited his purpose. Thus he would have the National Electric Power Company sell three properties to the Middle West at a good profit—$3,000,000 in one case. Of course there was no real profit. The Middle West owned the National. This thing went on all over the system, the scheming magnate in his high tower moving the light and power and gas plants of hundreds of towns around as his needs dictated, and piling up fictitious profits.

Why did he do this? In order to make the public believe that his companies were very prosperous, so that he might induce them to buy more and more millions of his stock. For instance, in 1931 it was announced that the year, so disastrous for business, had been the second most profitable year in the Middle West's history. This profit was put down at $11,000,000. But a large part of these profits were fictitious. Insull created some of them out of the air by merely moving one concern from the Middle West group over to the Public Service of Northern Illinois. He called it a sale, fixed the sale price at $15,000,-000, which showed a large profit for Middle West. At the time he did this, when he was showing these so-called record profits, his employees —collectors, mechanics, elevator man, clerks—were being driven at hot speed to sell stocks to their friends and relatives and to buy themselves. And when this campaign was going on—in December, 1931— Insull knew that his great business was bankrupt.

The chief profits of holding companies come from the dividends of the companies they own. Insull was always able to still further pad his profits by having these subsidiary companies declare stock dividends. These stock dividends would be handed over to the Middle West and put down as profits at the market value of the stock. This is a violation of the rules of accounting of the New York Stock Exchange. Everyone knows the market value of a stock does not represent its true value. It may be too high or too low. In 1928 and 1929 the market was outrageously high. The New York Stock Exchange has roundly condemned this practice. But Insull companies were loaded with such fictitious profits.

Every man who owns an automobile knows its value decreases each year. That's called depreciation. If you leave out the depreciation or minimize it you are fooling yourself and your creditors. That's what Insull did. Seven per cent is the well understood fair rate of depreciation in utility accounting. Insull put it at five in the Middle West, thus padding his assets and surplus each year for several millions. In 1931 he announced a profit on his rapid transit company of $207,-000. *But he allowed no depreciation.* Had he done so that profit would have been turned into a deficit of over a million dollars.

And now let us see the vast structure as it begins to crumble. This began in 1929. First we must understand that around 1928 Insull came face to face with the question of holding fast to his control of his great corporations. It is doubtful if in 1928 his own wealth was more than twenty-five or thirty million dollars at the most. That was not enough to control more than a fraction of the stock of his companies.

Insull saw this danger. He observed that large blocks of stock of his companies were being bought by various investment trusts. One of these was in the hands of Cyrus S. Eaton, one of the most daring of these new promoters. Insull therefore immediately organized his first investment trust—the Insull Utilities Investments, Inc., in which he ultimately gathered some $245,000,000. That pretty much insured his control. He turned over to it the holdings of himself, his wife and his son in his companies. These amounted to only $9,765,000. In return he got 40,000 shares of preferred stock at $100 and 764,000 shares of common in Insull Utilities at $7.50. He got besides an option to purchase 200,000 shares more at $15. Ultimately these shares went to $149 before they declined. At one time his paper profit on these common stock holdings amounted to $130,000,000. They were worth $143,000,000. He had other profits on another investment trust he organized later. This is what Insull referred to when he said the day he left Chicago that he had been worth $170,000,000.

One other fact you must understand. It is the key to the whole story. Insull always raised funds for his companies by one method. He issued rights to his stockholders. Each year in each publicly owned company he would give stockholders the "right" to subscribe to additional stock. Thus in midsummer, 1929, Insull announced that stockholders of Middle West would be allowed to subscribe to 450,000 new shares at $200 a share. If you were a stockholder you would readily see that Middle West shares were then selling on the Chicago Stock Exchange for $350 a share. Of course you would exercise your rights to buy for $200. These rights were issued each year. Millions of dollars poured into the Insull offices. But you must see one thing very clearly. To work this system, the price of the stock must be kept up on the market.

Now we may see Fate at work upon the Insull edifice. In the summer of 1929 he put out this issue of 450,000 "rights." Middle West was selling for $350 a share. All looked lovely. Then suddenly the storm broke. The fatal day—October 24, 1929—when the era of eternal prosperity came to an end, saw the stock crash. Middle West stocks started down. Insull, by this new issue of rights, proposed to raise around $90,000,000—a huge sum. October twenty-fourth when the crash came, Middle West was selling for 350. A week later it sold for 300. Insull's financing had to be completed by November fifteenth. By November ninth Middle West was down to 240 and falling fast.

Insull sat in his office those days, querulous, excited, angry, torn between the coming pageant of the opera opening and the necessity of keeping his stock from falling below 200. His brokers in La Salle Street were instructed to keep the price above 220. He had to pour millions into the market to peg the stock above this price. To get those millions he had to get immense loans from his banks and to pledge the stocks of his various companies.

The night of the opening of the opera Insull got bad news in his box. One of his brokers went to him when the lights were down and told him of the wave of selling which carried prices down that day and of the millions needed to support the market. Two days later the financing was all completed and Insull was safe—for the time being.

Then came the diastrous year of 1930. This year Insull had heavy financing to do for Commonwealth and Public Service of Northern Illinois. The prices of all stocks were toppling. Dark forebodings of the coming depression filled La Salle Street. But Insull shut his ears to them. While other industrialists trimmed their sails, Insull put out more canvas. He planned improvements amounting to $120,000,-000. He bought more and more utility companies. He borrowed incessantly.

Then came rumors of mysterious fights. The world loves the stories of reckless battles on the stock exchange—giant traders flinging millions of dollars onto the floor to capture control of some company. There had been tales of battles between Insull and Lowenstein; between Insull and Cyrus Eaton.

What actually happened is even more dramatic—more significant, more unusual than a stock-market fight. Insull was buying all stocks offered, right and left, to hold prices up. Eaton, who needed money, had plenty of stocks but most of them were going down fast. The one that was remaining up was the Insull stock.

So he decided to let Insull buy at the high price. Instead of Eaton buying against Insull, he was really dumping stocks on him.

Insull borrowed huge sums to make these purchases. But he hadn't bargained on such immense offerings as this. He could not permit the stocks to sag in price. So he sent for Eaton. The Cleveland banker declared himself ready to settle at 350 a share. He had about 150,000 shares at the time and Insull balked, but Eaton threatened to dump them all on the market and break the price of Insull's stocks. Insull capitulated.

After this he was no longer able to support the market. He had not the means. The prices of all stocks were swept down in the avalanche of liquidation which shook every stock exchange. As the prices of his stocks went down, the banks from which he had borrowed money clamored for more collateral. Insull had to put up more and more stocks until finally he had pledged practically every share belonging to all his corporations. In the end Insull Utilities Investments, Inc., had assets which had shrunk to $36,000,000 and liabilities of $226,000,000. This is a sample of what happened to these other corporations. Everything had been pledged to get money to keep up the price of stocks on the stock market. Pegging the market was the implement which delivered the final mortal thrust. No, it was not the depression which destroyed the Insull empire. It was Samuel Insull himself, transformed from a perfectly good utility operator into an insatiable and reckless promoter by the poison of easy profit.

THE LAST OF THE FREEBOOTERS

by Alexander Klein

Despite the valiant and perennial efforts of Robert Louis Stevenson, Charles Laughton and assorted Hollywood craftsmen, the age of piracy, of grand larceny on the high seas, appears very remote to most of us, a relic of Elizabethan days that went out long before sails gave way to funnels. Yet, within the memory of living men, nearly two decades after the *Monitor* met the *Merrimac*, occurred one of the most audacious and hilarious, if unconventional, episodes in the annals of piracy. Admittedly, this last, anachronistic echo of the golden age of buccaneering lacked the traditional elements of blood and thunder. In place of these were substituted the smoother techniques of the confidence man, combined with a certain imaginative grandeur.

One day in February, 1880, William Griffin, a ship's engineer, was nursing a glass in a Glasgow waterfront pub, when he was engaged in conversation by a man who introduced himself as Joseph Walker of the firm of Henderson & Company, Ship Brokers. Walker mentioned, among other things, that a wealthy client of his, named Smith, was interested in chartering a steamer for a Mediterranean cruise. If Griffin heard of a likely vessel available, Walker would be much obliged for the information. There also might be a good berth in it for Griffin. The cruise would not take place until the following winter, Walker explained, but Mr. Smith—being a relation of W. H. Smith, recently First Lord of the Admiralty—was a finicky client so Walker was already scouting around for both ship and crew.

Walker's search for an appropriate vessel ended in October. The Highland Railway Company had something that seemed to fit the bill perfectly, a 170-foot steamer, the *Ferret*, which they had at one time operated as a commercial pleasure cruiser. To the officials of the Highland Railway Company Walker appeared both prosperous and businesslike. He stated quite forthrightly that his client, Mr. Smith,

had not been in the best of health for some time, but that the extended sea voyage in the sunny Mediterranean was expected to bring
him around again. Since Mr. Smith was a relative of the former First
Lord of the Admiralty, it was understandable, however, that Walker
would personally have to make certain that the ship chartered was
adequate. Walker visited the *Ferret*, found her in shipshape order
and satisfied himself that she was capable of the twelve knots claimed
for her. The Highland Railway Company, in turn, obtained from
Walker Mr. Smith's references, including his bankers. The references
were contacted and gave Mr. Smith every recommendation, and
Mr. Smith's bank account was reported in order and of an ample
enough nature to make doing business with him a pleasure. A
charter rate of £275 a month was agreed upon and Walker handed
over a draft cashable three months later at Mr. Smith's bank.

Walker now got busy making all the arrangements for the cruise.
He went to the leading ship chandlers of Glasgow, provided the necessary references—which again proved gilt-edged—and ordered a
large supply of stores of all kinds. The bill came to over fifteen hundred pounds and Walker, apparently according to prevailing
custom, again paid with a draft on Mr. Smith's bank, callable in
three months. To please the fastidious tastes of the wealthy relative
of the recent First Lord of the Admiralty, Walker next had to make
the rounds of the best firms in town to purchase all sorts of delicacies
and conveniences, including many bottles of fine wines and cham-
pagnes, large quantities of the most expensive cigars, and the best
china and silverware.

Walker engaged a full crew, carefully interviewing each prospect.
Among them was Griffin, the ship's engineer whom Walker had
promised a berth months before, a master named Wright, and a
first-class ship's carpenter who had come particularly well-recom-
mended and had been selected in preference to some half dozen
other applicants. Walker, himself, took on the job of purser and
general factotum.

One blustery day in October, 1880, Mr. and Mrs. Smith, in whose
behalf so much activity had been buzzing for weeks, came aboard.
An hour later the *Ferret* steamed out of Glasgow and headed for
the balmy Mediterranean.

Shortly after the ship passed through the Strait of Gibraltar,
Walker had Wright, the captain, order all but one of the *Ferret's* blue
lifeboats painted white. The *Ferret's* yellow funnel was painted

black, with a red star near the top. Wright explained disgustedly to the perplexed crew that Smith—a nervous type of blue-blood—had taken a sudden dislike to the blue and yellow color scheme.

That night Walker and Smith, aided by Captain Wright, lowered the one remaining blue lifeboat and set it adrift. They also commended to the waves a dozen lifebuoys, several casks and some parts of deck fittings that Wright had previously ordered the carpenter to repair in the expectation that they might be conveniently left about for casting away. When some of this flotsam was found and reported, it might well be considered evidence that the *Ferret* had been shipwrecked, particularly if the ship disappeared completely.

Thereafter, Walker and Smith would be able to move about with relative freedom in distant ports, deal profitably in various cargoes and, at the appropriate time, sell the steamer for a handsome figure.

Before getting to work in earnest to disguise the *Ferret*, Walker, Smith and Wright felt they had to make some sort of definitive explanation to the crew. Wright called the crew together and admitted to them that the story about Smith's aristocratic and whimsical distaste for blue and yellow had been a fabrication. Now, however, he had been authorized to tell them the full truth. In reality Smith was an important American government official who, as a result of recent political upheavals in that barbarous land, was temporarily in hiding because he knew too much about certain shady governmental transactions. Smith, Walker told them, had purchased the *Ferret*, incognito, through Walker. However some of Smith's political enemies might still be on the trail, so the ship would now have to be disguised and its name changed. Each crew member was then called separately into the captain's cabin and assigned an alias, so that, when they put into any port, no familiar name from the roster of the *Ferret* could give them away. In the privacy of the captain's quarters each crew member, left hand on the ship's Bible, right hand upraised, was also required to swear himself to silence and secrecy.

At this point another touch of the traditional freebooter made its appearance. Smith, Walker and Wright brandished revolvers under the nose of each crew member, threatening to blow out his brains if he attempted to interfere with their plans or allowed his tongue to wag too loosely when they put into port. Since Smith's life was at stake, Walker added, there would be no hesitancy in acting on their threat. For proper co-operation, however, Smith would pay not only the standard sum originally agreed on, but a nice bonus.

The entire crew was now set to work repainting the ship. At every visible point the name *Ferret* was removed and the ship's new name, *Benton,* painted in its place. Then, one night, with lights screened, they slipped out past the straits and made for the island of San Antonio at Cape Verde. At this out-of-the-way port the ship's carpenter, so carefully chosen by Walker, supervised a major repair, the shifting of the deckhouse aft from amidships. This considerably altered the over-all aspect of the ship. The registered number of the ship was also changed. All the time they were in port none of the crew was allowed ashore.

It was now late in December, some two months since the *Ferret* had sailed from Glasgow. Before leaving Cape Verde, Walker and Smith purchased a large store of provisions, paying, as was their custom, with a London draft on Smith's bank. A Christmas celebration was held aboard ship, complete with champagne and plum pudding. Then, on December 26, 1880, the *Benton,* née *Ferret,* steamed out of Cape Verde headed for Santos, Brazil. At Santos, too, the crew was kept aboard ship. Smith, however, did go ashore and managed to obtain a commission to carry a cargo of some four thousand bags of coffee to Marseilles.

On January 11, the *Benton* put to sea again. Well out of sight of Santos, Wright changed the ship's course for Capetown. En route, the crew—probably the busiest painters in maritime history—changed the ship's name to *India.* This, of course, called for a change in the name on every lifeboat and on all lifebuoys.

They proved very fortunate in their choice of cargo. For Wright had made a major error and they ran out of coal many knots short of their destination. So instead of drinking up their anticipated profits, they burned them. Before the ship reached Capetown they burned over four hundred bags of coffee, the *India's* funnel, now green with red stripes, spreading an aromatic haze across the South Atlantic.

Meantime, Walker and Smith, who had had the foresight to place a printing plant aboard, along with a large supply of stationery, government stamps and other like necessaries, were preparing appropriate bills and letterheads to enable them to dispose of the rest of the coffee. In Capetown, Smith and Walker auctioned off the remaining 3,600 bags of coffee. After paying the auctioneer's commission they were left with a neat profit of £10,250. Now, at last, buccaneering was beginning to pay off in ready cash rather than just cigars and champagne.

Things, however, were not going as smoothly as planned. The *Ferret* lifeboat and other memorabilia had been found and Lloyd's had actually paid the Highland Railway Company for the ship's loss. But the steamer had been sighted and recognized off Malta, after the wreckage had been found. Moreover, the drafts with which Walker had paid for the vessel's charter and the stores had been sent in for payment at the bank, only to be returned in every case marked "No such account." Smith had, of course, taken all the money out before sailing. Further investigation showed that, except for the bank reference which had been bona fide at the time given, all the other references were fictitious creations of the fertile Walker and Smith. So the alarm went out to the police and to Lloyd's agents everywhere. And in the newspapers of the principal port cities of the world advertisements appeared offering a reward for any information that would lead to the discovery of the stolen ship.

Walker and Smith had a confederate in England who cabled them the bad news, by means of a prearranged code. So in Capetown they tried to sell the *Ferret*, now somewhat re-architectured and rechristened the *India*. But no buyer was forthcoming, so they quickly steamed out of port. They decided to make their next port of cal! Mauritius, some two thousand miles from Capetown in the Indiar Ocean.

In Capetown they had taken on a new seaman. By the sort of coincidence which in another context would be attributed to Beelzebub, this seaman had once shipped on the *Ferret*, before her metamorphosis. As he later testified, he sensed something familiar about the vessel from the start. But it was the loose discipline, the extraordinary liberality aboard the ship that really made him suspicious. Finally, when he discovered that he was allowed to help himself to a spot of grog whenever he was so minded, he decided there was something definitely phony going on. Snooping around, he soon found traces of the name *Ferret* in some of the remoter portions of the vessel, where lazy crewmen had done an imperfect painting job.

Walker and Smith, meantime, prepared themselves to change the ship's name as needed. They made out several sets of ship's papers and had several sets of aliases ready to provide for the entire crew. At Mauritius the crew was again kept aboard ship. And once again the entire ship was repainted. No cargo being obtainable, the *India* soon sailed away in search of fair game at other ports. To those at Mauritius who asked where they were headed, Walker, Smith and Wright declared they were "clearing out for Guam," which is the nautical equivalent for "none of your business."

The next leg of the *Ferret-Benton-India's* odyssey took her to Port Albany, Australia, and then to Melbourne, where they arrived on April 20, some six months after they had first steamed out from Glasgow to the accompaniment of the cheerful *bon voyage* waving of a Highland Railway official. Walker and Smith went ashore to try to sell the ship, leaving Captain Wright and the crew aboard ready to steam away at a moment's notice.

Lloyd's inquiries about the *Ferret* had, of course, reached Melbourne. Now Walker and Smith's overcaution proved their undoing. It struck one police official as very odd that none of the *India's* crew came ashore. The fact that the *India* always had steam up seemed even more suspicious. The official decided to look up the *India* in Lloyd's register. No *India* was listed.

The ship was immediately taken in custody by the harbor police. Smith, Walker and Wright were nowhere on board; they had evidently gotten wind of trouble and lit out. Within a few weeks, however, all three land-bound buccaneers were apprehended, Wright in a Melbourne pub, Walker and Smith, separately, in smaller towns to which they had fled.

Aboard the stolen vessel officials found copies of messages originally sent and received in code, including these:

Get out of port, somehow, or fire and sink her.

Game is up. Destroy or hide everything, and make yourself scarce.

At the trial some of the crew testified that Walker had confided to them his intention of going pirate in earnest, of seizing, by means of a ruse, a ship carrying gold bullion from Australian mines and in one stroke making all of them wealthy for life. Walker, acting as his own attorney, denied this and further defended himself by pointing out that, according to his charter agreement with the Highland Railway Company, he had an unexpired option to buy the *Ferret*, an option he had been planning to exercise. When Walker was cross-examined about the real reason he had chartered the ship, he immediately came up with an imaginative story about a gun-running contract he had negotiated with the Peruvian government, then at war with Chile. From the proceeds of this contract, Walker said, he would be able to pay all his creditors, if the Melbourne court would only let him go about his lawful business. But Walker's inventiveness cut very little ice with the court. The crew, including the first recruit, Griffin, was freed. Walker and Smith were sentenced to seven years imprisonment, Wright to three and a half years. The sentences were for the cargo and provision frauds and for entering a ship under a false, unregistered name. As for the ship-stealing charge that had been so widely advertised, because of the purchase option Walker had shrewdly included in the contract, the court was unable to convict.

There is one glaring omission in all the records about this last piece of buccaneering. The records mention a Mrs. Smith who boarded the *Ferret* in Glasgow, along with her husband. Thereafter, the sea seems to have swallowed her whole, leaving the romance department entirely to the tender mercies of the only true keepers of the buccaneering faith our civilization can boast, Mr. Laughton and the latter-day Walkers and Smiths whose typewriters generally do their clicking within hailing distance of Hollywood and Vine. At any rate, from October to April, 1880, a moribund tradition had flickered to dazzling life, and, compared to the good old days of Kidd, Blackbeard and the beckoning scaffold, the revivers of that tradition had come off practically scot-free. After all, how many people, even nowadays, get more than a total of a six months' vacation in three years—and all of it on the high seas? Evidently, Walker, Smith and Wright decided not to push their luck too far—or else they were letter-perfect in their next attempt—for, after this single meteoric odyssey, their names never again appear in the annals of crime.

THE GREAT CORPORATION SWINDLE

by Craig Thompson

When F. Donald Coster's $8,000,000 swindle was finally exposed, it caused a famous old American corporation to be suspended from New York Stock Exchange listing. Even more astonishing to New York business executives was the revelation that Coster's real name was Philip Musica, and that, as Musica, he had had a fairly prominent first career right in New York City. Moreover, Coster's gigantic swindle had been carried out right under the noses of his innocent associates and despite the scrupulous supervision of a noted and reputable firm of accountants. Thus, in more ways than one, Musica-Coster qualifies as a master at deception.

He was a testy little man who wore shoes with heels that added an inch to his stature and spats that matched his pants. He had a broad, flat owl's face with black eyes that roved restlessly behind his glasses, and a brain so cunning that it enabled him to be, at the same time, the president of an $86,000,000 corporation and the master swindler of the century.

In his sixty-one years he used many identities, but the one he made most infamous was the one he furnished the unsuspecting editors of *Who's Who in America*, for their 1938-39 edition. It ran: "COSTER, Frank Donald, corpn. official; b. Washington, D. C. May 12, 1884; s. Frank Donald and Marie (Girard) C.; Ph.D. U. of Heidelberg, 1909, M.D. 1911; m. Carol Jenkins Schiefflin, Jamaica, L. I., May 1, 1921; practicing physician, N. Y. C., 1912-14; pres. Girard & Co. Inc. (successor Girard Chemical Co.) 1914-26; pres. McKesson & Robbins, Ltd.; dir. Bridgeport City Trust Co., Fairfield (Conn.) Trust Co.; Methodist. Clubs: N. Y. Yacht, Bankers, Lotos, Advertising (N. Y.), University, Black Rock Yacht (Bridgeport), Brooklawn Country."

Seldom have so many lies been told in so short a space. The

man's name was Philip Musica, not Coster; he was born in Naples, Italy, not Washington; in 1877, not 1884. His wife's name had been Carol Jenkins Hubbard, not Schiefflin, and they were married in 1926, not 1921. Elmira Reformatory and Tombs Prison, not Heidelberg, had been his universities, and he had never been closer to the practice of medicine than as a conveyor of alcohol for the bootleg trade. He was neither a Methodist nor a member of most of the clubs he listed.

But he most assuredly was a director of the two banks he named and the president of McKesson & Robbins, an old-line drug house which, in 1937, transacted nearly $150,000,000 of business. In that sketch the gap between the true and the false was the measure of the shrewdest, most complex swindle in American history.

Unique among thieves, Coster was a creative man with an eye for solid, durable construction. When he acquired control of McKesson & Robbins, it was a small manufacturing firm. He expanded it into a giant; and though he plundered it rapaciously, weakened it dangerously and embroiled it in one of the most resounding scandals in commercial history, he could not destroy it. When Coster was exposed, the company he built was suddenly deprived of book assets of $21,000,000, or nearly one quarter of its supposed wealth. But in the hands of the men Coster brought into it, McKesson & Robbins is today sounder, richer, more flourishing and respected than it ever was.

Philip Musica had been six years old when Papa Antonio and Mamma Maria bundled their pitifully scant duffel, spent most of their savings for steerage tickets and moved from the slums of Naples to the equally redolent slums of New York's lower East Side. Antonio's move was inspired by dreams of wealth. Though these did not soon materialize, he did prosper in a small way, acquiring a little shop of his own and putting a few dollars by for his old age. What pleased him even more was that Maria, childless for ten years following Philip's birth, began having children again. A daughter, Louise, was born; then Grace, Arthur, George and finally Robert, twenty-three years younger than Philip.

As a boy, Philip was fascinated by a small print shop run by his father's closest friend. He hung out there by the hour, watching the printer convert type, ink and paper into impressive, important-looking business forms. Ultimately Philip founded a long career on forged, or phony, letterheads and other printed papers, all of which

had to originate in some little shop such as this. Even the old printer's identity eventually became a part of Philip's life. He was Fer-
nando Costa, the only traceable source for the name, F. Donald
Coster.

At about the time he attained his majority, Philip persuaded his
father to put up his meager savings for a joint venture into the import
business. They called it A. Musica & Son, and specialized in Italian
foodstuffs such as cheese, pasta and sausages.

When the Musicas received a shipment of goods, Philip would have
false invoices and bills of lading made out to show only a fraction
of the true weight. Then a customs inspector would be bribed to
substitute the originals of these for the true records supplied to the
customs service by the shipper. When this had been done, the Musicas could take copies to the warehouse or the pier, and claim their
merchandise by paying duty on only a part of its actual value. It
amounted to duty-free entry of about half their imports and permitted them to undersell competitors without any sacrifice of profits.

Though Antonio's thick, upswept mane and luxuriant beard turned
white in the process, the Musicas came up fast. In a few years their
business climbed from nothing to a gross yearly turnover of $500,000.
From the slums they moved into a spacious house in Brooklyn, with
landscaped grounds, horses, stables and a carriage house. Most resplendent of all was Philip, who now became one of the swellest of
swells. He took up opera in an assiduous way, becoming a sometime
crony of the great Enrico Caruso, and was frequently seen wearing a
silk hat, white tie and scarlet-lined opera cape in such gilded preening
places as the Peacock Alley of the old Waldorf.

The scheme that supported this gaudy show of new riches was
a good one in its reprehensible way—it went on for nine years.
But in 1909 it was uncovered, and Antonio and Philip were indicted.

Now thirty-two, Musica was a dapper little man with a certain
social polish. This came from expensive clothes, a reserved manner,
a quiet voice and a punctilio that was deferential without being
servile. When he dramatically entered a plea of guilty, taking the
blame for everything and exonerating Antonio of all guilty knowledge—even though the evidence included twenty-six false invoices
with Antonio's signature on each—he got credit for possessing nobility of spirit as well. Antonio was freed; Philip was fined $5,000 and
sentenced to a year in Elmira Reformatory, then used for Federal
prisoners. But such was the impression he made that President Wil-

liam Howard Taft was persuaded to pardon him when only five months and fifteen days of the term had run. Musica returned to the import business and a bigger fraud.

His next scheme was more complex and more quickly detected. He set up a business in human hair—in wide demand because of the high coiffures women wore at the time—and using the commercial paper that accompanied his shipments, he stole $600,000 from twenty-two banks. For this he spent three years in jail. And so, from one piece of criminality to another, he moved into his middle forties. Then national prohibition opened a new field for him.

The first step toward the creation of F. Donald Coster was taken in Brooklyn, in the second year of the prohibition era, with the formation of the Adelphi Pharmaceutical Manufacturing Corporation. Calling himself Frank Costa, Musica set up the Adelphi with $8,000 borrowed from his mother—probably part of the loot from the hair swindle.

As a manufacturer of drugs, Costa obtained a federal permit for five thousand gallons of alcohol a month, which he used to make hair tonics, dandruff removers and furniture polishes. To remove the scents, soap, oils, waxes and coloring matter, all a customer had to do was run an Adelphi product through an ordinary still. Then the alcohol could be cut with water, color and flavoring added, and one gallon of "dandrofuge" made into nearly two of "fine old Scotch whisky, just off the boat."

The trouble was that Costa could not get along with one of his partners, Joseph Brandino. In the quarrels that arose, Brandino alternately threatened to beat him to a pulp or tear him into pieces. Costa became so terrified that he tipped the Treasury Department's Alcohol Tax Unit to the true nature of Adelphi's business, and the permit was revoked.

"It's too bad, Joe," said Costa, "but that's the end of it."

Only it wasn't. Some years later, noting the meteoric rise of F. Donald Coster, Brandino blackmailed him for $3,000 on threat of exposure. Coster paid, and kept on paying until, at the time of his death, the cumulative count of Brandino's hush money came to more than $100,000—an average of about $10,000 a year.

Coster finally emerged in Mount Vernon, New York, in 1923. There he rented a small, two-story brick structure for another dandrofuge factory he called Girard & Co. Purportedly the enterprise belonged to an elderly chemist named P. Horace Girard. To give the federal

investigators a check point on Girard, Maria Musica, a widow by
now, and her younger daughter, Grace, assumed the name and
moved to Westbury, Long Island, where they lived in a house listed
as P. Horace Girard's home. As Coster found his feet and Girard &
Co. prospered, the ghostly Horace was gradually laid away. But
for the rest of her days Maria Musica remained Maria Girard.

In fact, the creation of Girard & Co. signalized the end of a name
for all the survivors of old Antonio. Arthur Musica now became
George Vernard, agent for a fictitious firm called W. W. Smith &
Co. George Musica became George Dietrich, and Coster's right
hand. Robert, now twenty-three, also took the name Dietrich and
worked close to George. After ten years of going their separate ways,
Girard & Co. reunited the multi-aliased Musicas in a common enterprise. All, that is, but Louise, who got married and moved out of the
family orbit.

Because of his alky permit, the Mount Vernon police paid Coster
almost weekly visits. With a joke and a flourish, Dietrich would
produce the order book and the delivery receipts. Behind façades
of respectability, many a business house was carrying on a thriving
back-door traffic with the bootleg world, and these, of course, were
Coster's better customers. But the biggest buyer of all was W. W.
Smith & Co.

Coster's new enterprise would have died in infancy had anyone
investigated Smith & Co. The only evidence of its existence was a
one-room Brooklyn office occupied by George Vernard and a typist.
Much of the alcohol that flowed into the Girard factory flowed out
again to commercial warehouses designated on Smith & Co. orders.
Bootleggers' trucks then picked it up, paying Vernard in cash, while
he, in turn, paid Girard by check. At the same time, Vernard made
out and filed in his office sheaves of phony papers which indicated
that the stuff had been shipped to buyers all over the world. Coster
was betting everything he had at stake that no investigator would
unravel this complex trail to the point where falsity became apparent. He remained, for fifteen years, on the winning side of that bet,
and during that time nearly $8,000,000 passed through George Ver-
nard's bank account.

By December, 1924, Girard & Co. had come along nicely enough
to give Coster big ideas. His first move was to invite the impeccable
Price, Waterhouse & Co., one of the most highly respected accounting
firms in the country, to conduct an audit of his books.

The auditor who was sent to Mount Vernon may never have realized it, but both Coster and Dietrich watched him with hawklike
concentration—not to hide anything, but in the hope of learning
something.

What they learned was that, as a matter of established practice,
an auditor did not check a company's inventory, but accepted
whatever tally of stocks on hand the company officers offered. As
for the audit, it showed Girard & Co. to be a tidy little business with
assets of $279,000, gross sales of $252,000 and net profits of $33,300.
Coster took it to his Mount Vernon bank and asked for a $100,000
loan. Regretfully unable to advance the sum, the bank introduced
him to a Wall Street man named Julian Thompson.

Of all the people touched by Coster's schemes, Thompson comes
closest to being the tragic figure. He was a sensitive romantic, who
wore pince-nez with a crew cut, and divided his talents between
business and the arts. A competent playright, one of his plays, *The
Warrior's Husband,* raised Katharine Hepburn to stardom. As an
investment broker he also raised Coster to the heights and then,
discovering his thefts, tore him down again. Nor did he long survive
Coster's downfall, dying a year or so thereafter of a complex of ailments.

In retrospect, Thompson's shattering sense of guilt can be traced
to his first contact with Coster. The meeting took place in Coster's
office. Upon the walls hung two masterpieces of printing-press forgery
—phony diplomas attesting the fictitious Heidelberg doctorates. Coster talked skillfully of drug manufacture and only fleetingly of hair
tonic. In addition to a copy of the audit, he gave Thompson two lists
—one of customers and the other of references. Brazenly, on each
he included W. W. Smith & Co. Had Thompson done more than
sample these lists or had his sampling included Smith & Co., the
story might have been different. In the end, this was the omission he
could not forget nor forgive himself.

But at the time Thompson became a Coster booster. "You're too
small for Wall Street now," he told Coster, "but maybe I can help."

To that end, he arranged a meeting with officials of the Bridgeport
City Trust Company. With his slightly old-fashioned clothes, his earnest, punctilious manner and his Price, Waterhouse audit, Coster captured the Bridgeport bankers. Not only did they lend him $80,000 of
the bank's money but added $27,500 of their own to buy 275 shares
in his company. Girard & Co. moved to Bridgeport, upped its alco-

hol withdrawals to 15,000 gallons a month, and turned in a banner year in 1925. Sales jumped to $1,100,000, profits to $250,000, and the bank loan was repaid. Word spread that F. Donald Coster was a wizard.

He was, too, in his fashion. During that 1925 year-end audit a Price, Waterhouse accountant noted that Smith & Co. owed Girard & Co. $22,500, and was moved to ask George Dietrich just what this Smith & Co. was. For reply, Dietrich pulled out a report by Dun & Company, one of the predecessor firms of Dun & Bradstreet, that characterized Smith & Co. as a globe-girdling trading concern, itemized properties it owned from Montreal to Bombay as worth about $7,000,000 and gave it top credit rating. A nickel telephone call would have proved the report a forgery. But it was so expertly done, that the auditors, thoroughly familiar with such reports, unhesitatingly accepted it as genuine. Thirteen years passed before anyone thought to spend that apocalyptic nickel.

Coster, meanwhile, had focused on McKesson & Robbins. Established in 1833, this firm had grown old without growing big. But it had one thing Coster needed—a good name. Negotiations were begun, a price agreed upon, a stock issue floated, and eventually Coster handed over a check for $1,100,000 in exchange for a corporate identity which raised him above suspicion. By the end of 1927, with the details of consolidation completed, the annual audit showed him in control of a $4,100,000 manufacturing company, drawing 25,000 gallons of alcohol per month and earning $600,000 a year net profit. What the auditor did not discover was that the big swindle had also begun.

What Coster did has since caused sweeping changes to be made in auditing practices, and added millions of dollars to the costs of operating America's business, but at the time it was not the custom for an auditor to go into the warehouses and stock rooms, and count the bales and bottles on hand. Having ascertained this one fact, Coster made the most of it.

The swindle was based upon a fictitious trade in crude drugs, each transaction of which was carried through a chain of many steps. The responsibility for hoodwinking the auditors fell to George Dietrich, whose office was next to Coster's and whose devotion to his job was such that on one occasion he went into a hospital at the close of one business day, had his tonsils removed and was back at nine o'clock the next morning. During eleven years Dietrich looked at all the incoming mail. He had to, because he could never risk letting someone else see it first.

In a typical transaction Dietrich would make out a McKesson & Robbins order to P. Pierson & Co., Montreal—one of five nonexistent Canadian warehouses he used—to purchase for the McKesson & Robbins account a quantity of, say, oil of lemon. Next he would clip to the carbon of the order an invoice on a printed P. Pierson form showing that the purchase had been made. Then a receiving ticket would be made out, to show that the goods were stored at the Pierson warehouse. After the bill had been duly entered on the inventory book, then, as an account payable, a letter would be written to Manning & Co., Montreal—a fictitious bank—authorizing it to pay Pierson. There then would be added to the file a printed Manning & Co. form certifying that Pierson had been paid. This completed the phony purchase, except that, on the books, McKesson & Robbins now owed the nonexistent Manning & Co. thousands of dollars for nonexistent goods in a nonexistent warehouse.

The next step was to sell the stuff. To start the new phony-paper chain Dietrich would notify W. W. Smith & Co. that McKesson & Robbins had, in Pierson's warehouse, a quantity of oil of lemon. There then would appear on Dietrich's desk an exquisitely printed Smith & Co. form saying that the oil had been sold. In the same way and with the same detail that he had built up a sheaf of papers to record the purchase, Dietrich built up another file to record its disposal, ending with a Manning & Co. statement showing payment by the purchaser. Supposing the fictitious sale price of the nonexistent goods to be $100,000, Dietrich would send a check on a real McKesson & Robbins bank account to Smith & Co. for $750, representing a sales commission of three quarters of one per cent. This George Vernard converted into cash, which came back to Coster.

The printer who made the phony forms was never found. But the blanks were kept in Vernard's office and all typed by one girl, who used seven different typewriters. When asked if she ever felt strange, working on all those different letterheads with a separate machine for each, she replied, "Oh, no. I thought they were holding companies or somp'n."

To complete the setup, Vernard maintained an office at the Montreal address of Manning & Co., where another girl kept one of the loneliest vigils on record. Perhaps twice a year she received two or three letters from Price, Waterhouse asking for a verification of the McKesson & Robbins balance on hand and a list of the company's stocks in the five warehouses. Such letters were mailed to Vernard, who sent back a packet of fat envelopes, all addressed to Price, Waterhouse in New York. These she stamped and dropped in the mail—and thus the swindle went on through the years. It was so good that the auditors, all honorable men, called Dietrich's crude-drugs division "the best-run department in the business."

Having developed his scheme, Coster saw that the only way it could ever be made to pay big money was to make McKesson & Robbins a big company. It would be manifestly absurd, and a sure source of suspicion, for a little company to carry on its books big sums tied up in crude drugs stored in foreign warehouses. Coster's lifetime drive had been toward bigness and he had now created a situation in which being big was his only way out.

In 1928 most of the drugs used in the United States were sold through locally owned and operated wholesale houses. It was Coster's idea, which he broached to Julian Thompson, to weld these into a nationwide chain under the McKesson & Robbins banner. "Now," said Thompson enthusiastically, "you are big enough for Wall Street."

With promises of financial aid from two investment houses, Coster undertook to gather in the wholesalers. Wheedling, bragging, cajoling, pleading, even at times showing them McKesson & Robbins' fictitious inventory of nonexistent crude drugs to prove how solid a firm it was, he put the merger through. In return for some cash—provided by the public through purchases of McKesson & Robbins preferred stock—and large chunks of common stock, the wholesalers transferred ownership to McKesson & Robbins.

Coster was so successful that by the middle of 1929 he stood astride an $80,000,000 Goliath, composed of forty-nine of the most-respected jobbing houses in the country, a $5,000,000 manufacturing division turning out 238 different products and a crude-drug division which dealt strictly in fraud. To these, after repeal, was added a liquor division, which, almost overnight, became the largest liquor-distributing agency in the country.

As president of the new giant—third largest drug house in the world—Coster fixed his salary at a modest $40,000 a year. "I'm not interested in making money," he explained to the eighty new vice-presidents who surrounded him, "I live for this company."

His mode of life bore witness to the lie. Back in 1926 he had gone one afternoon to a little church in Jamaica, Long Island, and there married the divorced sister of his onetime partner, Leonard Jenkins. Though many of his new associates stood quite high in the social world, the Costers made no efforts to use them for social climbing. They did not entertain much, and seldom went to night clubs or any other public gathering places. Installed in an eighteen-room, stucco-and-tile house in Fairfield, Connecticut, which Coster bought for her, Mrs. Coster raised chow dogs.

Coster's only extravagance was a 134-foot, second-hand yacht, which, to honor his wife, he called the *Carolita*. The vessel was old, and had previously been used by Marconi, the wireless man, and John Hays Hammond, Jr., the inventor, as a floating laboratory.

It could not be said that many of Coster's directors genuinely liked him, but, considering the way he lived and the long hours he spent at his desk, they did believe he told the truth when he said he lived for the company alone. As an executive he was irascible, sometimes arrogant, and a tireless memo writer. In the factory, his chemists had to throw out most of his ideas for new products, for, despite the Heidelberg diploma on his office wall, Coster knew next to nothing about medicine. In the merchandising field, his ideas were similarly bad, and almost as frequently thrown out. Some that were tried proved to be costly errors.

Nonetheless, Coster's directors came to believe that he was indispensable. Largely, this was based on his crude-drug operations. Year after year, no matter how badly things went in other departments, the crude-drug division always turned a profit. True, the profits kept on being plowed back into more crude drugs, but all those assets on the balance sheet looked mighty comforting. "Coster," they told one another, "is the greatest authority on crude drugs alive." Thus, it was Coster's thievery that kept his job secure.

This was the façade, the external picture. Behind it Coster lived in a nightmare world of worry, vigilance and frenzied manipulation. His greatest crisis, next to his last one, came only a few months after he finished putting the merger together. Buying on margin, Coster had plunged far beyond his depth in the greatest bull market in history. When it finally broke, in October, 1929, he was faced with total ruin just as his greatest adventure was getting under way. To save himself, he cranked his swindling machinery into high gear and in one three-day period he stole $634,000.

The irony of it was that his thefts saved his company. For, to steal so large a sum so fast, Coster had to increase by many millions the company's inventory of nonexistent crude drugs. As these appeared on the balance sheets as company assets, McKesson & Robbins looked to be in sound condition. While self-appointed committees of stock or bond holders, guided by eagle-eyed operators out to make a killing, threw hundreds of companies into bankruptcy or receivership, no one lifted an eyebrow at McKesson & Robbins.

The business recession of 1937, and not the great depression, doomed Coster. Fearful that the United States economy had hit another bottomless skid, McKesson & Robbins' directors ordered a general conversion of stocks on hand into cash. Coster was told to turn at least $2,000,000 of his crude-drug stockpile into dollars. But Coster, who had no drugs to sell, could do so only by pouring $2,000,000 cash into the company treasury and dropping an equal amount of nonexistent items from its inventories. This he could not or would not do.

Julian Thompson became Coster's nemesis. Back in 1929, Thompson had left Wall Street to become McKesson & Robbins' comptroller and treasurer. It was his duty to see that the orders of the board were carried out. When months had passed and there had been no sign of reduction of the crude-drugs stockpile, Thompson demanded to know why.

"I told those fellows to cut down," Coster replied. "I'll just have to give them hell."

Still more months passed while Coster figured a way out. He cut his thefts to a whisper and proposed borrowing $3,000,000, purportedly for various company improvements, but, more likely to get funds by which he could liquidate part of his phony stockpile. But before the company could borrow, Thompson had to swear that every item on the balance sheet was, to his knowledge and belief, a true statement.

As a result of a chance discovery, he had begun to wonder if that was so. The discovery was simply that, although the company had $21,000,000 worth of drugs in five Canadian warehouses, there was not a penny's worth of insurance on any of it. Bracing Coster with this, he was airily dismissed.

"Oh," said Coster, "W. W. Smith takes care of that."

For the first time, Thompson cast his mind back over all he knew about W. W. Smith and came up shaken. He had seen the Dun report, but he decided to spend that nickel. Learning that it was a forgery, Thompson went to Montreal, then to call on George Vernard, and finally back to Coster.

With the truth at last on the table between them, Coster leaned back and said, "What is it that you want, Mr. Thompson?" It was then, after fifteen years of association, that Thompson at last saw Coster for what he was.

But it was Coster who had the steel in his make-up. "You," he told Thompson accusingly, "are deliberately trying to wreck this company. If you do not sign that certificate [for the $3,000,000 loan] I shall throw the company into receivership."

McKesson & Robbins was Thompson's creation too. But he did not sign. . . .

The following morning Thompson went before a committee of the New York Stock Exchange and told what he knew. McKesson & Robbins was suspended from the big board. By late afternoon half a dozen investigations had been opened. In ten days Philip Musica had been completely unmasked.

In his Fairfield home, on the morning of December 16, 1938, Musica stood before a mirror with a pistol in his right hand. The calves of his legs touched a bathtub behind him, the rim of which was just below his knees. The sound of a shot slammed through the house, and the force of the bullet in his head slammed Musica back and down into the tub, where his blood ran vividly onto the white porcelain and down the drain. Even in suicide, he wanted to be a tidy man.

For a time, the survival of McKesson & Robbins as a going business was a touch-and-go matter. But Musica had limited his thievery strictly to the crude-drug manipulation, and the core of the company was sound. More than that, the company had become so important a part of the drug industry's distributive system that other manufacturing firms supported every effort to keep it alive. With the company placed in capable, energetic hands, it not only survived but grew steadily stronger until, today, it boasts a whopping $40,000,000 undistributed surplus.

The amount that Musica stole from McKesson & Robbins was eventually fixed at $2,900,000—the other $5,000,000 that went through Vernard's bank account probably represented bootlegging operations —and only $51,000—the value of the yacht and a piece of real estate —was ever recovered. The search for the missing money went on for years, and the searchers finally were convinced that much, if not most, of what Musica stole he paid over as blackmail to people who knew him when.

Philip Musica's widow refused to acknowledge the past and the truth that made him kill himself. She had his body laid away in an ornate Long Island mausoleum and caused the marble slab that covered it to be carved with this enduring alias: "F. Donald Coster, 1884-1938."

HOW MADAME HUMBERT TOOK FRANCE

by Alexander Klein

Had a straw-vote been taken in France during June, 1902, to determine the most popular woman in the country, there is little doubt
that a short, stout, yellow-skinned and quite homely fugitive from
justice named Thérèse Daurignac Humbert would have walked off with
the palm. In fact, the chances are good that she would have come
out near the top in a popularity contest in any literate country in
the world. For the world had just learned that Madame Humbert
had, for some twenty long years, been leading the celebrated and
wealthy circles of France by the nose, and, thereby, lived the life of
Riley, Mrs. Astor and Croesus rolled into one.

Making appearance do the work of reality is, of course, no uncommon, nor necessarily dishonorable, role for a woman. But the
grand manner in which Madame Humbert carried it off has rarely,
if ever, been rivaled. Composers have sometimes undertaken to re-
strict themselves to a single theme and its variations, in order to
produce a virtuoso piece. Madame Humbert created a single incident, and then wrote, produced and directed around it a real-life
drama that unfolded with innumerable variations for twenty years.
She, herself, also played the stellar role throughout; but, from time
to time, she introduced into the drama—in the flesh—leading social-
ites, jewelers, financiers and Cabinet Ministers. These were augmented by certain key off-stage characters who, through the agency
of Madame Humbert, were the prime movers of the entire two-
decade charade.

Madame Humbert began life as Thérèse Daurignac, the elder daughter of a poor peasant family. Later her mother opened a linen shop in
Toulouse. In the early 1880s, Thérèse, already in her middle twenties,
orphaned and unmarried, with no prospects in hand, announced
one day to her neighbors that she had just had a remarkable windfall. She had, in fact, inherited $20,000,000, equivalent to over 100,-

000,000 francs. To all who wished to see it, she freely showed the properly attested copy of the will signed by a Robert Henry Crawford. Crawford, she explained, had been an American millionaire. Some years ago, while away on a trip, she had sat in the same railway compartment with Crawford. He had fallen ill, some sort of food-poisoning, which, but for her prompt application of certain peasant remedies, might have been fatal. Afterwards, noting his dependence on her, she had spent several days nursing him back to health. She had thought nothing more of it since. But, now, bread cast upon the waters had come back gilded. There were some legal complications, to be sure, but in a short while the money would be hers.

Among those who rejoiced in her good fortune was a man named Frédéric Humbert, whose father had once been Minister of Justice and, afterwards, a vice-president of the Senate. Thérèse had met Humbert casually a number of times. Even if she had been the sort of lower-class beauty that can excite passion in the upper-class male beholder —a role for which she decidedly did not qualify—the chances are Humbert would not have been interested in anything more than a temporary affair; certainly his family would never have approved the match. Now, however, Thérèse was a celebrity, a wealthy heiress. Frédéric Humbert took new notice of her, became, apparently, genuinely interested, pressed his suit and was accepted.

Thus, in the space of a few short weeks, provincial, lisping, stout Thérèse Daurignac made an enormous social leap. In addition to the millions due her under the conditions of Crawford's will, she was privy to the more modest finances of her husband. While the Crawford will was still being probated in America, the newly-weds—with the husband's money—purchased a mansion on the fashionable Avenue de la Grand Armée, and a country estate.

Nice work and fast, but, as far as Madame Humbert was concerned, only the prelude to the real drama. So far all had been smooth sailing, but a drama must have conflict. Madame Humbert now introduced the conflict—the essential master-stroke of the whole plot—in the form of a second will made out by this same American millionaire, Robert Henry Crawford. In this will—brought to her attention, Madame Humbert said, by the interested American parties —the twenty million dollars were left for division into three parts, "One to go to Marie Daurignac (Madame Humbert's under-age sister); one to my nephew, Henry Crawford; one to my nephew, Robert Crawford; with the provision that these persons invest in France a capital sufficient to secure to Thérèse Daurignac an annuity of 30,000 francs per month."

This second will also expressed the millionaire's dying wish that one of his nephews should marry a Daurignac, thus uniting the two families. This union was one of the necessary conditions to be fulfilled before the division of the estate could be legally permitted. Meantime, according to a special authorizing document, which Madame Humbert had also received, "all title-deeds and securities constituting the assets of Mr. Crawford's estate are sequestered and placed in charge of Monsieur and Madame Humbert, until at Mademoiselle Daurignac's attaining her majority all the heirs mentioned shall come to an amicable agreement for an equitable transaction, or until, in default of such a transaction, the Courts shall have pronounced finally as to the rights of each."

All the heirs were thus, legally, prevented from immediately disposing of any of the Crawford securities. Accordingly Madame Humbert had a special safe built in her bedroom and, in the presence of a notary, deposited in the vault the 100,000,000 francs in approved securities that had been transmitted to her guardianship. The notary certified to the entire transaction. He watched her open the sealed outer packages in which the elaborately sealed envelopes of securities had been sent. He supervised the placing of the entire batch in the safe. He then signed an official document, stating categorically that not a single share of stock had been palmed by Madame Humbert, but that the entire 100,000,000 francs' worth had gone into the safe. Madame Humbert immediately sealed the safe in the notary's presence, and this, too, was certified. Henceforth, under a legal agreement with the two Crawford nephews she was not permitted to open the safe under penalty of forfeiting all claim upon the estate.

Madame Humbert had now obtained legal certification that she had a large treasure in her charge. She had also effectively barred any further immediate examination of that treasure. Meantime, the out-of-court legal battle over the conflicting wills, and the execution of the financial and romantic conditions of the second will—should it be the one validated—flared up between Madame Humbert and the Crawford nephews. Henry and Robert Crawford went further: they actually disputed Madame Humbert's right to hold the securities in escrow, going so far as to impugn her honor. Madame Humbert fought back. She hired the best lawyers in France and paid them well. The two Crawford nephews apparently knew how to choose good lawyers, too. The ebb and flow of the Humbert-Crawford out-of-court, trans-Atlantic legal wranglings—carried on via a staccato stream of letters and documents—kept cropping up in the French newspapers for years.

All this firmly established in everyone's mind—if anyone had any doubts to begin with—the bona fide nature of Madame Humbert's inheritance. No matter how the legal battles would eventually be decided, Madame Humbert and her sister were certain to come into a lot of money, sooner or later. But Madame Humbert was impatient with the delay. Within a few months after the Crawford nephews' legal entrance on the scene, she began to borrow money. Just as her inheritance had been enormous, so, proportionately, were her requests for loans. And her audacity was rewarded. Had she inherited, say, $5,000 in the same manner and attempted to borrow $1,000 on the strength of it, chances are she would have been refused or subjected to rigorous investigation. But with $20,000,000 in her safe, and her loan requests starting with one million francs, all went swimmingly.

Bankers and jewelers accepted without qualms her notes marked, "Payable after the conclusion of my actions-in-law." After all, each note was also countersigned by Marie Daurignac, the alternative heir and prospective bridegroom of a Crawford nephew; it was a three-way foolproof situation, and the rates of interest to which Madame Humbert agreed were quite generous. One Lille banker, alone, advanced her 7,000,000 francs (around $1,500,000). Over the years she obtained loans from a dozen other banks, for sums ranging from one to six million francs. All told, in twenty years, she borrowed and spent some $12,000,000.

This sort of financing enabled Madame Humbert and her husband to live in the grand manner. They maintained three magnificent country estates and a large yacht with full crew. When the opera box formerly held by Baron Haussmann became available, the Greek Ambassador was among those who put in his bid; but Madame Humbert was given the nod. The Paris salon of this stout, poorly-educated, reedy-voiced, but iron-willed provincial woman became a gathering place for notables of the day: writers, actors, painters, judges, distinguished members of the French Academy. Madame Humbert also invested widely in real estate, some twenty-five houses in all, and in fine paintings. Frédéric Humbert, a mild, subdued man, dabbled as a painter and generally kept in the background; he did, however, manage to get himself elected to the Chamber of Deputies.

In one sense, Madame Humbert's continued success in obtaining huge loans year after year had some of the quality of the legendary rat-cat farm, a kind of perpetual-motion, money-producing principle. The basic principle of the rat-cat farm is that the cats eat the rats and the carcasses of the skinned cats are in turn fed to the rats; thus the proceeds from the sale of the cat pelts and other by-products is all neat profit. And this goes on indefinitely. So with Madame Humbert. With the huge sums she had borrowed initially she lived a glamorous social life on a royal, palatial scale. She became a personage, her wealth no longer a question-mark, but the most advertised reality in France. To lend her money at high rates of interest became a pleasure to which more and more French bankers succumbed.

The real estate investments, made with the borrowed funds, also proved helpful, as security for new loans. On one occasion, in applying for a loan, Madame Humbert had a notary prepare a list of her physical assets—apart from the 100,000,000 francs in the safe. The list took up fourteen pages and was proudly qualified with the phrase, "All clear of mortgages."

Nevertheless, between 1882 and 1902 Madame Humbert's inventiveness and ingenuity were constantly put to the test. Under her tutelage, her master creations, Robert and Henry Crawford, became a most litigious pair, and the Crawford wills probably the most disputed documents in the history of legal inheritance. Again and again the Crawfords would be on the verge of accepting some compromise, only to boggle at the last moment and renew the suit. Frequently verdicts were handed down in favor of Madame Humbert. But the Crawfords repeatedly found legal bases for appeals.

At the same time the Crawfords—as Madame Humbert presented them in assorted letters and documents—were basically generous, and quite ardent about Marie Daurignac. In fact, romantic rivalry between Robert and Henry for Marie's hand was one of the perennial obstacles to a settlement. Fortunately, Marie Daurignac remained docile and available throughout, never once, to any of the creditors' knowledge, becoming enamored of some French swain.

Frequently, when a creditor pressed for payment, Madame Humbert would have the good fortune to receive a letter from one of the Crawfords directly, or via the attorneys, indicating that the marriage of Marie to Robert or Henry—as the swing of the pendulum would have it at the particular moment—was imminent. Never did so many wait so breathlessly and so long for the consummation of a marriage-of-convenience—for, of course, the Crawfords in America and Marie in France had never met. However, even mad Americans, independently wealthy though they might be, the French bankers felt, would sooner or later want to dip their hands into Madame Humbert's safe and extract their share of the precious securities.

In ensuing years the Crawfords did pay flying visits to France, meeting Marie and finding her very charming, dining with the Humberts, preparing to testify in person in the French courts so as to speed the conclusion of the suit. But the globe-trotting Crawfords would run off each time on some important errand or sudden whim before anyone else ever got a chance to meet them.

Occasionally, too, Robert and Henry Crawford, by way of apology for all the trouble they were causing Madame Humbert, would take up some of her I.O.U.s at par from uneasy creditors. When Madame Humbert had paid off such loans, her credit usually became so good again that she was able to obtain loans elsewhere far exceeding what she had returned. Such Crawford generosity seemed to be dependent on Madame Humbert's charm, for it frequently occurred while the nephews were visiting her, or shortly thereafter. Thus, while people never got to see the two American dandies, they did see their money, as good an earnest of their real existence as anyone could ask for.

All these years Madame Humbert—despite her unfashionably stout figure, the disadvantage of a scanty education, an ineradicable provincial accent and a thin, lisping voice—in addition to enjoying all that money could buy, was also enjoying something money alone could never have purchased her: her role as one of the great celebrities of her generation, a celebrity to which women of equal and even greater wealth could not attain. All of France was Madame Humbert's stage. Quite apart from the secret role she played as writer, producer and director of the drama, as creator of most of its characters, she also played a double role right on stage. Her first public role was the one also played by her sisters in the social whirl, a *grande dame* in high society. Her second special public role was that of litigant in the trial of the century.

And the character of this second special role afforded her opportunities for a wide range of dramatic effusions: frustration or hatred as a result of the incredible obstinacy of the Crawfords; determination to make a brilliant thrust and bring things to a speedy, happy conclusion; joy at the impending marriage of her long-patient sister, Marie; sorrow at the troubles she was causing—temporary though it was—to some anxious banker; conspiratorial confidence as, in later years, she consented, finally, to show some particularly pressing creditor the actual securities in the safe.

In showing the securities, Madame Humbert would betray tremendous agitation and repeatedly swear the banker to silence.

"If the Crawfords hear that I've broken my agreement and opened the safe," she would say, "all will be lost."

After drawing the curtains and locking the bedroom door, she would use heated knives and needles to remove the seals from the safe. Then she would take out a sealed packet or two, open them with the hot needles and reveal the French Five Per Cents inside, as well as certificates by notaries vouching for the conversion, say, of 85,000,000 francs into five per cent securities.

"What more do you want?" she would ask. Then she would carefully reseal the packets, and close and reseal the safe, all the while anxiously entreating the creditor not to tell a living soul that she had broken her agreement with the Crawfords.

Bankers, being human, did talk, sometimes to other creditors, sometimes only to their wives, who, in turn, told others. And, in cases where a banker did heed her warning to keep silent his new confidence in regard to the huge sums due him from Madame Humbert, or the new loans be made, caused a chain-reaction among other wavering creditors.

At times Madame Humbert had to resort to more conventional techniques. In one instance when a banker became extremely aggressive and insistent in the presence of several other creditors, and there was real danger that he might start an avalanche of foreclosures, Madame Humbert simply became very ill. Whether French gallantry or fear of causing the death of their last best hope for a return of the millions due them, led the creditors to withdraw is beside the point. In ensuing days Madame Humbert sought out each of the creditors individually and succeeded in placating them.

Toward the middle of the second decade's run of her historic drama, Madame Humbert occasionally lapsed into tearful admissions to creditors from whom she was seeking further loans. She had to have more money to pay the lawyers, she explained; if she were forced to retreat now, the Crawfords, with their ingenious American lawyers, might succeed in disinheriting both herself and her sister. It was sink or swim for all them now. Justice, however, was definitely on her side; if she persisted she would certainly triumph. Most bankers, approached with this gambit, gave until it hurt.

If Madame Humbert had persisted in, or been able to maintain the legal combativeness of the Crawfords all might have gone well for many more years, possibly for the rest of her life. However, either because of faulty strategy, or, perhaps, because she got bored with the basic line the drama had been following and daringly attempted a further variation, Madame Humbert eventually ran herself into what proved to be a blind alley. For more than fifteen years she had been retaining a battery of lawyers to carry on a legal campaign against the two American phantoms, Henry and Robert Crawford, antagonists whom the lawyers had never met in the flesh. Her lawyers now began to press Madame Humbert's American creations to the wall. For Madame Humbert's inventive ingenuity did have to operate within the laws pertaining to inheritance, and by now she had exhausted practically every aspect of those laws applicable to her drama. To avoid winning the suit and having to open the safe, Madame Humbert had to begin applying delaying tactics in her own right. She created a new, apparently solid stumbling-block by insisting on highly unreasonable conditions to which the Crawfords vigorously objected. For example, to satisfy her standards of investment safety for the guaranteed annuity, specified in the second will, would have been virtually impossible.

But these and similar conditions which she was forced to insist on, to counteract her lawyers' pertinacity, were so patently outrageous or, in some instances, so trivial that many began to see them for what they were, delaying tactics. The noted jurist, Waldeck-Rousseau, then Premier of France, took time out from the embroilments of the Dreyfus case to point out Madame Humbert's strange disinclination to win her suit, to take possession of the riches she had so long been denied. Premier Waldeck-Rousseau also stressed, publicly, the astonishing fact that no one in France other than the Humberts had ever seen the Crawfords, either the late millionaire or his nephews. Why, none of the creditors, or Madame Humbert's own attorneys, failed all these years—and even now with the Premier's warnings and mockeries ringing in their ears—to arrange a check on the existence of the Crawfords in America is one of the many mysteries about this case that will probably remain unanswered forever.

A partial answer lies in the exalted role to which Madame Humbert had succeeded in elevating herself, and in the presumed unimpeachability of her distinguished father-in-law, the former Minister of Justice. And Madame Humbert, of course, redoubled her attack. She produced the provincial magistrate who, many years ago, had supervised the placing of the securities in the safe. The magistrate swore he had seen and counted the securities and that they added up to well over 100,000,000 francs.

For five years after Premier Waldeck-Rousseau had practically called her a swindler and warned the country against her, Madame Humbert continued her gay, grand, demonic, but increasingly more difficult role. She took shrewd advantage of the reputation of her distinguished chief counsel, Maître Du Buit, who seemed to have complete confidence in her.

Maître Du Buit, however, also proved the boomerang Madame Humbert could not sidestep. Some of Madame Humbert's creditors had come upon hard times. Due to the large sums outstanding with her they were forced to be unduly harsh with other debtors, two of whom committed suicide. Several of the men who had lent her huge sums now went bankrupt themselves. The Humbert case was well on its way to becoming a national scandal. There were whispers, too, that high government officials were involved. Finally, Maître Du Buit forced the issue, declaring that to terminate the unwarranted rumors he, himself, would open the safe in the presence of his client's chief creditors. When Madame Humbert reminded him that, according to her agreement with the Crawfords she would forfeit all claims to the estate if she had the safe opened, Maître Du Buit reassured her. He cited a point in French law whereby the public, official circumstances under which the safe would be opened, and the necessity to do so in order to clear Madame Humbert's honor would combine to frustrate any attempt by the Crawfords to claim the estate as forfeit.

Two days before the appointed date, a fire broke out in Madame Humbert's house. The safe was fireproof so all could proceed as planned. But Madame Humbert said the fire had so unnerved her she needed rest; her lawyer would take care of the matter while she went to the country.

On the fateful day a half dozen of the leading bankers in France, Monsieur Cochefort, head of the Paris Detective Bureau, and several of his colleagues, and Maître Du Buit gathered in Madame Humbert's bedroom. The seals were removed, the doors swung open and out came the famous packets of securities. The securities, quite genuine, came to a grand total of five thousand francs. In addition Maître Du Buit and the bankers found an empty jewel case, a copper coin, a brass button, several worthless deeds and a number of yellowed newspapers of early 1880s vintage.

The swindle of the century had run its full course. But the architect of the drama, Madame Humbert, along with her collaborators, Frédéric Humbert and her two brothers Emile and Romain Daurignac, had fled the climax.

While the police of several countries searched for the fugitives, all France—and soon all Europe and America—told and retold the sensational details about the case that the press provided. At long last the French authorities cabled to America and instituted a search for the famous Crawfords. There were no Crawfords of any sort to be found at 1202 Broadway, New York City, the address Maître Du Buit supplied. And of the particular Crawfords being sought there was not the slightest trace anywhere.

The four fugitives were apprehended in Spain. The actual bare facts of the swindle added up to details about letters sent via agents, American lawyers' stationery printed and used liberally, and the like. The magistrate who had sworn he had seen and counted the securities had, apparently, testified to the truth as he saw it. He had seen some securities, he had counted the rest of the packets of equal size; Madame Humbert's social status had sufficed to make this appearance assume solid reality in his mind. It is far from certain that all who took part in the twenty-year swindle were brought to trial. Many felt that Humbert père, the former Minister of Justice, must have lent a hand at some phase of the proceedings. Then, too, the possibility of American accomplices was widely mentioned. But the curtain had fallen on the main drama. All the rest was epilogue. Madame Humbert and her husband Frédéric, who had originally been a dupe but gradually became a willing accomplice, were each sentenced to five years in prison. Thérèse's two brothers got three years apiece.

Correspondents at the trial marvelled at the contrast between the audacity and magnitude of the twenty-year hoax and the insignificant appearance of its perpetrators. Foreign correspondents in particular, had expected to see their version of the typical French charmer, or, at least, a grande dame of the old school. Instead, they saw a stout, homely, stubborn Frenchwoman, whom one correspondent—presumably to convey his utter disappointment—described as "the typical French cook."

Nevertheless—or perhaps all the more so—European newspapers and magazines gave the case tremendous coverage. Hundreds of cartoons appeared on every facet of the adventure. French bankers, who, despite their wealth and power had rarely been mentioned at any length in the press, now became, through the agency of an ex-peasant girl, nationally known figures in the supporting roles of Madame Humbert's dupes. Most of these creditors took the whole thing very hard. But one banker, owed some 3,500,000 francs, stole the limelight and became a minor national hero by taking it all very philosophically. In an interview he was quoted as saying: "Oh, I'll be paid back somehow, one of these days. And, if not, well, I shall have had the privilege of serving a truly gifted woman."

Among the many feature stories that appeared at this time was one by an English governess who had once been in charge of the Humbert's only child, a girl. The Humbert daughter, according to the governess, had been brought up with the strictest propriety. Once, when the governess reported that her charge had been guilty of a small fib, Madame and Monsieur Humbert, in the governess' words, "were thrown into such a fever of anguish that they wept in despair."

But the public did not need such tidbits to rationalize their cheers for Madame Humbert. Her fantastic feat was justification enough, as far as they were concerned. And many serious journals of opinion (like *The Spectator* and *The Nation*) echoed the popular reaction. One journal, for example, wrote shortly before the trial: "Let us hope this gifted woman may be spared the rigors of long and obscure exile from her beloved Paris."

Madame Humbert's imprisonment was relatively short, but her days of stardom were over. Like an old trouper, though, she stayed in character. Interviewed upon her release, she announced that the courts had wronged her, that the Crawfords would appear in due time to vindicate her and re-elevate her to eminence. However, Madame Humbert's audience had turned their attentions elsewhere, and the stage on which she had played, so brilliantly and so long, her improvisation on the theme of the Big Lie, was soon to play host to grimmer, vaster national and international variations on the same general theme.

A MAN OF GENIUS

by Charles Mackay

In the second decade of the eighteenth century the seemingly enormous potentials of the Mississippi Scheme in France and the South Sea Company in England gripped the popular imagination, and a fantastic speculative fever engulfed both nations. Both enterprises failed within a few years, ruining many thousands. During the height of the bubble in England the man who showed the most genius and, in our considered opinion, still holds the championship, is the one whose secret project Charles Mackay summarizes here by way of putting a period to these adventures in deception.

Innumerable joint-stock companies started up everywhere. They soon received the name of Bubbles, the most appropriate that imagination could devise.

Some of them lasted for a week or a fortnight, and were no more heard of, while others could not even live out that short span of existence. Every evening produced new schemes, and every morning new projects. The highest of the aristocracy were as eager in this hot pursuit of gain as the most plodding jobber in Cornhill. The Prince of Wales became governor of one company, and is said to have cleared £40,000 by his speculations. The Duke of Bridgewater started a scheme for the improvement of London and Westminster, and the Duke of Chandos another. There were nearly a hundred different projects, each more extravagant and deceptive than the other.

Some of these schemes were plausible enough and, had they been undertaken at a time when the public mind was unexcited, might have been pursued with advantage to all concerned. But they were established merely with the view of raising the shares in the market. The projectors took the first opportunity of a rise to sell out, and next morning the scheme was at an end. Maitland, in his *History of London,* gravely informs us that one of the projects which received great encouragement was for the establishment of a company "to make deal boards out of saw-dust." This is no doubt intended as a joke; but there is abundance of evidence to shew that dozens of schemes, hardly a whit more reasonable, lived their little day, ruining hundreds ere they fell. One of them was for a wheel for perpetual motion—capital one million; another was "for encouraging the breed of horses in England, and improving of glebe and church lands, and repairing and rebuilding parsonage and vicarage houses." Why the clergy, who were so mainly interested in the latter clause, should have taken so much interest in the first, is only to be explained on the supposition that the scheme was projected by a knot of the fox-hunting parsons, once so common in England. The shares of this company were rapidly subscribed for.

But the most absurd and preposterous of all, and which shewed, more completely than any other, the utter madness of the people, was one started by an unknown adventurer, entitled, "*A company for carrying on an undertaking of great advantage, but nobody to know what it is.*" Were not the fact stated by scores of credible witnesses, it would be impossible to believe that any person could have been duped by such a project.

The man of genius who essayed this bold and successful inroad upon public credulity, merely stated in his prospectus that the required capital was half a million, in five thousand shares of £100 each, deposit £2 per share. Each subscriber, paying his deposit, would be entitled to £100 per annum per share. How this immense profit was to be obtained, he did not condescend to inform them at that time, but promised that in a month full particulars should be duly announced, and a call made for the remaining £98 of the subscription. Next morning, at nine o'clock, this great man opened an office in Cornhill. Crowds of people beset his door, and when he shut up at three o'clock, he found that no less than one thousand shares had been subscribed for, and the deposits paid. He was thus, in five hours, the winner of £2,000. He was philosopher enough to be contented with his venture, and set off the same evening for the Continent. He was never heard of again.

Date Due